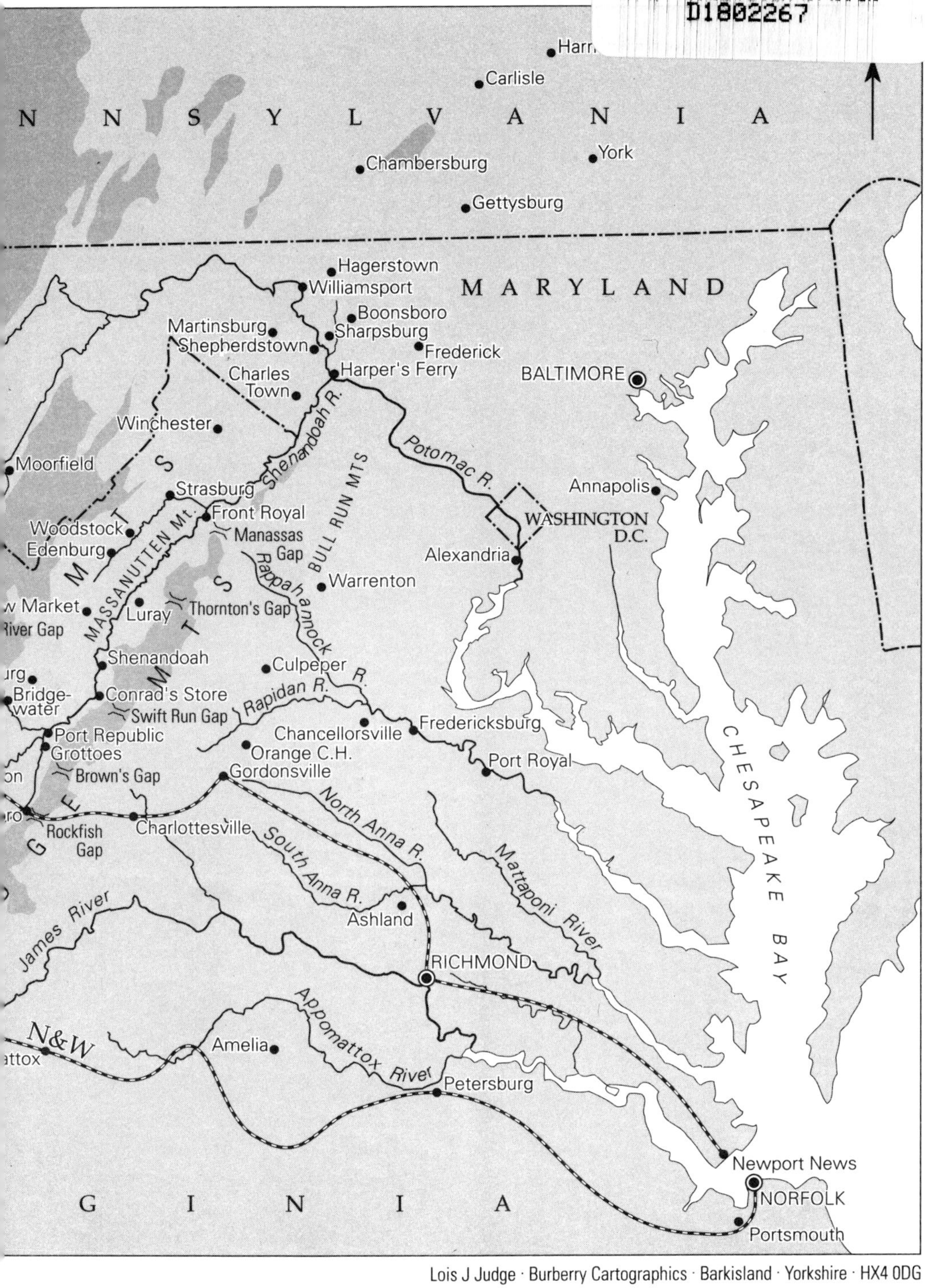

Lois J Judge · Burberry Cartographics · Barkisland · Yorkshire · HX4 0DG

The young Jedediah Hotchkiss.
Mary Baldwin College, Staunton, Virginia

JEDEDIAH HOTCHKISS

Rebel Mapmaker and Virginia Businessman

by

Peter W. Roper

*Foreword
by
Archie P. McDonald*

WHITE MANE PUBLISHING COMPANY, INC.

Copyright © 1992 by Peter W. Roper

Foreword copyright © 1992 by White Mane Publishing Company, Inc.

ALL RIGHTS RESERVED—no part of this book may be reproduced in any form without permission in writing from the publisher, except by a reviewer who wishes to quote brief passages in connection with a review.

This White Mane Publishing Company, Inc. publication
was printed by
Beidel Printing House, Inc.
63 West Burd Street
Shippensburg, PA 17257 USA

In respect for the scholarship contained herein, the acid-free paper used in this book meets the guidelines for permanence and durability of the Committee on Production Guidelines for Book Longevity of the Council on Library Resources.

For a complete list of available publications
please write
White Mane Publishing Company, Inc.
P.O. Box 152
Shippensburg, PA 17257 USA

Library of Congress Cataloging-in-Publication Data

Roper, Peter W., 1923-
    Jedediah Hotchkiss : rebel mapmaker and Virginia businessman / by Peter W. Roper.
      p.   c.m.
    Includes bibliographical references and index.
    ISBN 0-942597-26-5 : $29.95
    1. Hotchkiss, Jedediah, 1828-1899. 2. Cartographers--United States--Biography, I. Title.
GA407.H67R67   1992
526'.092--dc20
[B]   92-9456
                                                                                   CIP

PRINTED IN THE UNITED STATES OF AMERICA

To

Fletcher Collins, Jr.

and

his wife, Margaret

Acknowledgements

Two people are responsible for the existence of this book, not for its content, for that responsibility is mine, but for the fact. If Walter Ristow had not put together, and published, a collection of articles describing interesting maps and atlases in the collections of the Geography and Map Division of the Library of Congress; if Clara LeGear' had not been the author of one of these, then, probably, I would have remained in ignorance of the very name of Jedediah Hotchkiss, let alone his achievements. In 1972, the Library of Congress published *A la Carte. Selected Papers on Maps and Atlases*, compiled by Walter W. Ristow. It included a reprint from the November 1948, issue of the *Library of Congress Quarterly Journal of Current Acquisitions*, an article by Clara E. LeGear: "The Hotchkiss Collection of Confederate Maps." The description of the maps, recently acquired by the library, was enough in itself to stimulate further inquiry, but the glimpses provided of the life of the man who drew them made such inquiry imperative. I resolved to find out more. Then, in 1973, Archie P. McDonald published Hotchkiss' Civil War Journal, under the title *Make Me a Map of the Valley*, with copious notes and, in its introduction, offering the most comprehensive review of Hotchkiss' life hitherto published. Three years later an article appeared in the *Virginia Magazine of History and Biography*, authored by Jerry B. Thomas, entitled "Jedediah Hotchkiss, Gilded-Age Propagandist of Industrialism," describing an aspect of his postwar life. These two publications served to keep interest alive, by confirming that here was a man worth searching for.

For a Yankee to serve in the Confederate army was intriguing enough, but when that Yankee was from a family which first set foot on New England soil in 1638, from a family of strong religious belief with a record of public service, it commanded attention. When, without higher education or formal training as a teacher, he established schools and became a teacher of teachers; when, without formal training as a surveyor, he became the foremost mapmaker in the Army of Northern Virginia; when, by self-education he established himself as an authority on the geology and mineral resources of his adopted state; when, virtually single handed, he published monthly for six years a mining, industrial, and scientific journal; wrote books on the geography of Virginia;

wrote and lectured on the campaigns of the Civil War—we have no ordinary man. If, alongside those achievements, we recognize his powerful religious faith, missionary zeal, and sense of duty, all allied to compassion for the human condition, we know we are dealing with an extraordinary person. This combination earned him the respect of his contemporaries, and the trust of the rich and powerful. It has enslaved the author.

In 1980, a business trip to the United States allowed me the opportunity to see the Hotchkiss Map Collection, and to learn of the wealth of manuscript material deposited in the Library of Congress. Fortunately most of the *Papers of Jedediah Hotchkiss* were available on 60 reels of microfilm; this at least made the material transportable and potentially accessible to me in the midlands of Britain. The good offices of the County Library of Nottinghamshire made accessibility a fact. From April 1981 until the autumn of 1984 there was a steady transatlantic traffic in microfilm.

By 1985 it was clear that further progress could be made only by visiting the U.S.A. to see for myself the places familiar to Hotchkiss, and to examine the sources of information immobilized in museums, libraries, and archives.

For four months I traced his life on the ground: from his birthplace in Windsor, Broome County, N.Y., to Mossy Creek and Churchville in Virginia. I followed his military career, his postwar life in Staunton, and in a sense his afterlife, the history of his maps so providentially preserved by the efforts of an obscure provincial librarian.

In the course of this, and on a later visit in 1987, I was able to meet many of the people who had so kindly answered my queries by correspondence. My thanks are given, without constraint, to all whom I pestered with questions, but special mention must be made of Dr. Fletcher Collins, Jr., the present owner (with his wife) of the Hotchkiss house in Staunton, who persuaded me to write this account, repeatedly made me welcome at The Oaks, provided the very necessary editorial advice, and joined in the search with enthusiasm.

It was equally fortunate that another surviving building associated with Hotchkiss, his birthplace, was the home of Charles English, who, as a Civil War enthusiast, had more than a passing interest in the family who once lived there. In turn he was able to direct me to Bernard Osborne, local historian, and to Marjory B. Hinman of the Roberson Center, Binghamton, N.Y. The help and advice of all three is gratefully acknowledged.

In Virginia, and especially in the Shenandoah Valley, there was great interest shown in my quest; people responded generously with information, the loan, and even gifts, of Hotchkiss material. In Churchville, these included Mrs. Bowers, Rev. David McDonald, minister of Loch Willow Presbyterian Church, and Mr. and Mrs. Bear. In Deerfield, Virginia, Mr. and Mrs. Alfred M. Graham made available for study many letters relating to the Hotchkiss map collection. These letters and photographs have subsequently been given to Mary Baldwin College Archives. The Grahams also kindly allowed the inspection of Hotchkiss heirlooms passed to them by Mrs. R. E. Christian, the only Hotchkiss grandchild. In Grottoes, Virginia, Mrs. Debbie Diehl provided photographs and historical notes, and Mrs. Wisher allowed me to examine her collection of historical materials and loaned a copy of *Shendun News*. In Staunton, William Pollard, librarian of Mary Baldwin College, provided services too numerous to mention; suffice it to say that nothing was too much trouble. Mrs. Barbara Jennings, formerly reference librarian, Staunton Public Library, facilitated the loan of microfilm copies of the *Staunton Spectator*. Mrs. Katherine Bushman proffered advice on local archive material and drew my attention to the biographical sketch of Dr. John P. Hale in the second and third editions of Hale's *Trans-Allegheny Pioneers*. David J. Brown, executive director, and other members of Historic Staunton Foundation, Inc., located sources of information. David Schwartz rephotographed an old photograph of Loch Willow School. In Lexington, Dr. William Pusey III, former dean of Washington and Lee University, assisted with the abstraction of information from the Lee papers in the University Library.

The help of the staff of the Library of Congress, and of the Alderman Library, University of Virginia, was indispensable and is gratefully acknowledged. I owe a debt of gratitude to James Flatness and Richard W. Stephenson of the Geography and Map Division of the Library of Congress, not only for their help with the Hotchkiss Map Collection, but in answering many questions. In particular my thanks are due to Mr. Stephenson for his critique of a draft of the chapter on Hotchkiss' mapmaking activity. The staff of public libraries in Richmond, Winchester, Waynesboro, Virginia; Charles Town, West Virginia; and of academic libraries at the Virginia Polytechnic Institute and State University at Blacksburg, and the Virginia Military Institute at Lexington, all provided useful material in my search for Jedediah Hotchkiss.

To Benjamin Franklin Cooling III, I am indebted for valuable comments on my assembly of this material.

The abundance of data, coupled with the variety of interests, has made the presentation of this life of Hotchkiss a daunting one. To do it full justice would require a team of experts, each familiar with one or other of the tasks which he undertook, and to which he gave so much of his time and talent. What I have sought to do is to draw attention to this variety, and to indicate by examples the significance of his contribution to its component parts, while at the same time attempting to uncover the nature of the man. Inevitably this will leave some readers dissatisfied, but may stimulate others to probe more deeply into particular aspects of his life.

Foreword
by Archie P. McDonald

In the summer of 1959, Frank E. Vandiver introduced me to Jedediah Hotchkiss. Vandiver, my major professor at what was then called the Rice Institute, located in Houston, Texas, thought it time I started on my master's thesis. Since I hardly knew what a master's thesis was, he kindly suggested that I edit the Civil War portions of Hotchkiss' voluminous journal.

Vandiver had "discovered" Hotchkiss' role in the success of General T.J. Jackson's Civil War career when writing *Mighty Stonewall*, and thought that gentleman deserved more attention from the guild of historians working on the war. In the beginning I had only a microfilmed copy of the typescript prepared by Hotchkiss, and so it was a "journal," not a diary, because he had added and deleted information from the original when he found out more or when first impressions proved false. Eventually Vandiver cut down my obligation for the thesis to the first two years of the war, and then T. Harry Williams and Louisiana State University allowed me to finish the work and called it a dissertation.

Vandiver's introduction of Hotchkiss was a great blessing for me. Not only did I employ Hotchkiss' journal as a vehicle to obtain two advanced academic degrees, but under the published title of *Make Me A Map Of The Valley. The Civil War Journal of Stonewall Jackson's Topographer* it became what kindly has been called a "contribution" to the literature of the war. Most importantly, this allowed me to learn about, and to come to admire, much about this important nineteenth-century soldier, topographer, businessman, and humanitarian.

The biographical introduction to *Make Me A Map Of The Valley* was appropriate for the format, and contained much of what may be found in Peter Roper's biography for the first thirty-seven years of Hotchkiss' life. But even for that period, Roper has found out much more about Hotchkiss' business affairs, and certainly he has gone far beyond my modest accounting for Hotchkiss' varied activities in the Reconstruction era and afterwards. Roper had access to archival materials, family descendants, even much of Hotchkiss' own papers and maps beyond what was accessible thirty years ago, and he has incorporated these findings into a more complete biography. Its strength is in his accounts of Hotchkiss the entrepreneur, the developer, the visionary who labored to improve the educational level and economic condition of not only, but especially, Virginia and the rest of the South.

Even so, the character of the man followed a constant course. Certainly one reaction to reading Roper's story of Hotchkiss' various business enterprises, most of them unsuccessful in his lifetime, would be that he was an unsteady man, at least in the sense of a pay check or keeping his personal finances in order. The reason, one must conclude, is that he had a vision, and the hope to turn that realization into reality always led him onward even though his dreams often were not always fulfilled, at least as far as his personal finances were concerned.

Hotchkiss remained steady in other ways. Neither his travels nor his colleagues, some of whom may not always have been as religious as he, caused a waver in his conviction of Christianity and the commands over his behavior that this conviction required. A foe of liquor, a keeper of the Sabbath, a servant of the Lord, are all ways to describe this conviction. And he remained loquacious. Jackson himself commented that Hotchkiss talked too much, but as one who worked with his written words, and I suspect Roper would agree, he did not write too much, even though he did write quite a lot. While much of his journal covered mundane topics—and some would put his constant weather observations in this category—its sum is a rich reservoir of data about life in the nineteenth-century South, and especially for the action areas of the Army of Northern Virginia, II Corps, for the war years. Another word about the weather: it can be just as important for historical interpretation as anything else, as Hotchkiss' account of Jubal Early's raid on Washington in 1864 indicates. Early's loss of aggressiveness once the objective had been reached was due more to summer's heat and dust than anything else. Hotchkiss' words let us know that far better than Early's reports.

The primary value of this biography is the wider, and deeper, understanding it brings of Hotchkiss' role in the war and in the subsequent economic development of the Virginias. His family always desired this, and some of them felt cheated that makers of lesser contributions had won more fame because someone had gotten around to writing a biography of them. This is true for the majority of Jackson's staff, as well as other military figures. Charles Hotchkiss Osterhout wrote some of it, perhaps even my contribution of the published journal for the war years helped, but this is the first attempt to tell the story whole. As with any pioneering work, it is possible that in the future another will pick up the story and tell it again. If they do, the effort probably will be limited to the military years, for it is difficult to imagine anyone wanting to, or needing to, plow again the story of post-war activities that is done so completely here.

For those who knew of Hotchkiss' contributions to the Southern war effort, perhaps even quite a bit, there is more to learn about him in these pages, more about his maps and the way he made them than has been told before, and more about his efforts as economic developer. Like most who have worked on Hotchkiss—and probably all other historical characters—it is easy to become sympathetic to the central figure of the story and forget shortcomings, and Roper is no different from the rest of us. With Hotchkiss, this is easy. He was an important part of the Confederate military effort in Virginia, and equally an important figure in Virginia's recovery after the war, and it is our obligation to him to make his contribution more appreciated.

List of Abbreviations

The following abbreviations to titles of source material are used in the endnotes:

H.P. Hotchkiss Papers located in the Manuscript Division of the Library of Congress, Washington, D.C. Specific documents are identified by the reel and frame number of the microfilm copy, e.g. 24/562.

H.A. Hotchkiss Papers located in the Alderman Library, University of Virginia, Charlottesville, Virginia.

H.C. Hotchkiss Collection located in the Mary Baldwin College Archives, Staunton, Virginia.

S.S. *Staunton Spectator*.

C.W.J. *Make Me a Map of the Valley. The Civil War Journal of Stonewall Jackson's Topographer*.

C.M.H. *Confederate Military History*.

O.R. *War of the Rebellion: A Compilation of the Official Records of the Union and Confederate Armies*.

Contents

Acknowledgements		iv
Foreword by Archie P. McDonald		ix
List of Abbreviations		xii
I	"I thought but to make a winter's sojourn here"	1
II	"Now don't take any counsel of your fears"	28
III	"Fields of fierce contention"	59
IV	Back to school, but not for long	86
V	The search for capital	109
VI	"Everything has conspired against me..."	127
VII	"What would the Virginias do without you?"	134
VIII	The Civil War Remembered	150
IX	Getting Coal to Tidewater	159
X	"...Is skillful with his pencil..."	188
XI	Family and Friends	222
XII	Assessment	233
Epilogue: The Maps		246
Endnotes		252
Bibliography		283
Index		290

CHAPTER I

"I thought but to make a winter's sojourn here"

DURING THE AFTERNOON of May 10, 1862, two days after he had defeated Union General Robert H. Milroy in the battle on Sitlington's Hill above McDowell, Major General "Stonewall" Jackson beckoned to his topographical engineer to follow him. The secretive general had important orders for Mr. Jedediah Hotchkiss which must not be overheard, even by other members of his staff. They rode a little way back and then turned into the woods. Jackson was anticipating the movements of his enemy and gave instructions for the blockading of Dry River Gap, a western approach to the Shenandoah Valley. Hotchkiss knew exactly what he had to do, and knew how to do it. With the dependable Sergeant S. Howell Brown he rode the 50 miles to Churchville, arriving about midnight. He briefed his friend Captain Francis F. Sterrett of the Churchville Cavalry, then went to his own nearby home, Loch Willow, for a meal and a rest. Early the following day the small force rode into the gap, and with axes and crowbars they so blocked the way with boulders and felled trees that this side door to the Valley was firmly closed to Union troops.

The job done, Hotchkiss and Brown rejoined Jackson who had now given up his pursuit of Milroy and was returning to the Valley to move against General Nathaniel P. Banks.

This small but typical action by Hotchkiss contributed significantly to the success of the Confederate general's famous Shenandoah Valley campaign.

He had served Jackson for a mere six weeks, but in that time had demonstrated his uncanny understanding of terrain and its role in military operations. This, coupled with his conscientious reliability would make him indispensable to Jackson and his successors in the Army of Northern Virginia.

Nearly twenty years later, in April 1881, he handed to a railroad president, Frederick J. Kimball, a topographical map which showed how a railroad could be constructed to reach Virginia's vast supplies of coal that would fuel the nation for decades.

Not a Virginian by birth, Hotchkiss applied his self-developed skills, in peace as in war, to give a lifetime of service to his adopted state. What follows is an account of this man and this service.

On the west bank of the Susquehanna River in Broome County, New York, a few miles north of the Pennsylvania line, lies the small village

Stone House, overlooking the Susquehanna, Windsor, N.Y., the birthplace of Jedediah Hotchkiss.
Author

of Windsor. On the opposite side, on a terrace dissected by a stream tumbling down the wooded hillside, is a substantial stone-built house. It was here, at the Stone House, that Jedediah Hotchkiss was born on November 30, 1828.[1]

For generations the Hotchkiss family, descended from Samuel Hotchkiss, an English emigrant of about 1638, had remained in New England, until Hotchkiss' great-grandfather, David, came to the Susquehanna toward the end of the 18th century from Connecticut. He was one of the earliest of the New Englanders to settle there after the Tuscarora Indians had been displaced by the Sullivan-Clinton expedition of 1779.[2] John Doolittle arrived in 1786 to settle on Sage Creek, upstream from the lands of the Allison Classright Patent, part of which David Hotchkiss was to acquire a few years later. The square piece of land of the Allison Patent, which, with a fine disregard to the geography of the region, straddled the Susquehanna, contained 3,400 acres.[3] Of these, David Hotchkiss bought more than 2,200. In 1798, he secured an interest in lands immediately to the north, and founded the village of Windsor on the west bank of the Susquehanna. David built his home, still standing, at what is now the corner of Main and Kent Streets. He left it to his son Frederick, and subsequently several generations of his family lived there. To his son Amraphel he deeded the part of his property which lay on the east side of the river, and some, if not all, of these lands later belonged to Amraphel's sons Stiles, Frederick, and Gideon.

In 1828, "6 to 7 acres of land more or less" were deeded to Stiles, and this included "the Stone House, distillery, mill and the house in which Thomas Dixon now lives."[4] This was the birthplace of Jedediah Hotchkiss. His mother was to call him Jed, the name he came to prefer and by which he was known for most of his life. He was one of ten children born to Stiles and Lydia Beecher Hotchkiss, three of whom died within ten days of birth. Of the seven who reached adulthood only three lived the biblically allotted span: George, Nelson, and Jedediah. Stiles, credited with having built the first distillery in Windsor, is variously described as being a farmer, a dealer in lumber, and a contractor on public works.[5] Although he had acquired the Stone House from his father for a nominal sum, it was not long before Stiles sold it to another Hotchkiss relative, the Thomas Dixon who lived close by. Whether the family continued to live in the Stone House is uncertain, but they were on that side of the river in 1845, for Hotchkiss records in his diary on December 27, 1845, that he went "over the river" to the village.[6]

Little is known about Stiles. It seems he was not a well man; letters written by members of the family frequently refer to his ill health. Nor was he as successful as some other members of the family, for he appears to have lived in rented property and later hoped that son, Jedediah, would use some of his capital to provide a home for his father.[7] This hope was expressed after Hotchkiss had left home and when life seems to have become financially difficult for Stiles and Lydia. The family moved from place to place in the vicinity of Binghamton until Stiles finally returned to Windsor in 1859.

The whole Hotchkiss family was deeply religious and had a highly developed sense of service to their fellows. Not only did David play a part in establishing the Presbyterian Church in Windsor, but he also donated two-and-a-half acres of land for its meeting house. Most members of the family subscribed to this denomination, and it was later to be a major influence in Hotchkiss' life too. Grandfather Amraphel and his wife, however, were Methodists, and it seems probable that Stiles and Lydia were also, since neither of them appear in the well-kept records of the Windsor Presbyterian Church.[8]

It is clear from surviving letters, that Lydia believed totally in the mercy of God. Overcoming the hardships and misfortunes of this life was, for her, the sure way to everlasting salvation. It was such faith as this, but tempered by his greater knowledge, which was to sustain her son. What he gained from his father is not known, for no letters between them are known to exist, nor are there any references to him in Hotchkiss' diaries or letters to help form an opinion. Perhaps Stiles' legacy was a want of caution which Hotchkiss acknowledged years later, in a letter to his eldest daughter, as being a family trait. "Our Family," he wrote, "needs to have its 'crumb' of caution improved by exercise—it is the one weak point in its character and has been for generations."[9]

Undoubtedly he would have been influenced by his grandfather and his uncles, including Dr. Jesse T. Hotchkiss who graduated from the medical college of the University of Pennsylvania in 1842, and who gave Hotchkiss a reference when the young man left Windsor in 1846.[10] Grandfather Amraphel took a strong and active interest in the welfare of the town and built its first grist mill. His uncle Gideon patented inventions designed to improve the performance of grinding mills. Uncle Frederick, highly successful as a farmer and lumberman, was active on behalf of Windsor and its supervisor at one time. Brother George, eleven years senior to Jedediah, was a farmer, but also operated a saw mill at Hale's Eddy, Delaware County, New York. This he sold in 1866 and bought a farm in Windsor. His son, also christened George, became a particular favorite of his uncle Jedediah, and it is reputed that Hotchkiss gave him a saddle once belonging to Stonewall Jackson.[11] Another brother, Nelson, was to play a more direct role in Hotchkiss' life, for both eventually settled and died in Staunton, Augusta County, Virginia. Sister Jeanette, fond of her younger brother, missed his company when he left for the South, and would have willingly kept house for him had he remained a bachelor.[12]

Of Hotchkiss' schooling there is little available evidence. It was almost certainly limited to that provided by District School Number 1 plus one year at the Windsor Academy, but he read widely, and one supposes that his grandfather and uncles had something to do with that. Reverend Hiram M. Gilbert, pastor of the Presbyterian Church, and Reverend W. H. Miller, minister of the Methodist Episcopal Church and principal of the Academy, must have played a major part in encouraging that interest in natural history which formed the basis for Hotchkiss' lifetime concern for the geology and natural resources of his adopted state. Dr. Jesse T. Hotchkiss, located in Philadelphia, was well placed to secure for him the scientific texts which he so enjoyed reading. On the other hand, *The Transactions of the State (N.Y.) Agricultural Society*, in which Hotchkiss read an "interesting" article on geology, most likely came from his Uncle George, the keen and progressive farmer.[13]

From a young age Hotchkiss attempted to keep a diary, a habit he revived at intervals throughout his life. In one of the earliest, started on his 17th birthday, science and religion, which were to be dominating influences, are associated in one revealing sentence: "My hours of solitude have been cheered by works of science, it has been my delight to study the works of nature and of Nature's God."[14] This diary was kept daily from his birthday November 30, 1845, until Sunday, January 4, 1846, during a bitterly cold winter and while he was attending the Windsor Academy.

The Academy opened its doors to pupils on November 8, 1845. The need for such a school in the village had been apparent for some time; the nearest academy was at Franklin, too far away to be of use to the Windsor community. Nine local citizens, including Carver and Gideon Hotchkiss, formed themselves into a board of trustees, secured financing, acquired a site, and built the school, using lumber from the abandoned Presbyterian Church. Prior to 1845, Hotchkiss may have received formal instruction not only at District School No. 1, but also at the "select school" which operated in the same building, and offered education beyond the primary level. The select school, the precursor to the academy, functioned only when there was a sufficient number of students and there were funds available to hire a competent instructor. When these two conditions were not met, local residents offered private instruction. One of these was Jeanette Hotchkiss who, in 1840, conducted a private school over a wagon shop in the village, and may have taught her 12-year-old brother.[15]

In his diary, Hotchkiss, then 17, described the Windsor Academy as being a three-story structure with the school on the second story. There was at least one large schoolroom, two recitation rooms, and enough desks to accommodate about sixty pupils, although, at the time, there were only twenty-five in attendance. He studied Latin, Greek, algebra, and geography, and used Davies' series of books on mathematics, Bullion's *Greek Grammar and Reader*, and Mitchell's *Geography*. The Academy's motto: "order and perseverance", was one which he could well have adopted for himself. Perseverance he had to an uncommon degree, and if he did not always achieve order in his life, he certainly tried for it. In spite of his eagerness for knowledge, school was not easy for him. He found Greek "difficult and hard," and "after being unused to learning lessons for a time and commencing again it comes very hard."[16]

Not all his reading related to nature and nature's God. It is something of a relief to read the entry for Sunday, December 14, 1845: "Spent the day at home reading, though believing that the novels are not fit reading for youth yet I became so engaged in reading one entitled "The Female Blue-beard" by Eugene Sue that I finished it before I quit though not intending to read it."[17]

During the summer of 1846 he spent some time putting together a magazine for the Academy entitled *Autumn Wreath*.[18] That suggested he expected to return to the Academy when the new session opened.

It seems likely that Hotchkiss' interests—with the important exception of religion—set him somewhat apart from his immediate family, so that when the opportunity arose to join a group of young men going to Pennsylvania to teach, he changed his plans. Beginning November 9, 1846 (when he was not yet 18), he taught a school of 35 boys and girls, the children of 25 families living in and around Elizabethville in Washington Township, Dauphin County, Pennsylvania.[19] Among the teachers was his particular friend, Ralph McKune, and together they made excursions to the coal mines of Lyken's Valley (which were just then being opened), learned the German language, searched for Indian relics, and pursued an interest in natural history.

After the Elizabethville school closed in the Spring of 1847, he and McKune undertook a major expedition into Virginia. To pay for it they obtained a commission to canvas for subscribers to Mitchell's *Atlas*, maps, and other geographical publications. For five months the two young men travelled, mainly on foot, up the Shenandoah Valley, along the western edge of the Blue Ridge to Port Republic and Weyer's Cave, on the way stopping at the Shenandoah Iron Works, then via Staunton to Lexington and going as far south as Natural Bridge. They passed through the Blue Ridge along the James River to visit Lynchburg with its 6,000 inhabitants and 60 tobacco factories, then on to Charlottesville where they saw Jefferson's Monticello and University. Back into the Valley by Simmons Gap, they stopped again at the Shenandoah Iron Works before returning to the lower Valley and recrossing the Potomac on their way back to Elizabethville. Hotchkiss set down the details of the journey in his journal, commenting on people and places, the rocks and the scenery; pencil sketches of Harper's Ferry, Natural Bridge, Peaks of Otter, and James River Gap accompanied the diary entries.[20] It was a prodigious and momentous journey of about 500 miles in Virginia alone. Almost every day brought new experiences, sights and sounds, to an intelligent, inquisitive lad of not yet nineteen, sensitive to the beauty and form of the Valley landscape. His first railroad journey, the seventeen miles from Harrisburg to Carlisle. His first sight, at Hagerstown, Maryland, of slaves: "Today I have seen many slaves, but all appeared cheerful and contented." The dramatic scenery surrounding Harper's Ferry, his sitting up above it on a cliff, watching the Shenandoah tumble into the Potomac. The magnificently timbered Blue Ridge and Massanutten Mountains, squeezing the South fork of the Shenandoah into narrow Page Valley. The Caves of Luray and Weyer's Cave; the rich farmland; the iron furnaces. Everywhere there was evidence of Nature's bounty for man's use and enjoyment. It was not just a sightseeing trip. Hotchkiss and McKune worked and walked hard, selling subscriptions and maps, and we must suppose that sales were reasonably good, even though the diary entries about the number of subscriptions and maps sold are not detailed.

In the years to come, the place names in the diaries were to become famous, some legendary: Harper's Ferry, Winchester, Front Royal, Woodstock, Port Republic. He could not know that the contented slaves at Hagerstown, or the church at Port Republic with its "good sized cow bell...which makes a most delectable sound," would have other significances 14-15 years hence.

Nor did Hotchkiss have any idea how important were those two visits to the Shenandoah Iron Works. Meeting the owner, Henry Forrer, and through him, his brother Daniel Forrer of Mossy Creek, determined the course of his life. For without the patronage of the Forrers at that time, Hotchkiss might never have settled in Virginia. Who can say what the consequences would have been, not only for himself, but for the Virginias and even for the nation? It was Henry Forrer, presumably impressed by his talents and enthusiasm, who suggested that Hotchkiss should be tutor to his brother's children at Mossy Creek and so secured Hotchkiss for Augusta County, for Virginia, and for the South. The second visit to Henry Forrer lasted for about two weeks, because Hotchkiss was sick with a boil on his face which practically closed one eye. It was probably during this time that the brothers consulted and engaged Hotchkiss. The boil having subsided, the two young men resumed their business, finally returning to Elizabethville on November 10. Hotchkiss packed his belongings and returned south to arrive at Mossy Creek on November 19, 1847.

There was nothing extraordinary in Hotchkiss, a Northerner, becoming a tutor in a Southern home. A family with means would try to secure a broad secondary education for its sons at an academy. When the cost of educating several children at an academy was thought to be too high, or a suitable one too distant, the hiring of a tutor was a practical alternative. The presence of a tutor in the household, moreover, was valued as a status symbol, an indicator of a man's concern for the finer things of life as well as a sign of a comfortable financial position.

That so many tutors were from the North has been attributed to their availability and not to the lack of suitably qualified Southerners. In the South, access to the more desirable occupations of law practice, the ministry, and medicine was easier than in the North and so resulted in a shortage of people willing to be teachers. By contrast there was a surplus of Northerners who had suitable qualifications. Most of them regarded their sojourn there as being temporary, a regrettable, but necessary, interruption to their education. They were not professional teachers, were merely teaching for a year or so in order to provide the means of achieving another end. Hardly more than one in twenty remained in the profession. Hotchkiss was different in that he remained a teacher and that he stayed in the South. He regarded himself as a professional teacher with no other career in mind when he went to Mossy Creek. He may, of course, have hoped to extend his formal education, but only to improve his prospects in his chosen profession.[21]

The hospitality, respect, and friendship experienced by Hotchkiss was common to that extended to most Northern tutors. The ambiguities of the tutor's position, of which many of them were acutely aware, if recognized at all by Hotchkiss, were taken in his stride.[22] He was able to make an acceptable amalgam of the complex of roles: paid employee, guest, schoolmaster, family friend. So acceptable was it that he could speak later of the years spent in the Forrer home as "sunny places in the bright spring time."[23] Perhaps the culture shock was not so great for Hotchkiss as for tutors employed further South by plantation families.

Mossy Creek, lying within the Shenandoah Valley, was adjacent to the path of the pioneer families moving southwest from Pennsylvania.

The iron works there had been founded by Pennsylvanians, and many of the farmers were of Scotch-Irish descent. Their cultural roots were therefore not very different from Hotchkiss', and the nature of the land and the needs of the people tended toward mixed farming, not a plantation monoculture. In these circumstances slavery was neither so widespread nor so inhuman in its operation as further South or in the Tidewater area. That his employer was an ironmaster was not without significance; there was the common interest in rocks and minerals which they shared on numerous excursions. Reinforcing these acceptable conditions was Hotchkiss' love of and interest in the landscape of the Valley and his curiosity as to its geological origins. To live and work in the beautiful Shenandoah Valley would compensate for any disadvantages there might have been, but from the evidence available in his diaries there seems to have been none that he recognized.

The village of Mossy Creek, fourteen miles north of Staunton, takes its name from a small stream flowing from Augusta County in a northeasterly direction to join North River in adjacent Rockingham County. Henry Miller and Mark Bird came to this area from Pennsylvania in 1779 to build one of the early furnaces in the Shenandoah Valley. It was constructed on the northwest side of the creek, which was dammed to provide water power for the blowers of the furnace and hammers of the forge. (The dam produced a lake extending westward for about a mile to a point not far from Mossy Creek Church.) Daniel and Elizabeth Forrer acquired and settled on the Mossy Creek property in 1844, so had not been long established there before engaging young Hotchkiss as tutor to their children.[24] Their home was the substantial stone "mansion" built by Miller in 1784. It was there that Hotchkiss returned four days before he started teaching on November 23, 1847. He not only taught the Forrer children, but also those of nearby families. Within a month he had a "full number in attendance namely sixteen." Teaching occupied seven hours of each day from Monday to Friday; six were devoted to self-instruction, four to exercise and meals, and the remainder to sleep. This disciplined approach to the use of time—not a moment wasted—he observed throughout his life.[25]

Soon he explored the countryside, making excursions on Saturdays with Mr. Forrer. Naturally an early visit was made to the towers of Cambrian limestone, now called the "Natural Chimneys," a mere three miles away, and, then as now, a favorite place for visitors. In February, 1848, they went "to the mountains" to examine rocks; "The coal is seen in some six or seven places, and also the usual accompaniments of coal in the shape of fossil vegetables." An excursion of a different kind was on horseback to Staunton, where he visited Van Amburgh's menagerie then in town. He did not neglect his religious life. He attended Mossy Creek Church at the first opportunity, and frequently visited the Reverend John A. Van Lear, its pastor since 1837. Nor did he lack female company, for an entry in his diary for Sunday, May 14, reads: "In the evening I took a short ride to the Towers accompanied by Miss C. and Mary F[orrer]."[26]

By the new year of 1849 he was concerned with maintaining discipline among his pupils. Reluctantly, he resorted to the corporal punishment of offenders. Hotchkiss gave young Samuel Forrer "a good whipping for contradicting his teacher."

He recorded his interest in surveying and mapping. "Saturday, February 17, 1849: I spent this morning drawing a map of Augusta County." "Saturday, March 3: I employed most of the day in drawing maps.... In the afternoon made a measurement of a small field." "Saturday, March 10: Spent this morning in reading, collecting shells and drawing geological maps. In the afternoon John and I measured some land and run [sic] lines." A plot of one of these measurements signed "J. Hotchkiss" has survived in a file headed "Plot of D. Forrer's meadow by offsets," and annotated ca. 1848. His interest in natural history in the wider sense is clear from many entries in his diaries—a fine display of the Aurora Borealis in July when at Conklin, a drawing of the Moon and Venus as they appeared on January 27, 1849, the eclipse of the Moon on March 8. The following year he started a systematic record called a "Weather and Flower Table." Using one page for each month, he made a one-line entry each day in columns headed: "Sun, wind, rain, course of wind, colors, No. of plants." By March 1849 he must have begun to feel that he really was a Southerner, for he noted on the 23rd, after a visit he and Mr. Forrer had made to Staunton: "Mr. Forrer had his likeness taken by a Yankee."[27] Confirmation of his contentment with his life at Mossy Creek is to be found in a letter to his brother George, dated September 24, 1849. "I am doing very good business here, and think I shall continue for some time. My wages amounted to 300 dollars last year besides board, washing, roomlights and many more conveniences. There are horses to ride when I wish to go anywhere...I find a good deal of time for reading and study, which I gladly improve." There were some things he would have been happier without: "The fleas we have here torment in a manner I would hardly tell of for fear my truthfulness might be called in question."[28]

At the end of the 1851 school session, and after an interval of three years, he made another visit home—home this time being Kirkwood, close to Conklin on the Susquehanna. On his way he spent a few days sightseeing in Washington, D.C. He was there on July 4 when

President Millard Fillmore laid the corner stone of an extension to the Capitol building, and he listened to Daniel Webster's ninety-minute oration.[29] After the obligatory round of family visits, he attended the New York meetings of the American Association for the Advancement of Science at Albany, August 18-23. These meetings were important means of keeping up to date in a wide range of subjects, and it was at these that Hotchkiss met professional scientists who would be of help to him in the future, one such being Professor William Barton Rogers of the University of Virginia and the state's official geologist. A visit to an aunt and uncle at Syracuse, completion of business with his friend Ralph, and a trip to Niagara Falls—these occupied much of the remainder of his summer vacation.

Applications for admission to his select school at the Forrer's had frequently exceeded its capacity. When, for the 1851-52 session, he could provide for less than half the would-be pupils, Hotchkiss finally succumbed to the wishes of his friends and abandoned any thought of returning to the North. He "determined to stay provided [he] could extend [his] field of operation and take on larger numbers."[30] This could be done only if a more spacious building could be found, and as there was nothing suitable in the neighborhood he "conceived the idea of having the people unite in erecting an institution of learning." In the Spring of 1852 he canvassed the leading men of the area and in a short time had subscriptions totalling $2,000. Public meetings were held, addresses by distinguished advocates of popular education were delivered, the County was canvassed for aid, and funds were found in every quarter. The land was purchased, and a Board of Trustees and a building committee were appointed by the subscribers.[31]

Before this successful campaign, and not knowing what support he might get, he had a contingency plan for his own future if the community failed to respond. The eagerness of his search for knowledge must have borne the hope of attending a university or other place of higher education. This may well have been the "undertaking cherished from early life and not abandoned yet," which he referred to in June 1856 when he reviewed the events leading up to the foundation of Mossy Creek Academy. He had written to Reverend B. M. Smith of the Union Theological Seminary, Prince Edward, Virginia, who invited him to "attend an examination in college," and provided Hotchkiss with a letter of introduction to the faculty.[32]

The success of the canvass and the enthusiasm of his supporters, however, convinced Hotchkiss that he should stay. He wrote to his sister Jeanette, telling of his decision to make the "Old Dominion" his home. It was a decision that greatly upset the family. She replied, "It has made mother almost sick, she cannot speak of it without crying...." Everyone, she said, had some objection; Jeanette's were "very numerous." She was also convinced that "there was some *one* attraction" that kept him at Mossy Creek. If however this was not the case and Hotchkiss intended to keep Bachelor Hall, she was prepared to be his housekeeper.[33]

On September 11 the Trustees and the Building Committee met at Mossy Creek Church and signed the contract for the building of Mossy Creek Academy. The specification (actually dated September 18) called for the whole building to be "finished in neat, substantial and workmanlike manner...and the keys to be delivered to the Building Committee on or before the first day of December A.D. 1853."[34] Hotchkiss had chosen a site about a mile west of the Forrer mansion and close to the junction of present State Highways Nos. 747 and 613. It was a fine position on a knoll overlooking the lake formed by the damming of Mossy Creek. The finished Academy was a two-story building with internal dimensions of 40' × 66', a 6' basement and four-columned porches front and rear, extending the full height of the structure. The low-pitched roof was surmounted by a cupola or observatory. A central hallway between the porches separated the main schoolroom from two smaller rooms used as the primary school room and recitation room, respectively. It is probable that the classroom walls incorporated blackboards, for in a letter to the *Staunton Spectator*, September 1856, Hotchkiss described in detail the procedure for the preparation of a black plaster. The formulation included lamp black mixed with whiskey in the proportions of one pound of the pigment to one gallon of whiskey— probably the only good use Hotchkiss ever found for the spirit!

On March 14, 1853, Hotchkiss contracted with the Trustees to teach in the Academy building for the space of three years from the time of his "first occupation of the building."[35]

In July 1853 a leaflet was issued announcing the first session of Mossy Creek Academy, and advertisements appeared in the Staunton press. The editor of the *Staunton Spectator* commented, "The Mossy Creek Academy is a new institution built up by its efficient principal, MR. HOTCHKISS, who is doing much to advance the cause of education and deserves a liberal public patronage." The session was due to start on August 29 in the fine new building, built expressly for school purposes and soon to be complete at a cost of $4,000.[36] The schedule turned out to be optimistic, and the school opened in Mossy Creek Church. This decision, although supported by a majority of the congregation, caused considerable dissension, and some members never again worshipped there. The church was indeed not a satisfactory building for the school, and there were many complaints about the makeshift arrangements. Even when the Academy building was put into use in 1854 it was still not complete and complaints continued. Workmen were still on the premises, "thereby seriously interrupting the good order and quiet so essential to the proper management of a school." Indeed that first session was disastrous and strained the relationships Hotchkiss had established with a number of his keenest supporters.

The school attracted children from a large area, some coming from as far as Tazewell and Wythe Counties. As yet there was no boarding house managed by the school, so those pupils not living in the neighborhood boarded at local farms. Hotchkiss thought they were not properly supervised.[37]

Hotchkiss bought another piece of land west of the Academy plot extending to Brock's Lane (Highway No. 613). There he built a combined boarding house and residence. It was completed during the second session of the Academy (1854-55) and contained dormitories for 50 students, two to a room. Thus it was not until 1855, when all the facilities were available, and when Hotchkiss had recruited J. T. Brodt of Binghamton, N.Y. as associate principal, that a session opened under favorable circumstances.[38]

The Academy maintained a gruelling timetable. The workday started before 5 a.m., for one-and-a-half hours of private study was expected before breakfast at 6:30. Classes were from 8 to 12 and from 1 to 4 with private study from 6 to 9 p.m. The principal meal was at midday, supper being at 5 p.m.[39] Card playing and liquor drinking were strictly prohibited. Discipline combined "mildness and firmness," it avoided "harshness and unwarrantable severity," yet inculcated "strict order, prompt obedience, correct deportment and industry." The school was non-sectarian, but "founded on the broad principles of a common Christianity...therefore the lessons of the Bible are daily read in it...and all are required to attend Church on the Sabbath."[40]

Although Hotchkiss avoided the esoteric subjects which appeared in the catalogues of some academies, the number of courses offered was considerable, ranging from Greek to bookkeeping and from Latin to surveying. This combination of the old classical education with the more practical training appropriate to the needs of the day was typical of that provided by the academy movement then at its zenith.[41]

When Hotchkiss said at the end of the third session that there was little to regret he was referring only to the school as an educational establishment. Finances were another matter. Both Hotchkiss and the school were in a desperate state. In December of 1855 he conveyed to the trustees "the full right and title" of a lot of land "with all appurtenances thereto belonging," i.e., most of the land he had purchased

MOSSY CREEK ACADEMY & BOARDING HOUSE, AUGUSTA CO., VA.

Mossy Creek Academy, founded by Hotchkiss in 1852, was illustrated in the fourth annual catalogue for the year 1856-57.
Library of Congress

for the site of the Academy.⁴² In a separate deed Hotchkiss conveyed in trust to J. Howard McCue all the remaining land, as well as the Boarding House and all its contents, to secure debts totalling over $3,000. He could not continue much longer.⁴³

On February 22, 1856, he tendered his resignation to the Trustees effective at the end of the session. A strict construction of his contract would have required Hotchkiss to continue as principal until January 16, 1857, the third anniversary of the opening of the Academy building. But, he argued that "a liberal and honest" construction implied his "term of contracted service to close on the 20th of June." In this letter he made it abundantly clear that the Academy had brought "shipwreck" to his "temporal fortunes." "Justice to myself and I believe to others," he wrote, "would have compelled me to leave the school before this, for it has not paid its own expenses, leaving me without remuneration for three years of constant and, I trust, diligent labor besides a burden of debt that will demand all the energies of the best years of my life to liquidate."⁴⁴

This state of affairs had its origins in the nature of the contract between Hotchkiss and the Trustees. It required him to "furnish an adequate number of teachers for all the scholars that might attend said school, and charge for the same according to the rates established by" the Trustees. Thus there was no way in which Hotchkiss could ensure both professional excellence and financial viability. Since there could be no compromise on the former there was no option but to run into debt. He urged the trustees to charge fees that would bring the best teachers to Mossy Creek and "keep them there...for no school can prosper that changes its teachers every session." He was in no doubt that the Academy benefitted the community simply by its existence. It was an amenity which increased the value of the land holdings and brought money to the pockets of local people by their sale of goods and services to the boarders.⁴⁵

As for himself he would complete the terms of his engagement, if he was permitted to, and go elsewhere to seek to retrieve his fallen fortunes and save his name from reproach. This was no idle threat, for he had serious plans to go to California.⁴⁶ The opinions he had expressed in this letter of resignation he expanded upon in a farewell address to a large audience at the close of the 1856 session.

Hotchkiss reviewed the events which led up to the formation of the Academy, paying tribute to the support of the community. He described the problems which beset the first two sessions and drew attention to the more settled conditions which followed the completion of the Boarding House and the recruitment of an assistant. Although he did not wish to say much

> of the events which transpired during that [first] session and caused alienation of feeling, influence and co-operation among some that had been among the earliest and foremost friends of the cause of education here..., the matters of difference were acted upon and decided by the joint board of teachers on their own merits, and irrespective of persons or parties, ...for the thing contended for was *principle.*

Those must have been serious matters at the time, but Hotchkiss harbored no ill will and said, "I plant no seeds of rankling malice in my own bosom to produce there a crop of bitter fruits for my own eating, and if I think I have been misrepresented and mistreated, secure in the rectitude of my own intentions, I forgive and forget." There had been accusations of partiality in matters of religion, politics, and sectionalism. All these he vigorously refuted. He told his audience,

> The Bible is the first book here, as it should be in all schools, and the great principles of Christian faith, disconnected from *creed* or *party*, are here taught as the Alpha and Omega of education— as the only rules of conduct worthy of observance, and the only safeguard of society and liberty. There never has been, *and there never can be*, in this place an exercise, a lesson, or a lecture, sectarian in its tendencies—the principles of religion inculcated are those common to the great brotherhood of Christians, and on which they all unite, and those that have said aught to the contrary have said that which they did not know. The same may be said of politics—a lofty patriotism and love of country is inculcated—but no political sentiment peculiar to any party, are here promulgated— and we challenge any man to prove to the contrary. Selections from the speeches of dignified political speakers, are sometimes declaimed—but that is another matter—The charges of sectionalism that have been made go in the same category, and I have not been guilty of inculcating myself, or bringing any one here to inculcate sentiments inimical to this people, or unfriendly to the rights, or sentiments of any class of conservative American citizens.

Those suspicious of his Northern origins would not have been reassured by the recruitment of Brodt as associate principal.

But, it was not considerations such as these, which determined his decision to resign; he was driven out by the financial consequences of his contract. The school was underfunded. He reminded his listeners of "a homely proverb, but a true one, 'Money makes the mare go.'" The need of it was sadly felt. He repeated what he had told the Trustees, the rates of tuition were fifty per cent too low. His wages over the three years had not averaged $300 per year, no more than he had received when living with the Forrers. He told them,

> The pay is inadequate.... No man, competent and fitted to teach this school, can afford to do it for less than one thousand dollars a year, and he ought to have fifteen hundred, and why you ask. Because his labor is worth it, and the same amount of talents and labor in other professions would pay him more than that. You will pay a lawyer two dollars and a half for making a motion in court of five minutes duration, you will pay him fifty or one hundred dollars for defending a suit that may perhaps employ him *one* week or perhaps one day. You will pay the physician two dollars for a call and his services, for perhaps one hour, and your ministers are most of them quite liberally supported, when all the perquisites of their office are taken into consideration. I mention these professions because they are the only ones requiring the same kind of labor, in which the *brains* have more to do than the *hands.* Now let us compare the amount of labor required for each, and the qualifications necessary to fill properly each station. And now do not mistake my meaning, I am speaking of the *professional* teacher, of the man that intends to pursue that calling for his lifetime, and that makes preparation for it, that intends to fill up the measure of his usefulness here below, in training the intellects of the young, an employment second only to that which points to heaven and leads the way in its dignity, and second to none in the influences that affect society.... The teacher must have the same amount of general knowledge, to start with, that is required in other professions, he usually has more, unless we except some classes of clergy, and as a general rule, it will be found that the professional teachers have expended more time and money upon their education, than the professional lawyers, doctors, or preachers.... In laying his foundation, though, the teacher must go deeper, for it his business to explain *principles,* to give the reasons for those things that the others take for granted. He must not only possess knowledge, but the keys to knowledge; not only able to enter into the temple himself, but know how to lead in others.... If you wish to see teachers here

that will *educate* your children, and train them properly, for filling the exalted stations to which all may aspire in our favored land; and for filling that most exalted station upon earth, that of an *intelligent American Citizen*, you must pay the price of a good and durable article, and you will secure it—pay what you pay for services requiring the same talents, and then you will be well served and your children well trained."

He thanked in turn the Trustees, for many acts of kindness; his neighbors, "a kinder people...the sun in all its course does not shine upon;" and lastly his pupils: "We have aimed to instruct you well, to cultivate properly your minds and your hearts. Do not, by any subsequent course you may pursue, prove false to yourselves and to the pleasing hopes we indulge concerning you." He urged them to remember "that the fear of God is the beginning of wisdom."

There was probably much apprehension about the future of the school and great curiosity about what Hotchkiss would say. The speech was the most impressive event of the day and was listened to by an audience of "perhaps not less than a thousand or twelve hundred," some of whom had travelled a considerable distance to be there.[47]

On July 10, Hotchkiss put up for sale the Boarding House and all his personal property. But by this time his speech had caused people to think, and they thought how they could keep Hotchkiss at Mossy Creek. So when Reverend William H. Ruffner joined the considerable number of people who had gathered to see what was on offer, the handsome premises, the library, or the cabinet of minerals containing over 1,000 specimens, which Ruffner wanted, he was to be disappointed. Fifteen gentlemen assumed all of Hotchkiss' liabilities, persuaded him to retain his possessions, and to remain in charge of the Academy.[48]

The fourth session opened in September with Hotchkiss still the Principal as well as Professor of Languages and Mathematics.

When Jeanette suspected that a romantic attachment had induced Hotchkiss to make his home in Virginia, she had been wrong. However, by 1853, with the Academy built and the Boarding House under construction, the practical necessity of marriage would be apparent. After all who would supervise the cooking, cleaning, and other household chores? More importantly, pupils' parents would expect to see a normal and stable domestic scene, and mothers, in particular, would need the assurance that there was a woman present to care for the health and well-being of their sons.

The death of his friend Ralph McKune, sad though it was, provided the solution. Hotchkiss had first met McKune when they were together in Lykens Valley, Pennsylvania, and it is probable that he was introduced to McKune's girlfriend, Sara Comfort, at the beginning of their walking tour in 1847. There may have been further contact when the two young men met during Hotchkiss' visits to his family in 1848 and 1851. It is not improbable that Hotchkiss, his sister Jeanette, Ralph and his girl went riding together—riding with her brother was one of the enjoyments which Jeanette missed when Hotchkiss left home. Jeanette had certainly become friendly with the McKunes and it is from one of her letters that we learn of Ralph McKune's death. Writing from Great Bend in July 1852, she told her brother, "I attended a picnic at the cascade near the McKune's. We went over on the cars and they stopped on the Cascade Bridge and let me get off. I called at the McKune's but did not ask anything about Sara, for they were feeling so badly and I have not seen her since Ralph's death...."[49]

Sara, born February 14, 1833, lived at Lanesboro, not far from Conklin and Kirkwood or from the McKunes at Cascade. She was educated at Wyoming Seminary, Kingston, Pennsylvania, from which she graduated in July 1853.[50] The extent of the contact between them in the interval from the summer of 1851 to the time of their marriage in December 1853 is unknown. Presumably he wrote to her when Ralph died, and they continued to correspond. Hotchkiss did not visit his family in the summer of 1852 and there is no evidence to show whether he made a visit the following year, but we may assume that he did if only to propose to Sara and make arrangements for the wedding. This took place on December 21, 1853, at Hale's Eddy, Delaware County, New York, at the home of his brother Nelson, during the Christmas break of the first session of Mossy Creek Academy.[51] As the Boarding House was not completed until some time during the second session (1854/55) it is possible that Hotchkiss and his bride stayed with the Forrer's, and even that their first child, Ellen May (Nellie) was born there January 27, 1855. A second child, another girl, christened Anna Lydia, was born October 7, 1857, at the Boarding House.[52] This birth was a difficult one, and left Sara in poor health.[53]

By now Hotchkiss' association with the Academy was coming to an end. After the close of the 1856/57 session Hotchkiss and his associates sold the Boarding House to Thomas J. White for $5,000. At the same time Hotchkiss and his wife coveyed to White their entire interest in Mossy Creek Academy.[54] White assumed the position of Principal, but Hotchkiss continued as a teacher for the 1857/58 session. At the close of the school year he moved 18 miles to Stribling Springs so that Sara, who had been in poor health since the birth of Anna, could have the benefit of the health-giving waters. There he opened a select school with 20 pupils in the hotel where his family and most of the pupils boarded with Mr. Chesley Kinney, proprietor of the Springs.[55]

During this time, while Sara recovered, Hotchkiss planned his next venture, to establish another academy comparable to Mossy Creek. He had learned from his experience there, and no doubt hoped to avoid some of the difficulties. He would start with a separation of the duties of principal from those of manager of the boarding house; he would also reduce his dependence upon suppliers. He achieved both those ends by persuading his elder brother, Nelson, to join him in Virginia to manage a farm and boarding house.[56]

They found a suitable place on the outskirts of Churchville, seven miles northwest of Staunton. Here on rising ground, overlooking a willow-girt lake which gave it its name, was the imposing brick mansion of Loch Willow. This ten-room house, built in two stories above a ground-floor containing dining room, kitchen, storerooms, and other facilities, was suitable for the boarding of students; the nearby clapboard-clad log house was large enough to provide classrooms as well as to accommodate the Hotchkiss family, and the 312 acres sufficient to provide most of the culinary needs of a school community.[57] This property, acquired in November 1859, cost Nelson Hotchkiss $12,000, to be paid for in four annual installments of $3,000.[58]

The new school, which opened on the first Wednesday of September 1859, was run similar to Mossy Creek, with the same emphasis on self-discipline and diligence. "We will not tolerate any pupil addicted to dissolute and immoral habits." Thirty-eight boys attended during the first session, and Hotchkiss was assisted by Oswald F. Grinnan, a University of Virginia graduate.

Of particular interest were the departments of mathematics and physical sciences. In the former was taught, in addition to the mathematics, "Surveying, Theoretical and practical in all branches including Topographical Drawing." Pupils were told, "Surveying will be taught with practice in the field." The physical sciences included geography, geology, mineralogy, chemistry, astronomy, botany, and zoology. To aid in the teaching of these subjects there was "a carefully arranged Cabinet of Minerals of about one thousand specimens, an Herbarium of some one thousand five hundred specimens of plants, a good collection of Geological, Physical, Political Maps, Charts, plans, and sections; a set of Anatomical Plates, Chemicals, apparatus..."[59] The cabinet of minerals contained the collections Hotchkiss had made during his Virginia walking tour of ten years earlier, enhanced by the specimens collected while living at Mossy Creek.

Hotchkiss operated Loch Willow School on a sounder financial basis

Loch Willow School overlooking Churchville, Va., founded by Jed and Nelson Hotchkiss immediately prior to the Civil War. Photograph taken from "Certificate of Distinction" conferred on a pupil of the school.

than Mossy Creek Academy. Nevertheless by the end of 1859, the brothers had debts amounting to $3,105.66, and the second instalment of the purchase money was due in less than three-months time.[60]

To deal with this situation they conveyed all the property to David Fultz with the stipulation that if the debts were not paid by December 25, 1860, it would be his duty, at the request of the creditors secured by the deed, to sell the property.[61] The detail included in this deed of trust provides an insight into life at Loch Willow. As well as household goods, farm equipment, forage, and produce, the property list named eight slaves, four of each sex; Andy, Cyrus, Robert, William, Amanda, Susan, Margaret, and Mary. Of these we know from other sources that Amanda and Mary together with two children were hired from Thomas Crawford for a total of $105 for the year and Andy was hired at a cost of $125.[62] William was destined to accompany Hotchkiss during the war and to remain with him as a freedman when it was over.

Whether the brothers would have been able to extricate themselves from their financial problems and make the schools pay, we cannot know; the Civil War saw to that. It is possible that in the long term Loch Willow School could have been a viable business, but in 1859, when they conveyed all the property to Fultz, the prospects must have seemed bleak. A quarter of a century later Hotchkiss had forgotten the financial problems and described the time at Loch Willow as "successful and enjoyable."[63]

The chance encounter with Henry Forrer at the Shenandoah Iron Works had determined the pattern of Hotchkiss' life for the past 14 years. Now it was to be redirected and forever changed by the upheaval of the Civil War. The obscure schoolmaster was to become the aide to an obscure soldier-professor from the Virginia Military Institute. In the future, Lieutenant General Thomas Jonathan Jackson, a military genius, would become a Confederate hero, a legend, the subject of innumerable books and articles in which Hotchkiss would appear only as a footnote, but without whose knowledge, loyalty, skill, and sheer hard work the victories might well have been ignominious defeats.

How the war came, and why, have been the subjects of even more studies, but at rock bottom it had its origins in the evolution of two distinct perceptions of what represented the good life. One of these depended upon slavery. Negro slavery existed in the South because the climate, the land, and its crops combined uniquely in its favor. It continued because the lifestyle of the planters would be destroyed in its destruction.[64]

North and South might have continued a mutually critical, but peaceful co-existence, save for a third element: the Western Territories.

It was one thing to tolerate slavery where it was already established, another to permit its extension into those developing areas. For the Northerners moving west, the slave-owning Southerner presented unfair competition. To the Southerner, being prevented from taking his slaves was the same as excluding his horses. It was an attack on his way of life.

The situation was further complicated by conflicting views on the respective powers of state and federal governments. Southerners, in particular, were fiercely loyal to their home states. The threat to "states rights" implied in the Free Soil or abolitionist tendencies in the North was for many a sufficient reason to advocate secession.

About the time that Hotchkiss finished his schooling in Windsor, and before he went to teach in Pennsylvania, David Wilmot, a Democratic representative from the northern part of that state, moved an amendment to an appropriation bill then before the House which would exclude slavery from all lands acquired in the war with Mexico. This, the infamous Wilmot proviso, gave a new impetus to the Northern agitation against the South's peculiar institution. It initiated a series of events which culminated in the secession of the Southern states and the outbreak of civil war. Party loyalties were eroded, the Whig party was destroyed, the Democratic party split, and a new Northern party— the Republican party—born. The nation divided.

It was during these years of developing crisis that Hotchkiss reached maturity. He was barely 19 when he joined the Forrer household in Mossy Creek, thirty-two when he joined the Confederate army. During that time he had established himself as a respected schoolmaster. To do so he had to secure the support of the richer and more influential members of the local community. He could hardly have done it by adopting a "yankee" attitude; he had to be accepted as a member of the community. That he was so accepted is clearly demonstrated by the financial rescue mounted by fifteen friends at Mossy Creek.

Long before Alansa Rounds came to Loch Willow in September 1859, Hotchkiss had become a Virginian in all but birth. Alansa recalled the following conversation with her uncle as they rode from Staunton to her new home: "Uncle Jed said presently: 'Well Allie, how do you like old Virginia?' 'Oh, I don't like it I love it!' I told him. 'Yes I thought you would,' he answered, 'and I prophesy that you will admire the people as much as the scenery. I think Virginians are the best people in the world!'" Later in her recollections she wrote, "I rapidly became accustomed to colored servants. They swarmed everywhere, ...and I soon realized that I had been transferred *South* of 'Mason & Dixon's Line' to a peaceful, restful, happy land, and geographically, politically and socially new and refreshing to me. To find people 'behind the times' devoid of the restless 'hurry and push' of the North seemed a beautiful dream. The people, rich and poor, were warm-hearted and hospitable. The men so chivalrous in their bearing to women." Alansa was charmed by all she saw, including "The true, everyday life among the slave owners, where I saw and heard of no cruelty or oppression, and no one servant was overburdened, but each had their respective tasks. I fell in love with dear old Aunt Charity, the cook, and Amanda, the laundress. Then there was a dairymaid, a house maid, a table waiter and an errand boy, &c. &c."[65]

No wonder the people of the Valley wanted to maintain the status quo, feared the abolitionist threat from the North, and the secessionist talk from the deep South. Hotchkiss had been assimilated into this society, seduced by the delights of the Valley and the lifestyle portrayed in such joyous terms by Alansa in her memoirs. He shared its hopes and fears, and no doubt discussed the developing crisis with his friends and neighbors. He read the local newspapers.

In the verbal struggle between North and South, Virginia had a unique position, keenly felt. For thirty-six of the sixty years since the adoption of the Constitution of the United States of America, a Virginian had been President. "Southern by position, education, and feeling, and ready to defend [its] peculiar institution...at the proper time," Virginia was anxious to preserve the Union which her statesmen had done so much to create.

The strength of this feeling was not uniform across the state. To the north and west the ties to the Union were stronger than elsewhere. It was related to the economic importance of slavery in these very different regions. While Tidewater Virginia supported a plantation economy dependent upon slave labor, the mountainous west of the state was either sparsely inhabited, or, in the fertile valleys, had attracted farming communities in which slavery was of much less importance. Furthermore, the people living beyond the Blue Ridge were in large part descended from the Scotch-Irish or German families who had moved southwestward from Pennsylvania. Thus, there were cultural differences which reinforced the economic ones engendered by the different agricultural practices, themselves determined by contrasting physical geographies.

In Tidewater Virginia there were approximately equal numbers of black and white, but in the Valley only a fifth of the population was black. In Staunton, the main Valley town, with a population in 1860 of 3,875, just over a quarter of the inhabitants was black.[66]

These differences between western and eastern Virginia affected the politics of the state in the ante-bellum period. The balance of power lay in Tidewater Virginia. The western population had long been underrepresented, and felt isolated and neglected.

In Hotchkiss' Augusta County, another influence strengthened even further the local support for the maintenance of the Union. Staunton was the home of Alexander H. H. Stuart, Secretary of the Interior under President Fillmore. Although reserved and not a people's man in the populist sense, he was respected for his intellect and integrity. In times of crisis, men looked to him for guidance. He was a firm, earnest Union man.[67] The editor of the *Staunton Spectator* shared his ideals, and it was from this weekly newspaper that Hotchkiss learned of the developing crisis.

He had no difficulty associating with the conservative opinion of the *Staunton Spectator*, nor with the Whig politics of Stuart. He actively supported the Know Nothing party in 1855, and the Constitutional Union party in the presidential elections of 1860. On the other hand, as a Northerner, he had to defend himself against the charge of being an abolitionist.[68] In fact in his letters to his mother he defended slavery, finding biblical support for the practice.[69] Like so many Virginians, he saw no reason why the slavery issue should rend the Union.

Only after John Brown's raid on Harper's Ferry did the editor of the *Staunton Spectator* depart from his conservative stance. Answering the question "What should Virginia do?" he wrote that the Commonwealth should "adopt every peaceful measure of defence and protection within the Union and the Constitution, and then when all these fail, go out of the Union and fight for her rights." But it was not long before he abandoned secessionist talk and again urged Virginia to fight for its Constitutional rights within Union.[70]

Consistent with this stand, the paper supported the Constitutional Union party in the Presidential election of 1860, in which Virginia was one of only three states to vote for the party's presidential candidate, John Bell and his running mate, Edward Everett. During the election campaign Bell and Everett Clubs were formed "as an efficient means of disseminating useful information to the people."[71] The Hotchkiss brothers were active members of the Churchville Club which took part in one particularly "Grand and Glorious Rally" when, in spite of the rain and mud, people came to Staunton in their "hundreds from all directions...to testify their deep devotion to the Union." The newspaper reporter concluded his description of the event by saying, "If the destiny of our country and the fate of the Union was in the control of Augusta, the watchman on the tower of Liberty might confidently exclaim, 'All is well...the country is safe.' "[72] Unhappily Augusta was not in control, and the country was not safe.

The election of a "Black Republican" president might signal the dissolution of the Union; but there were still some prepared to make the effort to save it. Within three weeks of Lincoln's election, friends of the Union in Augusta County, irrespective of party allegiance, had met twice and expressed their views in a series of resolutions. The last of these eight prolix statements appealed to the politicians in Richmond "to bend all their energies to keep Virginia to her moorings as the 'Flagship of the Union' and to induce her...to use her power and influence to preserve...the harmony of the Union and the integrity of the Constitution."[73]

While attempts were being made to divert North and South from a collision course before Lincoln's inauguration on March 4, event followed event in rapid succession. One by one the other states had seceded and formed a Southern Confederacy with a constitution; a capital, Montgomery, Alabama; and a president, Jefferson Davis.

South Carolina had taken the lead by leaving the Union on December 20. Since then its forces had occupied coastal forts at Charleston, and threatened Fort Sumter in the harbor.

In his inaugural address, the new President made clear his opinion that no state could on its own decision leave the Union. Therefore, he as President of the whole of the United States would ensure that its laws would be "faithfully executed in all the States." He had the authority and would use it to "possess the property and places belonging to the government." The particular property he had in mind was Fort Sumter, still held by the Union, but in need of reinforcement and supplies. One expedition had been made and failed; Lincoln authorized another. When news of this reached Charleston, the authorities there unsuccessfully tried to persuade its commander, Major Robert Anderson, to evacuate the fort. At 4:30 a.m. April 12, 1861, a ring of guns, installed by General Pierre Gustave Toutant Beauregard, opened fire and after 34 hours of bombardment forced the garrison to surrender. The conflict had begun.

Lincoln waited just long enough to be sure of the facts of the case and then authorized Simon Cameron, his Secretary of War, to call out the militia. On April 15, Cameron wrote to the state governors to request the immediate mobilization of 75,000 men for three months' military service. The Virginia quota was 2,340. Governor John Letcher's reply was prompt: "I have only to say that the Militia of Virginia will not be furnished to the powers at Washington for any such use or purpose as they have in view. Your object is to subjugate the Southern states...You have chosen to inaugurate civil war...."

Two days later the Virginia convention, which had first met on

February 4, and which had been urging a conciliatory policy, reconvened and adopted by 81 votes to 51 an ordinance "to repeal the ratification of the Constitution of the United States by the State of Virginia." This decision had to be put to the people in a referendum arranged for May 23, but action was not deferred—indeed could not be deferred—until then. Nor was there a need. Lincoln's call for 75,000 men had wrought a dramatic reversal of sentiment. The people in Augusta County "indignantly resented the proclamation...considered war as rudely and recklessly forced upon them, and they not only accepted the issue, but, inflamed with rage at the insult, they flew to arms."[74]

Even before the decision of the convention was announced, ex-Governor Henry Wise had made plans with the officers of the state's militia and volunteer companies for the occupation of Harper's Ferry and capture of the armory there. John D. Imboden's Staunton Artillery was one of the units involved in the maneuver, and it was not long before other companies in Augusta County were mustered for service. By the end of April, Colonel Thomas J. Jackson of The Virginia Military Institute had been appointed commandant at Harper's Ferry where, seventeen months before, he had commanded V.M.I. cadets as part of the guard at John Brown's execution. Six companies were ordered to report to him there, including that of Hotchkiss' neighbor, Captain Francis F. Sterrett's Churchville Cavalry. In Staunton, a company of Home Guard was being drilled in fine style by Major Robert D. Lilley, who was soon to command the Augusta Lee Rifles. Oswald F. Grinnan, Hotchkiss' assistant at Loch Willow, organized the Ready Rifles of Augusta, and was later to command Company I, 5th Virginia Regiment.[75]

Virginia and the Valley were mobilizing for armed resistance to Northern aggression. It would soon be time for Hotchkiss to close his school.

CHAPTER II

"Now don't take any counsel of your fears"

THE SCHOOL REALLY closed itself. Older pupils had volunteered for military duty, the younger ones were anxious to be with their families at this uncertain time. Before the official close of the session at the end of June 1861, Hotchkiss had seen those pupils safely home, some through Federal lines into Maryland. On June 26, he gathered up his surveying and mapping gear, and drove a wagon of military supplies some 150 miles across the Appalachian ridges to Camp Garnett at the western foot of Rich Mountain.[1]

The Appalachian mountain range provided a natural defense against Federal attack from the west, but this difficult country was penetrated by two routes, one along the Great Kanawha Valley, the other from Wheeling to Parkersburg along the Baltimore and Ohio Railroad eastward to Grafton and then southeastward to Staunton. General Robert E. Lee sought to block those routes by concentrating below Charleston and at Grafton, using lesser forces for observation at points between those places.² His immediate adversary, Major General George B. McClellan, had established his headquarters at Cincinnati from where he organized two regiments, at Wheeling and Parkersburg. On May 26, military operations began, following the Confederate destruction of bridges on the Baltimore and Ohio Railroad (the B&O) northwest and west of Grafton. Superior Federal strength forced the Confederates from Grafton to Philippi, and subsequently from that town also, to fall back through Beverley to Huttonsville. The Federals occupied Beverley. This disastrous start to the defense of the South, an event known as the Philippi Races, was exploited by the Union as a "very considerable victory," on the strength of which McClellan mounted the first rung of his ladder to military fame.³

Meanwhile Lieutenant Colonel Jonathan M. Heck had been assembling reinforcements at Staunton. On news of the retreat from Grafton, Lee immediately increased the size of this force and appointed Brigadier General Robert S. Garnett to take command in the northwest of Virginia. Garnett organized the motley collection of Confederate soldiery into two regiments: one, later to become the 31st Virginia, under the command of Lieutenant Colonel William L. Jackson; the other, the 25th Virginia commanded by Lieutenant Colonel Heck. Also under Garnett's orders were the New Market Battery of four guns and the Churchville Cavalry. Leaving three companies at Huttonsville to guard his communications, he made a forced march on the night of June 15 to Beverley. Here he detached Heck's regiment, two guns and the cavalry, and sent them by way of the Parkersburg Turnpike to a point at the western foot of Rich Mountain to form the defensive position, known as Camp Garnett. General Garnett moved forward with Jackson's regiment to Laurel Hill. With these locations properly defended he "held the gates to northwestern Virginia."⁴

Hotchkiss delivered the supplies to Captain Franklin F. Sterrett's Churchville Cavalry, and offered his services to Colonel Heck, who referred him to General Garnett at Beverley. The General sent him to Camp Garnett where, on July 3, Heck assigned him to topographical duties, ordering him to map the camp and its vicinity.⁵ Hotchkiss had nearly completed the triangulation and measurements necessary for the preparation of an accurate topographical map, when, on the evening of July 9, the enemy started its movement against the Rich Mountain position, forcing a Confederate retreat in which he lost all his surveying instruments, notes, maps, and baggage, and barely escaped capture.

In this retreat Heck directed Hotchkiss to lead the column through the pathless forest up and across Rich Mountain. In the vanguard was

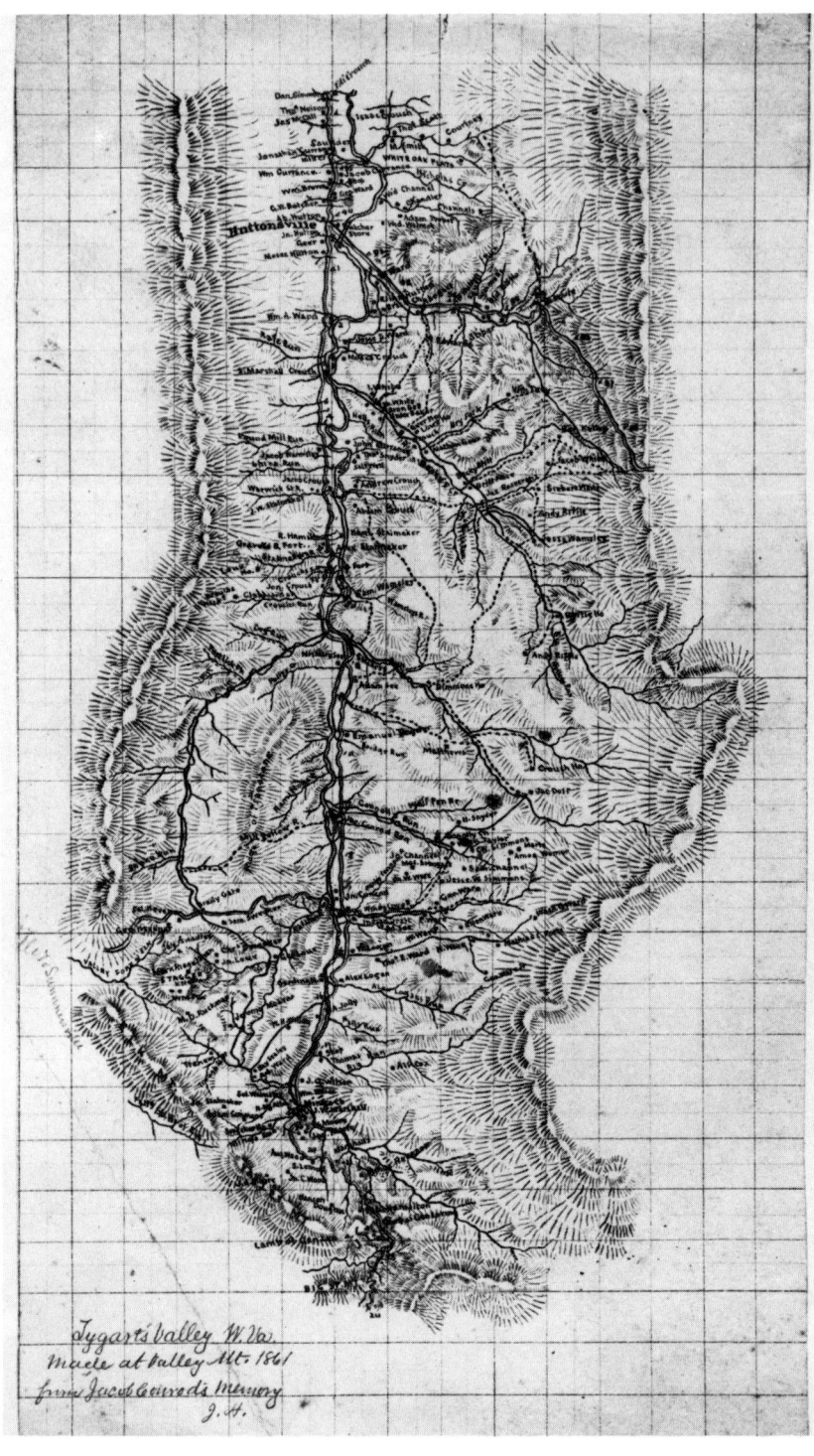

Tygart's Valley, the earliest of Hotchkiss' Civil War maps known to exist. A fair copy drawn at Loch Willow in the winter of 1861.

Alderman Library, University of Virginia

Captain Robert D. Lilley's Augusta Lee Rifles. Hotchkiss' earlier reconnaissance for the map proved invaluable. He was able to select a passable, though difficult route through the laurel swamps near Roaring Creek, then across the rocky and heavily wooded spurs of Rich Mountain. The conditions were atrocious, the night dark and cold, the rain poured down in torrents, and the way was often barred by fallen trees and dense thickets. Early on, the column was challenged by a low whistle from the enemy. Hotchkiss replied; the troops moved quickly but quietly forward, and escaped recognition. When daylight came, the leading company was two-thirds of the way to the top of the mountain, but to his great surprise, Hotchkiss found that, instead of the whole command, he was followed by only a portion of Captain Lilley's company and a few other men, some fifty in all. Unknown to Hotchkiss there had been a change of orders, but, due to the darkness of the night and the steepness of the way, a staff officer sent to halt the column was unable to reach its head, and so interposed himself in the midst of Captain Lilley's company and divided it.[6]

Hotchkiss and his little band eventually met up with other remnants of Garnett's force, including the Churchville Cavalry, and retreated farther to Monterey. They arrived there on July 15. The following day, the men of the Augusta Lee Rifles elected Hotchkiss an honorary member of their company for his services in bringing them safely over Rich Mountain. On the 17th he was appointed Acting Adjutant of what was left of the 25th Virginia Regiment.[7]

The Regiment marched eastward to McDowell where it camped for a week before returning to Monterey. During this time Hotchkiss "was quite ill from exposure," so ill that on the march back to Monterey he was unable to ride his horse, and had to be carried on a baggage wagon.[8] At the end of the month he resigned the adjutancy and was put on special duties for General Henry R. Jackson to make a map of the region. Later when Jackson wished him to continue working on the map as a private detailed to him, Hotchkiss refused, and went off in search of General Loring at Valley Mountain, who commissioned him a lieutenant of Engineers and assigned him to topographical duties.[9] The following day, August 21, he began work on a map of Tygart's Valley for Generals Lee and Loring.[10]

The weather remained appalling, with almost continual rain; when not raining, a dense mist covered the heavily timbered mountains. The wet, the lack of shelter, the poor rations, and the unsanitary conditions combined to undermine his health. He was "quite ill" at the beginning of September, and though he recovered from this "typhoid attack" he was so sick by the middle of the month that on September 17 he arranged to start homeward.[11]

Part of the large map of the Shenandoah Valley showing North River and Dry River Gaps blockaded by Hotchkiss in May 1862. The obstruction of these gaps contributed to the success of Jackson's Valley campaign.

Library of Congress

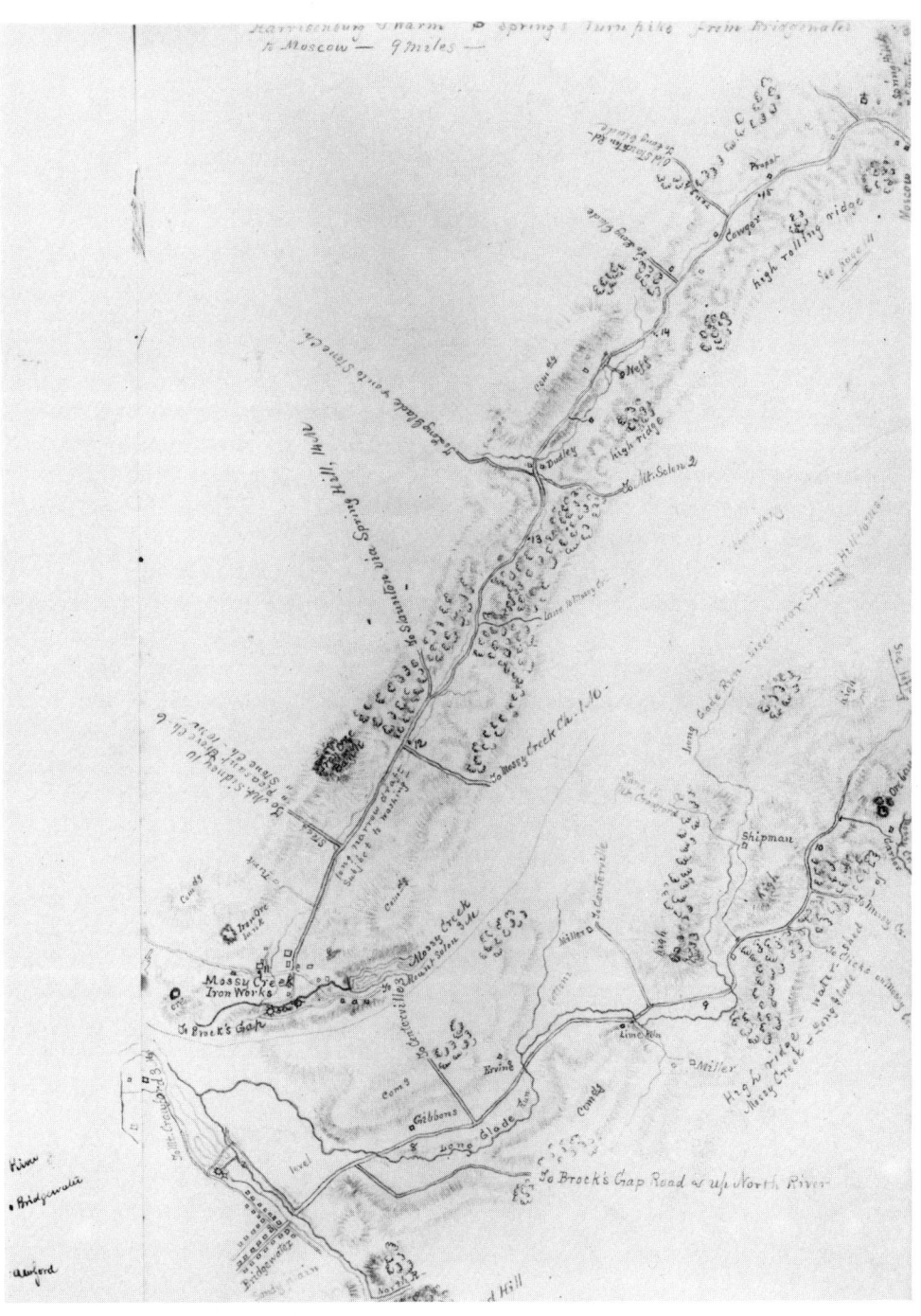

A page from Hotchkiss' war time note book. Harrisonburg & Warm Springs Turn Pike from Bridgewater to Moscow.

Hotchkiss Map Collection #1, page 13, Library of Congress

So ended Hotchkiss' introduction to warfare. It might well have been final. Capture at Rich Mountain was avoided by a combination of skill and luck, surviving typhoid fever was providential and unusual.

He remained at Loch Willow until March 1862. During this six-month convalescence he did a little tutoring, wrote his report on the retreat from Rich Mountain, and redrew his first wartime map, the map of Tygart's Valley, as ordered by Generals Lee and Loring.[12]

Fit once again, Hotchkiss wrote to his friend, Colonel William S. H. Baylor of Staunton, on the staff of General Thomas J. (Stonewall) Jackson, and requested suitable employment as a topographical engineer. Baylor thought that there would be no difficulty in this, but advised him to seek an interview with the General. Governor Letcher's call-out of the militia in the Shenandoah Valley provided the opportunity. On March 17, Hotchkiss joined the three Regiments of the Augusta County militia assembled at Staunton. Colonel John H. Crawford, the senior officer present, appointed Hotchkiss Adjutant with the immediate task of organizing the march down the Valley. After three days of warm and dusty marching, the new recruits went into camp at Mount Airy. Hotchkiss, in the company of another officer, rode forward toward Hawkinstown to appraise General Jackson of the arrival of the Augusta Militia. The men were then mustered into the service of the Confederate States for the duration of the war.

On March 26, Hotchkiss was ordered to report to Jackson who, after some general conversation about Hotchkiss' topographical work in northwestern Virginia, said to him, "I want you to make me a map of the Valley, from Harper's Ferry to Lexington, showing all the points of offence and defence in those places. Mr. Pendleton will give you orders for whatever outfit you want. Good morning, Sir." So began Hotchkiss' "career as Topographical Engineer of the Valley District of the Department of Northern Virginia, while that was Jackson's separate command, and then as Topographical Engineer of the Second Corps of the Army of Northern Virginia, under the respective Commands of Gens. Jackson, A. P. Hill, Ewell, and Early."[13]

Throughout the war in Virginia, Union generals frequently overestimated the size of the armies opposing them. The Confederate generals knew that they were outnumbered. The respective reactions to these perceptions determined the course of the Virginia campaigns. Union generals tended to mass their forces; Southern generals could not win by such tactics. Only by maneuvering to separate the enemy's formations, and by defeating them in detail could they hope to drive away the aggressor, invade his territory, and force him to the conference table. Lee and Jackson were brilliant practitioners of this strategy.

The prosecution of a successful campaign of maneuver not only requires an efficient organization and command structure, but also a detailed knowledge of the country over which the army has to move. The army commander needs to know the width, depth, and speed of rivers, the quality of roads and tracks, the shape of the ground—all of those features which can be used to help or hinder movement of the opposing forces. It was his knowledge of the Shenandoah Valley in particular, together with an ability to describe, sketch, and map topography, which made Hotchkiss indispensable to his generals.

He demonstrated his skills to Jackson shortly after the battle of Kernstown. This battle, although a strategic victory for the South, was a tactical defeat for the general, and Jackson had retreated to Narrow Passage Creek where he formed a defensive line. Hotchkiss examined the country along this creek and "reported it unfavorable for defense." He found that the position could be easily turned by several roads and that it would be difficult for an army to fall back speedily from that point. A few days later he reconnoitered Stony Creek and "the country from Massanutten Mountain across to Little North Mountain and found it a good one for defense." He mapped the area for Jackson and "advised him to make a stand there," advice which the general accepted.

This, the first professional encounter between the two men, established a relationship which few others ever achieved with Jackson. Here was the trained soldier, a West Pointer, well versed in the theory of military operations, and now, with 12-months' battle experience, accepting the advice of schoolmaster Hotchkiss whose military service was limited to a few rough-and-tumble weeks in the Appalachians. In unhesitatingly accepting the Stony Creek line, he paid tribute to Hotchkiss' skillful description of the terrain. Jackson held that position for sixteen days, ample time to form an opinion about it, but did not move until Union forces under Banks launched a full-scale attack.

From then on until his mortal wounding at Chancellorsville, Jackson made full use of Hotchkiss' eye for country, and entrusted him with many missions, sure in the knowledge that they would be properly executed.

To appreciate his value to successive commanders of II Corps, it is necessary to keep in mind the main events of the war in Virginia. Naturally enough the conquest of Virginia, the occupation of Richmond, the capital of the Confederacy, dominated the minds of the politicians in Washington. It was not just because the South was at their backdoor; Virginia was the most industrially advanced of the Confederate States, the one most able to produce the munitions of war. Eliminate Virginia, and the ability of the South to resist the might of the Northern states would be critically reduced.

McClellan, now commanding the Army of the Potomac, had decided that Richmond could be more easily taken from the east than by a direct thrust from the north. So while maintaining pressure from this direction he embarked on an ambitious amphibious operation to land his magnificently drilled and equipped army on the peninsula separating the York and James Rivers. The Confederate task was to keep as many Union formations as possible engaged elsewhere in order to prevent the creation of an overwhelming enemy force. Jackson succeeded in this, first by convincing the Union high command that he was stronger than was the case. Jackson may not have attacked at Kernstown had he known the strength of the opposition, but the fact that he did was interpreted in Washington as demonstrating the existence of a serious threat which could not be ignored. The following three months were occupied by a most remarkable series of maneuvers which were to mark Jackson as one of the greatest of field commanders. After Banks' attack on the Stony Creek position, he made an orderly retreat southward up the Valley, apparently reducing any threat to the Union reinforcement of McClellan. Banks therefore did not follow, and was further kept in ignorance by the cavalry screening Jackson's movements.

The threat to the Valley was not only from a northerly direction, but also from the west. A combination of the western and northern forces had to be prevented. Jackson took his six-thousand men out of the Valley, not westward but eastward over the Blue Ridge. Then, using the Virginia Central Railroad, he returned to the Valley at Staunton, moved westward, defeated General Robert H. Milroy at McDowell, and pursued him to Franklin before once again returning to the Valley to deal with Banks. In the defeat of Banks, Jackson made the topography of the Valley his ally. The distance between Winchester and Staunton is about 100 miles, the width of the Valley between the Blue Ridge to the east and the first ridges of the Appalachians to the west about 15 miles. Within the Valley, and running along its length for 50 miles is Massanutten Mountain. This feature was worth an army to Jackson. It provided him with two routes, the well-developed route along the turnpike to Winchester's front door, and the narrower more difficult route on the east side of the Massanuttens, down Page Valley to the side door. Banks had established a strong defensive position at Strasburg and firmly blocked the way to the front door, but the "tradesman's" entrance through Front Royal was only lightly held. Jackson moved directly toward Strasburg, then crossed the Massanutten Mountain, swept through Front Royal and wreaked havoc on Banks as he retreated pell-mell through Winchester, Jackson not stopping until the remnants of the Union army were north of the Potomac.

Now Jackson was in peril. Fremont's army of 15,000 was at Franklin to the southwest, Shields with 10,000 was just east of the Blue Ridge in the vicinity of Manassas Gap, within 25 miles of Strasburg, 50 miles behind Jackson. Jackson was trapped. But the speed, skillful use of cavalry, and good staff work on Jackson's part, combined with the difficulty the Union generals had in co-ordinating their movements, foiled the Union plan.

Jackson escaped, moved up the Valley, lured both Fremont and Shields deeper into hostile territory, kept them on opposite banks of the Shenandoah, and defeated them separately on successive days at Cross Keys and Port Republic, before joining Lee to frustrate McClellan on the peninsula. Between March 23, the Battle of Kernstown, and June 24, when Jackson left the Valley to join Lee, his army (never more than 17,000 strong) had marched over 550 miles, and defeated armies having a combined total of 55,000 in four major engagements.[14]

Before the withdrawal from Stony Creek, Hotchkiss was sent to a point where he could observe the deployment of the enemy and estimate their size and deduce their intention. The army fell back up the Valley, rounded the southern end of Massanutten, crossed the South Fork of the Shenandoah River, and went into camp on Elk Run on the road leading to Swift Run Gap. The route across Massanutten Mountain from New Market to Luray in Page Valley, which Jackson was to exploit a few weeks later, was a threat to his flank and rear once his force was south of New Market. To prevent, or at least delay, any possible assault from this direction, Jackson ordered Hotchkiss—hardly just a mapmaker—to go and burn the "Red" and the "Columbia" Bridges across the South Fork of the Shenandoah, on the roads leading from New Market eastward, if they were not already held by the enemy. He was to take to aid him all the cavalry he could find on the way. He took along with him his assistant mapmaker, Sergeant S. Howell Brown. At Shenandoah Iron Works he found his cavalry. Many of them, including their commander Captain Macon Jordan, who had been a pupil at Hotchkiss' Mossy Creek Academy, were drunk on applejack. After a short halt at Henry Forrer's, they went down to the river where Hotchkiss instructed Brown to prepare the Red Bridge for burning, but not to fire it until Hotchkiss had time to reach the other bridge. He then rode off with the companies of Captains Macon Jordan and George F. Sheetz toward the Columbia Bridge.

Sheetz's reconnaissance revealed no enemy at the bridge, so he was sent with about 50 men to burn it. At the same time Hotchkiss sent a detail to fire yet another bridge still farther down the river. Hardly had this been done when Sheetz and a few men came dashing back, at full gallop, pursued by the enemy. Hotchkiss succeeded in getting Jordan's men into the road to meet the attack, but at the first fire they ran away and could not be stopped. Hotchkiss escaped, made his way to the Red Bridge to warn the men there and to deploy them to meet the enemy, but they did not come on. Brown had burned the Red Bridge, but the other two remained intact. In a letter home describing this "escapade with Jordan," Hotchkiss said he had never seen a more disgraceful affair: "all owing, no doubt, to the state of intoxication of some of the men, and the want of discipline among them."

The following day, although it was Easter Sunday, he was making a map of the locality around Elk Run, but the next two days he was in the saddle again on reconnaissance work for Jackson. His report was accompanied by a map of his route, and the positions held by the enemy at Columbia Bridge.

Jackson remained below Swift Run Gap for ten days before moving toward Port Republic, preparatory to crossing the Blue Ridge at Brown's Gap. This afforded Hotchkiss an opportunity for a visit home. Apart from the joy of being with his family again, he was anxious about them on two counts. Shortly after his first meeting with Jackson, he learned from Sara that Nellie and Anna were very ill with scarlet fever. There were many anxious days before he heard that their recovery was certain. He shared that worrying time with colleagues who were to be less fortunate as this pestilence took its toll. Now he wanted to reassure himself that Nellie and Anna had fully recovered. He was also fearful for his family's safety. Not only were the Union soldiers at Harrisonburg, 12 miles away, but Federal units operating in the Appalachians were getting dangerously close. General Edward Johnson was barring their way at West View, a mere six miles from Staunton, but Federal cavalry had been to Jennings Gap, within four miles of the Hotchkiss Loch Willow home. Hotchkiss combined a visit home with a mission for Jackson. He was to meet General Johnson, find out the military situation on his front, and report back. By the time he did so Jackson was ready to move. A mixed force of infantry, cavalry, and artillery was sent to demonstrate against Banks in the neighborhood of Harrisonburg to cover the evacuation of the Elk Run camps and the march to Port Republic. With an escort of cavalry and a company of the 10th Virginia, commanded by Captain William B. Yancey, another former Mossy Creek pupil, Hotchkiss observed the reaction of the enemy from the summit of The Peak, the southernmost point of Massanutten Mountain. By the time he reported back that the enemy remained inactive, Jackson's army was on its arduous march through the mud and quicksands at the foot of the Blue Ridge. In company with the General and all the staff, he was engaged "with a whole regiment of men mending the worst road [he] ever saw in the Valley of Virginia." So bad were the conditions that it took three days to move the army the 15 miles to the entrance to Brown's Gap with its good, dry, turnpike over the Blue Ridge.

While the army made its surprise and comfortable return to the Valley on the cars of the Virginia Central Railroad, and Jackson set up his headquarters at the Virginia Hotel in Staunton, Hotchkiss again met with General Johnson, and reconnoitered the position of the enemy beyond West View.

Jackson's march to deal with the threat from the west began on May 7 when he and some of his staff rode out to join General Johnson's men moving along the Staunton-Parkersburg Turnpike, slowly pushing back the enemy's forward troops. The turnpike crosses the grain of the country, twisting and turning as it ascends and descends a series of serrated ridges separated by deep valleys. It was a country ideally suited for defense and ambuscade. One defensive position, Fort Johnson, was sited at the summit of Shenandoah Mountain, formerly a Confederate stronghold; it was now thought to be held by Union troops. Jackson ordered Hotchkiss to take a party of skirmishers on a flanking movement on the right, while another officer, Colonel T. H. Williamson, did similar duty on the left. They discovered that the enemy had abandoned the position and retreated to the next ridge. There they repeated the arduous task of checking the flanks of the route. Later, to speed the progress, Jackson sent Hotchkiss ahead with a party of skirmishers to each bend in the road. If the way was clear, a wave of his handkerchief was the signal for the march to be resumed.

In this fashion the advance came to the summit of Bull Pasture Mountain, within three miles of McDowell. Hotchkiss took Jackson "to a projecting ledge of rocks from which the enemy's position was visible and pointed out to him the details of the locality, supplementing this with a sketch map made on the spot showing the details in a general way of the topography" lying before them.[15] It was too late in the day for Jackson to mount an attack. So after instructing Hotchkiss to find a route to bring artillery to the top of Sitlington's Hill to the left of the turnpike, and Johnson to deploy his men in a defensive position, he sent his staff to the rear, intending to assault the Federal positions at McDowell the next day. He remained with Johnson. But the Federal general, Milroy, attacked before Jackson's assault was ready. In the ensuing vigorous battle, the Federals were driven back, but only after much confused fighting in which General Johnson was wounded, and 450 Confederates killed. Hotchkiss, hearing the sounds of battle of battle while resting at headquarters after his reconnaissance, immediately galloped the three miles back "to the top of Bull Pasture Mountain where I found Gen. Jackson all alone, in the road at the gap." Hotchkiss was at once ordered to deliver to General William B. Taliaferro, who had succeeded Johnson, the order to hold on until Jackson came up with the Stonewall Brigade. But by this time the fight was over.

The following day Hotchkiss went forward to reconnoiter, only to find that the enemy had retreated along the Bull Pasture River toward Franklin. He spent the rest of the day sketching the former battlefield on Sitlington's Hill and examining the surrounding country.

During the pursuit of Milroy, Jackson gave Hotchkiss another important task. He told him, "General Banks is in Harrisonburg, General Fremont is at Franklin, there is a good road between them. Gen. Fremont ought to march to Gen. Banks, ...I want the road between them and Dry River Gap blockaded by daylight tomorrow so he cannot do this.... Now don't take any counsel of your fears." With the reliable Sergeant Brown, Hotchkiss rode the fifty miles to Churchville, arriving about midnight. There he ordered Captain Frank Sterrett to assemble his men, and then rode home where he and Brown fed themselves and their horses.

When Sterrett reported, Hotchkiss and Brown were ready to move. They went by way of Mossy Creek to the vicinity of Ottobine Church, not far from Dry River Gap, where Hotchkiss recorded that they "obtained axes, crowbars, etc. from the farm houses of the vicinity, many of whom I knew personally." The party pushed forward to where the road to Franklin passed through a rocky gorge. There he directed the men to fell trees, and roll rocks into the road as they slowly moved back toward the Valley. Those operations were completed just before daylight. Thus, in the course of a few hours the road was effectively blockaded for some distance. Hotchkiss concluded the account, "Having completed the duty assigned me, on the morning of the 11th we retired to the vicinity of Ottobine where we got breakfast and fed our horses and rested for a short time."[16]

The success of this operation was demonstrated two weeks later when Fremont was ordered to Harrisonburg to cut off Jackson's withdrawal from Winchester. Colonel Albert Tracey, a Union officer with Fremont, described in his journal the difficulty of complying with this order. Apart from a lack of transport, a lack of provisions, and floods, "the road southeasterly to Harrisonburg was impeded by bridges ruined, culverts torn away and trees felled across—the whole to an extent tending to involve great embarrassment and delay."[17]

Hotchkiss made his way back to Jackson, who by this time had retraced his steps and was in the vicinity of McDowell on his march back to the Valley. Jackson sent him to overtake the advance of the army which was on its way to Staunton, and turn it toward Jennings Gap and Stribling Springs. Having done that, he was to find quarters for the General and his staff at Lebanon White Sulphur Springs. Once again he was close to home and on May 16, a day of fasting and prayer proclaimed by President Davis, Hotchkiss rode to Loch Willow, meeting on the way a wagon-load of his people coming out to visit him. The next day the army camped on the banks of North River, opposite Bridgewater, with headquarters at Mount Solon.

It was here that Generals Jackson and Ewell planned the brilliant operation which resulted in the recapture of Winchester and the rout of Banks' army.[18] Banks was encouraged to believe that Jackson would attack his defensive line at Strasburg, to which he had fallen back, closely pressed by Jackson's cavalry. The deception was strengthened by detaching part of Ewell's division to join Jackson.

Whatever route Jackson might take, he had to cross North River, which was too deep to ford. Hotchkiss solved the problem for him by proposing that farm wagons should be pushed into the river one behind the other, closed up, and planked over. Simultaneously, Hotchkiss, in company with Lieutenant Keith Boswell, rode down the Valley to reconnoiter the enemy's position, climbing to the summit of the Three-topped Mountain at the north end of Massanutten Mountain. With a cavalry escort, he went down to the enemy's lines at Pugh's Run, in sight of the enemy pickets. That may have been part of a deception plan, because by this time Jackson was in Page Valley within ten miles of Front Royal. Other than obtaining a reliable report that Banks had not moved, and hence his own movements undiscovered, there was little information that Jackson needed from that front—indeed none that his cavalry could not have provided.

Returning from this reconnaissance, Hotchkiss found orders at Columbia Bridge instructing him to report to headquarters. After an early start and a ride of 44 miles, he arrived at Front Royal just as the Federals were forced across the two forks of the Shenandoah. The following day Jackson ordered him to take a party of cavalry down the Cedarville-Middletown road to find out where Banks was. He soon struck the Federal pickets. Calling up, in succession, cavalry, infantry, and artillery, Hotchkiss pushed on toward Middletown and reached its vicinity in time to assist the larger force sent by Jackson to cut Banks' retreating column. His role in the Battle of Winchester and the expulsion of Banks from Virginia is not revealed in his diary. He made no entries for the

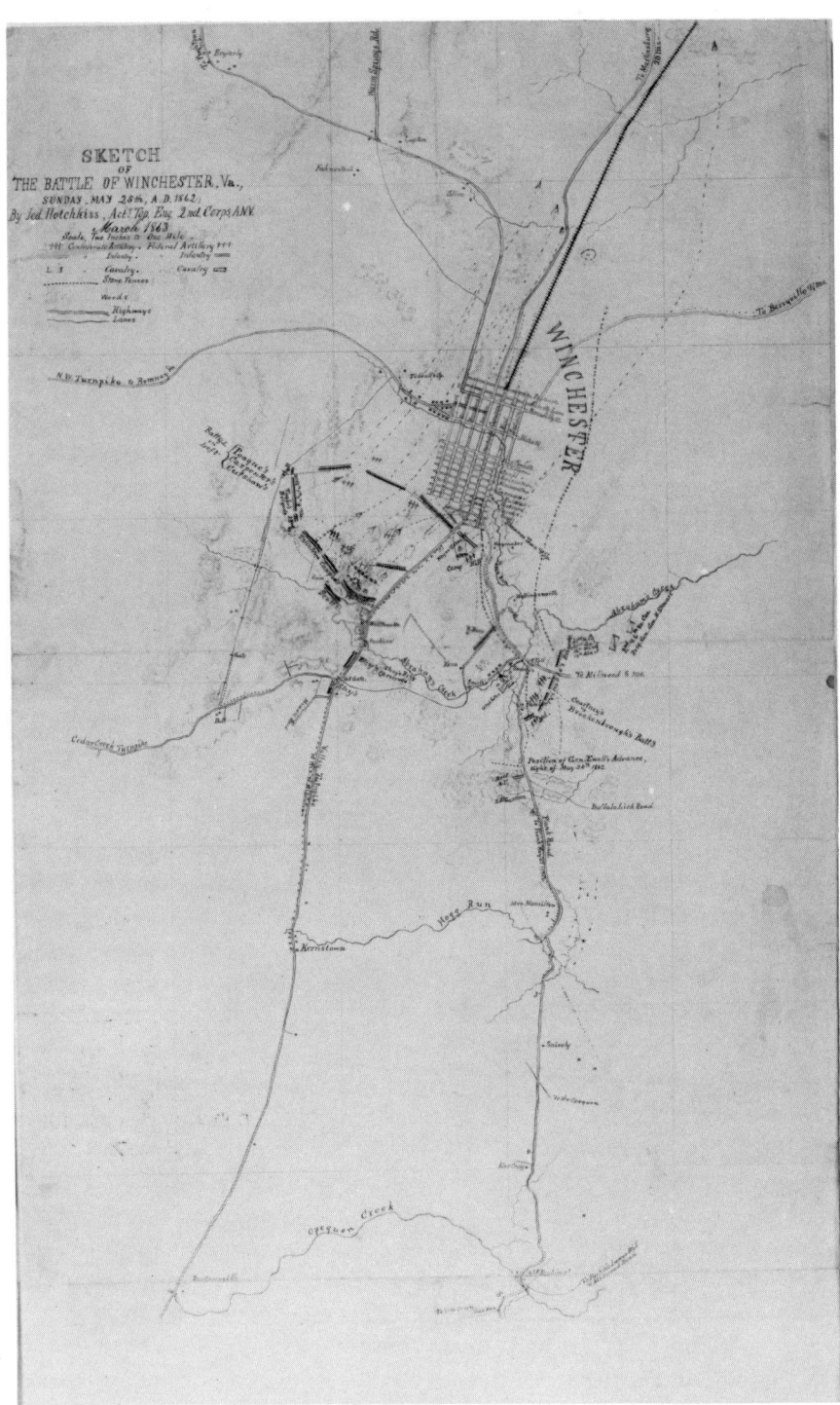

Battle of Winchester, 1862. Map made in March 1863 to illustrate General Thomas J. (Stonewall) Jackson's report. This is one of three maps donated by Hotchkiss' granddaughter, Mrs. Ellen Christian, to The Handley Library, Winchester, Virginia.
Jedediah Hotchkiss Collection, Winchester-Frederick County Historical Society Archives

five exciting days from May 25 through May 29, but on the 30th recorded that he was with the 5th Virginia Regiment who were skirmishing with the enemy not far from Harper's Ferry. There he "got chased by a Yankee cavalryman, and as [he] had no arms [he] made good use of his horse."

Jackson had achieved all he could. He had forced the diversion of thousands of Union troops from their intended march on Richmond to deal with his apparent threat to Washington. It was time for him to go. In the withdrawal, Hotchkiss was again entrusted with important missions. Jackson's army was dispersed over an area extending from Front Royal to Winchester and to the Potomac. It now had to be concentrated, brought onto the Valley pike, and hurried south before the Union pincer movement closed the main route to the safety of the Valley. Hotchkiss was sent to lead the troops operating in the neighborhood of Harper's Ferry to Winchester where Jackson would stay as long as he could. But if the enemy got there first Hotchkiss was to bring them "round through the mountains." Jackson did not spell out what route he was to take. He trusted that Hotchkiss' local knowledge and topographical flare would meet the occasion. They were not put to the test. At Winchester, Hotchkiss found neither Jackson nor the enemy. So the troops continued their march and joined Jackson at Newtown, 10 miles north of Strasburg. All had marched 28 miles, some 35.

The destruction of Banks yielded great materiel as well as psychological benefits. The Confederates had seized large quantities of small arms, ammunition, and food (some of it on the hoof). Jackson was determined to move those captured goods back if he possibly could. His movement up the Valley was determined by the speed at which his train of horse-drawn wagons, hampered by the booty, could move ahead of his troops. The difficulty was that, double-banked and well closed up, the whole column occupied 7-8 miles of road. "The train got in great confusion," wrote Hotchkiss, "and the General sent me to go along with it and get it in order, and direct that no wagon should stop to water, etc., and keep all to the right and in motion."[19]

While the army withdrew, keeping Fremont at bay, and protecting its flanks by the destruction of the bridges that Hotchkiss had been unable to burn in April, Jackson was planning how to deal with the twin threats posed by the Union forces moving down both sides of the Massanutten Mountain. Hotchkiss was consulted several times about the country in the neighborhood of Port Republic. As the army turned eastward round the southern end of the mountain, Hotchkiss was sent to The Peak to observe the movements of the enemy down Page Valley. Later he reported to Jackson that their advanced formations were encamped near Conrad's Store. Meanwhile, the army enjoyed "a well earned and much needed rest beside the bright water and in the green pastures, and park like forests along the road between Cross Keys, ...and the north bank of the river at Port Republic."[20] Hotchkiss made a map of the surrounding country and maintained communication with the signalman he had posted on The Peak.

At that point Jackson had completed his withdrawal. The moment had come to prevent the junction of the two Federal armies. The battle of Cross Keys on June 8, skillfully managed by General Ewell, defeated Fremont's larger, but ineptly led army, on the west side of the Shenandoah, and so permitted a concentration of force to deal with Shields' troops moving up the east bank of Shenandoah's South Fork.[21]

The plan was nearly ruined, with potentially diastrous results, on the morning of June 8. While all was quiet in Jackson's camps near Port Republic, and just as the General was mounting his horse to ride to Ewell's command, a detachment of Shields' cavalry, with two sections of light artillery, drove in the Confederate pickets. They forded the river to capture the village. One gun turned north to seize the south end of the bridge carrying the road to Cross Keys, the other south to attack the ammunition train parked outside the village. "Providentially, Jackson had time to ride rapidly across the bridge before the street was occupied by the Federal cavalry, but a portion of his staff was captured and affairs were in a critical condition for a short time."[22] Jackson soon gained control of the situation and drove the intruders back across the river. Hotchkiss, exhausted, was resting in his tent near the wagon train when the excitement began. Although sick with a violent headache, a consequence of the arduous duty of the previous days, he was soon helping to strike the tents and load the headquarter's wagons; this done, he mounted his horse and rode rapidly up the river out of range of the enemy guns. When the panic subsided he went to Cave Hill from where he had a good view of the battle of Cross Keys.

With Fremont neutralized, and the position at Port Republic secured from any further assault, Jackson now turned on Shields' forces. This Federal army had struggled along the western foot of the Blue Ridge, hampered by the rain-swollen streams which crossed its path. The advance had reached Lewiston farm six miles below Port Republic. There the Federals selected a strong position, siting their guns on a level cut into the hillside for a charcoal hearth. It was protected on the left by a dense forest extending toward the Blue Ridge, and in front by a ravine cut by a fast-flowing stream.

Jackson crossed the river, as he had North River, on a Hotchkiss-style footbridge of wagons. This time, however, it was not so well constructed

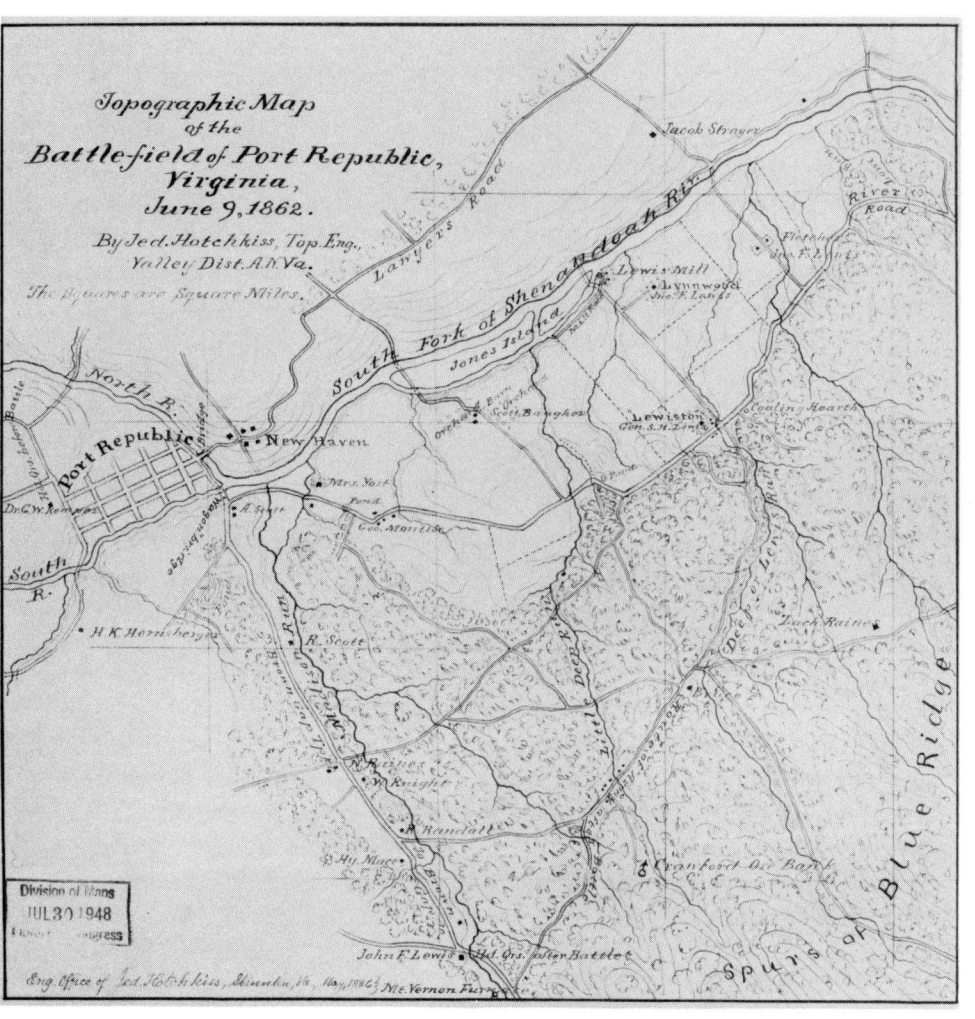

The Battle of Port Republic. Map prepared for William Allan's *History of the campaign of General T. J. (Stonewall) Jackson in the Shenandoah Valley from November 4, 1861 to June 17, 1862*, first published in 1886.

Hotchkiss Map Collection #96, Library of Congress

and caused some delay. That and Jackson's impatience nearly brought disaster. Winder's Brigade, which had opened the attack on the Federal position, was subjected to a devastating fire from the guns on the coaling. It was in this situation that Jackson ordered Hotchkiss "to take General Taylor around those batteries."

"The head of Taylor's column was promptly turned to the right, and in concealment, marched as rapidly through the woods as the rough character of the ground and the thick growth of young timber would admit." Hotchkiss intended to position Taylor's brigade for a flank attack. But before he could complete the movement Winder's situation had become so desperate that only an immediate assault on the battery could save him from defeat. It was decided to charge the guns from across the ravine. Taylor's men, "although opposed by a galling fire of musketry and artillery at short range," captured the battery, but only held it after a desperate fight in which the position changed hands several times.[23]

The elimination of the batteries turned the tide of battle, and the Federals were soon in full retreat. On orders from his general, Hotchkiss led Jackson's tired army through the woods to Mt. Vernon Furnace, then up to Brown's Gap. While the army rested, secure in the folds of the Blue Ridge, Hotchkiss had one more service to perform before the Valley Campaign could be said to be over. He had to examine the South River fords to discover whether the army could recross. He found the water too deep to enable the caissons to cross and keep their boxes dry, and so recommended that the fords be filled up with stones, a procedure which he supervised at two points, one for the fighting units to cross near Port Republic, the other for the baggage train above Weyer's Cave at Patterson's Mill. On June 12, three days after the battle of Port Republic, Jackson moved his troops into "the noble park-like oak forests between the forks of the Shenandoah, in the vicinity of Weyer's Cave and Mt. Meridian, where for five days of splendid June weather, he rested, recuperated and refitted his army."[24] Hotchkiss also rested and recuperated.

Jackson's Valley Campaign of 1862 ranks among the greatest of military feats. To have taken part in it, even in a lowly capacity, would become a matter of great pride, comparable with that evoked by service on D-Day, or at Iwo Jima. Hotchkiss, who had been as close to the commanding general as anyone could be, recalled and relived the experience time and time again. Important though it was as a military operation, the interaction of those two men, the loquacious Hotchkiss and the taciturn Jackson, was even more remarkable. Hotchkiss' admiration for Jackson is understandable. Jackson was a professional soldier who Hotchkiss assumed would know his trade, and experience supported that assumption. On the other hand, Hotchkiss was a schoolmaster, an amateur mapmaker, a self-taught surveyor with no engineering experience. Yet Jackson employed him on important military tasks. Jackson had others who could be regarded as better qualified for at least some of those assignments. S. Howell Brown was a skilled surveyor. James Keith Boswell entered the service of Virginia as a civil engineer, and served with General John Magruder before being assigned to Jackson's staff. Hotchkiss' combination of age, maturity, and ability to communicate, must have made an immediate impression on Jackson, and he demonstrated his knowledge and intuitive understanding of the importance of topography in warfare within days of their first meeting. Jackson was as certain in his choice of staff as he was in the disposition of his troops, or in his reading of the intentions of his enemies. Whatever the mechanism by which Jackson made his judgments, it brought to his service a man who would perform the tasks assigned to him with skill and imagination, regardless of rank and station.

The time had come for Lee to concentrate his forces at Richmond to meet the threatened attack of the Army of the Potomac. Returning from an abortive journey on June 17 to meet General Thomas T. Munford, Hotchkiss found Jackson's army gone from its camp. He caught up with it at Rockfish Gap in the Blue Ridge on its way to join Lee. In spite of all the turmoil of the past three months, Jackson had not forgotten his first order to Hotchkiss. He now sent him back to the Valley expressly to continue the work of "preparing an accurate map of that important military field."[25] For three whole weeks, Hotchkiss was able to give all his attention to this task. It was a peaceful, relaxed interlude during which he spent time with his family, visited neighbors and friends, and watched the ripening harvest. This sunny time ended on July 15, when, at 10 p.m., after a full day's work on the map, he received an order from Jackson calling him to Gordonsville.[26] A new phase in the war was about to begin.

Lee had successfully repulsed McClellan in a bloody seven-day battle. Now a new threat was developing. From the armies of Fremont, Banks, and McDowell, the North had organized a new force under Major General John Pope. With the departure of Jackson from the Valley, two corps of this force crossed the Blue Ridge at Chester Gap to threaten Gordonsville and Lee's lines of communication and supply with the Valley.[27] To deal with this threat and to "suppress Pope," Jackson was detached from the Richmond front. It proved no easy task, but eventually the Confederacy defeated Pope by one of those daring divisions of forces which characterized the Lee-Jackson partnership. On that occasion the maneuver culminated in the Second Battle of Manassas. Never was a boastful general so confused, so thoroughly "suppressed," as Pope. Lee immediately took advantage of the situation and marched his victorious army north, crossing the Potomac into Maryland on September 5. Twelve days later the contending armies met in bloody conflict in the gentle countryside along Antietam Creek. The battered but undefeated Confederate army withdrew across the Potomac to the relative safety of the Valley.

In contrast to the campaign in the Valley, Hotchkiss played little part in the events leading up to the Second Battle of Manassas and the invasion of Maryland. Except for the selection of a concealed route by which the army could be moved prior to the battle of Cedar Run and reconnaissance duties during that battle, he was employed almost exclusively in mapmaking.[28] In particular Jackson asked him to make as many maps as possible of the country between the Rapidan and the Potomac.

When the time came to carry the war into Northern territory, Lee gave Jackson the task of destroying the garrison of 11,000 Federal troops at Harper's Ferry. In that operation Hotchkiss, on September 13, established a line of signals from headquarters to General John George Walker, whose brigade was located on Loudoun Heights. After the surrender of the Federal garrison, Jackson joined the remainder of the army on the east bank of Antietam Creek, leaving Hotchkiss to assist in the destruction of the bridges across the Potomac, and in the collection of arms.

On the day of the Antietam battle, September 17, Hotchkiss went to Charles Town "and transacted some business there, then on to Shepherdstown and found the battle raging around Sharpsburg." It would seem that he was not at that time in close touch with Jackson, and was unaware of the development of the campaign.

He did not recross the Potomac until the day after the battle. When he did so he found that Jackson wanted a reconnaissance up the river. He found a guide and located the position of the enemy pickets. When he could go no further up the river on the Maryland side, he crossed back to the Virginia shore and continued his reconnaissance as far as Terrapin Neck. He sent his report to Jackson by courier; then, after supper, he assisted in the posting of a strong picket of all arms sent to guard Shepherds Fork. He returned to Shepherdstown intending to cross the river there to seek Jackson, but was forced by the press of horses, wagons, and ambulances to make his way along the river's edge and cross by the ford at Boteler's Mill. Falling in with General Jeb Stuart, he learned that Jackson had received his report, and went with Stuart to Shepherdstown. Hotchkiss then lay down "in the street of Shepherdstown, beside a fire some soldiers had kindled, and slept for two hours, being very weary."[29] The whole army crossed the Potomac during the night of September 18. Hotchkiss wrote in his diary, "Our recrossing of the river without any loss, must be considered one of the most successful military movements."[30]

McClellan did not make a serious attempt to follow Lee's army, so Jackson was able to remain in the lower Valley, virtually unmolested until late November. The two-month respite from military activity allowed Hotchkiss to escape from the verminous camps to enjoy his favorite activities, roaming and mapping the countryside, sketching its topography, staying with friends, and renewing old acquaintances. He even managed to make two visits home. One, just before he rejoined Jackson's staff near Fredericksburg, was to get over a bout of sickness following a chill. Hotchkiss had not been well since the army returned to Virginia. The troops, assembled on the south bank of the Opequon Creek, took advantage of the stream to wash off the dirt of their long marches and battles from their bodies and their clothes. Hotchkiss, also cleaned up, later complained in his diary, "I am not well; cleaned up too much after being so long dirty, I suppose." There was much jaundice in the camp, and Hotchkiss spent the greater part of late September confined to bed.

His topographical duties gave him some relief from the squalid conditions of the camp as he rode out to map a fine country on "a genuine October day." He enjoyed "the bracing air, the fine wild grapes, and the mountain scenery." That fall was exceptionally dry, and as Hotchkiss rode home later that month, he noted that "the Great Valley [was] almost desolate from the drought." November brought cooler weather, with flurries of snow, and Hotchkiss began to find sketching cold work. Nevertheless he persisted with his exploration of the unmapped portions of the Valley, as well as some areas immediately to the east of the Blue Ridge. It was during his return into the Valley via Swift Run Gap toward the end of November that he became so thoroughly chilled that he became ill with headache and sickness. He decided to go home for the weekend. On the way he found orders at Staunton for him to report to Orange Court House at once, "but was too unwell to obey." Home and medicine ensured that he felt much better on the following Sunday so he started back to camp that afternoon. It was his thirty-fourth birthday, and he was reluctant to go. He "left home with a sad heart," for the army was gone from the Valley and the fate of both was uncertain; he did not know when he would be home again.

For over a month the Federal Army of the Potomac remained in Maryland, not crossing the Potomac in force until October 26. Then it did so east of the Blue Ridge, to occupy an area stretching south to the Rappahannock. The following day Lee moved Longstreet's Corps up the Valley, to cross the Blue Ridge at Chester Gap and continue southeast toward Culpeper Court House, where Longstreet established his headquarters on November 5. Jackson did not move from the neighborhood of Winchester until November 22, by which time the Army of the Potomac had concentrated opposite Fredericksburg, and Lee was obliged to move his army to prevent a crossing of the Rappahannock at that point. Slowly the players took their places for another contest. This time there was to be no uncertainty in the outcome. A catastrophic defeat awaited the North at Fredericksburg on December 13, 1862.

It took Hotchkiss four days to ride to Jackson's headquarters at Guiney's, eight miles south of Fredericksburg. Once there, Jackson requested a map of Caroline County; no chance now of getting back to the Valley. Not much chance either of making the map, for he was again required for reconnaissance tasks, eastward downriver to Port Royal, as well as in the vicinity of Fredericksburg. The new Federal commander, Major General Ambrose Everett Burnside, opened the attack across the Rappahannock just before dawn on December 11, and attempted to establish pontoon bridges under the cover of heavy artillery fire. He eventually succeeded at Deep Run one-and-a-half miles below the town, and was able to move some troops across, but did not develop his assault until two days later. Lee and Jackson examined the situation early on December 12 and made plans to meet the attack. Hotchkiss and S. Howell Brown joined Jackson as he examined the terrain on both sides of Deep Run, and later in the day Hotchkiss accompanied him as he rode down to the Rappahannock from Hamilton's Crossing to examine the country adjacent to the river bank. Everything was ready for the morrow.

Hotchkiss wrote in his diary: "*Saturday, Dec. 13th.* [1862] We were up at an early hour and off to the battlefield by daylight; the tents were struck and the wagons loaded up and sent to the rear. All our troops were early in position; ..." The diary entry continues as if confident of the outcome. Lee, Jackson, Longstreet, and all the Confederate troops had good reason for optimism: they were fighting a defensive battle from a superb position which the enemy had decided to attack head on. Unless the Corps and Divisional commanders made serious mistakes the outcome was plain. After a red and fiery sun drove away the early morning fog, the carnage was completed under an almost cloudless sky. That night, overhead, was a grand auroral display, one of the finest Hotchkiss had ever seen, but in the valley of the Rappahannock the thick white mist had returned, penetrated only by the screams of the dying. It seems incredible that Burnside seriously considered renewing the attack on Sunday. Fortunately he was dissuaded, but even so kept his battered divisions across the river for two whole days before accepting defeat.

Jackson established his winter headquarters on the grounds of "Moss Neck," Richard Corbin's house between Fredericksburg and Port Royal. The following four months were happy ones for Jackson's military family, for its members were able to enjoy all the amenities available to the wealthy plantation family living there. There was a good library, good company. Hotchkiss' friendship with members of Jackson's staff developed during this time. Notable among these officers were Colonel Alexander Swift ("Sandie") Pendleton, Colonel William Allan, and Lieutenant James Keith Boswell. With Allan he would talk of maps and battles, discuss "what added to the charm of reading history," and read to one another books from the Corbin library, thus laying the foundation of their post-war co-operation. The young, unmarried, staff officers were particularly appreciative of the social life afforded by the presence of Kate Corbin and her friends. Pendleton fell in love with Kate and they were married a year later.

Here Jackson, with the help of Colonel Charles James Faulkner, wrote his reports of the battles and marches of the preceding year, and Hotchkiss was kept busy drawing maps as illustrations. On the whole it was a happy time for Hotchkiss. The victory at Fredericksburg had uplifted his spirit as it had done for the whole army. He confided no complaints to his diary when he returned from home leave either at Christmas, or in February. He enjoyed the work and the opportunity for prolonged discussion and debate with his companions, particularly his conversations with Jackson.

Hotchkiss' report-writing required him to question many officers about the position or movement of their formations, to settle just where a particular unit was at a particular time. There was lively discussion in trying to settle the differing recollections of that incident-packed year of 1862. It was obvious to Hotchkiss that he was handling the raw material of history, and it was during that time at Moss Neck that he began to think of writing an account of the battles. He noted in his diary for the last day of January, "Rec'd a letter from Harrison asking for maps, etc. of our battles, —which I must refuse, as I intend to write myself."

The four-months respite from active combat was punctuated by several events concerning his family or his friends, which disturbed this idyll. His own problem at this time concerned the Loch Willow property. It had to be sold because there was simply insufficient income to pay the outstanding installments on the mortgage. Nelson and his family lived in the "mansion." Their presence, a mere hundred yards up the hill from Jed's more modest home, was a comfort to Sara, and Hotchkiss could have some peace of mind knowing that his family was being looked after. Nelson, however, did not want to stay in Churchville. According to his daughter Lora, writing long after the event, Nelson had received threats from some of his Northern acquaintances when the Union troops had come close by during the spring and summer of the previous year. Although, following the battle of Fredericksburg, the enemy had left the Valley, there was no guarantee that they would not be back. It was a risk Nelson was not prepared to take. Considering the risks to which Hotchkiss had been exposed almost daily, it must have been hard to understand his brother's behavior, and no doubt Sara was scathing in her comments.

Hotchkiss had eight days' leave at Christmas, which he used mainly for family business, the hiring of servants, and the settling of accounts, but it is probable that the brothers discussed the future of the farm at that time. During further leave in February the farm was put up for sale, and although they received a good bid, they were not satisfied with the offer and put off the sale to the end of the month. Early in March both Sara and Nelson wrote Hotchkiss despondent letters, possibly because no sale had been made. They regretted that they had not accepted the earlier offer. The letters added to his distress, for they arrived just when his position in the army seemed to be in jeopardy.[31] He was so upset that he confessed to his diary, "I did no work to be mentioned, —being too much disturbed. Alas, alas," he said, "what am I coming to? But there is a just God and He always sustained me and brought good out of evil, and glory be to Him." Thus he composed himself. The expected better news was not long in coming, for he recorded on March 25, "Got a letter from my brother and heard he had sold our farm, and he will soon move.[32] Hotchkiss hoped that all might prove to be for the best.

Military duties often brought him into contact with old friends, colleagues or one-time pupils from his days at Mossy Creek. Not all of these occurred under the most propitious circumstances, but few could have been more distressing than the visit he made to the guardhouse of the 10th Virginia Regiment. Locked up was Samuel J. Forrer, son of Hotchkiss' patron and friend, Daniel Forrer, charged with desertion. Execution by firing squad could be the penalty if the charge was proved. Hotchkiss, armed with a pocket full of tracts and Testaments, rode down the river through a lush green countryside, peachtrees in full blossom, and thought of the young Sam of fifteen years before. He remembered his stubborn will and wayward disposition, and telling him that he would "come to the gallows unless he radically changed his notions of right and wrong." This prophesy Hotchkiss was now to do his best to frustrate. He found his "young friend thoroughly cut down, deeply mortified at his situation." Young Forrer claimed that he had attempted to cross the lines to secure medical supplies, had passed himself off as a British subject, was arrested, and then attempted to escape. Hotchkiss saw the young man's commanding officers, and then some members of the court which was to try him. He could only hope that Sam would escape death and receive only some severe punishment. Exactly what the outcome was we are not told, but, whether due to Hotchkiss' intervention or to the defending attorney, John B. Baldwin, Sam survived, saw service at Gettysburg, and lived into the next century.[33]

The Confederate defensive position at Fredericksburg was so strong that only by a flanking attack could it be taken without an intolerable toll in killed and wounded. Burnside made two further attempts to cross the river before he in turn was replaced, on January 22, by Major General Joseph Hooker. The first attempt was planned to take place at the end of December. A cavalry expedition was to turn Lee's left flank, disrupt his lines of communication, and conceal the main point of attack which was to be a crossing of the Rappahannock at Seddon's, down river from Fredericksburg. Opposition from within his own army scuttled this plan. The second more realistic plan called for turning Lee's left with the mass of Burnside's army, an operation which his successor would adopt at the end of April. What might be possible in the spring was impossible in the winter. On the day after the movement began, the weather intervened, a terrible rain and snowstorm set in, streams rose rapidly, water flooded the low-lying lands, and the roads were soon converted into deep mud. Long before the columns reached the fords of the Rappahannock, Federal wagons, artillery, even horsemen, were mired in great numbers. Burnside's "mud march" achieved nothing but the final ruin of his military reputation.[34]

Hooker too was thwarted by the weather. He had intended to launch a major cavalry raid against Lee's lines of communication on April 13, but heavy rains made the fords of the Rappahannock impassable, so that the raid was delayed until the end of the month to coincide with the major offensive. At General Jackson's headquarters all was calm. Hotchkiss was more concerned about his horse which had wandered off, and in the contents of a box of provisions, which his servant William Gearing had brought from home, than in any movement there might be among Hooker's troops on the other side of the Rappahannock. Jackson had his wife and child visit him during the week preceding the battle, even when Lee's intelligence indicated that the Federal offensive was imminent. That was not a sign of slackness, or complacency—there could be no room for either in an army which knew that it was outnumbered 2 to 1—but was an acceptance that the initiative was with Hooker. Furthermore the winter months had been well used in refitting the army, and the morale of the troops was high. Lee, Jackson, Stuart, the whole army, were confident that they would react effectively in the coming attack.

Early on Wednesday, April 29, Hotchkiss learned that the enemy had crossed the Rappahannock. "Soon the sounds of coming strife, musketry and artillery, were heard by all." What they heard was a diversionary attack across the river below Fredericksburg. The main assault was being developed farther up the river where Hooker had pushed two corps across at Kelley's Ford. By nightfall these columns had reached the Rapidan. On the right, Jackson's corps, with the exception of Early's division, which was already there, moved up from Grace Church and Moss Neck to the vicinity of Hamilton's Crossing to contain the Federal bridgeheads below Fredericksburg. Hotchkiss worked on a map of Caroline County in the morning, then rode along the defenses, before being ordered back by Jackson.

The intentions of the enemy were now clear. No major attack was being developed below Fredericksburg, so Lee sent Anderson's division in the direction of Chancellorsville to meet Hooker's main thrust, and at the same time protect United States Ford on the Rappahannock. While the unequal forces moved to meet each other in a clearing in an otherwise dense and almost impenetrable forest of scrubby oak and pine which had given this region the name of the "Wilderness," Hotchkiss was hastily "striking off eight maps" of the country between the Rappahannock and its tributary river, the Rapidan. Hardly had he done this than he was ordered by Jackson to find a feasible route by which the corps could be moved to Salem Church on the plank road from Fredericksburg to Chancellorsville. This reconnaissance took most of the moonlit night of April 30/May 1. By the time he reported back to Jackson at 4:30 a.m., the troops were already on their way, and the wagons about to be off to Guiney's. Hotchkiss followed on later with Brown, overtook the army at Tabernacle Church, finished the maps and supplied them to the divisional commanders. By the end of the day all of Jackson's Corps, apart from Early's division which was left to contain the enemy below Fredericksburg, was within a mile and a half of Chancellorsville. This rapid movement completely disrupted Hooker's own planned advance and he was forced back into the protection of his strong defenses. Generals Lee and Jackson with their staff, including Hotchkiss, slept that night at "the top of the hill where the furnace road turns off."

It was here at an early hour that the two generals took stock of the situation and agreed to the flanking movement which was to mark out the Chancellorsville battle as their most brilliant victory, the true pinnacle of Confederate military endeavor, but bought at an incalculable price, the mortal wounding of its principal architect.

Hotchkiss, in his diary, described the events of that day:

> *Saturday, May 2nd.* The Generals were up at an early hour and had a consultation, in the pines on the top of the hill where the Catherine Furnace road turns from the Plank Road, sitting on Yankee cracker boxes which the enemy had left there. I went down to Mr. Welford's where General Stuart had his quarters, and ascertained the roads that led around to the enemy's rear and came back and reported to Generals Lee and Jackson, who consulted and examined the map and then started the Second Corps down by the furnace, Rodes division in front, and went on to the Brock road, and then up it a piece and into a private road, and so on to the Plank Road and across both Plank Roads to the Old Turnpike and formed our line of battle at the (Lucket's) house and with three lines of battle fell on the enemy's rear at Talley's at precisely 6 o'clock, and after an infantry fight on our side, of 32 minutes, the enemy using infantry and artillery, we routed them and drove them completely from the field and some three miles beyond driving them out of two lines of entrenchments and on to some breastworks....[35]

What Hotchkiss didn't say was that Jackson had taken 28,000 of Lee's army on a 12-mile march, leaving his commander with only 14,000 men to oppose Hooker's 70,000. The risks were enormous; had Hooker divined the true intention of Jackson's movement Lee's army could have been destroyed. The gamble paid off. Although the movement was detected, its meaning was not, and Jackson's men burst upon unsuspecting Northerners, eating supper, their arms stacked.

Hotchkiss did not immediately join Jackson's marching column but remained at headquarters to copy a map for General Lee. This done, he caught up with the advance and then, from time to time, made "sketches showing points reached in the march." These Jackson included in his dispatches to Lee. He remained with Jackson during the assault.

The attack, centered on the Old Turnpike Road, was made by troops extended to the right and left of the road, advancing through dense thickets of scrub. By the time they had come within two miles of Chancellorsville the Confederates' leading divisions had become a confused mass. It was time for their third division, A. P. Hill's, to take up the advance. During the lull in the battle while that division came up, Jackson, accompanied by some of his staff and couriers, rode forward to reconnoiter. Hotchkiss rode beside Jackson until they "reached the old school house in a little opening in the wood from which the line of Federal timber works was visible...."[36]

At this point Hotchkiss left the general's party to investigate a road which turned off to the right. He soon found himself in front of a Federal line of battle covering Hazel Grove farm. Swiftly withdrawing, he sought the cover of the woods and galloped back, behind the line that Hill was forming along the abandoned enemy works, toward the turnpike. As he approached this road he heard a volley fired by the troops to his right. Realizing that it was aimed in the general direction that Jackson had taken, he put spurs to his horse and rode on rapidly until he "came upon Jackson and his party on the left of the road in the open space made by the junction of the numerous roads that there meet." It was light enough for him to see that several of the staff were helping Jackson off his horse and that he was badly wounded. Hotchkiss "hastened back for an ambulance and some spirits and found Dr. McGuire and sent him forward."[37]

Hotchkiss' diary makes no reference to Jackson's reconnaissance, saying only "by accident our men fired into each other and by that fire General Jackson was wounded," and that he, Hotchkiss, went in search of McGuire. That Hotchkiss was with Jackson when he moved ahead of the pickets, but not when the volley was fired, was revealed in a letter he wrote Hunter McGuire, October 8, 1898.[38]

Later that night Hotchkiss went to the Wilderness Tavern, where General Jackson "was yet in a state of stuper [sic] from the shock he had received, not having rallied enough to have his wounds dressed." At midnight Hotchkiss started back to Lee's headquarters to report the tragic outcome of an otherwise spectacular success. It took all of four hours to make this journey, making a wide detour to avoid the enemy who had penetrated the space between Jackson's force and the divisions remaining with Lee. When he arrived he found that the news of the wounding of Jackson had already reached General Lee, who "was much distressed and said he would rather a thousand times it had been himself. He did not wish to converse about it."[39]

After resting awhile and breakfasting with Lee, Hotchkiss was sent back with a message to General Stuart, who had taken over Jackson's command, to press the enemy vigorously and make juncture of the two wings of Lee's army. This done, Hotchkiss started

> to look for my friend Boswell, whom I had not seen or heard of since the fight. I went to where the General was wounded and there I found him, some 20 steps in advance, by the road side, dead, pierced through the heart by two balls and wounded in the leg. I was completely overcome, although I expected it from the state of his mind before, expecting to be killed in this fight. His body had been riffled of hat, field glasses, pistol, daguerreotype, &c., but his look in death was as peaceful and as pleasant as in life. I procured an ambulance and took him to where the General was, at Wilderness Tavern, and with many tears buried him in a grave which I had dug in the family burying ground at Elwood, the family home of Major J. Horace Lacy, by the side of General Jackson's arm which had been amputated and buried there. We buried him just as the moon rose, wrapped in his martial coat, Rev. B. T. Lacy making a feeling prayer. Brown, who assisted me, the two men I had employed to dig the grave, Mr. Lacy and myself were all that were present. I wept for him as for a brother; he was kind and gentle and with as few faults as most men. Peace to his memory.[40]

The following day, Hotchkiss, with a party of pioneers to clear the road of obstructions, was sent in front of the ambulance which took Jackson from Wilderness Tavern to Mr. Chandler's house at Guiney's. There the General stayed and appeared to improve. On Sunday, May 10, he succumbed to pneumonia and died. In his diary Hotchkiss recorded, "Much to our grief General Jackson died today, at 3½ p.m.; lost to his country, but to himself, he has won his crown immortal and we may fondly hope he may still plead, as he pleaded here, for peace."

Following the wounding of Jackson, some of the momentum of the battle was lost. But the initiative had been wrested from Hooker. Although his troops fought a desperate battle, they were unable to prevent the link-up of the separated parts of Lee's army, which then forced them out of their strong defensive position at Chancellorsville. Lee was successful in preventing the juncture of the Federal corps at Fredericksburg with the remainder of the army holding Chancellorsville. Hooker admitted defeat, and withdrew across the Rappahannock at United States Ford during the dark, wet night of May 5.

Hooker's departure had caught Lee by surprise. Earlier that day he had sent Hotchkiss to determine the location of the roads leading to this ford in preparation for an attack to cut the Federal line of retreat. But when, at 3 a.m. on the 6th, a Confederate division moved to dislodge the enemy from their strong positions protecting the road to the ford, it was clear that they had gone. Hotchkiss was sent with this intelligence to Lee, "who did not much credit the report of the enemy's retreat," but sent Hotchkiss back to tell General Stuart to press on. Lee followed, only to have it confirmed that Hooker had made good his escape.

So closed the battle of Chancellorsville, the last and most brilliant of Confederate victories in Virginia, the end of a partnership, which, but for the mortal wounding of Jackson, might have given the Civil War a different and more beneficial ending. For Hotchkiss it was the end of a fourteen-month association which was to be an inspiration throughout his life. He was particularly receptive to Jackson's practice of his faith, devotion to duty, asceticism, and self-discipline, for these were characteristics which Hotchkiss admired.

As a field commander Jackson had no equal. Never again, however good the plan, was there the verve, the energy, the sure touch in its execution. Hotchkiss held the view that after Jackson's death the Army of Northern Virginia was never the same again, and cited the failure at Gettysburg and the increase in desertions.[41] To biographer Henderson he wrote, "I was engaged in no great battle subsequent to Jackson's death in which I did not see the opportunity which, in my opinion, he would have seized, and have routed his opponents."[42] As a symbol of southern nationalism, he was second only to Lee. Hotchkiss once quoted an old soldier who wrote to him saying that the death of Jackson "knocked our main prop from under us and robbed our beloved sunny southland of its brightest Jewel. Had Stonewall lived the Confederacy might have been today one of the proudest nations of the world." Hotchkiss commented, "The old fellow voices the opinion, one may safely say, of nearly all the old soldiers of the Confederate army. They thought so when Jackson died, and the survivors of that army, and many others besides, think so still."[43]

CHAPTER III

"Fields of fierce contention"

WHILE HOTCHKISS mapped the battlefield of Chancellorsville, Lee reorganized his army and planned his next moves. By the end of the month, both men had completed their tasks. The Army of Northern Virginia, some 75,000 strong, now comprised three corps: I Corps under James Longstreet; II Corps, Jackson's old corps, commanded by Richard S. Ewell; and III Corps, by Ambrose P. Hill. On June 1, 1863, there was a conference of Generals at Lee's headquarters, and on the 3rd, with Longstreet's corps leading the way, the army began the march which was to take it to Gettysburg and its first defeat. Two days later, the II Corps headquarters broke up their camp at Yerby's, where it had been for the past month. A. P. Hill's corps remained for a little longer in the neighborhood of Fredericksburg to guard the rear, then joined the long column moving toward Maryland.

Hotchkiss sat beside General Ewell in his buggy as they rode through the Wilderness on the way to Culpeper, Hotchkiss pointing out the more important locations in the Chancellorsville battle. Ewell had lost a leg during the Second Manassas campaign, and returned to field duties only after Hooker's defeat, so was much interested in Hotchkiss' description of a battle he would have relished. At this time Hotchkiss probably knew more than anyone else about the sequence of events and the locations of the troops in that encounter.

Ten days later, Ewell's cavalry was at Chambersburg, Pennsylvania, and his infantry about to cross the Potomac. On the way two divisions of II Corps again liberated Winchester, an action watched by Ewell and his staff, including Hotchkiss, from the top of a hill on the Millwood road. Hotchkiss served almost exclusively as a topographical engineer that day, providing Ewell and his divisional commanders with maps and route information, and making a map of the Winchester battlefield for the corps commander before moving up to the Potomac.

On June 28, the day Major General George G. Meade replaced Hooker, General Ewell set up his headquarters in the United States barracks at Carlisle, Pennsylvania. Here he hoisted the Confederate flag, an occasion of particular significance to the general for he had commanded that army post; there was a little ceremony with speeches from Ewell and some of his subordinates. "Quite an animating scene," remarked Hotchkiss. II Corps had reached its most northerly incursion into Union territory. Its advance units were within three miles of Harrisburg, and John B. Gordon's brigade of Early's division was at Wrightsville on the Susquehanna. But just as Ewell was planning to advance on Harrisburg, he received orders from Lee to move on Gettysburg, twenty-five miles to the south. Hotchkiss was close to the leading division of II Corps and recorded the opening day of the battle and Ewell's initial success.

> We pressed forward and soon engaged the enemy on the hills west of Gettysburg. A. P. Hill attacked on our right at the same time. At 11 A.M. firing of artillery by Hill; 11.30 infantry firing by Hill: 11.45 Rodes line of battle advanced—Iverson in front. We were moving in column along the crest of the hill. At 12M. the enemy driven back and Hill advancing; 12-20 Hill's artillery brisk on the right; 2½ P.M. Early's artillery opened up on the left; 3¼ P.M. Early's Infantry advanced and swept gallantly up to the town; Rodes advanced on our right and had severe fighting with enemy on the [....] road. The enemy shelled our position on the hill and compelled us to retire; but our artillery played on them with effect just before Early advanced.... Early's line was thrown into some disorder by his advance and he reformed at 4 P.M. and moved into the town at 5 P.M. Heavy firing took place on our right. Rodes entered at about the same hour as Early and we followed into the town, meeting a crowd of prisoners

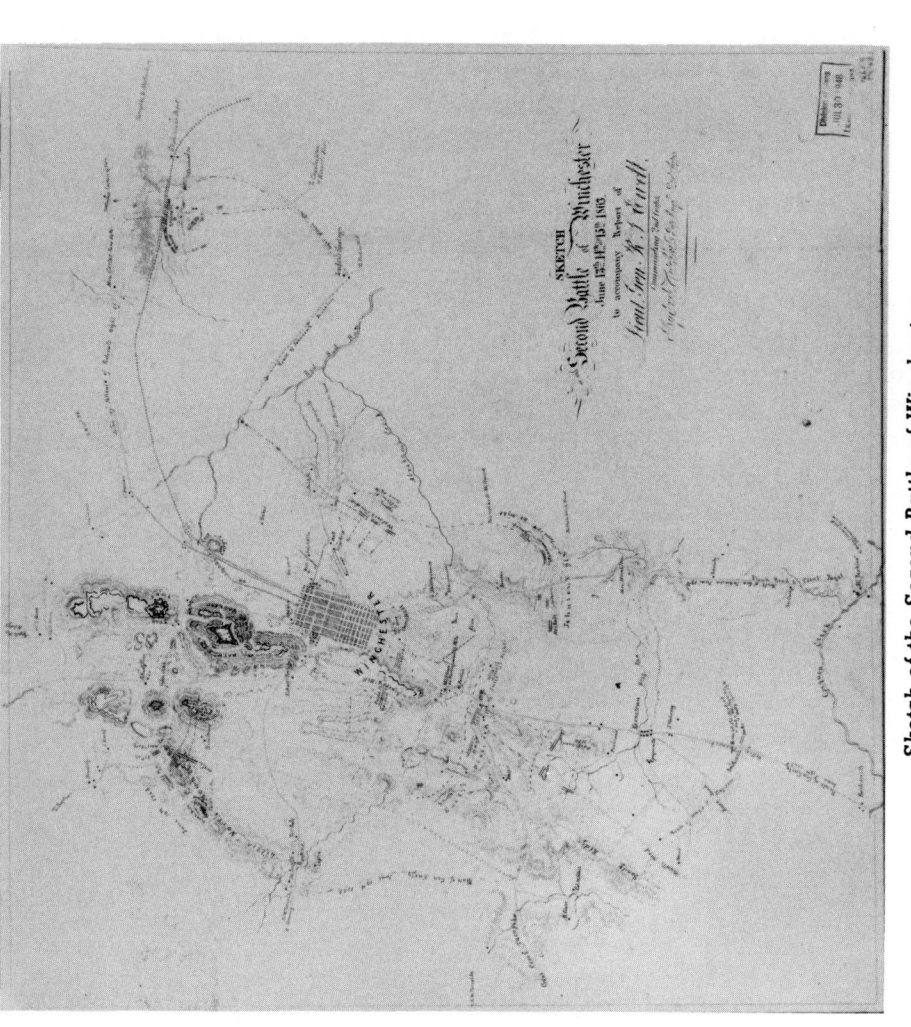

Sketch of the Second Battle of Winchester
Hotchkiss Map Collection #155, Library of Congress

coming back. Gen'l Lee came up about 4½ P.M. ... The pursuit was checked by the lateness of the hour and the position the enemy had secured in a cemetery.

Unfortunately, Hotchkiss did not write as detailed an account of the events of the next two days, which marked the turning point of the war. However, he did make some significant observations. On July 2, "General Lee was at our quarters in the A.M. and there planned the movement, though not in my opinion very sanguine of success." "At 4 P.M., Longstreet, having come up on the right, A. P. Hill being in the centre, and Ewell on the left, we made a vigorous attack on the enemy, although not a simultaneous one, and drove them from some of their positions; but they had strongly entrenched the hills on which they were and we did not succeed in gaining their main works."

Hotchkiss described Pickett's famous charge of the third day in brief, but telling phrases.

> The attack was furiously renewed and we drove the enemy from their works, but our supports were not near enough and the enemy rallied and regained them. Pickett's division took the hill on the right, but Petigrew failed to sustain them. We were repulsed on all sides; only gained a little ground from the enemy who kept closely in his works and did not advance. Our loss was very great, the men fighting with desperation and great valor. Many were killed and wounded.... The Generals had a council at General A. P. Hill's headquarters on the Cashtown Road, about sundown, and decided to fall back.... I met Pickett's division, returning after the battle, that night, scattered along the road; no officers and all protesting that they had been completely cut up.... There was a general feeling of despondency in the army at our great losses, though the battle is regarded as a drawn one.[1]

In later years Hotchkiss ascribed the failure at Gettysburg to a number of factors. The more important ones were Lee's lack of knowledge as to the whereabouts of the Union formations due to the absence of Jeb Stuart's cavalry, and the failure of Early to follow up his successful attack through Gettysburg on July 1. "This lack of energy and failure of concerted action by Lee's corps commanders lost to the Confederates the great advantages gained during the day, which if followed up in 'Stonewall's' way would, in so far as one can forecast events, have resulted in crushing the Federal army in detail...." Other reasons were the failure to occupy the Round Tops, and the slowness of Longstreet to start the attack on July 2. By the time Longstreet was ready, the "most opportune time for the assault had passed." He censured Ewell for his over-optimism, and failure to attack at the same time as his fellow corps commanders.[2]

Hotchkiss had not been employed during the battle, but this was to change as soon as it was over, for at 2 a.m. on July 4 he was working on a map of the country back towards Virginia, and was later active in the selection of the defensive line that Lee constructed between Hagerstown and Williamsport on the Potomac to protect his retreat. This done, he took a party, at the request of Major Michael ("Mike") Harman, (the Chief Quartermaster of II Corps, whom Ewell had told "to get the baggage train across the river or he wanted to see his face no more"), Hotchkiss made a causeway on the Virginia shore to aid the crossing of the swollen river.[3] He had considerable trouble in completing it, but in the middle of the afternoon of July 12 the difficult and dangerous task of ferrying the wagons began. Fortunately, during the night the water level fell and the river became fordable at Williamsport. The next day the baggage trains completed the crossing, to be followed by the artillery. As the light faded, the infantry moved up to the river, the cavalry taking their place along the lines. Hotchkiss saw his wagon ferried across the river and returned to headquarters. He later crossed the river by the pontoon bridge at Falling Waters to join the headquarter's wagons on their way to camp some four and a half miles from Martinsburg. The infantry crossed in the early hours of the 14th. By then the river had dropped sufficiently at Williamsport to allow the men of II Corps to wade across, albeit with the water up to their armpits, and to move into camp between Martinsburg and Falling Waters.

Shortly after the return to Virginia, Lee ordered a large reduction in the baggage accompanying the army. "A necessary thing," wrote Hotchkiss, "as our wagons, ambulances and artillery extend over 50 miles of road when on a march." All of II Corps headquarters' baggage was now to go into two wagons, which meant that Hotchkiss had to send his own wagon away, retaining only such mapping gear as he could carry in his saddle bags. Stripped of its excess impedimenta, the army continued its withdrawal so that by end of the month it was once again east of the Blue Ridge and behind the Rapidan. Hotchkiss was an observer rather than a participant during that retreat. There was little opportunity for mapmaking, and the only operational duty he recorded was the posting of pickets at Browntown to give warning of any approach of the enemy from Jenkins' Gap in the Blue Ridge.

In a number of respects the following two months were similar to those of the previous winter at Moss Neck. Report writing and mapmaking generated the same kinds of conversation among staff officers of II Corps. But there was no Jackson. Nevertheless he was the subject of much discussion. The defeat at Gettysburg demanded the question, what would Jackson have done? Would he not have assaulted and overrun the Federals in their positions in the cemetery on the first day? Hotchkiss recorded that the pursuit was checked by the lateness of the hour, but at Chancellorsville, Jackson's assault did not start until 6 p.m. and he was preparing to renew it at dusk. Early's division moved into Gettysburg at 5 p.m. with several hours of daylight left in which to secure the defeat of his enemy. However strong the defenses at 5 p.m. on the 1st, they would be much stronger by 5 a.m. on the 2nd. Jackson would not have given his adversary that opportunity.

Jackson was the Southerners' hero. They wanted to know as much as they could about him. He was a hero, also, to those who had served him, and there were some who would write about him. Among these was John Esten Cooke, one of Jeb Stuart's staff officers. Cooke sent a copy of his *Life of Stonewall Jackson* to Hotchkiss, asking for his comments. Hotchkiss read the book carefully, discussed it with his fellow staff officers, particularly with Pendleton, and heavily annotated it, often quoting Pendleton. While dissenting from some passages on Cooke's account, Hotchkiss and his colleagues were "rather gratified at the tone of it." After the war, he bound it with other published material, as well as with his own collection of reminiscences, to make one volume.[4]

With headquarters not far from the scene of the battle of Cedar Run, the overture to the campaign against Pope of 12 months before, it was natural that those involved should go over the ground again. On Monday, September 7, Hotchkiss "started at an early hour and rode to the battlefield...recalling the scenes of that eventful period."

Later that day, after "sketching awhile," he went on to see Jeb Stuart at his headquarters at Culpeper. They talked about the Pennsylvania campaign. "Stuart said he had been much blamed by those that knew nothing about it." If he told his side of the story, Hotchkiss did not record it, so the blame remains.

Hotchkiss suffered from an attack of dysentery that day. Nevertheless he rose early the following morning to examine the route to the old battlefield. By the time he returned to camp he could hardly ride. He went straight to bed, called in Dr. Hunter McGuire, and applied for sick leave. He spent the next 24 hours in bed, and missed Lee's review of II Corps. But on September 10, helped by his colleagues, he started for home, Samson Biddulph Robinson going with him on the railroad as far as Gordonsville.

His companion had been transferred from the 7th Louisiana Regiment immediately following the Gettysburg battle to assist Hotchkiss as a mapmaker. He was to remain with Hotchkiss throughout the war and into the early years of peace, becoming, perhaps, his closest friend, and taking the place that might have been Ralph McKune's or Keith Boswell's had they lived.

Under the care of two doctors, Hotchkiss remained in bed for ten uncomfortable days before making a slow convalescence. A trip into Staunton on September 26 proved to be premature, for the following day he spent "at home not feeling very well." Fortunately he had applied for, and was given, a ten-day extension to his leave during which he made rapid progress, and enjoyed visiting his friends and neighbors. He went out to Mount Solon to visit John Marshall McCue, and spent a night there before going on to Bridgewater to see his old Irish servant, Richard Gibbon. On his way back he called on Daniel Forrer at Mossy Creek, found there young Samuel, who had just returned from Gettysburg where he had been taken prisoner, as well as other of his former pupils.

It is not surprising that, when his furlough ended, he "was very reluctant to leave home." Especially when so many cares devolved upon Sara, who was often quite unwell from rheumatism.

Hotchkiss returned to duty on October 6. There is a gap in his journal from that date until October 20. Such a gap is always disappointing but in this case doubly so, for it coincides with the last major offensive campaign which Lee mounted in Virginia.

For two months, the Army of Northern Virginia had occupied a defensive position along the Rapidan from the neighborhood of Orange Court House eastward toward its confluence with the Rappahannock. Meade had made no attempt to bring it to battle, and it was therefore time for Lee to do something. Once again he sallied forth, but this time could not maneuver around the Union army, nor compel it to stand and fight. The only serious engagement occurred between Hill's corps and the enemy rearguard at Bristoe Station, in which Hill's men were repulsed with heavy losses. Before October 20, Lee had withdrawn to the Rappahannock.

Hotchkiss' next entry is puzzling. He wrote that he "Spent the day in camp verifying a map of Culpeper County and was much fatigued from being over the table all day, as I have not been used to it for some time." What had he been doing during those two weeks? If he had not been drawing maps, and was engaged in other duties, there would be nothing unusual in that, but they had never exhausted him before. More likely he had still not recovered his health, and, although back in camp, was not back to work. However, whatever he may have, or have not, been doing during those unaccounted days, he was busy with his cartographic duties until the Yankees forced Lee's army to retire once more behind the Rapidan early in November. Hotchkiss assisted the withdrawal on the night of November 7 by leading General Edward Johnson and his division to a defensive position to protect the approaches to the river crossings. When daylight came he helped select a line to be fortified by all three divisions. That done, he found a suitable crossing for the wagons, and had a ford and footbridge made. The troops remained in their fortifications during the day, "the cavalry fighting at the front." With the wagons safely across, the infantry withdrew about dark. Hotchkiss rode ahead with Pendleton to establish a new corps headquarters at Morton Hall, a few miles south of the Rapidan at the head of Mountain Run. Except for a few days at the end of November this was to remain the headquarters of II Corps until the opening of the Wilderness Campaign in May 1864.

Those few days were occupied by the battle of Mine Run. Meade, having done nothing of note for nearly four months, crossed the Rapidan at Mine and Jacob's Fords in an attempt to turn Lee's right flank. Lee selected a defensive position along the west bank of Mine Run, a small stream running northward to the Rapidan, and waited. At about 8 a.m. on the last day of the month, as if to salute Hotchkiss' birthday, the enemy opened up with artillery "quite furiously—keeping it up at intervals, all day, but not doing much damage." No assault developed that day or the next. The following day nothing could be seen of the Yankees. They had retreated across the river. Military activity for 1863 was over.

There was one more staff job for Hotchkiss to do before he could go on leave. He accompanied Pendleton in a three-day search for suitable winter camps. That concluded, on December 19 he went to Army Headquarters at Orange Court House, got his furlough approved, drew his pay, and received orders for maps from Colonel William P. Smith, Lee's acting Chief of Engineers. His absence from camp was not to be all holiday. He spent many days at the drawing board in the comfort and warmth of his own home and office.

To all intents, the war ceased during the winter months. Both armies gave victory to the weather, so some semblance of normal life was possible. The main domestic tasks at this season of the year were the settling of accounts and the hiring of servants, but before he did either, Hotchkiss sold his roan mare for $600, and made another visit to his old servant, Gibbon. When he had been on sick leave in September, Hotchkiss had suggested to Gibbon that he should come to Loch Willow, and renew their old association. For some reason Gibbon was now reluctant to join the Hotchkiss household. This must have been a disappointment. For with Nelson no longer living nearby, Sara had to rely on neighbors, not always immediately available in times of emergency.

Hotchkiss was back in camp by January 16, only to be ordered to return to the Valley to "reconnoitre for defences." He set up a topographical office in Staunton, then spent two months roaming the Appalachian mountains to the west, sketching the roads, and locating the farmsteads, ridges, rivers, all those features necessary for the revision of existing maps to make them useful to the army. He varied his fieldwork with days in the office where he worked on his notes, instructed his assistants, or made maps to the orders of General Early or Colonel Smith. With the field work completed, Hotchkiss spent a further month at Staunton, near enough to go home for weekend visits; indeed, he sometimes worked at Loch Willow instead of at the office. About this time, Christian W. Oltmanns joined the mapping team. Like Robinson, he had been serving in Taylor's Louisiana brigade, but in the Fifth Regiment. After university and professional training in Hanover, he had emigrated to America, obtained employment in the United States Coast Survey, and was in New Orleans when the war began.[5] In the post-war years, he was to become a somewhat wayward member of Hotchkiss' wide circle of friends and associates. Meanwhile he was to give valuable service which Hotchkiss acknowledged in his reports.

That approximation to a peacetime civilian routine ended in April when Hotchkiss closed the Staunton office, and in company with other members of the staff, prepared for the hard work which Lee predicted for the 1864 campaigning season.

It started on May 3, a year after the Battle of Chancellorsville, and a little to the west, but in the same kind of country, covered with oak and pine, choked with a dense undergrowth. Grant expected Lee to retreat to the defenses along Mine Run as soon as the freshly equipped Federals crossed the Rapidan on the pontoon bridges at Germanna and Ely Fords. Lee's force was only a little more than half the size of Grant's. But he would engage him in the tangle of the Wilderness, which favored defense and nullified Grant's superiority in artillery. Two days of hard fighting, during which Hotchkiss carried orders, reconnoitered lines, and sketched the battlefield, stopped Grant. But this was not 1863, and Grant was not Hooker. Leaving only one pontoon bridge in place across the Rapidan, he moved his army to the left in an attempt to get between Lee and Richmond. Lee anticipated the move, marched rapidly to Spotsylvania Court House, arriving there just in time. There the Confederates created a strong defensive position, an arc of trenches, which

Grant's frontal assault made famous as the "bloody angle." Hotchkiss described the events of May 12 in his diary:

> At 4 A.M. the enemy massed and advanced on our center, with a tremendous force, and broke it for the moment, capturing 20 pieces of artillery that were just coming into position, having been withdrawn during the night; ....Many of Johnson's Division were captured, Gen. J. among them, and many were killed. The scene was terrific, for several hours, before we regained the line of works we had in the rear of our front line. We drove the enemy out of most of them; they only held a salient. We got up reinforcements and drove them back and successfully resisted all their attacks, which were incessant from 4 A.M. to 1 P.M.; then came a little lull and the fight was renewed until 4 P.M. The panic at one time was fearful, and nearly the whole of Johnson's Division came pouring back to the rear, and many of them were captured; but Gordon and some others filled up the gap and received the shock of the enemy's attack and broke them every time. It rained very hard a good portion of the day, with thunder and lightning, but it made no difference in the fighting and the musketry and artillery were incessant. We lost many valuable lives. I spent the day, with many others of the staff, rallying and sending in again the broken fragments of Johnson's Division and giving orders in reference to wounded, etc., in the vicinity of the battle ground. Grant was foiled in the purpose he had in view....

The armies remained facing each other for a further nine days. Then, after another abortive attempt to break Lee's line, Grant again tried to turn Lee's right flank. Lee responded as before. A two-day march, on the first of which Hotchkiss had the task of getting the ambulances and ordnance wagons on the road ahead of the rear guard, put the army across the North Anna, at Hanover Junction. At this point Hotchkiss attended the conference of Generals called by Lee to consider where to hold a line. Hotchkiss gave his reasons for favoring the line of the Virginia Central Railroad, and was ordered to go with General Smith and the engineers to examine the ground. They rode throughout the night of May 23 to select the line to be fortified. Although the Federals crossed the river they made no serious attack, judging the Confederate position to be too strong. Grant repeated his leftward movement, yet again Lee moved to meet him.

Each of these movements brought Grant nearer to Richmond, and this one was to finish at Cold Harbor, a mere 10 miles from the

Confederate capital, near enough for Hotchkiss to send his servant, William, there to buy cherries! Grant and his generals thought that the Confederates were whipped, that one major effort would defeat Lee and end the war. That major effort was made on June 3. "Late in the P.M. the Yankees made a grand attack on our lines in front of Gaines Mill, ..., but were repulsed with much loss." "Confederate rifle fire tore the Federal columns and inflicted a resounding defeat—the most unrelieved and tragically costly one the Army of the Potomac had suffered since it crossed the Rapidan."[6]

When the battle was over the opposing generals had much to think about. In the hope of weakening Lee's army still further, Grant had increased operations in the Shenandoah. He hoped that threat to the Confederates' supplies, and lines of communication, would make Lee detach some of his meagre force to deal with it. So far Lee had not done so. Grant, on the other hand, had run out of space. The swamps of the Chickahominy precluded any further turning movement toward Richmond. But for once he caught Lee by surprise, not in attack but in withdrawing, giving up this unprofitable field for another with better prospects south of the James River. As Grant made this move, Lee detached II Corps with its newly promoted commander, Lieutenant General Jubal A. Early, to deal with the Union forces operating in the Valley.

On June 13 the whole corps started for Lynchburg to begin a campaign which Hotchkiss later described as "among the most remarkable and brilliant of the Confederate war in Virginia and Maryland."[7] Hotchkiss went to Richmond to collect supplies from the Engineer Bureau, then joined the march at its first camp near Auburn Mills on the South Anna. The troops were in fine spirits, glad to be out of the trenches and marching toward the Valley. Hotchkiss corrected his map as he rode in warm weather along the dusty roads, and no doubt would have continued to do so, had he not fallen so sick that he had to ride in an ambulance. At Charlottesville the Corps boarded the cars of the Orange and Alexandria Railroad to complete the second half of the journey in a matter of hours. Once in Lynchburg, Hotchkiss, though still not well, went in search of maps of the vicinity, and made copies for the divisional commanders.

As a result of poor staff work by Early's command, the Federal forces under David Hunter were permitted to retreat into the mountains. With Hunter gone, II Corps started the march which was to bring it to Winchester on July 2, and across the Potomac on the 5th, to spend a day in front of Washington on the 12th. Hotchkiss said that as they approached the Federal capital, Early told some of the troops that he

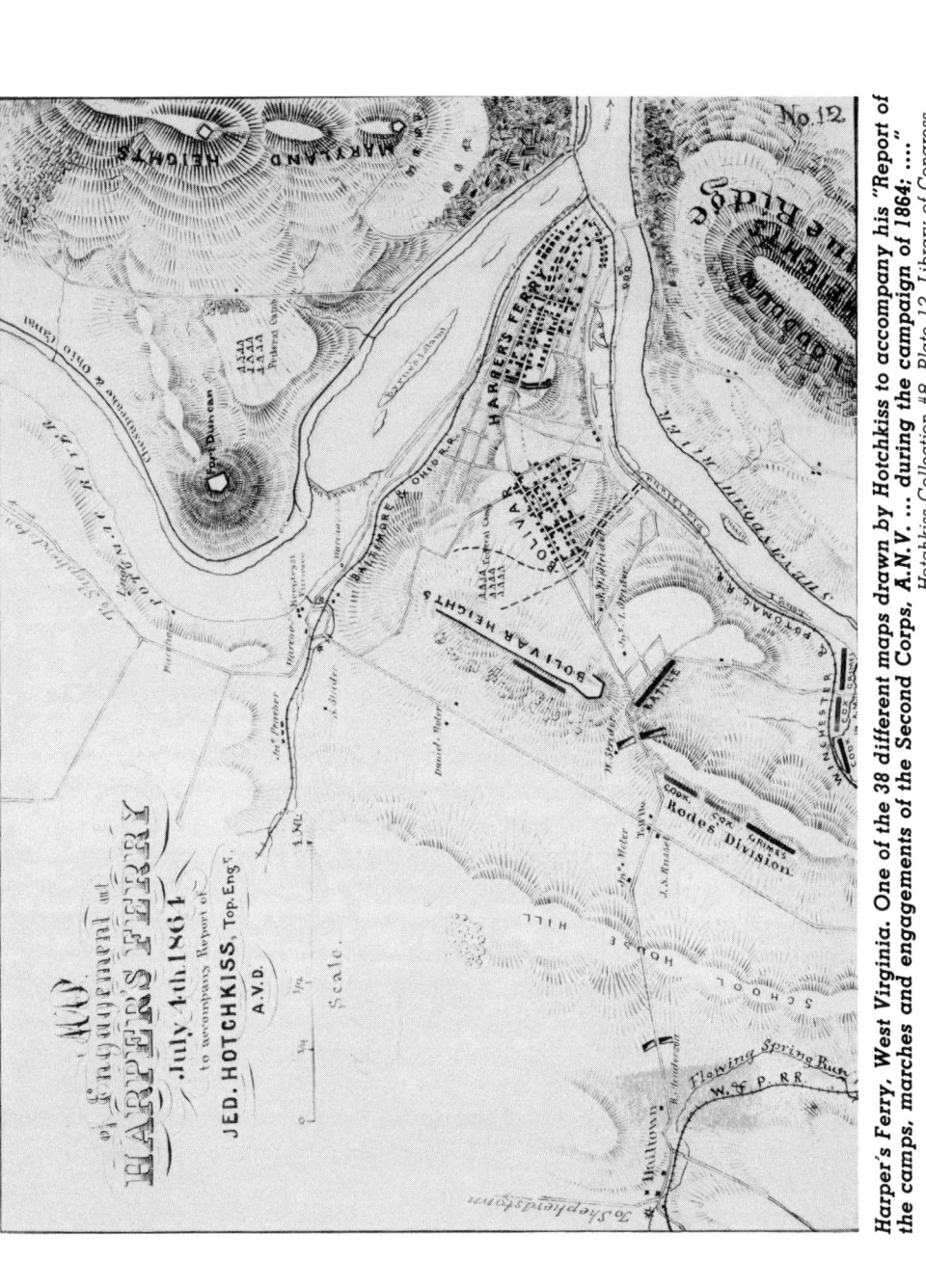

Harper's Ferry, West Virginia. One of the 38 different maps drawn by Hotchkiss to accompany his "Report of the camps, marches and engagements of the Second Corps, A.N.V. ... during the campaign of 1864; ...."
Hotchkiss Collection #8, Plate 12, Library of Congress

would take them into the city, "but they were so exhausted by the intense heat and dust that he made no decided attack; only skirmished some." The ease with which he had made this march must have momentarily kindled a fantasy of a triumphant entry into the nation's capital. A night's sleep and sober reflection resulted in a more sensible decision, namely to return to the Valley. That was accomplished without too much trouble. Ten days later the corps was strung out on the Valley turnpike north and south of Strasburg. But Early was not going to withdraw any farther than necessary. On July 28 he reversed his march, drove his pursuers back to the Potomac, and launched a cavalry raid across the river which was to reach and raze Chambersburg in Pennsylvania. Simultaneously, he took his main force on an excursion into Maryland, had another look at the Sharpsburg battlefield, then marched to Hagerstown before returning to Virginia via Williamsport.

The audacious raid toward Washington, and the depredations in Maryland and Pennsylvania, roused Grant. He appointed Major General Philip Sheridan to destroy Early, and put the Shenandoah Valley to the torch. From then on, with one notable exception, II Corps was on the defensive and would not again impose its will on the fortunes of the battlefield.

In the second week of August, Sheridan pushed Early back to Strasburg, but then withdrew through a countryside he smudged with the smouldering ruins of farms, homes, and mills—a sign of what was to come to the rest of the Valley that fall.

For most of the time since leaving the trenches at Cold Harbor, Hotchkiss' main assignments had been to provide route information, and record the movements and engagements of the corps. With the exception of a few days in July, when the troops marched from Lexington to Winchester, his diary provides a full record, not just of his own employment, but of the whereabouts of the several divisions under Early's command. Occasionally there is a comment on the behavior or performance of a particular unit, as for example of General Stephen D. Ramseur's loss of some 400 men and 4 pieces of artillery in an engagement with General William W. Averell at Moorefield. "A disgraceful affair" he called it.[8] Mostly the diary is factual; the entry for Friday, August 26, 1864, is more typical of its content:

"We spent about half the day at Shepherdstown, then marched back to Leetown, Ramseur in advance, followed by Rodes, Gordon and Wharton. Our cavalry came to the vicinity of Shepherdstown, having found the enemy in force to oppose their passage at Williamsport. They had an artillery duel in the morning, Anderson had a fight near Charlestown in the P.M. Headquarters in the orchard at the old General Lee house.

Colonel Boteler spends the night with me. Robinson and Oltmanns worked awhile at maps. Fine day. Windy and some rain at night."

There were some incidents that merited an entry, but were ignored. Thus, the day before arriving in front of Washington he noted, "I got some maps from Frank Blair's House, by order of the Lt. General," but there is no mention of the looting of the wine cellar of this luxurious house, or its destruction by fire two days later. In view of the outcry at this particular piece of vandalism, it is a pity that Hotchkiss had nothing to say.

Although mapmaking to aid maneuver, or to record engagements was his main responsibility, Hotchkiss was used for other duties, perhaps not so frequently or so importantly as in Jackson's campaign. Thus in the withdrawal toward Strasburg in August, he noted "About noon I guided Gordon across country, by a route I had selected in the A.M., to the pike near Kernstown and took him to a position near Newtown." The following day he spent "reconnoitering and carrying orders, and at night took Colonel Jackson and his cavalry to the Middle Road and posted them for pickets." When Sheridan withdrew a few days later, Hotchkiss "took Forsberg's small brigade to the Middle Road and threw them out to the left and drove the enemy from the hills in front...then reported, and Wharton's division was sent there. I put it in line to advance against Bower's hill. Then saw it go in and take the hill."

These were minor assignments. His most brilliant contribution to this campaign was still to come. To put it in context it is necessary to describe the events subsequent to the arrival of Sheridan.

Sheridan had withdrawn from Strasburg in the mistaken belief that Early was about to be reinforced. When, on the contrary, Early lost men for the Petersburg front, Sheridan set about a major offensive. On September 19, as Hotchkiss was returning to camp following a visit home and to Staunton for maps, Sheridan attacked the forces of General Early on the Berryville pike, not far from Winchester. After what he described as a most stubborn and sanguinary engagement, lasting from early in the morning until 5 o'clock in the afternoon, Sheridan achieved complete victory. The following day as Hotchkiss rode through New Market, he heard of the "disastrous battle" in which General Rodes had been killed, and at Rude's Hill saw his body. "A severe loss, his men along the road lamenting it deeply. Soon met trains of ambulances, and troops of wounded and stragglers filled the road all the way to Fisher's Hill, where I found the army in its old position."

Fisher's Hill, just south of Strasburg, was the anchor point of a line of defense works which stretched westward to the slopes of North Mountain. There, three days later, Early suffered an even more devastating defeat. Several times during the day of September 22, Sheridan gave every indication of mounting a frontal attack, but late in the afternoon turned Early's left flank. What happened then was described by Hotchkiss in terms which well convey the panic which can overwhelm the most battle-hardened troops.

At the same time a flanking force that had come on our left...moved on the left flank of our infantry—rather beyond it. The brigade there was ordered to move to the left, and the whole line was ordered to extend that way, moving along the line of breastworks. But the enemy attacking just then, the second brigade from the left instead of marching by the line of works, was marched across at an angle by its commander. The enemy seeing this movement rushed over the works, and the brigade fled in confusion, thus letting the enemy into the rear of Early's Division, as well as of Gordon's and the rest of Rodes': our whole line gave way toward the right, offering little or no resistance, and the enemy came on and occupied our line. General Early and staff were near by, and I with others went after Wharton...but it was too late. Our whole line had retreated before he got to the turnpike. The enemy opened a furious cannonade on him. Our men came back in a perfect rout, and so rapidly that the enemy was crossing the railroad before the head of the column got into the pike, even. It was then getting dark. I hastened back to try to stop the mass of fugitives on the top of the hill near Mount Prospect. General Gordon, General Pegram, and Colonel Pendleton with others came up. Colonel Pendleton and myself had gotten a few men to stop near a fence, there, and also two pieces of artillery, which were opened on the enemy. By the combined efforts of all a few men were induced to stop. The artillery was opened on the woods where the enemy was advancing and it checked them for the moment, but most of our men went on, officers and all, at breakneck speed. Wharton came along parallel to the pike and on the left, and kept some of his men together. He checked the enemy some, and a rear guard was formed from his division which made a stand at Tom's Brook, and gave the enemy a volley which made them desist from pursuit....Colonel Pendleton was mortally wounded soon after we made a stand on the hill. The rout of wagons, caissons, limbers, artillery and flying men was fearful as the stream swept down the pike toward Woodstock, as many thought the enemy's cavalry was aiming to get there by the Middle road and cut us off. I became alarmed for the bridges, lest they should be broken and stop the retreat, so I hastened along as best

I could and checked the speed of the train, which was fairly flying. I finally got to the head of the train at Hawkinstown and advised Major Harman to park beyond Mount Jackson. Then I went to the river, beyond Mount Jackson, and got Captain Hart, of the Engineer Company, to put out guards and stop the fugitives, a duty which he and Lieutenant Boyd nobly performed. I then laid down and slept two hours and fed my horse. I got there about 1 A.M. A fine warm day.

The headlong retreat was brought under control, to be followed by a more orderly withdrawal up the Valley. Hotchkiss' knowledge of the country as well as his experience with Jackson in 1862 was put to good use during the following days. On the 23rd a stand was made at Rude's Hill, but the enemy moved up the left flank on the opposite side of the river to make this position untenable. The army then fell back to near New Market, then gradually, in line of battle to Tenth Legion Church, where it kept the enemy at bay until after dark. Hotchkiss took orders to Major Harman about the movement of the wagons and assisted in getting them off the pike onto the Keezletown road. After dark the infantry retired by the same route. When the moon rose, he guided the wagon train to the safety of Brown's Gap in the Blue Ridge, to be followed at dawn by the rest of the army. Only the cavalry was deployed to delay the advance of Sheridan's troopers. Although the Yankee cavalry was successful in pushing forward to the Confederate lines, their several charges were repulsed by artillery fire. During one of the charges, Hotchkiss' horse was killed.

From the security of Brown's Gap, Early, advised by Hotchkiss and using routes he had reconnoitered, attacked the enemy cavalry camp located near Weyer's Cave and drove them away from between Middle and South Rivers. The surprise element of the attack was spoiled by the artillery opening up prematurely. This was as far as Sheridan dared to go; he faced the same problems which had beset Federal commanders in the past: the vulnerability of long lines of communication passing through a countryside peppered with hostile towns, villages, hamlets, and homesteads. His scorched-earth policy had added to the bitterness as he destroyed thousands of barns and scores of mills, in an attempt to deny Lee's army its winter rations. Hotchkiss described how the Yankees "made the night light with burning barns, haystacks, &c" as they fulfilled Grant's promise to turn the Shenandoah Valley into a barren waste so that "crows flying over it...will have to carry their provender with them."

During the first half of October, Sheridan withdrew slowly down the Valley, leaving a devastated land. Early's divisions followed close behind, taking every opportunity to harass the vandals, while Hotchkiss directed the engineer troops in re-stringing the telegraph line and in building bridges. By the 14th of the month Early was back at Fisher's Hill, and Sheridan was camped between Strasburg and Middletown, east of Cedar Creek.

If there is one battle which can be ascribed to Hotchkiss it must be the one which was to take place here on October 19, 1864. He had been used in the planning of other successful actions, notably while serving Jackson, but in this one he seems to have provided the inspiration.

This portion of the Valley is remarkable for two features: the dramatic northern slope of Massanutten Mountain which descends steeply to the Valley floor from the summit of Three Top Mountain; and the bend of the Shenandoah as it turns eastward to flow close to the mountain's flank. From the summit of Three Top Mountain could be obtained a clear view over a wide segment of the lower Valley, to the west and northwest the containing ridges of the Appalachians, to the northeast the crumpled patchwork of wooded hillock and improved, cultivated land of the Valley stretching toward Winchester, around to the east to the Blue Ridge. At any time a sight of great beauty, but never more so than at this time of the year, the golds, oranges and reds of the fall foliage merging on the distant mountains into a deep dusty pink.

More important to Generals Gordon and Evans, and "Captain" Jed Hotchkiss, sent there by General Early, was the view of the enemy camp across the Shenandoah River. Hotchkiss made a map of the position. Then he and General Gordon fixed on a plan of attack to suggest to General Early, a plan which they discussed fully as they came back to camp. After an "arduous journey," Hotchkiss supped with Gordon before returning to headquarters to report to his commanding General. It was an audacious plan made possible by the false sense of security felt by Sheridan's army in the protection afforded by the Shenandoah River. There seemed no reason for an attack from that direction. The rebels were at Fisher's Hill to the east of the river. Their proper defensive line was roughly along the wildly meandering Cedar Creek flowing southward to enter the Shenandoah two miles east of Strasburg. The plan, which Gordon put to the meeting of generals convened by Early on the following day, "assigned to each division its place and time of attack, almost precisely as it was subsequently carried into execution."[9]

Gordon, with three divisions, was to march after dark, from Fisher's Hill to a crossing of the Shenandoah, near its right, which the pioneer corps was to bridge for the men, move along and around the base of Three Top Mountain by a concealed pathway, and then, by fording the Shenandoah at Bowman's Ford, turn the enemy's left flank. Starting at successively later times, divisions under Kershaw and Wharton were to march through Strasburg, Kershaw's to turn off and position itself to cross Cedar Creek at Bowman's Mill, Wharton's to Hupp's Hill, where he would be able to support the other attacks. Rosser's cavalry was to move by the back road to engage the enemy's cavalry encamped on the right flank of their army. Those units of Early's force, numbering about 10,000, had to be in position and ready to attack from 5 a.m. At that hour Rosser was to start the assault, followed on the far right by Gordon, and then Kershaw. Hotchkiss made a detailed examination of the route to be taken by Gordon's division, and at twilight led a party of pioneers to clear a way for the troops, who began their move at 8 p.m.

At 5 a.m. the attacks began. Early achieved complete surprise. Kershaw's and Gordon's men swept through the camps of Sheridan's VIII and XV Corps and, rousing the sleeping soldiers from their tents, drove them in wild confusion across Meadow Run toward Middletown. Here the VI Corps made a stand, but were driven away by the vigorous use of artillery. By 10 a.m., Early's small force of 10,000 had secured a great victory over Sheridan's host of 50,000. Regrettably, that initiative was not exploited, and an opportunity which Hotchkiss thought that Jackson would have seized, was missed. From 10 a.m. until 4 p.m. the Confederates held a line through Middletown at right angles to the Valley Pike, "using some artillery on the right and left and advancing our skirmishers a little, but making no decided move."

One of the objectives, which was impossible of achievement, was the capture of the Federal commander. Sheridan had his headquarters at the Belle Grove plantation, and it was the task of the cavalry attached to Gordon's divisions, once they had forded the Shenandoah, to ride directly to Belle Grove to capture that man who made war on civilians. Unknown to Early, Sheridan had been summoned to Washington for consultation, so was in Winchester on his way back to his command. His arrival late in the afternoon, when order had already been restored, put heart into the men about to make a counter attack, which reversed the fortunes of the day and routed the Confederates. Hotchkiss described what happened:

> The enemy having had time to rally, had collected in rear of the large body of woods in our front and formed a line of battle and advanced at 4:30 P.M., obliquely to the left, and struck our

left, or rather between the two brigades on the left, where the line was weak and it gave way with little resistance, and was followed by all the rest of the line toward the left, and soon everything was in full retreat toward Cedar Creek. The artillery nobly fell back fighting and kept the enemy in check, and everything was getting off well, when, Rosser having fallen back, the Yankee cavalry crossed by Hite's old mill and came up to Stickley's and fell on our train and artillery just after dark, on Hupp's Hill, and dashed along, killing horses and turning over ambulances, caisson's, &c., as there was nothing to defend them and we had no organized force to go after them. Only a few Yankee cavalry did it all. They came as far as Spangler's Mill, and there tore up a bridge which had been broken and impeded our train, but had been repaired and we were passing over it. The general and staff got to Fisher's Hill and tried to rally the men. We succeeded in getting many of them into camp, but could get none to go back and recapture the wagons, &c., at Strasburg. Colonel Brown got eight or ten to go on and guard the stone bridge. We got 1,300 prisoners off safely. The general was very much prostrated when he learned the extent of our disaster and started the wagons to the rear, and sent for Rosser to come and cover the retreat. He sent me to Edenburg to stop the stragglers.[10] Thus was one of the most brilliant victories of the war turned into one of the most disgraceful defeats, and all owing to the delay in pressing the enemy after we got into Middletown.... I got to Edenburg and put the engineer troops on guard at the bridge to stop fugitives. A very fine day. Cool at night. I spent the day with the general; carried orders, &c. We had many narrow escapes. We were frequently fired at and much exposed.

The following day the disconsolate army retreated to New Market. Here Early established his headquarters and remained, except for one brief excursion down the Valley, until the army went into winter camps between Staunton and Waynesboro.

Early's bitter disappointment at the outcome of the Cedar Creek battle was given full rein in his letter, dated October 22, 1864, to the "Soldiers of the Army of the Valley." He had hoped to have congratulated them on a splendid victory, but had the mortification of announcing that by their subsequent misconduct all the benefits of the victory had been lost and a serious disaster incurred. "Had you remained steadfast to your duty and your colors the victory would have been one of the most brilliant and decisive of the war, —you would have gloriously retrieved the reverses at Winchester and Fisher's Hill and entitled yourselves to the admiration and gratitude of your country. But many of you, including commissioned officers, yielded to a disgraceful propensity for plunder, deserted your colors to appropriate to yourselves the abandoned property of the enemy...." Thus when the counterattack came, the lines were so weakened that those who had remained at their posts panicked and fled. In the extravagant language of the time he lashed them for their indiscipline and told them that those who had fought from Manassas to Cold Harbor, and especially those "who were with the immortal JACKSON in all his triumphs," were capable of better things. He finished his harangue with an appeal to his "fellow soldiers" to remember past glories, "the woes of your bleeding country, the ruined homes and devastated fields you see around you, the cries of anguish which come from the widows and orphans of your dead comrades, ...to render a cheerful and willing obedience to the rules of discipline, and to shoulder your musket again with the determination never more to turn your backs on the foe, but to do battle like men and soldiers until the vestige of the footsteps of our barbarous and cruel enemies is erased from the soil they desecrate and the independence of our country is firmly established."

But he too had fallen short of the Jackson standard, and he knew it. After the retreat to New Market, he sent Hotchkiss to Richmond with dispatches for Lee, but told him not to tell General Lee that the army should have advanced after reaching Middletown on the morning of the 19th.

This was the end of a remarkable campaign in which a ragged army had marched 1,670 miles and fought seventy-five battles and skirmishes since it left the vicinity of Cold Harbor on June 13.

The winter camps which Hotchkiss once again helped to select in the Staunton area were not occupied until December 19. Hardly had the troops moved in than a report that the enemy was coming up the Valley had them on the road again, Hotchkiss guiding Wharton's infantry by the shortest route to the Valley Pike. The threat turned out not to be serious. The Yankees retreated down the Valley when Rosser's cavalry made a surprise attack and routed them as they were saddling up. Just as well perhaps, for though most of the men marching with Wharton in a cold and biting snowstorm were in a good humor, they were "in no plight for battle."[11]

At last the army, and Hotchkiss, could settle into the winter routine. Hotchkiss was home on Christmas Eve. That year he entertained his closest military colleagues: Robinson, Oltmanns, Colonel William Allan, and Colonel Proctor Smith. "We had a very pleasant evening," wrote Hotchkiss, but he did not record any details of the Christmas dinner that Sara had prepared for them. Had he done so he might have revealed the hardship being suffered in the Confederacy at this time, but although Yankee soldiers had twice visited Loch Willow, and Hotchkiss had been fearful that it would suffer Sheridan's depredations, Churchville, being west of the Valley Pike, had managed to escape the attention of the vandals. Sara might have been able to raise enough to provide a meal suitable to the occasion. But there would be no tea, unless it was sassafras, and no coffee unless it was made from sweet potato, toasted brown, and ground to a powder.

The Confederate dollar was now practically worthless, and the great shortage of food made grain a better currency. So when Hotchkiss went into Staunton in search of servants, not only were they difficult to hire, "they were hired only for grain and at very high rates, men bringing 100 bushels of corn or wheat."[12]

Office work, at home or at Army headquarters in Staunton, occupied the whole of January and February of 1865 until, on the last day of the month, orders came to "Pack up" as the enemy was advancing.

By this time Early's command in the Valley had been reduced to about 2,000 men, many of whom were widely scattered on picket duty. Coming up the Valley, and on the morning of the 28th already reported to be at Mount Jackson, were 10,000 of Sheridan's troopers. In great excitement, headquarters at Staunton was packed up and stores made ready to be moved by train to Richmond. This might not even be possible. There had been a great amount of rain during the preceding days, the temperature had risen and the snow melted, the streams and rivers were running high, so high that the railroad bridge over Christian's Creek between Staunton and the Blue Ridge had been washed away. Early's pioneers under Chief of Engineers, Colonel William Proctor Smith, rebuilt the bridge in two days, completing it the day before the train was due to leave.

Late on the night of February 28, the enemy was reported to be farther south at Harrisonburg. Orders were issued to be ready to move at sunrise, but it was nearly noon before all the baggage got off, and the last train did not leave until late in the afternoon of March 1. Hotchkiss went with the wagons to Waynesboro and saw them across the South River, but he had to leave Staunton without his servant, William, who thought this to be a good time to get drunk, and, as Hotchkiss put it, "got out of the way."[13] Learning in Waynesboro where William might be, Hotchkiss rode back in the night towards Staunton, found him and his horse, and brought them both back to camp.

Waynesboro lies in the plain of South River, the southerly tributary to the South Fork of the Shenandoah, flowing between the town and the lower slopes of the Blue Ridge. A few miles to the east is Rockfish Gap; through this is the exit-road from the Valley. The Virginia Central Railroad, (later the C&O), crosses the river and takes a similar route but under the gap through Crozet's Blue Ridge tunnel. The only other river crossing at that time was a foot bridge two- or three-feet wide.

On March 2, enemy cavalry destroyed the newly completed bridge over Christians Creek, quickly overran the small picket at Fishersville, and came on toward Waynesboro. Wharton's division, supported by six pieces of artillery, had been deployed at an early hour to the northwest of Waynesboro, with the river behind, and was waiting in the constantly falling cold sleet. About two in the afternoon the enemy formed a line of battle about a mile in front of Wharton's men. Confederate artillery fire compelled them to fall back, but they reformed and, moving through some woods, turned the Confederate left flank, which made a feeble resistance and gave way, followed by the remainder of the line. Then ensued "one of the most terrible panics and stampedes" Hotchkiss had ever seen. "There was a perfect rout along the road up the mountain, and the enemy (all of the force being cavalry and mounted infantry) dashed rapidly forward into the swarm of flying men, wagons, etc., and pursued [them] over the mountain of Rockfish Gap, capturing over a thousand prisoners and all the artillery and trains."

Hotchkiss had just gone to a fire "to warm" when the stampede began. He got his horse and rode rapidly across the river, expecting to find artillery on the hill there and by its aid to rally the men who were crossing by the railroad bridge. To his surprise there was no artillery. Convinced that "all was lost," Hotchkiss collected his saddle bags and reports from his wagon and rode up the mountain at a gallop. "The road [was] full of fugitives and the foe yelling 'Stop! Stop! Stop!' behind and firing constantly." Before reaching the summit of the gap, he turned off to the right into the woods, made his way along the snow-covered mountainside to the top, and found a place to stay just before dark.[14]

Hotchkiss ascribed the responsibility for this debacle entirely to Jubal Early. "The General committed an unpardonable error in posting so small a force with a swollen river in its rear and with its flank wholly exposed." On the left there was a gap of some 200 yards between the end of the line and the river, as well as a body of woods that could, and did, conceal movements made by the enemy. Early had not made provision for a retreat, and all the artillery was on the Waynesboro side of the river.

Some of the enemy camped in Waynesboro, but the bulk of them went on toward Charlottesville. Fog and rain obscured the view until noon of the next day, but in the afternoon it cleared sufficiently for Hotchkiss to see that the enemy was still crossing the mountain. He remained where he was for another night, after which the road was clear enough for him to make his way back to Staunton. He rode through the wreckage of the ordnance train, and waded through the still swollen South River into badly damaged Waynesboro. Stopping only to eat, he went on to spend the night at Fishersville. He arrived in Staunton to find that Federal troops had rounded up many civilians and convalescent soldiers and were taking them down the Valley as prisoners. General Rosser with the few cavalry he had was following after them. Hotchkiss was sent to find more cavalry to join in the chase. He found them at Buffalo Gap and directed them toward Harrisonburg to join Rosser. The combined force, together with the assistance of partisans, secured the release of the prisoners, although their guards escaped.

While this, the last military operation in the Shenandoah Valley, was taking place, Hotchkiss went home, "fixing up after the losses at Waynesboro," and then went in search of his maps. Later he joined Rosser, who had returned to Staunton and now wanted to make his way to unite with the bulk of Lee's army defending the Confederate capital. Riding four days by a circuitous route brought them to Ashland on March 15. There Hotchkiss left Rosser and went into Richmond, taking with him dispatches for General Lee. Another four days were spent on military business in Richmond and in Petersburg, where he collected information for the report on the operations of 1864 from the divisional commanders of II Corps, whose troops were currently placed in the fortifications at Petersburg.

Ordered back to the Valley, Hotchkiss had sent William and the horses on their way, and now went to Lynchburg on the South Side Rail Road which was in such a condition that it took fourteen hours to complete the 100-mile journey. From there he intended to enter the Valley by boat on the James River Canal, but that waterway was unusable. He had to go to Salem, before turning toward Lexington, Staunton, and home. By then March was near its end, and so was the war. Hotchkiss and his assistants continued with their work amid rumors that the enemy was coming up the Valley, and that Richmond had been given up. Both were true. General Lomax, who had been ordered to take command of the Valley District, arrived in Staunton to impress teams to haul supplies to Lexington for Lee's army, which had now abandoned the trenches at Petersburg. Hotchkiss went with him to Lexington, and then to Lynchburg. They were there on Sunday, April 9, the day Lee surrendered to Grant at Appomattox Courthouse. Hotchkiss' diary entry for that day includes: "News came rapidly that our army lost most of its trains and artillery yesterday and that there was a fight this morning and the army has surrendered. It was confirmed late in the day and sadness and gloom pervaded the entire community. Gens. Thos. L. Rosser and Thos. T. Munford came in, late in the day, and the town is full of fugitives."

In spite of the news, Lomax and his division, Hotchkiss included, resumed their march toward Danville where General Lee was said to have gone, and it was not until April 12 that they "heard positively that Gen. Lee had surrendered himself." It was one thing for the army to surrender, another thing altogether for Lee to surrender. "This," said Hotchkiss, "had caused nearly everyone to give up all hopes for the Confederacy." It resulted in a complete demoralization, and Lomax's division "just melted away."

There was nothing more for Hotchkiss to do but to find his belongings and make his way home. On April 16 he met up with Robinson at Buchanan, and, after staying with the Reverend William H. Ruffner in Lexington on the way, together they returned to Loch Willow. On May 1, Captain Snyder, Acting Assistant Provost Marshal General, Army of Shenandoah, paroled Hotchkiss.[15] His soldiering days were over.

This and the previous chapter have described Hotchkiss' four years of military service, but have largely ignored the mapmaking activity which was his principal duty. This work is reserved for a later chapter where it is discussed as one important part of his contribution to the mapping of his adopted state. It is clear, even with this omission, that his services to the military operations of II Corps of the Army of Northern Virginia were outstanding. As a staff officer he acted as courier and planner, went on reconnaissance, engaged in special operations, supervised bridge-building and the construction of fortifications and telegraph lines. He aided the marshalling of the wagon-train at critical times, and helped to stem the stream of panic-stricken men retreating in defeat. If he had never put colored crayon to a sketch pad, if his services had been only as described, he had repeatedly earned the thanks of his generals. It is surprising, then, that he was never commissioned as an officer in the Confederate army.[16]

In July 1861 he had been made Acting Adjutant of the 25th Virginia Regiment, but this was no more than a gesture on the part of its officers and men. In the following month, General Loring appointed Hotchkiss Lieutenant of Engineers; again this was only a local decision, and the official application was rejected on the grounds that there was no vacancy. When he marched down the Valley with the militia to join Jackson, he was again acting in the capacity of adjutant. Throughout the Valley campaign he was a civilian member of Jackson's staff, and it was not until September 29, 1862, that he again applied to the War Department for a commission.[17] In his Diary he recorded, "I got a letter of recommendation from Lt. J. K. Boswell, and also one from Gen. Jackson, to the Secretary of War and applied for a commission in the Topographical Engineer Corps. I had a plain talk with the General; he said he thought my great fault was talking too much, but he gave me a good testimonial and hoped that I might succeed in the appointment, and at the same time asked that I might be assigned to him for duty." As a result Hotchkiss was granted a temporary commission entitling him to the pay of a Captain of Engineers. Even so it was necessary for him to get the permission of Lee to continue in his present duty with Jackson. He used, and was addressed by, the title Captain to the end of the war. To cite one example: in the correspondence between himself and Jubal Early concerning the reconnaissance of the mountains to the west of the Valley, the General always addressed his letters to "Capt. Hotchkiss," and Hotchkiss signed himself "Capt. & Top. Eng. 2nd. Corps." This was only a courtesy title, however; when in March 1863, there was a general order to enroll all civilian personnel attached to the army, Jackson had no option but to conscript Hotchkiss into one of the infantry companies. Hotchkiss protested to his general, but Jackson said it was an unpleasant duty imposed upon him. Had Hotchkiss been commissioned, as both men wished, that situation would never have arisen. Jackson not only allowed Hotchkiss to take his protest direct to General Lee, but also added his own remarks to the appeal. In spite of that support Hotchkiss was fearful of the outcome, and did no work to speak of that day, "being too much disturbed."[18] He need not have been. As soon as he obtained the interview, Lee ruled that Hotchkiss was already on duty, and sent him back to report to Jackson.

That absurd situation probably prompted another formal application to the Secretary of War made a week later. The application was endorsed by Boswell as follows:

> Hd. Qrs. 2nd Army Corps, March 13, 1863
> Mr. Jed Hotchkiss has been serving as Top. Eng. with this Army Corps since the 27th of March, 1862, and has rendered a large amount of valuable service. In the collection of topographical information I have never known his superior, I therefore, respectfully recommend that he be commissioned in the Prov. Eng. Corps and assigned to this command.
> (Signed) J. K. Boswell
> Capt. & Ch. Eng. 2nd Corps.

Jackson approved the letter and forwarded it to Lee.[19]

Earlier, while waiting for his interview with Lee, Hotchkiss had visited Jeb Stuart, and must have told him of his troubles, for the very evening that Hotchkiss returned to Lee's headquarters, Stuart wrote of his surprise at learning that Jackson's topographical engineer had never been commissioned. In spite of all those recommendations, the reply was the same as it always had been, and would continue to be, that there were no vacancies in the Engineering Corps. In part this was due to Confederate policy of distributing such appointments evenly among the states, but as the application of this policy had failed to the extent that in 1862 almost a quarter of the authorized posts were held by Virginians, Hotchkiss had very little chance of getting a commission. Eventually, in the last winter of the war, he was given the highest civilian appointment in the gift of the Chief of the Bureau of Engineers, namely First Military Assistant Engineer, a belated recognition of his services.

The title of "Captain" continued to be applied to Hotchkiss in the immediate post-war years. Thus Allan & Co., realtors, advertised in September 1865, that Captain Jed Hotchkiss would "prepare accurate maps for land owners."[20] Reasonably, the title was also used in a report of the Celebration of the Death of Stonewall Jackson, in which Hotchkiss was one of the parade marshals.[21] Just as often, though, he was referred to as Mr. Hotchkiss, as for instance in the announcement by Miss Mary J. Baldwin that her school would reopen on September 18, 1865, with Mr. Hotchkiss as professor of natural Sciences.[22] Although the parent of the Misses Nellie and Anna Hotchkiss was referred to in the 1871-2 Catalogue of the Augusta Female Seminary as "captain," he had already been "promoted," and furthermore this had been accepted by no less a personage than Robert E. Lee. The contract governing the employment of Hotchkiss as topographical engineer for the Board of Survey of Washington College, referred to him as Major Jed Hotchkiss.[23] The official announcement of this appointment used the same title, as did letters signed by Lee, as president of the college, and directed to Hotchkiss in the course of his work for that Board.

The title was used throughout the remainder of his life, and to his surveyors and mapmaking staff he became, simply and affectionately, "The Major."

The Hotchkiss Family: Nellie Hotchkiss, Jed Hotchkiss, Anna Hotchkiss, Sara Hotchkiss.
Mary Baldwin College, Staunton, Virginia

CHAPTER IV

Back to school, but not for long

HOTCHKISS, ACCOMPANIED by Robinson, arrived home on April 18, and quickly attempted to pick up where he had left off nearly four years earlier.[1] He distributed a printed handbill dated May 8, 1865, announcing that he intended "to resume the duties of his school on Wednesday 10th May at the Temperance Hall in Churchville."[2] Six pupils were enrolled and classes continued until harvest time in June. In July he concluded an agreement with nine parents (including the Harmans) to teach their children, fifteen in all, at $100 per pupil for a session of ten months, starting on the first Monday in September.[3] Because of the great shortage of money he was prepared to accept cereals as payment for his services, a bushel of wheat being equivalent to $1, and the same quantity of corn 75 cents. About the same time he learned that Colonel Michael G. Harman required a survey of his lands in Fauquier County.[4] During July, with the help of Robinson and his servant, William (now free), he surveyed Henry Forrer's Shenandoah Iron Works property, and in August spent 21 days surveying Mike Harman's land, charging $10 per day and expenses.[5] The following month the Hotchkiss family, plus Robinson, moved to Staunton to occupy premises on the corner of present-day Frederick Street and Central Avenue. Hotchkiss had rented this property for one year from Lyttleton Waddell Jr. for $300, with the option of renting for a further year.[6]

Miss Mary J. Baldwin's announcement that her school, the Augusta Female Seminary, would reopen on September 18, included Hotchkiss as Professor of Natural Sciences and Robinson as Professor of Penmanship on her list of the faculty.[7] When not teaching, Hotchkiss and Robinson filled up their time surveying farmlands put up for sale.[8] Hotchkiss also undertook surveying commissions for the newly formed real estate agents, Allan & Co.[9] The Allan of this company, the former Chief of Ordnance of II Corps, was the same William Allan with whom Hotchkiss would soon co-operate in an ambitious project to publish accounts of the battlefields of Virginia.

Other map work came to Hotchkiss from an unexpected quarter. At the end of August he received a letter from L. Rowland which referred to a meeting with Brigadier General Michie, "a class mate and intimate friend from West Point," who was anxious to obtain copies of Confederate military maps.[10] Hotchkiss would have saved himself a deal of trouble if he had written to Michie at that time. Two months later, Oltmanns, writing from New York, passed on gossip he had heard "that some lady has informed against you in Richmond as having in [your] possession maps and materials &c..."[11] On Monday, October 23, only days after receiving that news, a Federal detective arrived from Richmond bearing a military order requiring Hotchkiss to surrender his collection of maps. Hotchkiss "got rid of him by promising to go to Richmond next Thursday" and take his maps with him.[12] In the meantime he successfully sought the aid of such prominent men in Staunton as Alexander H. H. Stuart and John B. Baldwin to intercede on his behalf with Governor Pierpont.[13] He went to Richmond on Thursday, October 26, "taking along a large number of maps...made and collected during the war." The interview with General Michie on the following day resulted in some kind of understanding. What this was, Hotchkiss did not record, but soon after returning home, he put Robinson to work on county maps.[14] Hotchkiss made another visit to Michie in December, which was followed by a letter from the General setting out the agreement between them: "You will please work up for the Eng. Dept. from your notes maps of the Valley Counties of Virginia and such other sections of the State made important by military operations....Your compensation will be $5 per day."[15]

Published accounts of this matter state that Hotchkiss retained

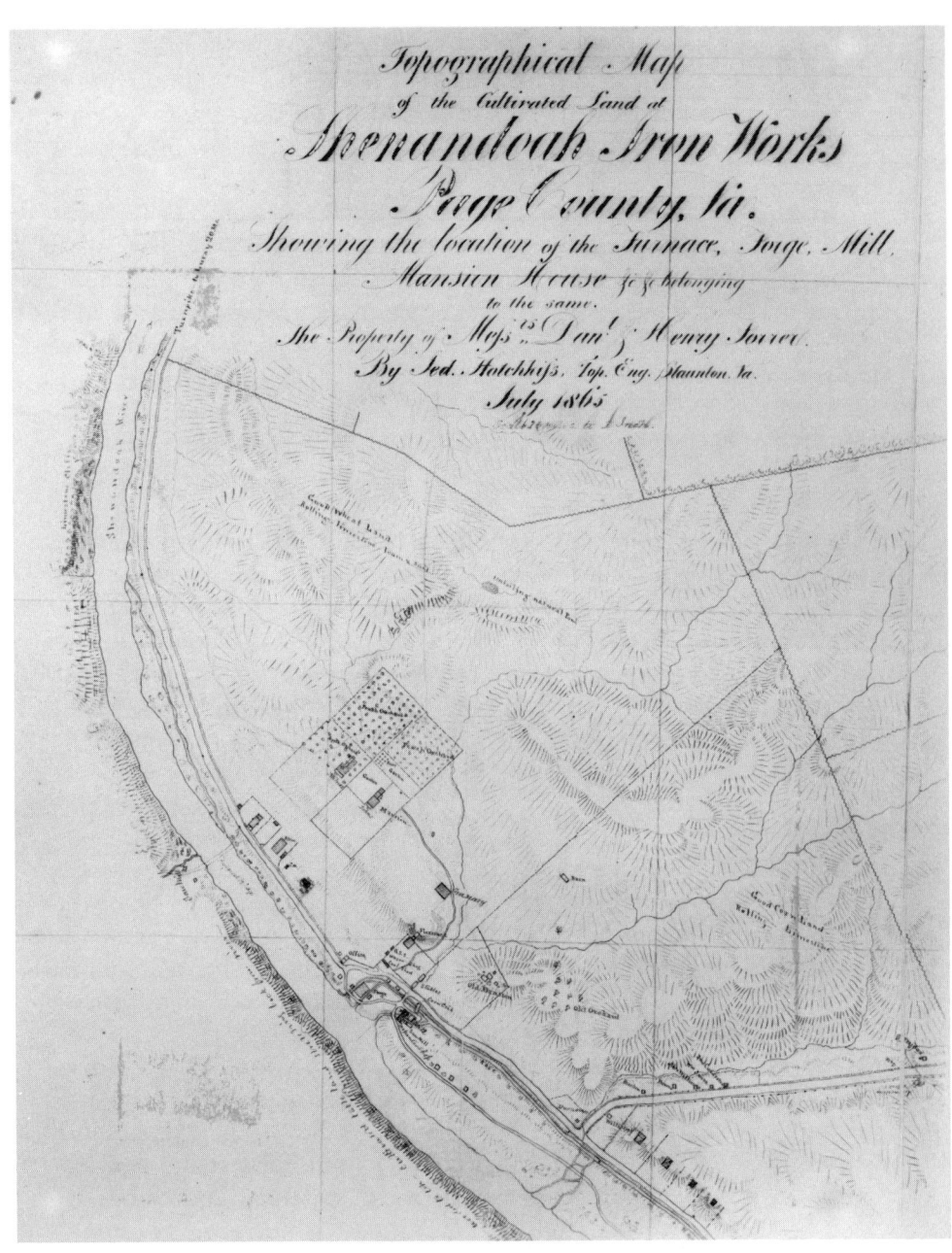

Part of the map of the Forrers' Shenandoah Iron Works surveyed in the summer of 1865.
Hotchkiss Map Collection #248, Library of Congress

Augusta County, Virginia. Part of the map made by Hotchkiss in 1865 under the direction of Brigadier General Peter S. Michie, but not published until 1875. Scale: ¾ inch to one mile. This portion shows the places where Hotchkiss made his home; Mossy Creek, Stribling Springs, Churchville and Staunton.

Library of Congress

his maps as a direct consequence of a personal interview with General Grant, but nowhere in the diary between October 23, when the detective called, and December 29, when Michie confirmed the agreement between them, did Hotchkiss make any reference to a visit to Washington, let alone to one to General Grant. It is inconceivable that he should have an interview with Grant and not record it. If Grant had any part in the arrangement, it must have been simply his approval of the action of a subordinate officer. This would explain the delay between Michie's first meeting with Hotchkiss and his official request.

A number of sketches of the life of Hotchkiss, published during the year following his death, referred to this incident. On March 8, 1899, the *Staunton Spectator and Vindicator* published the "admirable paper on the life of the late Major Hotchkiss," presented at a meeting of the Stonewall Jackson Camp Confederate veterans. This contained the statement,

> Hotchkiss' maps were seized by order of General Grant, ...But when Hotchkiss insisted on going to Washington with his maps, offering to copy them, Grant kindly ordered their return and paid for the work of copying.

In June 1899, the *Confederate Veteran* gave a different version.

> The United States Government demanded his maps, by order of General Grant. Refusing to deliver them he went to Washington, where after many rebuffs he saw General Grant in person, who ordered and paid for such copies as he required for his reports, and courteously returned them all.

Another account was published in the biographical section of *Confederate Military History, Volume III*, Virginia, 1899, which stated:

> An informer caused his arrest that fall, but he accompanied his cherished maps to Washington, and General Grant ordered their return, and paid for copying all he desired to use in his own reports.[16]

The next reference to this matter appears to be in *Encyclopaedia of Virginia Biography.* Vol. III, 1915:

> He placed his maps in security, as he thought, but their existence was reported to the Federal government, and a demand made for them by Gen. Grant. In a personal interview with Gen.

BACK TO SCHOOL, BUT NOT FOR LONG 91

Grant at Washington, Mr. Hotchkiss protested against the order, offering to make exact copies for the government; Gen. Grant offered to pay for such copies as he could use and ordered the originals to be returned.

It is this authority which has been quoted by later authors.[17] The supposed Washington visit may have its origin in a mistake made by Hotchkiss years after the event.

In 1886, the John A. Andrew Post No. 15 of the Grand Army of the Republic presented a series of lectures on the Civil War at Tremont Temple in Boston, Massachusetts. The sixth lecture, "Stonewall Jackson's Valley Campaign," was given by Major Jed Hotchkiss on Wednesday evening, November 24.[18] Among the Hotchkiss papers in the Library of Congress is an undated newspaper clipping of an article headed PILOT OF THE ARMY. Its opening sentence reads:

> The *Traveller*, a few weeks ago published, in connection with his visit to this city, a portrait and brief sketch of Major Hotchkiss of Staunton, Virginia, but since that time it has come into possession of further interesting facts regarding this gentleman's war career.

One of these was the map episode, which it describes as follows:

> That fall, on a statement made by an informer, his maps were seized by an order of General Grant; but when Major Hotchkiss, who insisted on accompanying them to Washington, protested the taking of his maps, and offered to make accurate copies of any of them that General Grant wanted, (he having sent for them to use in preparing his report) the latter kindly ordered their return, and then paid for making the copies he desired.[19]

The "further interesting facts" came from Hotchkiss. Elsewhere among the papers is an incomplete account of his life, majoring on the war years. This, although written in the third person, appears to be in Hotchkiss' handwriting. It begins: "Major Jed. Hotchkiss, of Virginia, the distinguished Topographical Engineer of 'Stonewall' Jackson, who is to lecture on the memorable Shenandoah Valley Campaign, of that famous Confederate General, on Wednesday evening, Nov. 24th, 1886, in Tremont Temple..."[20] Unfortunately the sketch only extends to the battle of Fredericksburg, but it is reasonable to conclude that the *Traveller's* information was derived from this, or a version of it. The newspaper's account of the attempt by the U.S. Army to secure the maps makes no reference to an interview with Grant, and only speaks of orders emanating from the general. The only discrepancy from the diary record is the visit to Washington instead of to Richmond. Thus, the notion of an interview with Grant is an elaboration made by the contributor to the *Confederate Veteran* and repeated in the *Encyclopaedia of Virginia Biography.*

It was to be expected that among those returning from the war would be a belief that a market would exist for first-hand accounts of skirmishes, raids, and battles, and thus a source of income. Some would feel the need to justify their past actions, others to eulogize some loved and lost commander; a few would recognise the future need for an accurate account of the campaigns. Many would require additional information to supplement their own remembrances, and Hotchkiss was one of the reliable sources all serious writers about the Virginia campaigns could call upon. General Robert E. Lee wrote to him on September 30 that he would "be much obliged...for any aid you could give me. Please let me know what battlefields you have plans of and what you can furnish me."[21] Earlier Campbell Brown had asked for maps of the Spotsylvania Campaign to be sent to him for his stepfather and former superior officer, General Ewell.[22] To General Thomas Rosser, Hotchkiss sent a map of western Virginia and the Valley.[23] He wrote articles for the *Valley Virginian* and collaborated with William Allan. The two men intended to produce a series of books on the battlefields of Virginia, the first of which would describe the battle of Chancellorsville. In order to achieve a complete account Hotchkiss wrote to his cousin and U.S. Congressman, Giles W. Hotchkiss of Binghamton, New York, for copies of the official Federal records, "Conduct of the War." He also wrote Hooker for his report of the battle. Neither of these requests was fulfilled, but that they were made was characteristic of Hotchkiss' thoroughness in seeking the facts.[24]

His determination to get back to a normal civilian life was shared by most Virginians. S. Howell Brown wrote to Hotchkiss, "Our old friends Hawks, Lack, Campbell and Co. are well and everyone seems to be struggling to get into the old business channels...." His farm, and that of his father, had been destroyed in the war and he was having to start all over again "without a hoof of stock of any kind or a $...." He too was looking for some additional source of income and hoped to publish a revised version of the only map he had saved from the wreck, "that of the Valley from Potomac to Staunton and from mountain to mountain."[25]

The devastation in Virginia had been considerable and the Valley had suffered greatly from the raids of Hunter and the scorched-earth policy of Sheridan. In Rockingham County alone, 30 houses, 450 barns, and 31 mills had been destroyed, and over 10,000 head of livestock carried off.[26] Indeed "From Harpers Ferry to New Market...the country was almost a desert. There were no fences...no cattle, hogs, sheep or horses or anything else...barns were all burned, a great many of the private dwellings were burned, chimneys standing without houses, houses standing without roof or door or window, a most desolate state of affairs, bridges all destroyed and roads badly cut up."[27] Of the 64 persons who had been engaged in business in Staunton, in 1862, 20 were dead, 30 had left town, and the remaining 14 were out of business or had changed their vocation.[28]

Nevertheless, in November 1865, Whitelaw Reid was able to report significant improvements: "Thanks to Northern loans...already the Virginia Central Railroad was open to Staunton and the Orange and Alexandria through its whole length over a score or more of battlefields."[29] The *Staunton Spectator*, whose presses had been destroyed by Hunter in July 1864, appeared in an abbreviated form twelve months later, and was being printed on new presses and with new type face during the first months of 1866.[30] The First National Bank of Staunton, using money borrowed in Baltimore, opened its doors again in September 1865, with Alexander H. H. Stuart as president and William Allan as cashier.[31]

A new enterprise called the National Express and Transportation Company was organized at this time by three Virginians, Colonel Harman of Staunton, Richmond banker Charles W. Purcell, and L. W. Glazebrook. According to Harman, this would be "the greatest company in the world" and would furnish employment for the officers and men who were the survivors of the war. True to its name, this was to be no sectional enterprise, and apportionment of the capital stock was made to Northern as well as Southern states. Hotchkiss was one of many who invested in this over-ambitious scheme.[32]

Throughout 1866 he was occupied with the variety of teaching, surveying, and mapping tasks begun the previous year. But the topographical work was becoming the more important part of his working life. As Robinson, writing to his friend David Boyd in Louisiana in March 1866, said, "We have done a good business in Surveying and Map Making since our location in Staunton—though money is still very scarce here & we have the material & means for building up one of the best business [sic] in this line I have ever known."[33] This view is supported by the entries in the Hotchkiss account book which shows that apart from the lucrative work for Harman, he had done work for Echols,

Bell, and Catlett, Attorneys at Law, who were to become important land speculators and developers; for James Crawford, and D. and H. Forrer; and for Brigadier General Peter S. Michie. For the last three months of 1865 he had performed topographical engineering work amounting to $745, significantly more than he was earning from his select school, and as well as employing Robinson he engaged C. W. Oltmanns at the end of November.[34]

In March 1866 Hotchkiss started yet another scheme. He acquired, on extremely favorable terms from Mike Harman, an undivided half-interest in a garden together with a house and lot formerly occupied by Dr. Hoge. Harman and Hotchkiss were "to be the joint owners for the purpose of planting and cultivating a vineyard sharing equally the expenses and dividing the profits that may accrue." In a column of the *Staunton Spectator* devoted to "Our Town," the editor noted "the spirit of helpfulness and enterprise" which animated the people, and that "Messrs Harman and Hotchkiss are now engaged in setting out an extensive vineyard in the suburbs of the town." Just what prompted that interest is not recorded, but the previous November, Hotchkiss had written a long article on "Vine Culture in Virginia" for the *Richmond Enquirer*.[35] The property on Institution Road, now East Beverley Street, was to become The Oaks, one of the most widely known private addresses in Staunton. The ten-year agreement only lasted eighteen months and in September 1867, Hotchkiss acquired the whole three acres to make it the family home.[36] Until then it is probable that he continued to live in, and operate his select school from, the Water Street premises, after negotiating an extension of the rental with the new owner.

During 1866, when time permitted, Hotchkiss worked on a history of the Fredericksburg and Chancellorsville battlefields and prepared maps for its illustration. His teaching and mapping activities slowed his progress, but by September he had received the proofs of his maps from the printers. He also had the proofs of the manuscript, for William Allan was expecting Hotchkiss to correct them. "Be sure you do it all right," Allan wrote on September 10. "Don't leave any blunders or I shall 'shoot' you. When will you have that thing printed? If you had used your usual energy it would have been done long ago. Try to get it out and be done with it."[37] Through Francis Smith, superintendent of the Virginia Military Institute, Hotchkiss had made contact with the New York publishing firm of Van Nostrand who agreed to publish the book.[38] It appeared in February 1867, but was not a success, for in July the publishers wrote to "General" Jed Hotchkiss, "We are sorry to say that the success in selling 'Chancellorsville' has not been very encouraging."[39]

The optimism shown by Robinson in March 1866 had evaporated by the end of the year. In a letter to Boyd he said that business was "very dull and collections hard to make." Robinson feared that the lack of funds might delay his return to Louisiana, but the following month he was in New Orleans and by March 1867 was engaged as acting librarian at Louisiana State Seminary, where Boyd was superintendent. Business may not have been as brisk as Robinson would have liked, but there is little doubt of the determination of the people of Staunton to overcome their difficulties and present at least an appearance of a successful and civilized community. By the beginning of 1867 there were two debating societies and a theater company in the town, and the Staunton Musical Association had just been formed. Hotchkiss frequently took part in the weekly debates of the Lyceum and occasionally addressed its members. At the end of December 1866 he lectured on "The importance of having correct maps of all countries," and the following April took part in a debate on the question, "Is a general free school system desirable in Virginia?" Hotchkiss spoke in favor of the motion, but it was defeated by 12 votes to 2![40]

For business growth the townspeople needed good communications and this meant good railroads. Soon after taking up residence at Mossy Creek, Hotchkiss had written to his brother, "They need communications to market very much...they have to send flour by wagon 80 miles before they can reach a railroad and you know the cost of transportation by wagon is very expensive."[41] By the beginning of the Civil War this distance had been shortened by the Manassas Gap Railroad, linking Strasburg to Alexandria, and by the tunnelling of the Blue Ridge for the Virginia Central. Both railroads suffered considerably at the hands of the contending armies, but while the Virginia Central was operating over its entire length by the spring of 1866 the Manassas Gap Railroad was still in ruins, and there was considerable interest being shown in establishing a new railroad throughout the length of the Valley from Winchester to Salem.

A public meeting in the Staunton courthouse on January 26, 1866, called upon the Virginia General Assembly to grant a charter for this purpose. The charter was granted in February and a convention of delegates from all the Valley counties met at Staunton in April for the purpose of securing sufficient subscription of stock to permit the organization of the railroad company. Not surprisingly, more than half the delegates were from Augusta County and included not only Alexander H. H. Stuart, who 30 years earlier had led the railroad movement in the Assembly, but also John B. Baldwin, John Echols, Michael G. Harman, William Allan, and Jed Hotchkiss. With the requisite amount of stock promised, the company was formed with Harman as president. A year later at the annual general meeting of stockholders, "On motion of General Echols, Dr. Graham of Rockbridge was called to the chair and Capt. Jed Hotchkiss appointed secretary."[42]

Hotchkiss also took an interest in another and more important railroad scheme; the extension of the Virginia Central, by 12.6 miles, to Covington, and its consolidation with the proposed, but unbuilt Covington and Ohio Railroad. A convention at Greenbrier White Sulphur Springs, newly reopened under the management of George L. Peyton, proprietor of Staunton's Virginia Hotel, was attended by Hotchkiss' associates, Echols and Bell, and they would have kept him informed.[43]

The same year saw other developments in Staunton in which Hotchkiss played a part and in doing so gradually established himself as a civic leader. On January 15, 1867, the Virginia General Assembly passed the act incorporating the Augusta County Fair "for the purpose of establishing and conducting fairs and other exhibitions of the natural and industrial products of Augusta County and of promoting enterprise, industry, economy and thrift among the people." The ten directors appointed by the County Court met in June, and elected John B. Baldwin as the president of the fair and "Major" Jedediah Hotchkiss its secretary. They purchased twenty-one acres of land lying to the east of Staunton on Lewis Creek in October and held the first fair the following year.[44]

In May 1867, he associated himself with three other educators in an attempt to set up a "Business College and Normal School" in Staunton.[45] This local venture was not successful, but another on an altogether grander scale had been in the mind of the philanthropist George Peabody, one which would affect Hotchkiss closely and be his financial life-line for years to come. Peabody had written to sixteen prominent men, North and South, including Robert C. Winthrop of Maine, General Grant, and the Honorable William C. Rives of Virginia, "Feeling that it was a duty and a privilege of the more favored and wealthy parts of our nation to assist those who are less fortunate...I give you gentlemen the sum of one million dollars...for the promotion and encouragement of intellectual, moral, or industrial education among the young of the more destitute parts of Southern and Southwestern States of our Union." He requested that Mr. Winthrop should be chairman. The Peabody Education Fund was born.

In July of 1867 Barnas Sears, the Fund's agent, visited Staunton and that August made it his base.[46] Hotchkiss and Barnas Sears were to become close friends, and Hotchkiss benefited from the patronage Sears could offer, especially in the difficult years after 1873.

Hotchkiss' interest in education, in the broadest meaning of the word, continued throughout his life, but it was during those years that he finally gave up the idea of re-establishing himself as a schoolmaster. He explained this many years later by saying that he "found after 4 years in the saddle, confinement irksome."⁴⁷ On the other hand the surveying and mapping of property, farms, and furnaces gave him just the combination of indoor and outdoor, intellectual and physical activity he needed. By the time he decided to give up his select school he had established himself as a topographical and civil engineer and cartographer. With the help of Robinson and Oltmanns he had completed work on six county maps for General Michie, two for W. L. Nicholson of the Federal Post Office, and had work in progress on sixteen others. He had also undertaken fieldwork on properties belonging to M. G. Harman, D. and H. Forrer, and a dozen other Valley property owners.⁴⁸

He seriously intended to publish his county maps. Even as early as August 1865 he had made an agreement with Frank Boylan, a former topographical engineer with the Army of Northern Virginia and now employed by J. D. Price & Co., Real Estate Agents of Harrisonburg, to collect subscriptions and supply topographical information for a map of Rockingham County. Boylan was to receive 30% commission. The project came to nothing and the contract was scrapped a year later.⁴⁹

One map which he did produce and publish was the attractive circular map "35 miles around Richmond" at a scale of approximately 3-miles-to-1-inch. In the top two corner spaces between the circular map and the rectangular border were vignettes of the Capitol of the Confederate States and the Washington Monument in Richmond, and in the bottom corners plans of the cities of Richmond and Petersburg. On the face of the map were shown the lines of the Confederate and Federal fortifications. Referring to this map, although calling it "10 miles around Richmond," Charles S. Bundy, writing in the Windsor Academy's magazine, *The Echo*, December 1909, claimed that it hung in every hotel and public hall in Virginia for years after the War of the Rebellion. Even if this was the case, the venture was not profitable and Hotchkiss never again engaged in map publishing on his own account.⁵⁰

What seems to have appealed to him most, and was profitable, was the examination and reporting on extensive real estate, especially if it had potential for mineral operations. The property owned by the Forrers was of this kind. After the survey of the Shenandoah Iron Works and its successful sale to the Honorable William Milnes, Jr., they commissioned Hotchkiss to prepare a survey and report on their Elizabeth Furnace Estate. This charcoal furnace, named after Daniel Forrer's wife, was built about 1863 on the line of the Virginia Central Railroad

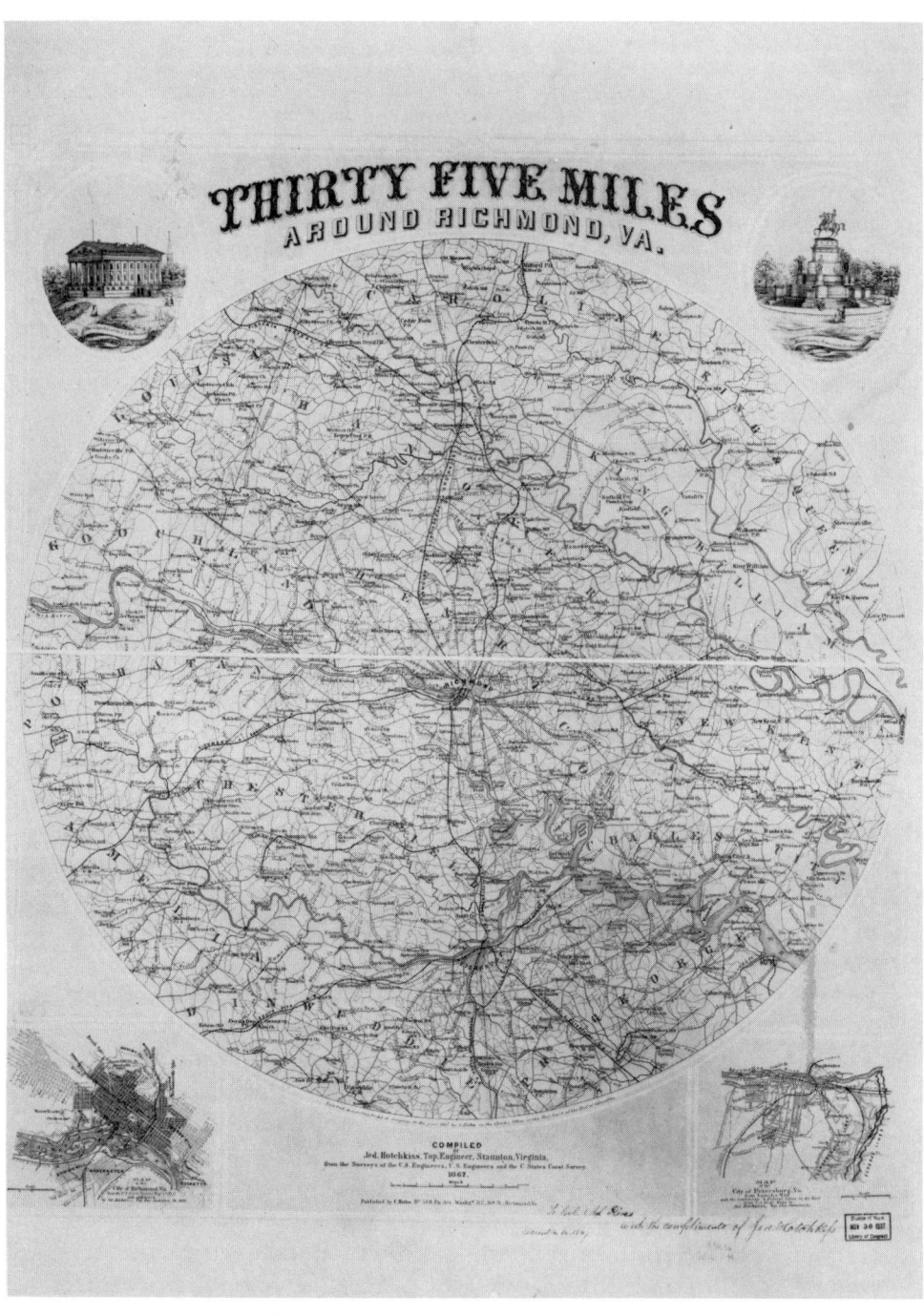

The first published Hotchkiss map, and said to have been widely distributed throughout Virginia.

Library of Congress

sixteen miles west of Staunton. The property, containing about 6,250 acres, was surveyed by Hotchkiss in July 1867, and from this he constructed a map on a scale of 1:23,500 (2.7 inches to 1 mile) with insets showing the general location of the estate, and a profile of the road to the ore banks. This map was lithographed by A. Hoen & Co. of Baltimore to accompany the 13-page report printed in the *Vindicator* Job Office in Staunton. The text of the report dealt successively with the location, topography, geology, and the iron ores, of the estate, and included chemical analyses of the ore and production statistics of the furnace.[51]

Hotchkiss had established a close relationship with Echols, Bell, and Catlett, who had a good real-estate business, and in March 1867 he rented an office on their premises which must have assisted co-operation with the partnership. This became even more effective by the formation of a new company, Echols, Bell, Catlett & Co., Real Estate Agents, which included "J. Hotchkiss" on its "card."[52] The notebooks he kept over the years 1867-8 give a detailed record of his topographical work, much of it directly attributable to his involvement with this firm. Among these are field books containing plans of lots and houses as well as more extensive surveys. Most of these are freehand pencil drawings, but the plat of John B. Hoge's lot at the corner of New and Frederick Streets is ruled in ink. Others are quite elaborate topographical sketches with streams shown in blue ink, and hill forms in pencil. From them we learn that he engaged other people to assist him: John A. McGuffin in March 1868 and in November of the same year M. A. Miller, who was to become one of his closest professional colleagues.[53]

By 1868, Hotchkiss was involved in yet another enterprise, this time with Washington College and under the direction of no less a person than General Robert E. Lee. Shortly after the end of the war Lee had been offered, and had accepted, the presidency of the college. He brought to it not just an illustrious name, but fresh ideas and a determination to re-create from the ruins of Hunter's vandals a first-class institution for the education of Virginia's young men. In April 1867 Lee presented his plan to the Trustees the results of his deliberations. It included the formation of nine departments and the election of four new professors. One of these was William Allan as Professor of Applied Mathematics. So, when in June 1868, on the recommendation of the Faculty, the trustees set up a Board of Survey "to gather exact information on the geography, mineral resources, industry and natural history of the South and particularly of the State of Virginia,—and to publish the same...," it is not surprising that it employed Hotchkiss as its topographical engineer. He was the obvious choice to prepare the "accurate topographical maps of the several counties of Virginia" the Board wished to publish, and he signed a five-year contract with Lee on June 29, 1868, to prepare "such maps as the Board may require." He was to receive no salary, but would be entitled to the profits from the sale of the maps to the public.[54]

Washington College was not the only institution taking an interest in Virginia's resources. Its close neighbor in Lexington, the Virginia Military Institute (V.M.I.), had its own ideas about a physical survey of the state. Both were responding to the general concern that in prewar days Virginia had neglected its natural wealth; they wished to provide a sound foundation for future development. Less altruistically, as both were desperately short of money, each saw their survey activities as a means of attracting funds available from the Federal land-grant appropriations under the terms of the Morrill Act of 1862.[55] Francis Smith, superintendent of V.M.I., had obtained the services of another famous Virginian, Commodore Matthew Fontaine Maury, as Professor of Physics and with specific responsibility for a "Physical Survey of Virginia."

Maury arrived in New York from England on July 14, 1868, and he and his family were invited by the proprietor to holiday at White Sulphur Springs where they would meet many distinguished Southerners, including Lee. The surveys proposed by the institutions were discussed by the two men and Maury concluded that their respective plans were complimentary to one another. This conclusion did not prevent Francis Smith from believing Washington College to be a threat; he even went so far as to warn Maury from having anything to do with Hotchkiss, whom he described as "a land speculator—or rather—employed in that interest. He is sharp and unscrupulous—so beware of him."[56]

Hotchkiss had already been in touch with Maury about a very different matter. As secretary, Hotchkiss was involved in making arrangements for the first Augusta County Fair, and had engaged Maury to be one of the speakers of this event. The fair was hailed as a "GRAND SUCCESS" by the *Staunton Spectator* which also reported that, "The most attractive and entertaining of the second day's exercises was the delivery by Commodore Matthew F. Maury of a very instructive address."[57]

In December following the fair, Lee told Hotchkiss that the Board of Survey desired "that the preparation and publication of the series of county maps should be commenced," and that it preferred "that those of Roanoke and Augusta should be first brought out."[58] At that time Hotchkiss had very little topographical information about Roanoke

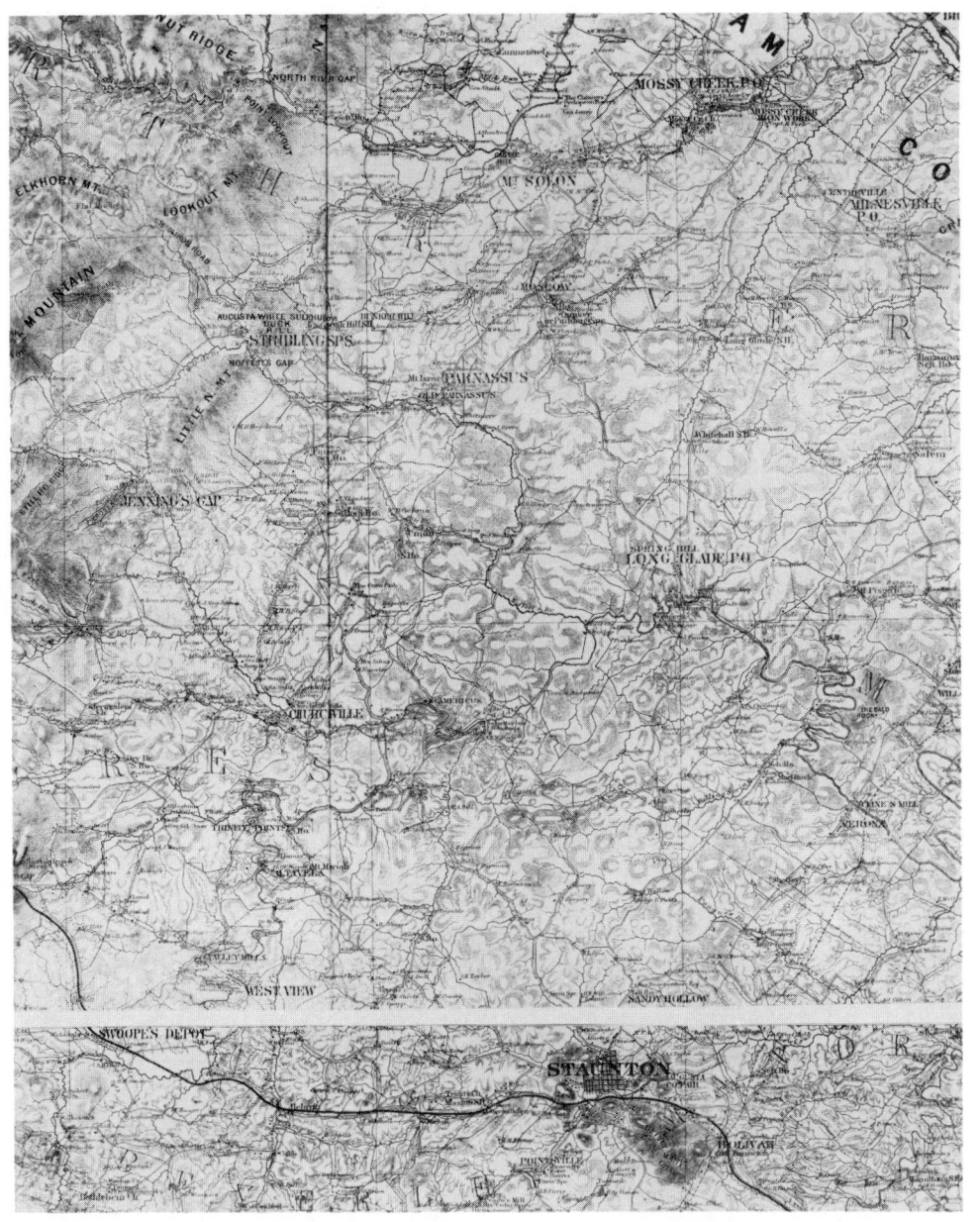

Augusta County, Virginia. Part of the map made by Hotchkiss for the Board of Survey of Washington College, and published in 1870. Original scale: one inch to one mile.

Library of Congress

County, certainly nothing to compare with the wealth of data he had accumulated on Augusta County, so it is not surprising that the Board soon decided that the cartographic work should initially be confined to that county. Even so, progress was slow, and although Lee was able to report to the Trustees in June 1869 that the mass of the work had been done, the map was not in the hands of the engravers until the following January. Indeed, Lee had written Hotchkiss in October 1869 that the faculty had hoped to have received it before then and wanted to know when they could expect to have it. He reminded Hotchkiss, "When you were last present at the meeting of the Board it was determined to prepare the Augusta map from the surveys at your command...." The Board thought it unwise to spend time on minute details of topography.[59] The finished map was in Lee's hands in time for his report to the Trustees in June 1870. For the second of the Board's projects, a map of Henrico and Chesterfield Counties (rather than of Roanoke County), Lee invited Hotchkiss to Lexington where he could work under supervision and without distraction.[60] By April 1870, according to a statement published in the *Richmond Whig*—attributed to an "officer of the Board of Survey," in addition to the nearly complete Henrico-Chesterfield map the Board had "the recent surveys from either Confederate or Federal sources of seventy-three other counties of the State, several of them in a condition ready for the engraver."[61] In fact, only the map of Augusta County was ever published by the Board, which itself ceased to function after Lee's death in September 1870. The treasurer's report to the Trustees, June 17, 1871, contains an item of $100 paid to Hotchkiss May 31, but the new president of Washington College did not mention the Board of Survey in his report.[62]

In fairness to Hotchkiss it should be said that the arrangement he had made with Lee was unsatisfactory to both of them. There was no immediate financial advantage to Hotchkiss, who would only receive the proceeds from the public sale of the maps, and hence had no incentive to make swift progress. More importantly, he had to undertake other commissions to meet his day-to-day needs.

The Virginia Military Institute was no more successful in its enterprise. Maury very quickly published in December 1868 his *Physical Survey of Virginia, Preliminary Report, No. 1.*, but although he continued the work and a second report was ready by May 1871, lack of funds prevented publication. A revised version was published in 1878, long after Maury's death, by which time Hotchkiss' own *Virginia, a Geographical and Political Summary* had been issued by the State Board of Immigration. Neither Washington College nor the Virginia Military Institute was successful in attracting land-grant monies. These went instead to Hampden-Sidney College and to Preston and Olin Academy at Blacksburg, which became the Virginia Agriculture and Mechanical College, later to develop into the Virginia Polytechnic Institute.

Not all the work which Hotchkiss did for the Board of Survey was wasted. He came to an arrangement with the magazine, *The Southern Planter and Farmer*, "To furnish a County map of some county of Virginia...for each month of 1871." The editor announced this by saying,

> At much trouble and expense the publication has secured the right to use the valuable series of MAPS OF THE COUNTIES OF VIRGINIA prepared by that eminent Topographical Engineer, Maj. Jed Hotchkiss, chief engineer on the staff of Gen. T.J. Jackson...these maps are made from actual surveys under the auspices of Washington College and its late President, Gen. Lee.

The *Richmond Whig*, January 4, 1871, reported that a new feature in this farming journal "is the publication of the [maps of] several counties in the State. This department will be under the care and supervision of Major Jed. Hotchkiss, topographical engineer of Staunton who is well qualified for the service. The present number contains a map of Louisa County with the history of the county, statistics, etc...." These maps were small, only 7 × 10 inches, and were reduced by the printer from a scale of 1:160,000 of the manuscript map to 1:240,000 in the magazine. Hotchkiss planned the production of at least nine of these, but only maps of five of them were published in the *Southern Planter and Farmer*, namely for the counties of Louisa, Buckingham, Orange, Hanover, and Surry. He prepared descriptive texts to accompany the maps of Louisa, Hanover, Surry, and Prince Edward Counties, but only those for Louisa County and Surry County were published. Only the map of Surry County carried an acknowledgement to the Board of Survey of Washington College.[63]

During the period when Hotchkiss was topographical engineer for the Board of Survey, important political changes took place in Virginia. The state had a new constitution and was once more one of the United States, its period of "reconstruction" over. Embedded in the Virginia constitution of 1870 were provisions for state responsibility for education, and early in that year the legislature arranged for the election of a state superintendent of public instruction. It was not the most popular post—indeed most Virginians were opposed to the concept of state education, especially its implications for the Negro population—so when William Henry Ruffner canvassed for the position there was no opposition and his nomination was confirmed by the Legislature, 141 to 1, on March 2, 1870. It is doubtful whether a better man could have been found for the task; the United States Commissioner for Education subsequently recommended in 1872 that Southern states study the Virginian program, and Barnas Sears reported in 1873 that Virginia led the South in respect to systems of public education.[64] This was the same Ruffner who had written in praise of Hotchkiss and his academy at Mossy Creek and had underwritten Nelson Hotchkiss' purchase of Loch Willow. Now he was to appoint Hotchkiss as Superintendent of Augusta County Schools. Although Hotchkiss held the post for less than a year, the fact that he was appointed at all indicates his reputation in educational circles.[65] Hotchkiss resigned this post in March 1871 to act as an agent for the publishers of a series of textbooks which had been approved by the state superintendent. For twelve months he applied his prodigious energy to persuading county superintendents, boards of trustees of schools, and others with local influence, of the merits of the Select Series of school text books. In this work he was in competition with a Colonel Withers, agent for a rival publishing company. Frequently they debated in public the advantages of their texts. Thus he recorded in his diary for Friday and Saturday, April 28 and 29, 1871:

> Went to Winchester on cars saw a number of persons there and discussed books. Addressed 75 circulars to Co. Supts at night and wrote description of Hanover Co. for Farmer and Planter.
> Spent day in Winchester—at 1 p.m. had discussion for 2 hours with Col. Withers in CH quite a large audience. Left at 3 p.m. for home which I reached about midnight.

That kind of schedule was by no means unusual. At the end of the previous week Hotchkiss had driven in a buggy the 65 miles to Luray. He spent the Sunday there, met the Page County board on Monday morning, and started back to Staunton at 1:45 p.m. to arrive home at 11 p.m. One hour later he left for Monterey where the following day he "addressed the people of Highland [County] on education and met board of trustees."

In doing this work he did not neglect the reporting and surveying of property. His civil engineering business was growing, he engaged a number of people to assist him with particular projects, and it was no longer convenient to work either in his house or the office at Echols, Bell, Catlett, and Co. By September 1871, he was planning to build a separate office on the plot on East Beverley Street. A month later, while Hotchkiss was mailing 1,000 circulars to school officers of Virginia and 200 to teachers of private schools, construction began. The office, occupied early in the following year, marked the end of the transition from school teacher to civil and mining engineer. Already he was closely involved with a report on the Dolly Ann Furnace property, a real estate commission of some magnitude, and his marketing of text books would cease with the completion of his report to Wilson, Hinkle & Co. in March, just twelve months after his resignation as County Superintendent.

Thus, in the years following the war Hotchkiss had tried a variety of occupations: school teaching, mapmaking, and publishing, writing, selling of real estate, topographical and civil engineering, educational administration, book selling, and viticulture—indeed almost anything that the application of his natural talents and knowledge could earn enough for him and his family. Only the vinegrowing did not seem to fit the pattern of his life; although he bought cuttings in May 1868, and had his old servant William Gearing plant them, and he was pruning in the vineyard in March 1872, it is unlikely that viticulture was ever a serious enterprise.[66] Perhaps its main purpose was to keep William occupied and away from drink.[67]

Common to all the other projects was a theme which would remain throughout his life: the gathering and dissemination of information. To find something out and tell it to someone was what he liked best, and if he was paid for it so much the better. By this time what he liked to find out and tell were the location of Virginia's natural resources, not as an academic exercise, not even for personal gain, though economic necessity must have been a sharp enough goad, but because they were there for man's use. Put there by God for that purpose, it was man's duty to make use of them. He had been given the skill to map and describe these resources; it was his duty to use these skills. He shared the regret of Maury and others that these resources had been neglected in the past, and he never lost an opportunity to aid in their exploitation. The Augusta County Fair provided one public occasion that gave, as we have seen, a platform to Maury from which to describe his vision of a great Virginia port for a fleet of vessels to carry away Virginian coal and iron as well as the products of its factories powered by the abundant water resources of the state. Hotchkiss made his own contribution at the fair with a prize-winning entry, "Essay on the water courses of Augusta County, in reference to Irrigation, and the Propelling of Machinery."[68]

The coal, the iron, the manufactures, the farm produce, all had to be got to Virginia's seabord by rail or canal; there were still some, including Maury, who were prepared to believe that canals could still provide a viable transport system, but it was the railroad that would determine the extent and rate of development of Virginia's mineral wealth. At that date the railroad of interest to Hotchkiss was the Chesapeake & Ohio, climbing over the Allegheny mountains, winding through the canyon of the New River to the Kanawha, the "Beautiful River of the Woods," on its way to Huntington on the Ohio River.

For sixty years the Kanawha had been the site of industrial activity. There were located the salt works where before the war twice as much salt was produced as in any other state. The brine was pumped from wells and evaporated; coal from nearby mines supplied the energy. It was for the transport of this salt and coal that the James River and Kanawha Company was created in 1832 from enterprises having their origins dating back to Revolutionary times, and designed to fulfill the dream of a link between the Atlantic and the Mississippi. Washington in 1784 saw political as well as commercial reasons for connecting East and West, and when President he showed a continued interest in the development of the James River route across the Appalachians to the Ohio. The new company was formed "to complete the improvement of the navigation of James River, and to connect that navigation with the navigation of the Kanawha."[69] By the beginning of the Civil War a canal had been opened alongside the James River as far as Buchanan, Virginia, and excavations extended toward Covington, but they were abandoned. In the meantime, the Louisa Railroad Company and the Blue Ridge Company (the state-owned concern which tunneled the Blue Ridge) had become the Virginia Central RR and had extended the line to Covington. The railroads were succeeding the canals.

The prospects of a rail link made the development of the Kanawha coal an exciting proposition, one in which Hotchkiss was determined to get involved.

The Chesapeake & Ohio railroad was formed in 1868 by the consolidation of the Virginia Central and the Covington & Ohio railroad companies with Colonel Edmund Fontaine as president. He was soon succeeded by General William C. Wickham who went north in search of capital, found (or was found by) Collis P. Huntington, and, "almost before Wickham, the C&O, and Virginia knew what had happened Huntington had won approval for a new financial scheme...which brought him the presidency of the C&O on November 27, 1869."[70] This influx of Northern capital brought Northern control, and soon Virginians were outnumbered on the board of directors by seven to four. One of these Northern directors was Pliny Fisk, of whom, and of his relations with Hotchkiss, more later.

The road west from Covington had to be constructed through wild and spectacular country and its building was an engineering triumph.

The surveyors, when marking the route through New River gorge, had to be suspended from ropes while making their observations, and engineering supplies were brought down the turbulent rivers on "batteaux." Huntington had made the descent of the Greenbriar and New River on one of these 60-foot long craft in 1869 prior to his presidency of the C&O, and so had first-hand knowledge of the difficulties which his engineers would have to overcome.[71] It was January 1873 before the last rail was in place, but in anticipation of this event Hotchkiss described the route in a long essay, published in *Scribner's Monthly* in the issues of December 1872 and January 1873. The articles were illustrated by many delightful drawings of people and places encountered along the way, made by the artists who had accompanied Hotchkiss on his reconnaissance.

Of the New River he had this to say:

> I thought it at first a convenient but unprofitable passage for a railroad—a haunt likely to be very famous among the lovers of grand and picturesque scenery...where...clear pure air and solitude would reward them with renewed health and vigor. Such indeed it will be, no doubt; for this hundred mile long crack in our planet deserves to rank among the famous sights; ...But as the train thunders along, if you examine the bluff or precipice across the river, you will...notice that the stratification of the rocks is very remarkable. The rocks lie in their beds evidently as they were deposited. There has been through all this country, no upheaval, no disorganization of the strata; ...Curious but unimportant do you say? On the contrary, it is both curious and important. For if you keep your eyes open...you will be made aware that out of the steep high bank there crops, at numerous points already laid bare, a coal seam, or perhaps several coal seams....Here by a singular fortunate chance, the miner digs straight into the mountain, the mine drains itself, and his dump cars deposit [the coal] by gravity at the pit's mouth.

The coal is so easy of access and so extensive in the New River and Kanawha region that "opposite Charleston...you may see the little ferryboat tied up to the river bank, and the deck hand shovelling coal from the vein itself into the steamboat's coal-bunker; every farmhouse has its coal heap—just as further west they have a woodpile near the house; and almost every farmer has somewhere on his land an outcropping coal-vein, from which he supplies himself."

Hotchkiss included in his article a section of Kanawha Coal seams at Armstrong's Creek, showing sixteen seams with an aggregate thickness of seventy-eight feet, one being eleven feet thick. Without the C&O almost the whole of this vast mineral wealth would have remained unused. Furthermore the coal and limestone lay within a hundred miles of some of "the richest and most important deposits of iron in the United States," but without the railroad "the ore, the coal and the limestone were separated by a barrier of distance too great to make their union possible." Between Kanawha Falls and the Ohio were the salines, at that time in the doldrums, some salt works actually being paid by other companies to remain idle, but with opening of the railroad Hotchkiss expected they would soon be in production again, sending their salt eastwards.

All that was needed to develop this rich area adjacent to the railroad was capital.

CHAPTER V

The search for capital

THERE WERE TWO places to go to raise capital: to the North or to Europe, and Europe meant England. England was the world's premier industrial country. Its capitalists knew all about iron, steel, coal, coke, and railways. They had invested in Virginia in the past. Now with the C&O well on its way to completion, this surely was the time to regenerate the interest of financiers on that side of the Atlantic.

On the outskirts of Staunton, not far from the new Augusta County Fairgrounds, was an imposing, if somewhat rundown, residence in a farm of 123 acres, called "Selma." It was owned by William Easton, an Englishman. He it was who provided Hotchkiss with contacts in England, and, as we shall see, a great deal of unwanted responsibility and financial worry. Staying with Easton in 1872 was a fellow countryman, Sidgwick, whose father, a wealthy lawyer, lived at Riddlesden Hall near Keighley in Yorkshire. Through him Hotchkiss would be introduced to a large and influential group of manufacturers and financiers.[1]

Before the *Scribner's* articles were published, Hotchkiss was on his way. Both the *Staunton Spectator* and the *Baltimore Gazette* noted his departure. The local editor hoped that Major Hotchkiss' visit to England would "have the effect of introducing capital and immigrants to the State." He was as "well acquainted with the character of the undeveloped resources of the State as anyone," and was "well qualified to make them known."[2] Together with William Easton, Hotchkiss crossed from New York to Liverpool, and arrived November 24, 1872.

Three events during his stay in England had an important effect on his future: his personal entanglement in the financial affairs of William Easton, the attempt to sell the Cabin Creek lands to Charles Easton, and his address to the Society of Arts. The consequences of his dealings with the Eastons were precise, painful, and quantifiable; those of the address quite the reverse, pleasurable but uncertain.

On January 29 he wrote to a friend in Virginia, "I had intended sailing for home yesterday but the Society of Arts, of which the Prince of Wales is President, has invited me to address it on Virginia, on the 19th instant [sic] and I have concluded to stay as they will publish a large edition of the lecture and so give much publicity to what I may say."[3] He spoke "On the Virginias; Their Agricultural, Mineral, and Commercial Resources." The address was full of facts and figures, far too numerous to be absorbed by the audience, but which provided a valuable record when published in the Society's *Journal*.[4] It was well received and those members present who had visited Virginia confirmed his description of the richness of the coal reserves. For example Professor David T. Ansted, an influential geologist, "could speak personally and positively as to the nature of the coalfields alluded to, which provided one of the greatest resources of mineral wealth of Virginia."[5] Mr. James Bowron, ironmaster from Newcastle, concurred with the remarks made by Ansted, and commented on his own experiences. Mr. Thomas Sopwith F.R.S. directed his comments to the speaker's mapmaking skills. He drew "attention to the maps by which the paper had been illustrated. The large map of Virginia, showing topographical features, was quite a model of its kind, and some smaller maps which he had seen, also by Major Hotchkiss, ...were of the same excellent character." The only jarring note was the intervention by the Secretary of the Council of Foreign Bondholders, who referred to the adverse effect on investment in Virginia if outstanding debts were not paid. He called on Major Hotchkiss to "press upon his fellow-citizens to take all the measures necessary to restore the position and reputation of the state."

That lecture, reached a wider audience through the London *Times* which acknowledged that Major Hotchkiss was "entitled to be heard with respect." But that paper too was more concerned about Virginia's financial integrity.⁶ What Hotchkiss had done was to make English investors aware of the potential of the West Virginia coalfields, and the *Times* now made frequent reference to developments in the two Virginia states. Thus is quoted the *New York Bulletin*, "...we have the prospect of an inexhaustible supply [of coal] being made at once available by the opening of the C&O railroad. That line runs through the heart of a coal and iron field, which in extent, its richness and its variety of these minerals is probably unequalled by anything yet discovered in any part of the world."⁷ The *Mining Journal* illustrated the potential effect of the mining of that coal on the English coal and iron trade when it compared the price of iron produced in Virginia, £2-16s per ton, with that of iron produced in various parts of England, between £4-7s and £7-3s per ton.⁸ As nearly a third of America's iron consumption was imported, and this almost wholly from Britain, the consequences for the future were clear. While that appearance before the Society of Arts enhanced Hotchkiss' reputation and increased his circle of acquaintances, it did not immediately put money in his pocket.

He had come to England with at least two specific propositions, the Elizabeth Furnace Estate which the Forrers had not yet sold, and a large area of coal lands on Cabin Creek, a tributary of the Kanawha. In the middle of January he made an agreement with Amasa Mason, Philip S. Justice, and James Bowron by which they would purchase three-quarters of the former property, then valued at $250,000, Hotchkiss to hold the rest. Subsequently Sir Antonio Brady, who had chaired the Society of Arts meeting, and who later gave Hotchkiss much needed material and moral support, became a fifth partner.⁹ That was a purely speculative deal and they intended to resell the property when it could be done profitably. There seems to have been no intention to put the furnace into blast. Unfortunately that arrangement had not been finalized before Hotchkiss, accompanied by Brady, returned to Virginia in mid-March, only to discover that another party had made a more advantageous bid. But by securing the intervention of the C&O through Pliny Fisk, Hotchkiss obtained extra time from the Forrers to effect the sale to his English partners. Brady returned to England with the new terms but was unable to complete the sale within the allotted time.¹⁰

The Cabin Creek matter became ever more complicated. It eventually left Hotchkiss in a legal morass from which he could not extricate himself for many years. Charles Easton wanted to buy that property and Hotchkiss made the arrangements for him. The negotiations were complex because the tract was in the hands of trustees to secure the debts of its owner, Augustus Pack. Hotchkiss found it "the hardest job

I ever undertook to get them to have a survey made by which to sell." Nevertheless, he provided the information Easton asked for, involved Pliny Fisk where necessary to give the C&O perspective, and made Sir Antonio Brady familiar with the negotiations. When Brady returned to England, he briefed Easton on the negotiations and obtained his agreement to the employment of Messrs. Miller and Quarrier of Charleston to investigate the land title. Easton wrote to Miller, requesting him to act on his behalf, and to bargain the price down because he claimed that the distance from the lands to the Kanawha had been misrepresented. That may have been an indication that Easton was having second thoughts about concluding the purchase; the distance was seven miles and not five, as previously reported. He did, however, advise Miller to get in touch with Hotchkiss in whom he had "the most perfect confidence." Eventually, when agreement had been reached, Hotchkiss cabled Easton, "Purchase perfected money wanted immediately." What Hotchkiss did not know was that six days earlier Easton had written to him, "I have received at last the long looked for information about Pack tract [Cabin Creek] and I am much obliged to you for the very exhaustive report which accompanied the papers. I fear that I have not got what I bargained for." He then discussed the imperfections of the deal and finally as a *postscript* said, "You will please consider the purchase abandoned." Hotchkiss had 14,000 acres of land and no money to pay for it![11]

While Charles Easton was vacillating, incompetent, and foolish, his nephew was shiftless, and probably an alcoholic. His financial affairs were in such a poor condition that he had to raise funds from a number of sources, using "Selma" as security. A trust fund had been set up, and William asked Hotchkiss to be a trustee. In view of the hospitality, the help, and the business that the Eastons had provided, it would have been difficult for him to refuse, and Hotchkiss reluctantly agreed. It is probable that the funds raised were to be used to acquire potentially lucrative enterprises in Virginia. For example, they invested in a property located on the extensive deposits of kaolin at Porcelain, in Augusta County. Hotchkiss considered that investment a valuable property. As he wrote Charles Easton, "one capable of yielding a large revenue if properly and skillfully managed." Hotchkiss thought William was bringing an excellent scheme with him to England.[12] It is probable that William's return to England triggered Charles Easton's concern about the wisdom of proceeding with the purchase of Cabin Creek. Certainly Hotchkiss thought so. For he wrote to Frederick Easton, "...your brother has not sent the money because William has made some sort of statements that, to say the least, have influenced and prejudiced your brother against me.[13] From England William wrote offensive letters to Hotchkiss, complaining about the lack of information about Cabin Creek, and the treatment of Mrs. Easton, whom he had left at home at "Selma."

There were difficulties with the trust which caused Hotchkiss to threaten to withdraw as trustee. He wrote William, "I am now experiencing what I anticipated and informed you when *you* asked me to become a trustee. If you read the agreement you entered into in London you will find that the money was to be applied for a specific purpose at *my* discretion...." He suggested that all the money that had been taken out of the trust fund should be paid back and that application should be made to the court for a change of trustee.[14] He took no action at that time, but continued to do his duty, in part perhaps out of concern for William's neglected wife. In the same letter in which he confirmed the purchase of Cabin Creek, he told Charles Easton of the death from cholera of William's infant daughter, Evaline. The misuse of the funds continued. The trust's lawyer demanded that Hotchkiss should sell "Selma" because Easton had failed to pay the interest on the loans. Hotchkiss repudiated any suggestion that he had breached his trust in the Easton matter. He told Sidgwick that William intended trying to sell "Selma" to his uncle: "I hope he will. I am only too anxious to have the matter settled."[15] Charles Easton did not oblige his nephew, and eventually the estate had to be sold outside the family.[16]

In spite of all those difficulties, Hotchkiss continued, not only to do business with the Easton family, but also to show them the utmost friendship. Charles Easton owned properties near Gordonsville including "Oak Hill" from which he wished to sell timber. He expected $7,000 from this sale which could be used, in part, for new speculations. To Easton's great disappointment, Hotchkiss only managed to raise a little over $6,000. Much of that money was needed for the third and final instalment on the purchase price. Hotchkiss made the payment and completed the purchase.[17] Charles Easton also asked him to handle the transfer of funds to yet another of his brothers, Alexander Easton. Charles Easton's son, Charles John Easton, planned a visit to America about Christmas time 1873. At the request of the elder Easton, Hotchkiss arranged for $1,000 to be paid into a New York bank for the young man's use. This done, he invited him to stay in Staunton to "give him a Virginia Christmas as a successor to the fine one I enjoyed so much last year in 'Old England'."[18]

The financial panic of 1873 and Virginia's state debt combined to cause the efforts of Hotchkiss and his friends to raise capital in England and America to fail. The causes of the financial panic of 1873 were many. Principal among these were excessive investment in railroads and financial practices which were questionable when not actually crooked. The financial difficulties, and more particularly the scandals, caused a loss of public confidence which became a panic when the well-respected and powerful banking firm, Jay, Cooke & Co., could not meet its obligations, and closed its doors on September 18. As is the nature of the financial web, a strand broken in one place immediately transfers the load to others, possibly less able to take the strain. So it was in this case. Fisk & Hatch, the financial backers of the C&O railroad, suspended operations the following day in New York, Philadelphia, and Washington, bringing down with it the First National Bank of Washington. On the 20th the New York Stock Exchange closed and remained so for ten days. By the end of the year business failures exceeded 5,000 and 89 railroads had defaulted on their bonds.[19]

It is hardly surprising that Pliny Fisk was distracted and paid little attention to the land business, a matter of considerable significance to Hotchkiss. When Professor Ansted visited him in October 1873, Hotchkiss had engaged him in making geological reports on a number of properties in the belief that Fisk would cover the cost until the properties were sold. Fisk's failure to do so was embarrassing: "I fear you put me in a bad or false position with Professor Ansted." Clearly those were not the times to secure investment from one's friends, let alone from the public at large. More important, then, to attract capital from abroad. Here the obstacle was the repayment of the Virginia debt. Hotchkiss had already heard the sentiments of the spokesman for the English holders of foreign bonds. They certainly had a grievance, but Virginia had almost insuperable problems, a legacy from the war and the separation of its western part to form the state of West Virginia.

By the beginning of 1874 the state was bankrupt, and her debt was increasing at the rate of $1,000,000 a year. A conference with bondholders to achieve some compromise failed, and the feeling grew that there was no alternative but to pay the debt.[20]

In those circumstances it seems surprising that Hotchkiss made another attempt to raise capital in England. Perhaps he argued that what he was asking for, and what he was offering, were entirely unconnected with the state's debt. He was offering lands underlaid with valuable minerals alongside a railroad with direct access to a deepwater port on America's eastern seaboard. All that was needed was capital to initiate their profitable development. Professor Ansted cogently expressed the same sentiments in an address to the Society of Arts in January 1874, soon after returning from his three-month visit to Virginia. In his opening sentences he drew attention to the "admirable account of the resources and statistics of the Virginia States" given by Major Hotchkiss to the society nearly twelve months earlier. The purpose of Ansted's lecture, he claimed, was not to repeat what had been said then, but to describe his own observations of the iron and coal deposits "laid open by the completion of the Chesapeake and Ohio Railroad." After discussing the location, geology, composition, and economics of the iron ores, he pointed out:

> As the demand for railway iron alone in America is greater than the present make of pig, it is manifest that there is an opening for a largely increased manufacture, even at high prices; and many years must elapse before the price will descend so low as to yield other than large profits to the Virginia ironmaster. Capital alone is wanted to develop the best resources of Virginia in the matter of iron. This capital cannot come fast enough, and iron works in Virginia, on the line of the Chesapeake and Ohio railway, if properly conducted, cannot fail of success.

He gave a detailed account of the coals of the Kanawha Valley, referring in particular to the deposits in the vicinity of Hawk's Nest, and to those exposed by the tributaries: Cabin Creek, Elk River, and Coal River. He drew attention to one of the few sites on the Kanawha where a new town could be developed, and alluded briefly to the salt manufacture, "At present...little developed, though of long standing, but no place could be selected better adapted for chemical works,..." He pointed out that there were tens of thousands of acres of valuable land covered in timber and abounding in mineral wealth which could be obtained now at low prices. "At a cost varying from three to fifty dollars per acre, property may now be acquired that, a few years hence, will be saleable at twenty times that amount."

Just as in the previous year, the voice of the Council of Foreign Bondholders detracted from the optimism of the principal speaker. Mr. Hyde Clarke, their spokesman, in a long comment acknowledging the geographical and geological facts, was emphatic that "it would be impossible for persons in England to invest money in Virginia until they were fully assured that public obligations would be fulfilled." A constructive rejoinder to this was made by another contributor to the discussion, "...the best way to help Virginia was by sending capital there, and...when she developed her resources she would be able to pay all her debts."[21]

This address, and the discussion which followed it, was a useful prelude to Hotchkiss' own campaign later in the year. In spite of personal as well as national financial problems, he continued identifying and securing options on potentially valuable real estate, making surveys and ensuring the validity of the vendors' titles. While some of this property was well described, properly mapped and ownership not disputed, that was not the case with the majority of the lands. (Even the Forrers' Elizabeth Furnace Estate was not entirely in order.)[22] Large tracts had been granted in a forested terrain of considerable topographical complexity. Most of those grants, dating from immediately after the Revolutionary War, had been surveyed by the most primitive of compass traverses. The boundaries were identified by marked trees, the following being typical of the description that Hotchkiss had to use to identify what he was buying and selling: "Beginning at (56) three white oaks Williams corner, thence N 24 degrees East 472 poles (118 chs) crossing Williams Mill run to a red oak (65) two hickory sapplings on a hill side, thence South 75 degrees West 80 poles (20 chs) to (66) two white oaks on a hillside, ..."[23] The difficulty of following such a description of metes and bounds eighty years after the original survey can be imagined. So too can be imagined the opportunity for the swindling of either party to a sale. Hotchkiss was meticulous in his surveys and his advice to his clients, and so built up a reputation not only for his outstanding knowledge of the Virginias, but also for straight dealing and honest reporting.

Writing to Sir Antonio Brady in February 1874, about the conditions under which he would undertake the purchase and re-sale of a tract of land, he said:

> I have just spent $4,000 on a survey of Cabin Creek land and while the results are most satisfactory, beyond anything I could have hoped,... it has given me a lesson I shall heed in regard to large tracts of West Virginia land. The only condition upon which I would undertake the Fleury land would be that a survey should be made at his expense and an abstract of title made showing what he really owns. *Then* I would examine and report on the mineral and timber value of the property for my share of the work—and get up the facts upon which a sale could be made. It will take 6 months of hard work by not less than 4 parties of engineers to make a satisfactory survey.... If owners will put up the money for the expenses I will have the work *thoroughly* done and settle all questions of title &c. Until that is done I would not give a farthing for anyone's opinion of the title, quantity of land or in fact *anything* about the property.[24]

He clearly described the difficulty of conducting surveys in West

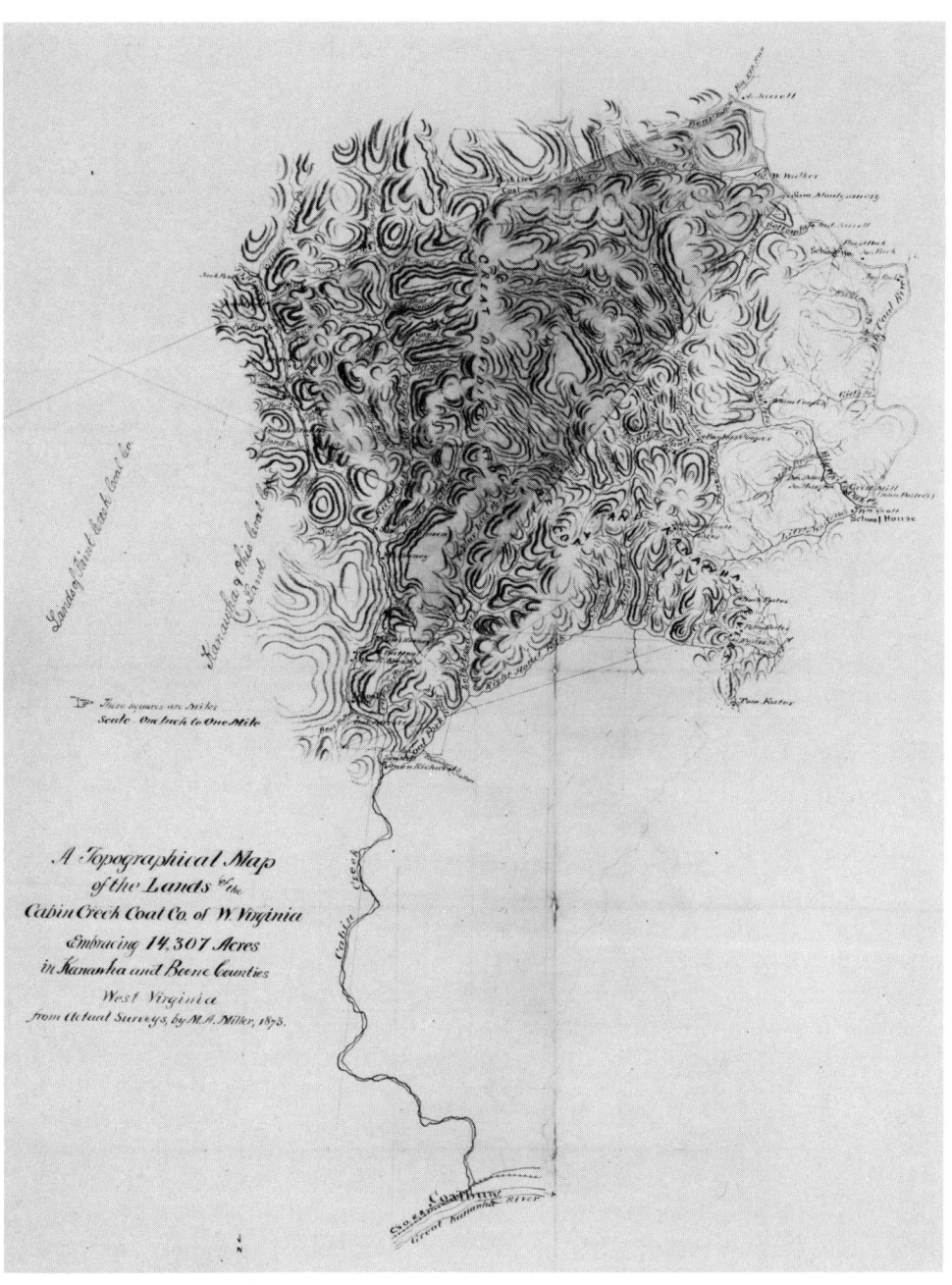

Cabin Creek Coal Lands, Hotchkiss' millstone. His failure to sell this property in 1873 was to be a source of trouble and embarrassment for many years.

Hotchkiss Map Collection #252, Library of Congress

Virginia to W. L. Nicholson, topographer for the Post Office. His example is almost certainly the survey of Cabin Creek.

> In answer to the question of the cost of a survey I need not say to you that there are so many items to be considered it is almost impossible to give an estimate, especially in West Virginia where the lands were so carelessly surveyed or not surveyed at all originally, making it necessary...to run simultaneously, the lines of the estate in question and those of the adjacent estates...I recently surveyed an estate of 15,000 acres in the Kanawha region...I had to have more lines of other estates run than of the estate in hand before I could decide how much land we had...In that we had to run over 500 miles of lines, one outside line had to be carried nearly 30 miles to find an old corner and settle a line 5 miles long....That survey, which was a complete topographical one, with map at 1-20,000 scale cost about $4,000.[25]

One of the most ambitious projects was the development of a new town to be called Kanawha City. In this project he worked with Dr. John P. Hale who had long been associated with the Kanawha salines. Hale was an innovator in both business and public affairs. He had introduced the first brick-making machinery into the Kanawha Valley, for example, and in 1870 laid in Capitol Street, Charleston, West Virginia, at his own expense, the first brick street pavement in America. He introduced the first steam packet boat on the Upper Kanawha River, the first theater in Charleston, its first public steam-laundry, its first daily paper and was the first to introduce the public delivery of ice in the city.[26] It was with this enterprising and friendly man that Hotchkiss became acquainted and with whom he would make many plans and share many misfortunes. They were involved together in the purchase of Cabin Creek after Charles Easton's withdrawal and in the sale of a property called Splint Coal. Hale was prepared to sell this off piecemeal, a procedure which Brady and Hotchkiss strongly disapproved of. In a letter to Pliny Fisk, who had now emerged from beneath the problems of the bank and the C&O, Hotchkiss said,

> I am sure we can never do anything with Splint Coal until there is a perfect survey. It is all *mixed up* and I can hardly understand it myself, but the doctor seems averse to letting me send my men to work it up in proper shape. Of course I shall do nothing there until asked and what is done must be at your and the Dr.'s instance.

In the same letter, written March 30, 1874, he also wrote, "My friend, we must decide about the Eng. trip. The Dr. seems quite anxious to go." Brady had suggested that the visit should be made in May.[27] Hotchkiss got his way over Splint Coal, and engaged W. M. Dunlap to "run the lines," and asked Hale to "see that he (was) provided with papers, assistance, board and lodging, &c. &c."

Another name which recurs in the Hotchkiss correspondence is that of John T. Cowan, a cattle breeder of Montgomery County, Virginia. His interest in the land deals was purely speculative. They first met in Richmond in January 1872 when Hotchkiss was there on textbook business, and to attend meetings of the committee on immigration. Cowan may also have been in the city for similar reasons, but both went to a meeting of the Agricultural Society. Knowing of Hotchkiss' expertise, it is probable that Cowan sought his advice on the selling of the coal lands he either owned or held options on. Cowan returned with Hotchkiss to Staunton, and stayed a few days during which time he made a contract with Echols, Bell, and Catlett to sell half his coal lands, Hotchkiss to have a quarter of the profits.[28] It was Cowan who held an option to purchase Pack's Cabin Creek lands prior to Hotchkiss' agreement with Pack in May 1873. It was on Cowan's behalf that Hotchkiss attempted to sell the land in England in 1872-3, and Cowan remained a substantial investor in the purchase following the failure to complete the deal with Easton.

Fisk, Hotchkiss, and Cowan met together on a number of occasions to try to resolve the financial and legal problems associated with this property. The 14,307 acres of Cabin Creek land was bought July 17, 1873, at $7 per acre, making a total price of $100,149. The terms of the sale required a down payment of 25% to be followed by three equal annual instalments plus interest payable from the purchase date. The legal expenses had amounted to $1,000, and of this Hotchkiss had paid $356.48 by a promissory note of Dr. Hale. His own expenses for the survey had been largely covered by $2,000 from Fisk and the same sum from Hale. These were to be repaid out of the first instalment on the purchase price. Most of the down payment had been provided by Cowan in the form of four notes payable at times varying from 30 days to 12 months, totalling $19,000, and Hotchkiss had also given his note for $1,850 at 90 days. Not until February 11, 1874, was this initial payment made to Swann and Knight, the trustees of the property, for Hotchkiss had no intention of making any payment until the property had been properly surveyed. That had not been completed until near the end of 1873, and it was not until the middle of January 1874 that he was able to write to Fisk, "making up the map...we find clean and clear 14,312 acres lying splendidly as to shape and accessibility."[29]

The deed for the land was made out to Hotchkiss, but was deposited "in escrow," awaiting the deposit of bonds for the deferred payments and the balance of the down payment. Having secured the property, he made a contract in which Cowan would buy one-third of the land, and Hotchkiss would receive a third of all profits arising from the sale of this third, but would retain control. Hotchkiss wanted to make a similar arrangement with other investors covering the remaining two-thirds, he "continuing to oversee the land and develop it and seek purchasers. I know there is no better investment in the country now that the land is free from all encumbrances." He was sure that he would soon sell' Cabin Creek in England at a good profit.[30]

With this ramshackle financing, Hotchkiss would need that money. He had also acquired a tract of 1,149 acres adjacent to the Cabin Creek land on similar credit terms, and there were other unpaid notes. He was so short of cash at this time that on one occasion when at short notice he had to travel from Richmond to Baltimore he found someone to cash a check and then wrote his Staunton bank, "Hope you will have it paid as I will put my account 'square' in a few days."[31] On another occasion he offered to settle a debt by means of a building lot he owned. "If you are disposed to trade a bad debt for a good lot—say so and I will meet you."[32] Shortly before he went to England he even attempted to recover the $30 prize money the Augusta County Fair had awarded him in 1868 for his essay on the Watercourses of Augusta County, but not yet paid.[33]

Sir Antonio Brady was once again in Virginia with a party of English industrialists seeking investment opportunities. Hotchkiss hoped to travel with Brady on his return to England, but depended on Fisk to finance the trip. Hotchkiss urged Brady to pay a visit to New River, and sent him an itinerary for his last week in the country to culminate with his departure from New York. He took another of Brady's party to Charleston, to interest him in the potential of that city and its environs, extracting a promise from him to build a soda-ash plant there. Those were hectic and anxious June weeks. On the 11th he wrote to Fisk, "Am home but badly used up from two nights out. Conclude by letter from the Doctor that he has gone on ready to sail. If so he can go with Sir A. or await me Wednesday... You know whether I can go Wednesday or not and can assure the Doctor." Hotchkiss wanted the financial arrangements between Hale, Brady, Fisk, and himself settled and he was quite prepared to leave it to the three of them to draw up the agreement, "*only everything must be agreed upon and signed before sailing.*"[34]

While he was dependent upon Fisk to finance the English venture,

THE SEARCH FOR CAPITAL 121

he was also relying on money from another source to meet other commitments, including family and household expenses. He and Barnas Sears owned land in the neighborhood of Staunton through which the Valley Railroad was seeking a right of way. Just when negotiations seemed to be coming to a successful conclusion the railroad management changed its mind about the route, and the funds which Hotchkiss was relying upon never materialized. To add to the turmoil, the discussions with the railroad caused him to be "dragged from Staunton to Baltimore twice and to Lynchburg and Charlottesville at different times all in the same week." His passage had been booked for the 20th and he hardly had time to catch the sailing. Telling Cowan about those past few days he said, "I did not have my clothes off but once in a week before leaving."[35] He had been anxious to see Cowan before going to England. There was a major disagreement between Fisk and Cowan which Hotchkiss had hoped to resolve. But all he could do was to write to Fisk, "It would be exceedingly gratifying to me if you and [Cowan] could meet and have a good fair talk without prejudice. I am sure it would do good...I want Cowan satisfied so that he will not make trouble."[36]

He must have felt an enormous relief when the *S.S. Batavia* drew away from the pier at New York. Whatever the chaos he had left behind in his domestic and business affairs there was nothing he could now do. He must relax, enjoy the voyage, and prepare for the work to be done in England. On this occasion he was accompanied by his 19-year-old daughter, Nellie, who had just completed her education at the Augusta Female Seminary.[37] Her interest and excitement about the trip would have helped to banish the financial problems from the forefront of his mind.

During the voyage we can imagine that he would think over all the events of the past fourteen months since returning home with some hope of English capital following him to Virginia. Hopes that were disappointed, in part because of the panic of 1873, in part because of the Virginia debt problem—both of them matters outside his control—but also because at the time he had little of substance to offer, only the promise offered by the new railroad access to New River and the Kanawha. This time he had detailed reports and maps of property which he had examined thoroughly. With him was Dr. Hale, whose knowledge and experience of the region should be a source of strength in their negotiations. Although, Brady, Hale and Fisk had not signed an agreement before they parted in New York, Hotchkiss was optimistic that this time he would not return empty handed. He would have new things to talk about too. He had not been content with furthering the developments along the line of the C&O, but had started the exploration of other parts of the vast coal field which extended to the south of New River. He had engaged Captain Isiah A. Welch to make a survey of land in southwest Virginia, which a decade later would initiate half a century of industrial activity.[38] Just before he left for England, Hotchkiss joined with others in the formation of the New River Railroad, Mining, and Manufacturing Company whose objective was to "connect the A.M.&O and C&O railroads and develop a splendid mineral country." The new road was to run from the mouth of the Greenbrier, near Hinton, to the New River depot in Montgomery County.[39]

He would also be thinking about the important work he had done for the state. In his cabin was a copy of a document to which his address to the Society of Arts could be called the prologue.

It was the direct result of the Immigration Convention which assembled at the Exchange Hotel in Richmond on Tuesday, December 12, 1871. Alexander H. H. Stuart presided over this two-day meeting, which had been given the task of making recommendations to the General Assembly of Virginia. A committee of ten, which included Hotchkiss, produced a report consisting of four brief sections. The first of these proposed that the Assembly should "cause to be prepared, published and disseminated...accurate and full descriptions of the physical elements and adaptations of the State." The second proposed that supervision of this task should be given to a board "which need not exceed three or four members," and "that as much as thirty thousand dollars should be appropriated, ...and wisely and efficiently supplied in said direction." These, as well as the other two more general recommendations, were unanimously adopted.[40] Throughout 1872 Hotchkiss promoted these proposals as essential to attracting capital and skilled labor to Virginia. Success came while he was away in England, for on March 29, 1873, an act was approved setting up a Board of Immigration whose first task was to be the preparation of a Geographical and Political Summary of the state.[41] In April the Board engaged Hotchkiss to compile the summary,

> because, in the pursuit of his calling as a topographical and mining engineer, he had devoted much time to acquiring accurate knowledge of the geography, the varied physical elements, the internal improvements and commercial capabilities, the agricultural, manufacturing and general industrial condition and resources of the State, and was believed to possess greater experience and aptitude for the work than any person known to the board.

In spite of all the real estate work he was engaged upon, he was able to deliver the entire manuscript to the Board on December 31. It contained in twelve chapters a description of the subjects enumerated in the act: "The territory of the State, and its form of government; the various character of its soil, its productions, its climate and its population; an account of its mineral resources, of its universities, its colleges, its public free school system, its religious advantages, and of its various lines of travel and transportation by water and by railroad."

The Board, in submitting the summary to the General Assembly, felt warranted in saying that the work was of the very highest value and interest to the state, that it constituted "a repository of most valuable information not to be found in any existing publication." In producing the text, Hotchkiss was able to use his experience in trying to sell real estate to those

> classes of persons that it is desired...should become interested in Virginia, that is capitalists, manufacturers, agriculturists, workers of mines, &c., and not only at home, but abroad, and so I [have] become familiar with the wants of those seeking information. ...there is a very strong desire for *well*-substantiated facts in regard to every subject in any way pertaining to the calling of the party seeking information.

Of fundamental importance was the "full presentation of the geology of the State," for this determined the character of the soils as well as the mineral resources. He therefore included a map of the results of the geological survey of the state made by Professor William Barton Rogers between 1835 and 1841. That map was the first to be published of his survey, and the first of a family of geological maps which grew in number and scale over the years. Hotchkiss had corresponded with Rogers since the summer of 1873, and Rogers had produced an outline geological map as early as September. He sent a colored copy to Hotchkiss. The base map did not satisfy Hotchkiss, so he made another more up-to-date map at a scale of 24-miles-to-one-inch. It was that one, colored by Rogers, which he used to illustrate the summary.[42]

In explaining the time taken to produce his draft, Hotchkiss pointed out that no similar publication existed from which to draw information. He had had to draw on "numberless sources." The main one was the 1860 census. The use of the later 1870 census would, in his opinion, have been a gross injustice to the productive capacity of Virginia, affected as it was by the Civil War and its aftermath. The use of the earlier census required the separation of data for West Virginia before he could start on identifying resources, production, and manufacturing statistics to each of the six grand divisions of Virginia. Some data he looked for in vain. There were no figures for the oyster catch, although it was taxed by quantity. The voluminous information available about the A.M.&O. railroad did not include a description of the freight carried from its stations; even statistics for the very important tobacco manufacturing plants in Richmond were not to be had for the year 1871. Considering the resources Hotchkiss had at his disposal, and the other demands upon his time, it would hardly seem necessary for him to have to explain why the board had to wait nine months.

The *Batavia* made the Atlantic crossing in 11 days, calling at Queenstown, where Hotchkiss mailed a number of letters to Virginia explaining why he had left without settling his debts. The ship berthed in Liverpool on July 1.

It is almost certain that father and daughter travelled immediately to London by way of the London & North Western Railway. They stayed at the Cannon Street Hotel, conveniently close to Sir Antonio Brady's office from where Hotchkiss conducted his business.[43] The most important first step was to settle the agreement between himself, Brady, Hale, and Fisk for the purchase and resale of Hale's Splint Coal property. As usual Hotchkiss was the intermediary, for his share in these deals was recompense for his survey, mapping, and reporting services, and it frequently fell to his lot to reconcile the different investors involved. It took the whole of July to achieve that agreement. Brady would not sign anything without his lawyer's support, and the lawyer was engaged on Parliamentary business. Hale was being difficult and threatening to go back home. Describing the situation to Fisk, Hotchkiss wrote, "I am worried more than ever I was in my life by the turn affairs have taken and sometimes wish I had never had anything to do with West Virginia lands...still I do not despair...but you *must* stand by me."[44] Agreement was finally reached, Hale agreed to sell the property to Brady, Fisk, and Hotchkiss for $400,000, and gave them until January 1, 1875, to complete the purchase. As for the resale, Hale was to pay 20% commission and to divide all that was obtained over $400,000 and the commission equally between Hale, Brady, Fisk, and Hotchkiss. As soon as the contract was signed, Brady and Hotchkiss gave a firm of London lawyers power to negotiate a sale at £200,000, or $800,000 at the then rate of exchange.[45]

Throughout the month he had to contend with the financial problems left behind in Virginia. Not only was he overdrawn at the bank, he had creditors pressing for payment. He still owed Allen and Dunlap for their survey of the Kanawha City Estates; worse still, a draft that Hotchkiss had sent them had been rejected by his bank. Now they were threatening to sue. Hotchkiss had allowed them the free use of his survey instruments and these they still had. If they were prepared to wait for their money, he was prepared to allow them the continued use of the instruments, but now at some charge, and "If you pursue any other course I must require an immediate return of the instruments or I shall consider them purchased by you at value."[46]

Of course some of the time was spent in more agreeable ways, and Nellie was enjoying herself visiting as many famous London sights as she could manage.[47] She had accompanied her father on a visit to the Sidgwicks at Newmarket and then to see Professor Ansted at his home in Melton, near Woodbridge, Suffolk. Hotchkiss would have wanted to hear a first-hand account of Ansted's address to the Society of Arts and its reception. Particularly he would want his opinion as to the current sentiment toward investment in Virginia. One thing he soon discovered was that the visit to England had been badly timed. His idea that he would quickly conclude his business and return home in September did not survive the month.[48] He found that August was the holiday month and all business in London was suspended, an exasperating situation. To Cowan he referred to "the holiday time in this holiday country" and went on to say, "If heaven was not more favorable to this country than to any under the sun I do not see how they would get along, it takes so much time to wind up anything."[49] Father and daughter made good use of this slack period with visits to Brighton, Crystal Palace, Windsor, museums, and art galleries, as well as undertaking a journey within the British isles.[50]

Back again at Cannon Street Hotel, Hotchkiss was anxious to get on with the business that had brought him to London. He started by trying to settle affairs with Maximilian Low. On his 1873 trip he had made a bargain with Low by which he was to find mineral lands in Virginia and West Virginia, buy them, and draw on Low for payment. In February 1874, he bought from C. J. Johnston and J. B. Peck 1,300 acres of iron land on New River and gave them a draft on Low which Low had failed to honor. Hotchkiss now sought, and secured, a new agreement.[51] Other schemes made little progress. The ambitious Kanawha City Estate scheme, although widely canvassed, generated no serious interest.

Hotchkiss found these negotiations hard going. Even the modest deal with Low fell through.[52] There was no shortage of money available for investment, but there was a lack of confidence in American affairs and in particular those of Virginia. In spite of these set-backs, Hotchkiss remained optimistic; he wrote to Fisk in September to say, "I see daily new fields here that could be cultivated if one had time to spend, and think I could eventually get up the same enthusiasm there was in 1873 when I had no lands to offer."⁵³

The reluctance of English financiers to invest in Virginia further prolonged his stay beyond the date he had envisaged for his return. In July 1874, when he wrote to his neighbor, General Echols, he had said he hoped to get through his business and be home in September. At the end of that month, when telling Cowan of the sale to Low, he said that he supposed Low would go out to Virginia about the first of November, a date when Hotchkiss wanted to get home.⁵⁴ That date came and went. Optimism gave way to despair when it became apparent that reluctance to invest had been replaced by refusal. He was desperately short of money, and what he had was borrowed. He noted in his diary on October 26, "Borrowed £20 of Reed. *My, my, how hard it is to get along*, poor Sara needs money now too—Am working as hard as I can but things go against me—God grant a change soon." Although he persisted throughout the winter he made no progress, but it was not until March 1875, that he finally gave up and boarded *The City of Chester* to sail home.

It was not due to lack of time or effort that the mission failed. Right up to the time of his departure he sought investments, and even on the short passage to Queenstown he negotiated for a survey and reporting commission.⁵⁵ The reason for failure he expressed in a letter written immediately after arriving home:

> Millions—I speak advisedly—have been lost to our State because of the vacillating course of legislation that has been pursued. I succeeded in modifying the last report of the Board of Foreign Bond Holders—but they still class our state among those that have repudiated, and backed by the all powerful press they declared that no English money shall come to Virginia until she settle, definitely, some financial scheme and place all her creditors on the same footing. This done, they say they will encourage the movement of capital to the state in all possible ways—I am authorized to say so by the Chairman of the Board.⁵⁶

One thing he did sort out in England was the Easton matter. He secured power of attorney over William Easton's affairs and an agreement to sell "Selma," settle the debts, and close the trust.⁵⁷ It was a long way to go to achieve so little, and from now on Hotchkiss took a sceptical view of the intentions of any English investors, or of those working in their interest. Years later he wrote to one such, "I have almost made up my mind that I will send a postal card to applicants for properties by English parties with just the word "no" on it, but I will give you another chance."⁵⁸

CHAPTER VI

"Everything has conspired against me..."

HOTCHKISS RETURNED to a United States still in depression following the panic of 1873, a condition that was to exist for the remainder of the decade.[1] A difficult time for many, for Hotchkiss it was ruinous. He had left for England in debt, and had only succeeded in increasing it. He had sold nothing, and had received no commissions. Now his creditors, many of whom were also in desperate straits, were combining to take action. Peck and Johnston were demanding the return of the deed of the 1,300 acres of iron land which he had failed to sell to Low.[2] Reluctant to do this he managed to negotiate a six-week extension of his option. The combination of creditors was not so easily handled, especially after the Augusta County court, in April, had appointed commissioners to determine exactly what real estate was owned by Hotchkiss.[3] Professor Ansted was one of his creditors. Pliny Fisk had not fulfilled his obligations to pay Hotchkiss for the professor's services; now Ansted's attorneys were threatening to sue. Hotchkiss replied that in normal times his property was worth three times his indebtedness, but a sale now would not realize the true value. Furthermore other creditors had a prior claim, and in any case the proceeds of a sale would only be realized over a three- or four-year period. It would be in Ansted's interest to await better times. Hotchkiss attempted to reassure him, "If I am left alone in three months after the revival in business and confidence I can pay off all I owe and have a handsome estate left."[4]

Not long after Barnas Sears settled in Staunton he and Hotchkiss jointly purchased land on the lower western slopes of what is now called Sears Hill, with the object of dividing it into lots for sale as building land. Altogether there were 45 such lots. But before any of these could be sold to meet Hotchkiss' debts, they had to divide the property. The 30 lots assigned to Hotchkiss were advertised for sale at public auction in 1878.[5] Excluding any commitments relating to the Cabin Creek purchase, his debts amounted to a little more than $3,500. He estimated that his property on Sears Hill alone was worth $34,510, probably a gross over-estimate, but certainly worth more than the $2,966 that was raised when the sale of all the available lots was completed in March 1878.[6] As Hotchkiss had warned, Ansted did not benefit from these transactions, and it was not until 1887 that his heirs secured payment.[7] Hotchkiss secured exclusion of "The Oaks" from that dispersal of his property by selling it to his daughter Nellie.

Hotchkiss lost no time in trying to sell in the United States the lands he had failed to dispose of in England. But it was a hopeless task and even when he had arrived at what appeared to be a satisfactory arrangement for the purchase of the 1,300 acres of iron land, Johnson and Peck refused to accept the money and Hotchkiss had to give up the deed.[8] As for Cabin Creek, that affair would all but destroy his friendship with Cowan, and continue to haunt him for many a year.

In the months immediately after his return, although despondent about the current situation, Hotchkiss continued to believe that sometime in the future the lands on which he, Fisk, and Hale had options would realize a profit. To Fisk he wrote on April 10, 1875, urging co-operation, "I again say there will soon be *large gain* and *No loss.* If we throw away all that we have and ignore all that we have done in good faith by all we must lose."[9] A week later he wrote to Sir Antonio Brady in optimistic style, but to Cowan and Fisk he revealed his concern. In reply to a complaining letter from Cowan he said,

> I note all you say...and can only say what I have said before, I am doing all I can. *There is no money here now—none,* the

railroad contractors owe here from $200,000 to $300,000 and the failure of the R. R. Co. to pay up has paralysed everything and everybody... I am worse off than anybody can be...but the times are sicker than any of us.[10]

To Fisk he wrote on May 14, "Matters cannot get any worse...The stagnation in business surpasses anything I have ever seen, and makes it almost impossible to do anything." In spite of this situation he claimed not to be discouraged and was able to see "a way of escape and a fair prospect for gain."[11] He conceded to Brady that "times here are very tight," that it was "almost impossible to convert anything into money," and "everything has conspired against me for some time past," but he was "working on cheerfully and will soon put a better face on affairs—just as soon as I can unload part of Cabin Creek."[12] He was just whistling to keep his spirits up—and those of his friends. In reality there was nothing to be done but persevere, keep his options on property before potential investors, and wait for the upturn in business which would come sooner or later. Replying to a letter from Fisk, Hotchkiss revealed his own desperate financial situation, which had been further aggravated by Fisk's failure to honor his obligations in the Cabin Creek purchase. "I should be more than glad to come and see you, but I can hardly get enough to stay at home—much less to go away. I do not know where I could get enough to pay my fare to Trenton and back."[13] Just how desperate he was at this time is illustrated by a scheme he put up to J. Taylor Ellyson. In the Hotchkiss-Allan book on the battle of Chancellorsville was a "fine likeness" of Stonewall Jackson which Hotchkiss could get reproduced at a few cents a copy. The coming state fair in Richmond with its large attendance would provide an excellent opportunity to sell, say 5,000 pictures at "10, 15 or 20 cents." Hotchkiss would be content with a fair share of the profits.[14] That scheme was later dropped.

In the meantime there were other matters to attend to. His responsibilities as a trustee of William Easton's property took up some of his time. Easton's Selma estate had to be sold, and his properties near Gordonsville put into good order and a tenant found for one of them. None of this was accomplished without trouble of one sort or another. Hotchkiss had arranged for an additional trustee to be appointed, ostensibly to provide increased protection of Easton's creditors in England, but primarily to protect himself against accusations of misuse of funds, or bad management of the property. His first attempt to put Selma up for public sale was frustrated by this trustee, E. R. Watson, an attorney at Charlottesville, who required assurance that the sale was in accordance with the wishes of Charles Easton and others involved.[15] The delay allowed Hotchkiss to offer it to friends and acquaintances; he suggested that Cowan and "Miss Lizzie" might buy it, "and have a nice home that is within a mile or so of somewhere. There is land enough for you to keep your fine stock on."[16] He also offered the whole estate to a local man for $22,000, but with Watson's agreement the Selma mansion and 32 acres were sold in front of Staunton's Courthouse for a mere $5,850.[17]

The *Summary of Virginia*, which Hotchkiss had been working on in the interval between his visits to England, still lacked its maps, and some chapters needed revision to meet the requirements of the Board of Immigration before it could be published. He had received a few enquiries about maps of Virginia counties, and these enabled him to give publicity to the maps he had for sale, as well as providing much needed cash.[18]

The most reliable, although intermittent, source of money was teaching, not children, but the teachers. This was done at the so-called county institutes held two or three times during the school year to give professional training to the teachers, or at the summer normal institutes conducted for four to six weeks in July and August. Both categories received support from the Peabody Fund so Hotchkiss' friendship with its director, Barnas Sears, ensured that he was paid for his services.[19] He taught at the Albermarle County Institute during the first week in August 1875, and in October was at Abingdon in southwest Virginia. There, at the three-day institute held in the Temperance Hall, he lectured on object-teaching, geography, grammar, and the "Best method of conducting a recitation."[20] He received $50 for this institute, but paid his own expenses.[21] At the end of January 1876 he lectured on geography and arithmetic at the three-day Teachers' Institute of the County of Augusta at the townhall in Staunton. His competence and popularity at these gatherings ensured continuing invitations which were not confined to Virginia, and he was asked to take part in institutes as far afield as North Carolina, Georgia, Mississippi, and Texas.[22] Indeed it would seem that he had difficulty in accommodating all the requests, for in March 1877 he accompanied Dr. Ruffner to four institutes in succession and could offer an inquirer only two days at the end of the month.[23] He charged $10 per day plus expenses for his services, so the Institutes were valuable sources of income, but they served other purposes. He had been commissioned to write a geography of Virginia; gatherings of one hundred or more teachers provided an excellent opportunity to promote his textbook, *Hotchkiss' Geography of Virginia*, published by A. Hoen & Company in 1877.[24]

Those years were not barren of real estate activity, however, for

Hotchkiss was engaged to report on a number of properties. One of these was the Guy's Run iron property of about 17,000 acres near Goshen on the line of the C&O. This had been through his hands in 1872, but was again for sale at the very reasonable price of less than $10 per acre. Hotchkiss considered "that as an iron ore property it [was] not excelled...by any on the line of the C&O."[25]

In a transaction free from any speculation, he reported on property owned by the Reverend Thomas Heywood of Elizabeth, New Jersey. That report took the form of a letter written around exquisite maps and sections of the copper mines owned by Heywood close to the Blue Ridge northeast of Gordonsville.[26]

On an altogether larger scale was the work he undertook for the Royal Land Company of Virginia, a company chartered in May 1876 for the purpose of working the deposits of anthracite coal on the mountainous western boundaries of Augusta and Rockingham counties.[27] From December 16, 1876, to April 17, 1877, he spent 76 days, at $10 per day, reporting on the lands owned by this company between Jennings Gap and Rawley Springs. They included the Dora coal mines. He made a map of Rockingham County and plotted on it the route of the railroad the company proposed building across the Valley and through the Blue Ridge at Swift Run Gap.[28] The original agreement envisaged a report of some 30 pages plus the map and costing no more than $800. However, once the work was underway the company wanted additional material to be included and a geological map to be prepared. That boosted the cost of producing 1,000 copies to nearly $1,400 and Hotchkiss had some difficulty in obtaining recompense.[29] Indeed, two years later, he wrote "one reason why I did not get my pay from the Royal Land Co. was because I had no order from the Pres."[30]

Not all the surveys he undertook were of mineral properties. By way of contrast, the Plan of Tinkling Spring Cemetery at a scale of 40-feet-to-1-inch (1876); "Oakenwold", a "first class brick dwelling, covered in slate," standing in 27 acres on Churchville Road in Staunton, (1877)[31]; and the "Map of the Drainage and Catchment Basin of Asylum Creek To Illustrate a Report on Water supply for the W. L. Asylum of Virginia" (1879)[32], all show the variety of his assignments. For Staunton, he produced a descriptive pamphlet of 47 pages extolling the virtues of this "energetic and flourishing little city of the hills." By those means Hotchkiss was able to earn enough to maintain the family and to advance his standing in Staunton and the state until business confidence returned.

Early in 1877, he thought he detected signs that the recovery might not be too long delayed, for he was able to tell a client, "I am very much pressed now for reports and have no minute to spare, which is a good sign of the change that is coming,"[33] and to another a few days later, "There is some activity now in leasing coal lands and some sales have been made. The general outlook is, I think, decidedly better."[34] Those were optimistic words written to encourage a more positive view of investment prospects.

The American correspondent of the London *Times* writing from Philadelphia on October 15, 1877, reported that liabilities due to commercial failure for the third quarter of 1877 were less than for the corresponding period of 1876. The figures were said to afford encouragement and the hope that the worst effects of the depression were over. But the turning point had not yet been reached, and iron and steel prices continued to fall, reaching their lowest in 1878.[35] Fortunately for Hotchkiss there were some who shared his belief that a resurgence of activity could not be long delayed. Alexander H. H. Stuart, when asked by a number of Staunton's citizens for his views on the prospects for a return to prosperity, concluded that the lowest point of the depression had been reached and predicted "bright prospects ahead."[36]

In May 1878, Hotchkiss was asked for a report on the Shenandoah Iron, Lumber, Mining, and Manufacturing Company, formerly the Forrers' Shenandoah Iron Works. That project earned him a useful $1,000 with the possibility of an equal amount if the company was sold before May 1, 1879.[37] However, it was not until 1879 that recovery began with a feverish activity. "Excitement and speculation took the place of the gloom and discouragement which...had been so familiar scarcely one year before, and the business of selling iron became close neighbour to that of gambling in stocks."[38] In October of that year Hotchkiss thought the worst had passed, iron was booming, and, with Cabin Creek in mind, hoped "that something could be done now with coal lands."[39] Everything indicated "an early resumption of...pushing forward the schemes that were underway in 1873."[40] The demand for iron and steel was now so great that not only was domestic production of pig iron at a record level, but over 280,000 tons of iron ore were imported. At no previous time had imports reached anything like these figures, never exceeding 100,000 tons in any one year prior to 1877. Price increases were equally dramatic as orders outstripped the ability of the iron masters to put the hundreds of idle furnaces back into blast. Prices of all categories of iron and steel more than doubled from the low levels of 1877 and 1878, and that of coke quadrupled from 90¢ to $4 per ton during 1879. If there was ever a time to push the resources of the Virginias, surely it was now. It was the time Hotchkiss had waited for.

The visit made in February 1879 by two gentlemen from the North who were interested in the Dora coal mines of the Royal Land Company illustrates his energetic promotion of mineral lands along the line of the C&O. They inspected the mines on a Friday and returned to Staunton the following day. As far as they were concerned that was the end of the mission, and were now on their way home. Hotchkiss had a different idea. He persuaded them to stay on, enticed them into his office, and lectured them on the iron and coal resources of the Virginias. On Sunday he had them for church and dinner, and then at *3 a.m.* on Monday he took them to Goshen where breakfast and horses were ready for them. "So we got an early start and had all of a fine day on the Guy's Run land...." They returned to Goshen for a late dinner and discussed iron matters again. Hotchkiss then suggested that they might see for themselves how cheaply coal could be mined and coked along the Kanawha. "They finally consented," wrote Hotchkiss, and off they "went to Covington for the night and the next day, a fine one, went to Cannelton...where they saw the mines in operation and also those and the coking at Fire Creek, Sewell, Quinnimont, &c."[41]

That personal instruction was obviously not enough. He needed a larger audience than his limited number of visitors and correspondents. He had to find some way of putting the facts before the investing classes. Hotchkiss began to think about producing a monthly magazine.

CHAPTER VII

"What would the Virginias do without you?"

AS EARLY AS FEBRUARY 1879, Hotchkiss was telling a correspondent, "I am often tempted to establish a *Virginias Mining Journal* that we may have the showing we deserve and to make known our great mineral wealth. But who will pay? Or where is the pay?"[1] He had already talked to a local printer, and had asked for a quote for the printing of a monthly edition of 1,000 copies of a 16- or 20-page journal in the style of the *Nation*.[2] Without considering the economics of the project, Hotchkiss ordered paper and type in July and expressed himself anxious "to get the first issue out and take the tide that it really seems is surely setting in."[3] But it was the end of the year before he was able to put together the first issue, which appeared in January of the new decade. That was a decade of intense activity for Hotchkiss, one in which he would make his most important contribution to the economic future of the two Virginias.

Appropriately, the new journal was entitled *The Virginias, a*

Mining, Industrial and Scientific Journal Devoted to the Development of Virginia and West Virginia. Hotchkiss described its purpose as being "The development of the resources of the great territory, 67,500 square miles in extent embraced in the States of Virginia and West Virginia...." He was convinced that no other region of equal extent in the United States had so much, and such variety of, unused mineral resources. What it lacked was the capital to develop and market these resources for the region to become an economic leader of the states. The most important of these latent resources were iron ore and coal, so *The Virginias* was to be "largely a Mining Journal striving to collect and publish full and reliable information concerning the mineral deposits of these states...." Because "scientific knowledge wisely applied" was the basis for development, he planned to devote a portion of the journal "to the presentation of scientific facts and statements relating to the Virginias." Nor were other enterprises to be ignored; agriculture, and in particular lumbering, were to receive attention; nothing that could be developed profitably seemed to escape his notice, not even bees.[4]

The journal was quickly established as an important contribution to public recognition of the potential of the region, and likely to bring business to a cash-starved population. The first issue carried 19 advertisements; by July the number had increased to 50; in its first year 60 advertisers had bought space; and in 1883, the journal's most successful year, 90. Who advertised gives some indication of the expected readership. By far the largest professional group was the lawyers, reflecting both the number of practitioners in the population and their indispensable role in land and property deals. No fewer than 14 different law firms advertised over the six years, some of them in practically every issue. Civil and mining engineers, analytical chemists, educational establishments, hotels, banks, and newspapers advertised regularly. Without doubt much of this support was essentially personal in character. Because Hotchkiss knew most of the advertisers, it is reasonable to suppose that, although they hoped to derive some direct benefit from advertising, they were providing financial support for a cause which they shared.

Among the educational establishments who advertised were the prestigious and influential University of Virginia, Washington and Lee University, and Virginia Military Institute. It was also their professors, past and present, who contributed good scientific papers, conferring stature on the publication.

For six years the journal appeared monthly and achieved a wide readership, extending to the principal sources of capital: New York,

Boston, Philadelphia, Liverpool, and London.[5] It was filled with facts of interest to the geologist and mining engineer, to the capitalist and speculator. Iron masters anxious to attract capital provided production statistics. In addition Hotchkiss culled facts and figures from the 1880 census data, reports of the Iron and Steel Manufacturers Association, and other publications. The output of furnaces was given in detail, including the number of days in blast. Quantities of ore, fuel, and flux used, and of pig iron produced gave valuable information about the efficiencies of different installations, and the quality of the ores. He obtained the quantities of the minerals carried from the railroads and thereby provided a record of the development of the Virginia coal industry.

That story of progress made *The Virginias* a prime means for drawing attention to properties on the market which Hotchkiss used to his advantage. Indeed he recognized that usefulness from the beginning as a way of financing the publication. When commissioned to prepare a report on a property, Hotchkiss negotiated with the vendor for it to be published in *The Virginias* where it would receive a wider circulation than would the limited-edition pamphlet normally produced in such cases. The vendor had the benefit of the larger readership, and Hotchkiss the funding of an issue of his journal. Often a specially enlarged edition helped his funding. The Van Buren Estate was an example of such a case. It was a large estate, 27,000 acres, near the northwest border of Shenandoah County. To accompany the three-page report describing the topography, geology, water resources, and history of the furnace, Hotchkiss produced a map at a scale of 1/80,000, depicting the topography, drainage, principal roads, and settlements, and another at a smaller scale to show the location of the property more clearly. A geological section through the furnace was shown at the foot of the map.[6] This was typical of the scores of such reports, practical examples of the exploitation of the state's resources. They were not confined to those of his own authorship. Thus the 39-square-mile Arcadia Furnace property was the subject of an account of its geology by Professor John L. Campbell of Washington and Lee University, as it was of several other contributions by mining engineers familiar with the area. The map published to illustrate these reports was a reduced version of one made in 1867 under the direction of Colonel T. H. Williamson, then professor of engineering at the Virginia Military Institute.[7]

Maps were an important feature of *The Virginias.* Not only were they included within the body of the paper, but were prepared and issued as special supplements. Always concerned about the inadequate maps then available, and hence the inability of investors to fully appreciate the significance of a property, or of some projected railroad development, Hotchkiss drew attention to the work of the infant U.S. Geological Survey, and to the maps published by others.[8] He gave favorable notice to a new map of West Virginia published by the *Wheeling Register* saying, "it is by far the best map of the State that has yet been published."[9] He also noticed the appearance of "A Map of the Great Dismal Swamp of Virginia" by Richard Lamb—"an accurate compilation," he called it. On the other hand, Professor C. Henry Roney prepared a map especially for *The Industrial Review* which Hotchkiss severely criticized. It showed "a grossly inaccurate" outline of the Ohio Coal Basin and "anyone seeking information...would be led entirely astray by this pretentious map."[10]

Of all the maps issued with *The Virginias*, none was more important than *Hotchkiss' Geological Map of Virginia and West Virginia. The Geology by Prof. William B. Rogers*, issued as a Supplement to the June-1880 number. This was based on the map that had accompanied Hotchkiss' *Virginia: A Geographical and Political Summary*, published in 1876. He published it again because the Board of Immigration, having spent more than three years dithering over the details, had only printed a limited number of copies of the *Summary*, and made no provision for advertising or marketing it. It was available from the state printers only on application.[11] This was hardly the way to stimulate the interest of anyone, let alone that of the potential immigrant with capital. The importance of the map was that for the first time the pioneering work of William Barton Rogers was made available in proper cartographic style to those able to appreciate it, and, perhaps, to profit by it. Not withstanding the title, it was Rogers' map and Hotchkiss gave handsome credit to the great geologist; a map "that will forever remain a monument to his genius as one of the fathers, if not *the father*, of American Geology." Hotchkiss claimed only "ownership resulting from its copyright publication, and from the preparation of the topographical map on which it is based."[12]

Hotchkiss' Geological Map was not the only service Hotchkiss did for his teacher. The annual reports of the survey being long out of print and difficult to find, he kept Rogers' work before the public by including in *The Virginias* extracts from them which had a contemporary interest. After Rogers' death in 1882, he assisted Mrs. Rogers in the production of a reprint of the papers her husband had written on Virginia geology.

Although Rogers' work provided a good understanding of the geological processes which had shaped Virginia, it was the location of exploitable minerals, especially iron and coal, which was of greater significance for the future, and of greater interest to Rogers at the time, as he pointed out:

> What surer foundation of permanent wealth and power of a community can be found than the store of coal and iron embosomed in the rocky strata of its hills and valleys, and what more efficacious stimulus to the mechanic arts, to industry in general, and to the advancement of all practical and profitable knowledge than the multifarious pursuits linked with the *manufacture of iron*?[13]

Hotchkiss had inherited that spirit which he was putting into practical effect, and through *The Virginias* was encouraging others to do likewise.

The existence of coal in western Virginia had been known at least as early as 1742 when John Howard and John P. Salling made the first recorded descent of New River on their way to the Mississippi. Later Dr. Thomas Walker in 1750 noted coal in the region of the headwaters of Tug Fork of the Big Sandy River, and Thomas Jefferson, 1787, referred to coal existing in many places "in the Western country."[14] Its extent, however, was not appreciated until Rogers' survey in which it was included within the fifth great geological division of the Virginias. He described this as being "the territory between the western limits of the state and an irregular line of mountain ranges as yet imperfectly determined, but nearly coinciding with the eastern front ridge of the Allegheny, the Greenbrier mountain and the great Flat Top mountain." No section of the state, he said, held out richer promise of valuable practical results once it had been systematically explored. He noted that the geological formations of the region were the same as those distinguished throughout the world for their deposits of bituminous coal, and that here in western Virginia the disposition of the rocks permitted ready access to the seams exposed in the sides of deep valleys.[15]

No serious exploitation took place until the 1880s. Hotchkiss, who possessed copies of the annual reports, was well aware of Rogers' work, and had sent Captain Isiah Welch to explore the headwaters of Laurel Creek in 1873. The region was so remote, so difficult of access, covered with forest, and deeply dissected by fast-flowing rivers, that substantial work would have to be done before this great wealth could be realized. The railroads, which were both transporters and users of coal, and one man, Frederick J. Kimball, provided that work.[16]

Kimball wrote Hotchkiss in 1879 inquiring about maps of Page and Warren Counties, presumably to assist in determining the route of the Shenandoah Valley Railroad. Hotchkiss in turn proposed that he should make a map of the country to be traversed by the road, and sought the help of Milnes to persuade Kimball of the merits of his suggestion.[17] That correspondence marked the beginning of a long and fruitful association between the two men. It led to the exploitation of the

Frederick J. Kimball, who made the Norfolk & Western Railroad the greatest coal carrier in the U.S.A. He relied on Hotchkiss' geological knowledge and map-making skills.
  Virginia State Library and Archives

A survey team of the kind that Hotchkiss used for his surveys in West Virginia.
  Jack M. Jones, Early Coal Mining in Pocahontas, Virginia, Lynchburg, Virginia

TYPICAL SURVEY CREW OF THE PERIOD
SOUTHWEST VIRGINIA IMPROVEMENT CO.
POCAHONTAS, VA.

Flat Top coalfield, and to the creation of one of America's great railroads.

The map of the Shenandoah Valley Railroad (S.V.R.R.) appeared in the March 1880 issue of *The Virginias*; accompanying articles described the mineral resources tributary to it. Kimball, who paid for the extra 1,000 copies produced to publicize the road, funded the issue. The following November, Kimball gave Hotchkiss the opportunity he had been looking for.[18] With the construction of the railroad in progress up the Valley toward Waynesboro it was time to plan the next phase, the link-up with the bankrupt Atlantic, Mississippi, & Ohio Railroad (A.M.&O.R.R.) which had absorbed the old Virginia & Tennessee in 1870. Hotchkiss responded to Kimball's first inquiry by sending a copy of his geological map on which he had marked the existing railroad and its proposed extension. An eight-page letter came with it describing in some detail the geology of Virginia. Kimball next asked for "a written opinion as to the best route." By best Kimball meant "the most economical in point of construction, and which will run in the closest proximity to the minerals."[19] A nine-page reply gave distances, grades, and specific information on the mineral deposits along the route of a railroad which would link with the A.M.&O. at or near Bonsacks.[20] Kimball eventually adopted a route close to that which Hotchkiss had proposed, but did not make the connection at Bonsacks. Instead the rails were laid on the other side of Read Mountain and the junction effected a few miles to the southwest at Big Lick, soon to become "the Magic City" of Roanoke. The next major event was the purchase of the A.M.&O., with considerable backing from English finance houses, by E. W. Clark & Co., who renamed it the Norfolk and Western Railroad (N&W). Kimball, who had replaced his uncle William Milnes, Jr. as the chairman of the S.V.R.R. in 1881, now took on the additional responsibility of first vice-president of the new organization. The first meeting of the N&W stockholders was held on May 3, 1881, but already Kimball was looking ahead, seeking a source of coal independent of the C&O. Again he wrote to Hotchkiss for advice. It was the acceptance of this advice which vindicated all that Rogers and Hotchkiss had said and written about the vast storehouse of wealth in the southwestern corner of the Virginia states. Hotchkiss' reply began,

> At the earliest possible moment I have constructed, and herewith hand you, a Topographical map showing what I conceive to be the best route, or routes, from the Norfolk & Western Railway to the Great Ohio Coal Basin, all things considered, and submit with same the following rema[r]ks on the railway routes and on the coals they will reach at the border of the Basin....

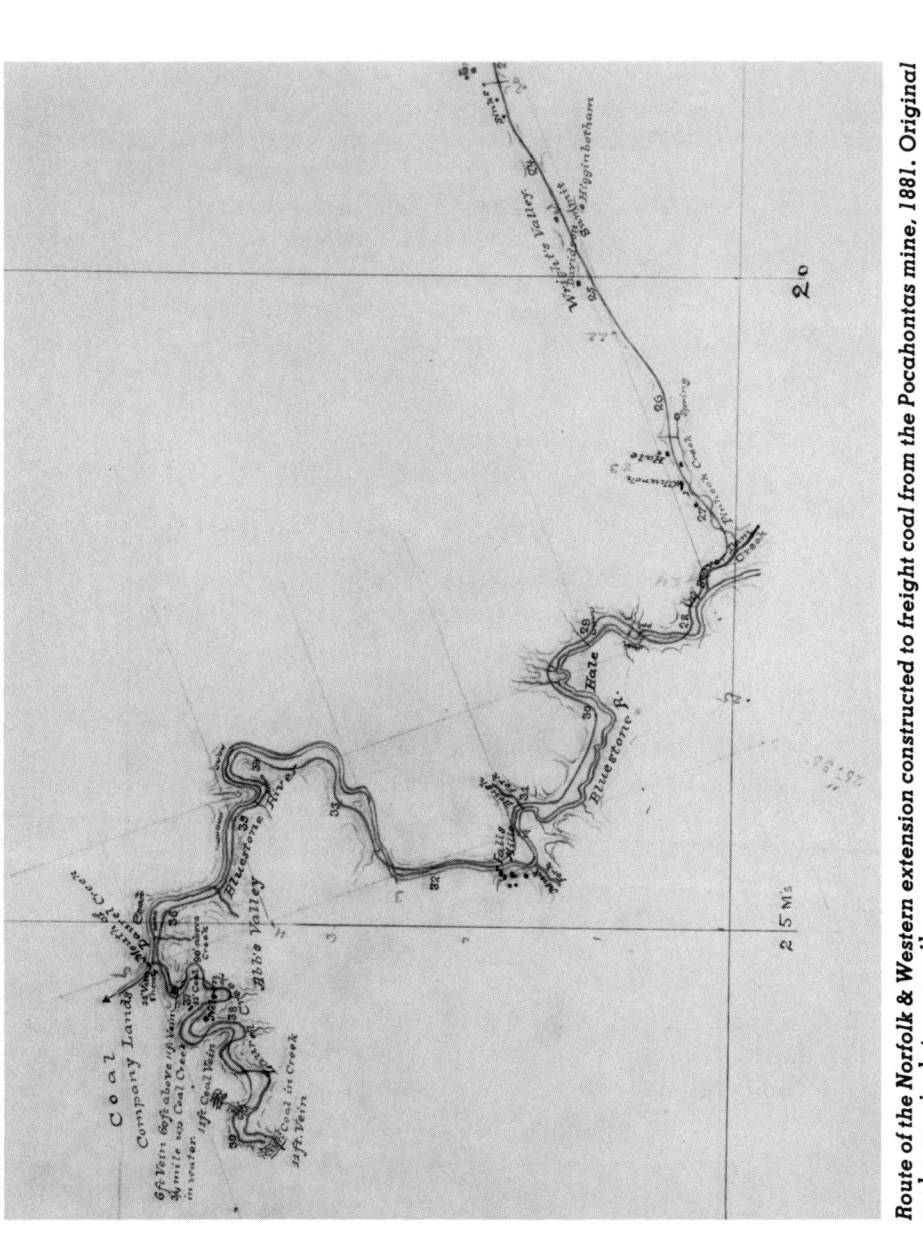

Route of the Norfolk & Western extension constructed to freight coal from the Pocahontas mine, 1881. Original scale: one inch to one mile.

Hotchkiss Map Collection #271, Library of Congress

He proposed two routes for consideration. The one preferred, and subsequently adopted, was down the New River to the mouth of East River and thence up that river and crossing over to the Bluestone and down to the fork with Laurel Creek. The other, leaving the New River at Wolf Creek, would have required the building of the railroad too far to the west before turning Buckhorn (East River) Mountain and running down Bluestone River. The advantage of these routes to the coal-field was that the coal-beds could be reached

> *near the level of their outcrops*; and then these outcrops *may be* followed northward for mining the coal and the point of vantage has been gained for crossing from the highest levels of the stream-valleys over to the Great Carboniferous Plateau, with its vast resources of timber and coals of many kinds, ...and thence down the *Big Sandy*...or down the *Guyandot* to the Ohio at Huntington, or down *Coal River*...and thence down the Great Kanawha to the Ohio to the railway systems of the west.[21]

In this long sentence Hotchkiss expressed his vision of the future and by doing so made a substantial contribution to its realization.

It was near the fork of Bluestone River and Laurel Creek that in 1873 Captain I. A. Welch, operating under Hotchkiss' instructions, had found, on the land of Mr. Nelson, that "a bed of coal had been driven into...that measured 9 feet in thickness from floor to roof." Hotchkiss marked on the map the location of this opening as well as three other exposures reported by Welch, and described in the letter to Kimball. Hotchkiss also quoted Welch's opinion that, ignoring coal beds less than three feet thick, there was an aggregate of readily mineable coal amounting to 30 feet.[22]

Soon after receiving that report, Kimball and other company officials rode, on horseback, over the ground with Hotchkiss, and saw for themselves the potential of that wild ravine-riven land. In June, Kimball had acquired the charters of four related companies who held franchises for railroads through the New, East, and Bluestone valleys. None of them had actually laid any tracks, but they held valuable options on coal lands. Kimball merged the companies into the New River Railroad, Mining, and Manufacturing Company, and began, under that name, the construction of a branch line from the N&W toward the coalfield in August 1881. Later this was to be integrated into the N&W as the New River division. At the same time another company, the Southwest Virginia Improvement Company, was restructured to develop the coal and timber. That company selected a site at Powell's Bottom, a widening of Laurel Creek a mile or so above its confluence with the Bluestone River, and here started to build the mining town of Pocahontas only 7 months after Hotchkiss had handed his proposals to Kimball.[23]

Hotchkiss followed closely the progress of both projects, reporting on them from time to time in *The Virginias*, including in it, for example, a map of the Flat Top Mountain coalfield showing the route of the railroad and the location of Pocahontas.[24] In July 1882 he noted that three sawmills were at work on the site, 80 houses and 100 coke ovens under contract, a large force of miners had driven gangways 800 feet into the seam, and output was expected to reach a thousand tons a day by the time the railroad reached the mine. The following October, he recorded that the New River branch had reached the mouth of East River. The remaining 36 miles to Pocahontas was completed on March 10, 1883, when Kimball and the chief engineer, W. W. Coe, drove in the last spikes and the first train arrived.[25] A day of great excitement, for it meant the end of isolation. "How anxiously we waited for that event and the arrival of the train," wrote the wife of the mine superintendent, "finally we heard the locomotive whistle down the line, and I can assure you no operatic music ever thrilled me as that sound did, and the freight train with its delapidated passenger car on the rear end was a beautiful sight."[26] A few days later, Hotchkiss, with Kimball and a party of officials from the railroad, made an inspection of the coal mines, tramways, coke ovens, and the other facilities of the first mining town in the Flat Top field. They found that about 9,000 feet of gangway had now been driven into the "big" or "Nelson" coal bed, and all the accessories for coal-mining and coking were nearly complete.[27]

On March 17, 1883, the first carload of coal, consigned to Mayor Lamb for free distribution, arrived in Norfolk to a display of flags and a salute from the Norfolk Light Artillery Blues.[28] By the end of 1883 nearly 120,000 tons of coal had been mined, of which just over a third was converted into coke, and monthly output approached 40,000 tons. From then on, coal output from this and the many other mines opened up along the creeks penetrating Flat Top Mountain steadily increased, reaching three and a quarter million tons in 1898, and a peak of over sixteen million tons in 1916.[29]

When it was clear that Kimball would build a railroad into the Flat Top region, Hotchkiss and his associates, Echols, Bell and Catlett, formed a syndicate to secure options on land along the Bluestone River. This river flows along the foot of the Flat Top escarpment. Its turbulent tributaries had cut the mountain into segments and provided access to the coal and timber. Hotchkiss engaged Captain Welch to survey this river system and locate the coal outcrops. The work of four teams of surveyors was completed early in 1863, and Hotchkiss incorporated their results in a new map of the region. Kimball, his railroad finished, made another visit to Flat Top mountain, guided by Hotchkiss and his map. This reconnaissance stimulated E. W. Clarke & Co. and other backers of the N&W to buy up the options of the Staunton syndicate and complete the land purchases. After some hesitation as to the best way of exploiting the coal deposits, they formed the Flat Top Coal Land Association. This did not mine the coal, but leased land to mining companies, deriving revenue as royalties on tonnage mined. Hotchkiss was a strong advocate of this policy, which later dominated the Appalachian coal industry.[30]

Throughout the remaining years of *The Virginias*, Hotchkiss continued to report on the developments in the Flat Top region. When tragedy struck the Pocahontas mine in the early hours of March 13, 1884, killing the whole of the night shift of at least 114, he immediately went to the site and made his own thorough investigation of the occurrence. His description of the scene, the account of the events immediately following the explosion, discussion of the possible causes, and his recommendations, were published in his journal. It was a lesson in careful objective observation which earned Kimball's praise. As he wrote Hotchkiss, "let me make my acknowledgements for the thorough manner in which you have referred to the terrible calamity at Pocahontas in the last issue of your "Virginias." What would the Virginias do without you? Your example of energy, perseverance, and thoroughness is admirable."[31]

By 1885 the hectic business activity of the earlier years of the decade had subsided, the shortage of iron had been eliminated and its price had dropped in consequence. That slowing down had a direct effect on *The Virginias*, and caused Hotchkiss to plead with the general manager of the C&O for support. "The hard times have caused a good many subscribers to drop off and advertisers to cease from advertising so my revenues have been greatly curtailed."[32] He seems not to have made a similar appeal to Kimball, who had his own troubles in 1885. When the Shenandoah Valley Railroad went bankrupt, he had resigned as its president. So possibly Hotchkiss thought that was not the time to ask for an extension of the support he was already getting. He did not finally cease publication, however, until the end of the year. Even then it was a reluctant decision, and he sought to perpetuate both the title and his personal contribution by coming to an arrangement with the weekly magazine, *Industrial South*.[33] Unfortunately, that cooperation was shortlived, for that journal failed by March 14, 1886.[34]

Although Hotchkiss contributed articles to national periodicals such as the *Coal Trade Journal*, he preferred to write for a permanent Southern journal, and it was the *Manufacturer's Record* of Baltimore which was to provide him occasional space to promote the mining interests of the Virginias.[35] That *The Virginias* had been successful in terms of providing information there can be no doubt. It had advanced Hotchkiss' reputation and made his name known far beyond Virginia's boundaries. Whether it was a financial success is another matter. Hotchkiss claimed that it was not, but it is unlikely that it was a major liability.

The people most likely to appreciate the value of Virginia's natural wealth and to direct capital to its exploitation were also likely to be members of the American Institute of Mining Engineers. In 1880, the Staunton City Council, probably prompted by Hotchkiss, invited the Institute to hold a meeting in its city, an invitation which was accepted for the spring meeting for the following year. That meeting, which took place at the end of May, comprised the usual combination of learned papers, excursions, and social events which *The Virginias* previewed in its May issue, given free to all participants. The arrangements for that meeting, which concluded at White Sulphur Springs, were largely the work of Hotchkiss, for which he received well-deserved praise. Professor Eggleston wrote to him: "You and your good people outdid yourselves and I am receiving intimations from all quarters of the country that the meeting in all points scientific and social was thoroughly appreciated."[36] Andrew S. McCreath, Chemical assistant to the Second Geological Survey of Pennsylvania, thought "the universal opinion must be that the Virginia meeting was a grand success."[37] The Institute met in 1883 in Roanoke. Again Hotchkiss published the programme and provided background notes in *The Virginias*, that time preparing a special map showing all the localities to be visited during the period of the meeting.[38]

The publication of *The Virginias* was additional to, and not in place of, his accustomed activities of reporting on property for clients, lecturing on Civil War topics, and lecturing at teachers' institutes. Two other tasks undertaken during this period bore directly on Hotchkiss' efforts to promote Virginia's resources. In 1880 he was appointed by Superintendent of the Census, General Walker, a special agent for the preparation of the mining statistics of Virginia and West Virginia for the tenth census. This provided a small income of $5 per day plus expenses and another $1.50 to pay an assistant. It greatly facilitated the collection of information for his journal, and increased the size of the audience he could reach. It was an acknowledgement of his authority in this field as well as a means of enhancing it still further. *The*

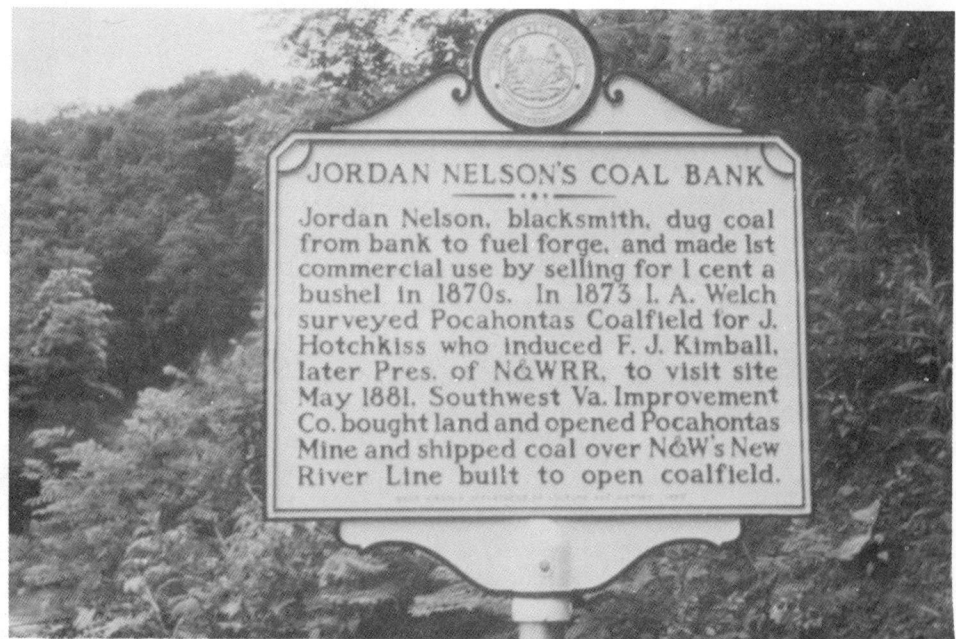

Historic marker at Pocahontas

Author

Jedediah Hotchkiss, 1884. Photograph on his exhibitor's admission ticket to the New Orleans Exposition 1884/5.

Hotchkiss Papers, Box 4, Alderman Library, University of Virginia

Commonwealth, announcing the appointment, said,

> General Walker, the Superintendent of the Census, never made a better appointment in his life than this, and we congratulate him on it. Major HOTCHKISS has devoted his time for thirty years to the study of our mineral resources, and has brought to the work great ability, and unflagging industry....Both Virginia and West Virginia owe him a debt...they can never repay.[39]

The other task enabled Hotchkiss to put on public view, as it were, the fruits of his endeavors, for in 1884 he was in charge of Virginia's mineral exhibit at the New Orleans World Cotton and Industrial Exposition. He had the task of collecting, labelling, and displaying all the specimens he thought appropriate to illustrate the theme. In addition he made his own personal contribution in the form of a series of large maps of the state depicting different aspects of its physical and social geography.[40] It is clear that at this time Hotchkiss was *the* authority on the economic geology and the topography of the Virginia states, so it is not surprising to find him being consulted not just by railroad builders, capitalists, and speculators, but also by the Director of the U.S. Geological Survey, John W. Powell, and his chief geographer, Henry Gannett.

That authority tempted him to make his one serious effort to enter politics. Hotchkiss, like the majority of white Virginians, supported the Democratic party. No self-respecting Confederate, in his opinion, could support the Republican party, which not only had been responsible for the terrible events of twenty years earlier, but since Appomattox had heaped misery upon misery on the Southern states, and had used a disreputable motley of scalawags and carpet-baggers to implement their policies.[41] But they were the party of capital, and strove to develop the industrial capability of the nation. One aspect of this was their attitude to duties imposed on the import of iron and steel. Naturally Hotchkiss was in favor of such imposts as providing protection to a developing industry. The Democrats, strongly influenced by the agrarian interests, were opposed. Hotchkiss was in a dilemma which he attempted to resolve by running as an independent candidate for the 49th Congress.[42] That raised a storm of protest, for while the local press had a high regard for Major Hotchkiss it considered him mistaken in running against John Randolph Tucker, the Democratic candidate. Hotchkiss' personal following could split the democratic vote and let in the Republican. Great was the relief when he withdrew. He was doing a splendid job as editor of *The Virginias*, and he would "have done himself a wrong and his party an injury, were he to have persisted in making the canvas in the face of his party and friends." The editor of Lynchburg's *Weekly Visitor* wrote, "We are glad to know the familiar name will still head the editorial column of *The Virginias*. Major Hotchkiss is in the best place for him, long may he remain in it and prosper. Congress could have given him nothing to compensate the State for the loss which would have resulted from his removal from the editorial chair."[43] A similar view was expressed by Kimball, who, on learning from Hotchkiss that he had withdrawn from the contest, replied, "I believe you can be of more benefit to Virginia in following out the purpose for which you have been engaged during so many years than you can in Congress."[44]

Before the end of the Eighties, Hotchkiss was to see some financial benefit from his real estate business. As the result of some good closings he was making progress in paying off his "panic year" indebtedness. In 1887 he had reduced his debt by some $15,000.[45] He confided to Professor I. C. White that he had "been quite busy in iron ore matters" during that year, and had "done quite well out of them."[46] Hotchkiss made similar remarks to Mrs. Rogers: "I have been quite providentially favored...in my business matters so that I am now more of a free man than I have been for a long time."[47] At the beginning of 1888, he told his nephew, Charles, he had recently finished a complete brick stable and had purchased two fine horses.[48]

But Hotchkiss had more ambitious plans than stables. Nothing less than the pulling down of the frame part of his house and building in its place a new one in brick.

While on a visit to Boston in February 1888, he discussed his ideas with Mr. G. H. Wetherell of the architectural firm Winslow and Wetherell. By May he had a fair notion of what he wanted. He sent the architects a set of plans and elevations which he asked Wetherell to "work into artistic shape." Hotchkiss wanted the house to be externally attractive, but this was to derive from simplicity and not from "what is usually called ornamentation." He wanted a "*thoroughly good* substantial dwelling."[49] A month later he wrote to the directors of Augusta National Bank, "I desire to begin building my new house at once. To do so with advantage I wish [to borrow] $3,000—say $1,000 July 16, $1,000 August 1, $1,000 September 1." As collateral he offered $5,000 of full paid-up stock of the Flat Top Coal Co.[50] It is an indication of his standing in his hometown that he was able to make these arrangements at so late a stage. Later, in December, he borrowed a similar sum from the National Valley Bank of Staunton, secured by stock certificates of the Flat Top Trust having a face value of $5,000.[51] The rebuilding did not proceed as fast as the planning. An unusually wet fall, problems

The Oaks, Staunton, Virginia.

Fletcher Collins, Jr.

with the plastering and the plumbing caused delay, but about a year after pulling down part of the old one, the grand new house was finished.

Now a Virginia Historic Landmark, and on the National Register of Historic Places, The Oaks remains today, much as it was then, a testimony to the man and his work: substantial, confident, dignified, yet full of interesting detail.[52]

CHAPTER VIII

The Civil War Remembered

OF COURSE IT could not be forgotten. No one who has been in battle ever forgets. There is no experience so demand-sharing as warfare. Long after the guns cease firing, and the citizen soldiers leave it to the politicians to squabble over the spoils, the survivors, the relatives of the living and the dead, need to mourn, to praise, to glorify the heroic deeds, the suffering, above all to recall the companionship in hardship, discomfort, pain, fear, and misery. Only a belief that the cause was worthy makes the grief bearable. So the myths are born.

Belief in the cause kept the South going when all the statistics showed that indeed the war should have been "over by Christmas," or certainly by the summer of 1862. That it was not was due to the skill of two men, Jackson and Lee, and the stubborn fortitude of the men they led. For the Southerners, defeat was not the result of poor generalship on their part, or of superior generalship on the part of the North, but of sheer weight of numbers of men and munitions pitted against them. They could view their performance with pride, and, pride being all they had left, they made the most of it.

The events are so long ago now that it is possible for that pride to be assimilated by the whole nation, possible to concentrate on the virtues of fighting for a cause believed in, and on the valor and self-sacrifice of those engaged with little notion of the real issues. To those involved it had been a matter of survival, keeping out the cold or the wet or the heat, not actually starving, wading rivers, hauling wagons through knee-deep mud, as well as the insanity of a frontal attack against a well-entrenched foe deploying superior firepower.

The remembrance of all this took many forms. The dead were collected and buried in the towns and villages they had come from. Their graves were disposed around a monument, or memorial, which became the focal point of parades in honor of the fallen. Those who had served in particular formations banded together to help each other, and the relatives of their dead comrades. The leaders, now in stone or bronze, took their places in squares, avenues, and cemeteries, their unveiling an occasion for the outpouring of heroic oratory. Alongside this effusion of emotion was also a desire to tell it as it was, or to set the record straight. Though Hotchkiss embraced the worship of heroes and of Southern honor, and could no more vote Republican than sup with the devil, his nature required him to know the facts, the truth as far as it was possible to know it. Thus Hotchkiss remembered the war, not only as a Confederate veteran entrancing his comrades with his "chalk talks," but as a close student of the maneuvers of the commanders he had served.

As we have seen, only a very short time elapsed after the surrender at Appomattox before he became involved in telling of the events he had witnessed and recorded in his diary. Apart from assisting those who had their own tale to tell, he joined with Colonel William Allan in what they hoped would be a complete account of the battlefields of Virginia. The first, and only, book in the series, was the history of the Fredericksburg and Chancellorsville campaigns published in 1867. Its lack of success deterred them from continuing the project, but neither gave up the hope of putting before the public the story of the battles, and of those who had shaped them. William Allan later published accounts of Jackson's campaign in the Valley, and of the 1863 campaign of the Army of Northern Virginia.

Until the very end of his life, Hotchkiss lectured on Civil War topics to a variety of organizations, including the Y.M.C.A., American Institute of Mining Engineers, American Historical Association,[1] National Geographic Society,[2] teachers' institutes,[3] as well as to camps and posts of war veterans. These lectures, illustrated by blackboard drawings, were generally well received, and well reviewed in the press. His favorite topic was "Jackson's Valley Campaign of 1862," a favorite with most Southerners, and all Virginians. For example his chalk talk on that subject delivered in Washington Hall, Charlestown, West Virginia, was anticipated as the "event of the week." The *Virginia Free Press* of that town reported that "With the aid of the blackboard, chalk, maps and an unlimited knowledge of the topography of the Shenandoah Valley, Major Jed Hotchkiss of Staunton, led a fascinated audience up and down that Valley...following Stonewall Jackson's lightning marches." The lecture was considered of special value because it was not the "product of speculation," but a careful statement of what Hotchkiss knew and had experienced. In the opinion of the reporter, "It had the additional merit of being embellished with genial humor, suggestive anecdote and patriotic eloquence."[4] The *Richmond Dispatch* described an occasion when Hotchkiss delivered this lecture to members of the Westminster Guild of the First Presbyterian Church in Staunton: "His audience was delighted with his eloquent and graphic descriptions of soldier life in the Valley. With his well known skill, the speaker outlined the peculiar features of the Valley of Virginia upon the blackboard and then made most vivid and realistic his thrilling sketches of the work of Jackson's 'foot cavalry.' For nearly two hours Major Hotchkiss held the breathless attention of his sympathetic audience."[5] In October 1878, Hotchkiss delivered his "famous lecture" to the Y.M.C.A. of Greenville to celebrate the first anniversary of its formation. According to the reporter, "A large body of the audience was composed of old soldiers of the Stonewall Brigade and some of them remarked at the close of the lecture, that so accurate, vivid, and lucid were his statements and illustrations that they felt as if they had just emerged once more from that memorable campaign."[6] Blessed with a good memory, he lectured without notes, and with a ready facility in the use of colored chalks he provided ample illustrations.[7] If a blackboard was not available, no matter, he brought his own, a flexible one which could be fastened to a convenient wall. In the absence of a wall, he arranged for a stand to be made to carry it, as he did when he gave a lecture to a party from the Anderson, Indiana, Public School when they passed through Clifton Forge on an educational trip.[8] Hotchkiss was especially anxious to talk to young people so that they could have a proper account of the remarkable events of the Civil War. The blackboard was not his only "visual aid"; he had a large map, 12 ft $\times$ 16ft, illustrating the Battle of Fredericksburg, drawn with paint and crayon on white cloth, now known as the "bedsheet" map.[9]

While most of his lectures received acclaim, it was not always the case. On one occasion after he had addressed a largely Republican audience in Morgantown, West Virginia, the editors of its weekly paper heavily criticized him for his Southern bias.[10] This was an exception, and not representative of most Northern sentiment, as was revealed by the reception of his contribution to the Lowell Institute's series of Civil War lectures in Boston in the spring of 1886, or of his address to the third annual meeting of the American Historical Association. In April of that year, in Washington, Hotchkiss addressed members of the association on "The Value of Topographical Knowledge in Battles and Campaigns." The *Report of the Proceedings* recorded that: "The lecturer sketched rapidly with colored crayons upon a large blackboard, the physical conformation of the Valley of Virginia, and described in a most graphic way, 'Stonewall' Jackson's Valley campaign. After the lecture, which was warmly applauded, Mr. Bancroft, with great enthusiasm, grasped hands with the Confederate officer and earnestly congratulated him upon the wonderful success of his description of a most remarkable campaign."[11] This response from the most eminent of America's historians must have been heartwarming indeed.

Hotchkiss enjoyed, too, the occasions when he lectured to Union veterans. When lecturing in Boston early in 1886 he met a number of Sheridan's officers with whom he discussed the Battle of Cedar Creek.[12] In the fall that year, a Grand Army of the Republic post in Boston made a nine-day trip around the Virginia battlefields. Hotchkiss accompanied the excursion, pointed out the places of interest along the route, and described the battlefields.[13] He was in Boston again before the end of the year to lecture at another meeting of veterans.[14] In 1890 he addressed a post in Philadelphia on "Jackson's Valley Campaign," and at Princeton University the same subject drew a good reception.[15]

At a special meeting of the National Geographic Society convened in February 1892, members discussed "Military Surveying during the Civil War." The principal contributors were Mr. Gilbert Thompson and Hotchkiss, who described their respective experiences with the Northern and Southern armies. As usual, Hotchkiss spoke without notes.[16]

Those lectures, always instructive and as accurate as Hotchkiss knew how to make them, were often presented as entertainments. People came to hear what they wanted to hear: great and exciting deeds in which the South had excelled. They were so successful that Hotchkiss was engaged to deliver them as fund-raising events, as he did, for example, at Berrysville at the beginning of 1893 in aid of the disabled Confederates of Clarke County.[17] "Jackson's Valley Campaign" had all the ingredients; an enigmatic leader, fast deceptive marches, close run battles, escape from the enemy's clutches, and ultimate victory over a larger foe. Here was the superior Southern strategy, and superior Southern tactics enacted by superior Southern fighting men. "It did the spirit good." Other campaigns had plenty of heroics, but even where clear Southern victories could be claimed, they were marred in some way. Fredericksburg was a static defensive battle, Chancellorsville displayed the military genius of Southern generals, but was spoiled by the mortal wounding of Jackson. The brilliant dash of Jubal Early to the very boundaries of Washington, in 1864, could not be separated from the defeat of Fisher's Hill or the debacle at Waynesboro. But Jackson's Valley campaign: there was unsullied, unqualified victory, against all the odds!

For most Southerners, whatever their status, the war had destroyed an accustomed way of life. In these circumstances it is not surprising that stories of its heroic defense offered an escape from a depressing reality. Hotchkiss had the knowledge, and the ability to tell these stories, to bring past deeds alive again, and in doing so, responded to the needs of ex-Confederates. That his lectures were appreciated by northern as well as southern audiences, in particular that his account of Jackson's Valley campaign was commended with enthusiasm by Bancroft, is evidence that they were not over-embroidered with southern bias.

Fortunately Hotchkiss' contribution to the recording of the war was not confined to delivering popular lectures, but was a continuing attempt throughout his busy life to find the facts. When he was in New Orleans visiting the Exposition he was able to find the names of three of the four stretcher bearers who carried Jackson from the field to the ambulance which took him to the field hospital at "Old Wilderness Tavern." He learned them from the janitor of New Orleans city hall, Robert McLaughlin, formerly Sergeant, Company B, 14th Louisiana Regiment, who had been in charge of the ambulance.[18]

Hotchkiss gave advice and contributed maps to many correspondents in the post-war years, but the most important and enduring of his historical work was that which he did for the War Records Office, in Washington, the help which he gave to Col. George Francis Robert Henderson, in England, and his authorship of Volume III of the *Confederate Military History*, completed just before his death.

His contribution to the work of the War Records Office was of two kinds, most of it related to the maps for the Atlas to accompany the *Official Records*, which will be dealt with in chapter X, but a small, though important element, concerned the records. Hotchkiss' *Report of Operations of the Second Corps of the Army of Northern Virginia and of the Valley District during the Campaign of 1864-5* had not been sent in before the war ended. In 1892 he sent to Major George B.

Davis, President of the Board of Publication of War Records, his original report covering the period May 3 to November 14, 1864, which he wanted returned. So he included a copy which differed from the original only in minor respects and which he wished to have accepted for publication in the *Official Records.* He also included a "Supplement Report" covering the operations from November 14, 1864, to April 12, 1865, and 38 manuscript-maps drawn during the winter of 1864-5.[19]

While these maps were being printed, a British army officer, Major (later Lieutenant Colonel) George F. R. Henderson of the Staff College, Camberley, was preparing to write a biography of Virginia's hero, "Stonewall" Jackson.[20] That study was to stand for three-quarters of a century as the authority on its subject, and the conduct of the war in Virginia up to Jackson's mortal wounding at Chancellorsville in 1863. At least some, and possibly a great deal of the credit for the accuracy of the Civil War chapters is due to Hotchkiss.

On one of his periodic journeys to the capitalists of Boston, New York, and Philadelphia, Hotchkiss met, in March 1892, William L. Chase, a friend of Henderson, and so began the remarkably fruitful correspondence that traversed the Atlantic until Henderson's two volume biography was published by Longmans, Green & Co. in October 1898. Chase followed the meeting with a letter containing 18 questions put by Henderson. These intrigued Hotchkiss who replied that they were "so suggestive and pertinent" that he "could not resist the temptation of saying a good deal." The result was a 34-page reply.[21] Later in the year, when Hotchkiss became fully aware of the task Henderson had set himself, he offered to aid him in any way he could, writing, "If you will send me the proof sheets or your matter type-written I will be glad to read it over and make suggestions as to statements, corrections, etc."[22] This was no idle offer; it is clear from the tone of this letter that Hotchkiss, in spite of all the other calls on his time, welcomed the opportunity of being involved in a project which he would have liked to have undertaken himself. Indeed, to Chase he had said that Henderson's questions could have been the spur that he had been waiting for to provoke him into writing about his "famous old commander."[23] The fact that someone else was to do just that was a matter of great pleasure to Hotchkiss—not something to regret as an opportunity lost, but one which would ensure that Jackson received the treatment his military feats deserved.

Early in 1893 Henderson was assigned to other duties which caused him to set aside work on his biography for a year, but in 1894 he visited Virginia and explored the battlefields of Cross Keys and Port Republic with Hotchkiss.[24] A fascinating experience that must have been for both of them: Henderson the professional soldier and military historian,

Hotchkiss, the gifted amateur who had taken part in the events Henderson was to write about. He described the ground, pointed out troop positions, the location of artillery, the skirmish line, relived the excitement, the fear, the exhaustion, the horror, but also, through his enthusiasm, demonstrated his pride at having served the Confederate cause under such a commander as Jackson. As the story was steadily recorded by Henderson, Hotchkiss, in his comments on the draft chapters, was able to remind Henderson of what they had seen together, and the significance of physical features on the conduct of these particular engagements. Thus when commenting on Henderson's Chapter IX, which dealt with the battles of Cross Keys and Port Republic, he was able to identify the bridge across North River by saying, "just where we crossed it when at Port Republic last Summer."[25]

It was not just the topographical detail that Hotchkiss corrected in his commentary; he was forthright in his statements as to the reliability of others. He commended Colonel Kelley's account of the Port Republic battle as being "a thoroughly accurate account of what happened," and advised Henderson to make his narrative agree with Kelley's statements.[26] On the other hand when, after reading an article in *Battles and Leaders*, Henderson asked the question, "Is General Imboden to be trusted?" Hotchkiss replied, "I do not like to say that my friend is unreliable; and yet the truth of the matter is that his statements will not bear the tests of criticism. He mixes dates, and states, as things done, events that happened long afterwards....He writes from a confused memory and never takes the trouble of verifying his statements by a reference to documents."[27] His severest criticism was reserved for Kyd Douglas, "the most unreliable of all the men who indulge in writing war recollections. He does not pay the slightest regard to the truth of history if he can, in any way, bring in Douglas himself as a prodigy....Douglas was very well sized up by a Pullman Car Conductor, not long ago, who asked me if I knew Col. Douglas—'The gentleman on whose staff Stonewall Jackson served.'"[28] By contrast Hotchkiss went to great lengths to ensure the accuracy of his recollections whenever his diary was incomplete. He had a long correspondence with General Thomas Taylor Munford to determine just where and when they met after the Port Republic battle, finally concluding that Munford was right and he was wrong.[29] Munford said of him, "Every now and then he finds that things don't fit and then he is honest enough to rub out and write it correctly."[30] There was a steady correspondence between Hotchkiss and almost anyone who could throw some light on battlefield incidents, or on Jackson's character, skills, and methods: Dr. Hunter Holmes McGuire and the Reverend Robert Lewis Dabney, both of whom had been on Jackson's staff; the Rev. Dr. J. W. Jones; the Rev. Dr. James R. Graham, with whom Jackson had lodged at Winchester, and who described Jackson as "the one great military general that our late Civil War produced"; General Fitzhugh Lee; and many others.

If there was a portion of the Valley Campaign of 1862 which fascinated Hotchkiss above all others, it was the concluding phase at Cross Keys and Port Republic. As we have seen, he played an important part in ensuring success. But he had been given vital tasks almost daily since the Valley campaign opened, so why did he give so much attention to these particular battles? Perhaps, simply, because they concluded the most intense period of activity he had ever experienced, followed by a month of calm, quiet work at the drawing board, a time for reflection. Was it the realization that disaster had been averted, not by Jackson's skill, but by chance, by God's mercy as Hotchkiss and his general surely believed? Whatever the reason Hotchkiss went to some lengths to establish what happened on that Sunday morning when the Federals had rushed into Port Republic, and Jackson and his staff raced for their lives, Hotchkiss roused the wagon train, and Carrington and Moore drove the enemy out. Not only did he seek accounts from participants of both armies, he wrote to his friend David Humphreys, then at the U.S. Geological Survey, for a map of the area to assist his memory of roads and lanes leading from the village.[31] When the sculptor, Valentine, came to Staunton to "look over the ground...for the equestrian statue of 'Old Jack'," Hotchkiss wanted it to be placed near Port Republic "where with a sweep of his long arm he ordered me to take Gen. Taylor around and take that battery."[32]

Henderson was grateful for the assistance given by Hotchkiss, frequently apologizing for the inconvenience and trouble he must be causing. Equally as frequently Hotchkiss would make such a reply as: "Please ask all the questions you care to ask without apologizing, I like to answer questions."[33] The questions and answers, draft chapters and copious comment, printer's proofs and corrections, flowed to and fro, until the great work was finished in 1897.[34] No author could have been better served.

Only a few could relive the heroic years by writing about them; the majority indulged their memories when they met their former comrades in the course of their daily pursuits, or through the more formal occasions of the memorial associations, the meetings of Confederate veterans, the celebration of Lee's birthday, and similar events. Hotchkiss took a part in these, and, in 1896, helped to found the Stonewall Jackson Camp No. 25 of Confederate Veterans in Staunton.[35]

Participation in the activities of the Camp provided an opportunity for Hotchkiss to indulge his romantic interest in the lost cause. His assistance to Henderson encouraged him to give serious consideration to writing of his experiences. For a long time he had collected material for such a project. In the summer of 1891 he was corresponding with Major Samuel J. C. Moore about the Port Republic battle. Hotchkiss asked Moore to send his account of the Federal raid in which Jackson was nearly captured, saying, "I am still gathering information, which I hope to have in my power to use some time in the near future in writing out my remembrances of Jackson's Valley Campaign." He also said that he did not know whether he would ever find the time to do so because he allowed himself "to get entangled first in one thing and then in another in trying to develop the resources of our old Commonwealth."[36] In addition to describing his own life as a topographical engineer with the Army of Northern Virginia, he wished to write about the 1864 campaign of Jubal Early which had not received the attention its audacity deserved. Unfortunately he did neither, but he was asked to author one of the series of volumes of the Confederate Military History edited by Gen. Clement A. Evans. In May 1897 he agreed to write volume III, *Virginia*, of the *Confederate Military History*, for the sum of $500 payable on delivery of the manuscript not later than the end of the year.[37] It was an impossible date to meet and, although Hotchkiss had by then collected together most of the material he required, it was not until January 1898 that he made a start on the narrative.[38] There followed much irritable correspondence between Hotchkiss and the publishers, interspersed with encouraging and appreciative letters from the editor, before the last of the manuscript was sent at the end of September. By this time the relationship between author and publisher had deteriorated to such a degree that Hotchkiss arranged for Adams Express to certify the date and hour of its dispatch and of delivery, to establish his adherence to the revised agreement drawn up in the previous August.[39]

It must have saddened Hotchkiss that this opportunity to pay tribute to the men of the Army of Northern Virginia should have been marred by bickering over the "impossible demands" of the publisher's business manager. The publisher required each chapter as soon as written and frequently pressed for delivery before Hotchkiss was satisfied with his work. Fortunately, judging by the result, these demands seem to have been frustrated by the combined efforts of author and editor.

CHAPTER IX

Getting Coal to Tidewater

THE SALUTE OF a battery of the Norfolk Light Artillery Blues on March 17, 1883, signalled, not only the arrival of the first carload of Pocahontas coal in the tidewater city of Norfolk, Virginia, but also the beginning of the great coal and coke industry of the western Virginias. It signalled, too, a significant shift in Hotchkiss' life. Hitherto he had worked mainly on his own or in short term collaboration with a few other independent men. He had not been employed by a large organization since being paroled in 1865. From now on, although he would still be involved in many individual schemes, more of his time would be devoted to the interests of organized groups of investors seeking profits from the coal deposits of the Ohio basin. Increasingly his skills were used in the development of these coalfields and in projects to carry the coal to the Eastern seaboard. He was to serve as promoter, director, consultant engineer, or manager of surveys in a number of coal land associations and railroad enterprises. Inevitably he was drawn into the politics of these organizations, the rivalries, the conflicting interests of different groups of investors, and the problems and idiosyncracies of colleagues and subordinates. As a result, his personal qualities came to be valued by his associates as highly as his technical knowledge and skills.

When the crazy new-town boom afflicted Virginia at the end of the '80s, Hotchkiss became enthusiastically involved, and attempted to harness that sudden outburst of speculative energy to further the larger purposes of coal extraction and transportation.

The roles he played during that period are well illustrated by his work for the Gauley, and the Guyandot Coal Land Associations, (just two of the half dozen he worked for,) the new town of Shendun, and the Virginias Railway Company.

With the opening of the C&O railroad in 1871, coal mining developed along the banks of the Kanawha, New River, and their tributaries. Of the latter the most significant was the Gauley; this drained a considerable territory of coal and timber lands north of New River which it joined to form the Kanawha. The ease with which coal could be extracted and transported in the vicinity of the railroad, in contrast with the difficulty of navigation on the Gauley, had left the Gauley's basin virgin forest. In 1890 Hotchkiss was actively involved in its development. His associates in this enterprise were his close Staunton friends, Henderson Moffett Bell and Richard H. Catlett, together with M. Erskine Miller, also of Staunton, and James Herbert Bramwell of New York. This group raised sufficient funds from investors in Boston, New York, and Philadelphia to begin to purchase tracts underlaid with good quality coal. They created the Gauley Coal Land Association with Hotchkiss as Manager of Surveys as well as a member of its board. At this time it was often referred to as the "Fay Association," after its most prominent investor, H. H. Fay of Boston, so distinguishing it from another association, the Gauley Coking Coal Land, or Robinson Association. The two organizations co-operated closely, eventually merging, and adopting the title Gauley Coal Land Association.[1]

That enterprise differed from other associations (e.g. the Guyandot Association) in which Hotchkiss had an interest in a number of respects, most importantly in not having close railroad connections, either financially or on the ground. Because without a railroad, exploitation of the coal and timber would be impossible, much of the work of that organization consisted of attempts to bring tracks into its territory. Once the survey work was under way, Hotchkiss not only sought the attention of the roads operating within reasonable distance of the Association's lands, but seriously considered the possibility of a road constructed just to carry coal from the Gauley region directly to the eastern seaboard. In November 1890, when Hotchkiss and his colleagues were negotiating with the Pennsylvania Railroad for the construction of a road from Mathias Point, to the coalfield and thence to link with the Kanawha & Michigan Railroad, they hired Professor Israel C. White to study both possibilities.[2] The following spring Hotchkiss approached President Melville E. Ingalls of the C&O to discuss the development of the lands between the New and Gauley Rivers.[3] The annual trip of the C&O directors provided a convenient opportunity for the meeting, but neither side was persuaded of the benefits of a co-operative venture. Nor was there a satisfactory response from the Pennsylvania Railroad. In Hotchkiss' view their proposals "would hand our region over to the C&O, a thing we wish to avoid as that road has never been a good one to promote mining industries."[4]

Moving south toward the same region was another important figure in the development of West Virginia's natural wealth, Johnson Newlon Camden, lawyer, land speculator, pioneer of the West Virginia oil industry, coal and railroad magnate, and former United States Senator. During the late 80's he had acquired control of a number of small narrow-guage railroads and consolidated them as the West Virginia & Pittsburgh Railroad.[5] Camden planned to convert the existing roads to standard guage and to extend them southwards from their present termini at Weston and Buckhannon by a switch-back route up the Cherry River into the land managed by the Gauley Coal Land Association and so provide a northerly outlet for coal and timber. These activities were welcomed by Hotchkiss who was particularly pleased with Camden's letter, August 18, 1891, enclosing a map and describing his plans. In reply Hotchkiss described the Gauley area as "undoubtedly the bonanza of the present time in West Virginia." He did not intend to rest content until that region was connected to deep water, and he was therefore anxious to meet with Camden to talk over a number of matters which he did not care to write about, but would discuss in private.[6] An opportunity for discussion occurred in October when Hotchkiss joined Camden's private train at Huntington to take him to Wheeling and Fairmont. After a day examining the Monagah mines, he went with Camden to Weston, over his new road, and then to Buckhannon. Thus he had plenty of opportunity to discuss Gauley matters, as well as to learn of the progress of Camden's railroad and his thoughts about its future route. The road was in operation to Braxton Court House and graded to Lane's Bottom (which name Camden immodestly changed to Camden-on-Gauley), where he intended to construct a saw mill capable of producing 40 million feet of timber a year. Camden had "about decided to extend his road down to the mouth of Cherry and thence across over to Marlinton by way of that river." It was possible, thought Hotchkiss, that the next year would see semi-bituminous coal being shipped out from Gauley mines.⁷

In contrast with those discussions was his detailed work as manager of surveys. No easy task in any circumstance, but made more difficult for him by three changes of engineers in as many years before one was found who could meet Hotchkiss' exacting standards. In spite of that turnover, it was in this work that his procedures reached their most sophisticated levels.

The first to hold the post was R. W. Harris, who had been working for the Guyandot C.L.A. That was something of a compassionate transfer; Hotchkiss thought that Harris' health would be improved in the higher regions of the Gauley.⁸ He was instructed to "begin a progress map on which you will plat, on a scale of 160 poles to an inch, each tract as soon as surveyed." He was to send a copy of this map to Hotchkiss weekly.⁹

The 1891 season opened with a number of changes in organization and personnel. Importantly, Hotchkiss decided to separate the surveying and cartographic functions. For the latter he engaged Frank Hamilton Anschutz, perhaps the best of all his mapmakers. Harris was replaced by E. W. Forster, a protege of Professor David C. Humphreys, and all was set for a good season's work. Indeed, in the twelve weeks to the first week in September, Forster's teams had surveyed the boundaries of 98 tracts of land totalling nearly 16,000 acres as well as about 26 miles of river.¹⁰

However, there were problems with the survey. One season was enough for Forster and he resigned at the end of the year. It was enough for Hotchkiss too. He told Humphreys, "I have been greatly disappointed in your Mr. Forster. He has proved himself unworthy of commendation."¹¹

In the new year Hotchkiss hired John Rapelje, a topographical engineer with the N&W.¹² The standard of work improved. On March 7, Hotchkiss described Rapelje's report for February, as being "in excellent shape."¹³ Hotchkiss sent him a map of the Gauley ruled with a grid of numbered squares, and suggested that Rapelje prepare a similar map "so that when you want to mention any particular thing you can say it is in a certain square. You can also make a little tracing of that particular square to locate anything by adding the name, etc." Although there were a few problems, and data was not processed as quickly as he would have liked, Hotchkiss found Rapelje a most excellent and energetic man. Under his direction 28,385 acres were surveyed up to May 7.¹⁴ By September they had surveyed over 150,000 acres in three seasons. In addition to mapping the boundaries of individual tracts, they ran lines to establish their relative disposition. Hotchkiss instructed Rapelje to make stream and road surveys, advising him to take advantage of the low water conditions in October to do the more difficult work. To the trustees, he explained that the surveys would permit the construction of a more accurate map of the region which he believed would be of great advantage to the Association. By the close of the season Hotchkiss told them, "I have never been able to accomplish more with a proportionate force, in the same length of time, and consider the Association is under many obligations to Supt. Rapelje and his assistants for what has been accomplished."[15] At the end of January, he wrote to Rapelje, "Thanks for your admirably gotten up report of operations of 1892," which showed that 358 tracts totalling 92,144 acres (144 square miles) had been surveyed, involving 1,130 miles of line being run at a cost of $15,217 or 16.5 cents per acre.[16] In that season Rapelje managed to survey more land than had been accomplished in the two previous seasons taken together. He was a highly experienced topographical engineer who, nevertheless, listened to and acted on Hotchkiss' instructions. Hotchkiss demonstrated his confidence in him by reversing the earlier policy of separating surveying and mapping functions, and sent Anschutz to Rapelje's headquarters to work up the surveyors' field notes.

When Hotchkiss said that he was determined to find a way to move Gauley coal and coke to deep water, he was not making small talk, but was being carried away on the wave of enthusiasm which had broken hysterically along the western mountains of Virginia at the end of the eighties. Suddenly, after decades of half-hearted attention to the potential of Virginia's natural wealth, people were falling over themselves to invest, not just in new enterprises, but in new towns. The efforts of Hotchkiss, and others who shared his vision of a vital Virginia industry based on iron and coal, at last seemed about to be rewarded. The railroads had led the way, particularly the N&W. The development in a matter of a few years of the village of Big Lick (the junction of the Shenandoah Valley road with the N&W), into the city of Roanoke, with its iron works and machine shops, and a population of 15,000 in 1888, provided the example for other settlements up and down the Valley. Not that an existing village was necessary to make a start. Buena Vista, taking its name from the charcoal furnace not far away, sprang up from a greenfield site. Other places—Glasgow, Clifton Forge, Basic City, (Waynesboro)—all competed with each other to attract investors and industry, each claiming itself to be the city of the future. Naturally, Staunton, as the most prominent town in the Valley, was not to be left out of that feverish movement toward wealth, nor was Hotchkiss who had done so much to prepare the way. Under the chairmanship of M. Erskine Miller there was formed the Staunton Development Company, whose board of directors included Henderson M. Bell and Jedediah Hotchkiss, to develop land east, north, and west of the town. Hotchkiss did not stay long, partly because of differences with the management, but mainly because he became more deeply involved with another enterprise, The Grottoes Company.[17]

At the foot of the Blue Ridge, on the east bank of the Shenandoah, the Norfolk & Western railroad passed through a settlement of farms and houses called Liola. Its claim to fame was Weyer's cave which Hotchkiss had first visited in 1848. That cave had long been famous, the Valley Railroad located a few miles to the west, had made excursions to it easier, and now in the '80s it had a railroad and hotel almost alongside it. The railroad did not adopt the local name, but more appropriately called their halt The Grottoes. Between the river and the railroad was a stretch of level land. To the east of the road rose the spurs of the Blue Ridge, between two of these was Mount Vernon Furnace, as well as a way over the Ridge by Brown's Gap. It was a place ripe for development both as a site for industry and as a tourist center.

The promoters of a scheme to build a town there included Bell, Catlett, Bramwell, and Randall, who were already investors in the Gauley associations; and A. D. Wright of Charlottesville. By April 1890 their plans were well advanced. Hotchkiss arranged for Professor Humphreys to supervise the surveying, marking lots, and mapping of 1,200 acres of the site.[18] The Grottoes Company was formally organized on May 6, 1890, with Hotchkiss president, and his son-in-law, Allan M. Howison, secretary.[19] The following day its General Manager, Frank E. Randall of New York, issued Circular No. 1, offering for sale 15,000 shares, having a par value of $100 per share, at $50 per share. These could be secured by a down payment of a mere $5, the balance to be paid off by nine monthly instalments. Although the prospectus was not issued until July 14, already local people had subscribed for $50,000 worth of stock before the middle of May, and Hotchkiss was confident of an early placement of all the stock.[20] By the end of July the mapping had made good progress and Hotchkiss expected the laying out of streets to go ahead rapidly.[21] He was already thinking about organizing an electric power company to be in operation as soon as wanted.[22] The subscription books were closed on September 19, and the allotment of business and residence lots to each of the subscribers who held five shares or multiples thereof was made on October 14. Hotchkiss, delighted with this occasion, wrote, "Everything passed off pleasantly and everyone is satisfied with the results. I am quite sure the management is. We sold 200 lots and received an average of about $640 a lot....Everything is active and there is no doubt that we will make this one of the most prosperous and attractive places in all the South."[23]

Hotchkiss' *Spring Report of the Conditions of The Grottoes Co.* addressed to the stockholders legitimately claimed substantial progress; 1,025 acres had been laid out in lots for the business portion of the town, now called Shendun, 51 miles of streets and alleys had been graded in the business district, and several miles of streets bordering the 600-villa lots were nearly completed. There was in operation 2.66 miles of street railway, with a bridge of sufficient size and strength under construction to carry it across South River toward the caves.[24] The foundations for the electric light and power plant, built from stone quarried on the company's land, were in place, two brickworks were in operation or near completion, and the largest carpentry shop in the state was busily at work. A brush and broom factory was expected, as was one designed to manufacture plaster. A paper, the *Shendun News*, printed on modern presses, had been published weekly since the end of October. In all, over a dozen industries were operating or would soon be doing so in the new town of Shendun. The correspondent of the *Rockingham Register*, who made a visit there in March, was "utterly astonished at the progress made since last fall." He had been rather skeptical as to the future of Shendun, but after one visit he felt assured it had a great future.[25] His optimism was shared by a committee of Lynchburg stockholders who examined the property and the books of The Grottoes Company and reported it to be "in fine condition, its Managers alive to the interests of the stockholders, economical in expenses, prudent in making investments, and giving the very best attention to all the different operations of the company."[26]

What, then, happened between March and September to transform the situation to one presaging ultimate failure? It seems that stockholders defaulted on their subscriptions, or on their payments for lots, or both. This reluctance to pay up was due to a strongly held belief that the promoters of the company held an undue proportion of the assets. In August, Hotchkiss called for a meeting of stockholders to be convened to settle the question and, if desired, to form a new management to "take steps for the prompt collection of the sums due."[27] In spite of the promoters relinquishing a substantial part of their interest, the stockholders voted in a new board and ended Hotchkiss' presidency. His successor was Edmund S. Ruffin, a lawyer from Norfolk, grandson of Edmund Ruffin, Virginia's distinguished agriculturist.[28] Undoubtedly Hotchkiss was greatly upset by this turn of events, but, faced with losing his office in any case, he accepted Ruffin as a good choice, as one who had done a great deal to reconcile discordant elements.

That harmony between the promoters and the new management did not last. Some features of the agreement reached at the beginning of September could not be realized by the promoters within the 30 days required. This was not due to any lack of will on the part of Hotchkiss and his friends, but to the complicated network of ownership of the assets involved. Ruffin threatened to sue. In a letter to a stockholder, who had played a prominent part in achieving the compromise, Hotchkiss wrote in December, "I am very much surprised at Mr. Ruffin's conduct in this matter. He took office only on the condition that we would harmoniously work with him for the general good and now he becomes the leader of a band of delinquents in an attempt not only to damage us but to destroy the assets of The Grottoes Company."[29] Hotchkiss was so disturbed by the state of the affairs of the company that he circularized the stockholders seeking support for a change in both management and policy. He reminded them he was one of the largest stock and lot holders in The Grottoes Company, and owner of a substantial interest in the Mount Vernon Iron property, thus interested in the prosperity of Shendun. If stockholders shared his concern, they were invited to send him their proxy for the forthcoming annual general meeting. His circular brought a vitriolic response from Ruffin. In the letter notifying stockholders of the meeting, he referred to the "insidious attack on the management and the contemptible appeal" for votes; for those who were present at the September meeting he thought it would "only cause a smile of derision."[30] Hotchkiss did not want to be president, but he was prepared to be a member of a small board of local people.[31]

Ruffin planned to return to his law practice, so a change of leadership was inevitable after the annual meeting on May 26, 1892. The new president was J. W. Rumple. Hotchkiss' reaction was that Shendun had "once again fallen into the hands of the Philistines."[32]

One of the practical problems which hindered progress was the absence of a general manager. At the insistence of New York stockholders, Frank E. Randall had been appointed to this position, but, from the start Randall was reluctant to exercise his duties. This had little effect while Hotchkiss performed much of the day-to-day management in his usual energetic style, but after his removal from the board the need for a general manager became increasingly clear. At the 1892 annual meeting, Hotchkiss unsuccessfully proposed Edmund C. Pechin for president, but now he took extraordinary steps to secure his appointment as General Manager. Pechin had recently resigned from the Virginia Development Company, which he had been looking after on behalf of E. W. Clark & Co., and was just such a man as Hotchkiss wanted to take care of matters at Shendun. Because The Grottoes Company could not pay the sort of salary Pechin had a right to expect, Hotchkiss suggested that individual stockholders should contribute to raise $2,500 as part of the salary, the company contributing a similar amount, contingent upon satisfactory service by Pechin.[33] Both Pechin and the board approved of the idea, and by the end of August he was appointed General Manager.

It was a shortlived appointment, for the stockholders failed to meet their obligations and in November Pechin resigned having accomplished nothing. This was the final attempt to breathe life into The Grottoes Company, but it did not mean that Hotchkiss was ready to abandon Shendun altogether. He owned lots in the town; more importantly, of the 30,000 acres originally controlled by The Grottoes Company, 25,000 was formerly the Mount Vernon tract in which he had a substantial interest. All but the 57 acres lying to the west of the Norfolk & Western R.R. were taken back by Hotchkiss and his associates in the settlement of the dispute between the stockholders and the promoters. Hotchkiss needed Shendun to succeed if he was to do anything with the Mount Vernon tract. If a railroad was built through Shendun he had little doubt that its prosperity would be as great as that of any town in the Valley, not even excepting Roanoke.[34]

In January 1892, while the promoters were still arguing with the board of The Grottoes Company over progress of the settlement, a charter for a new railroad company was on the desk of Governor McKinney.[35] The incorporators were Miller, Hotchkiss, Bell, and Catlett. The charter provided for the construction of a railway from any point on or between the York and Potomac Rivers to the West Virginia line. To build the road another company was organized under a separate charter. Much of the year was devoted to setting up that construction company, and negotiating a contract between it and the Chesapeake, Shendun, & Western Railroad (CS&WRR), as the new road was called. Hotchkiss hoped that a road could be built eastward from the West Virginia line through Harrisonburg, to Shendun, pass over the Blue Ridge at Brown's Gap, eventually reaching tidewater at Gloucester Point on the York River.

Within West Virginia, Hotchkiss had to depend upon existing railroads to make the coalfield connection. There were two roads which might be persuaded to do this; Camden's WV&P, and H. G. Davis' West Virginia Central & Pittsburgh railroad. In May 1892, Hotchkiss accepted an invitation from Davis to travel over his road and inspect the coalfields it served, but nothing emerged from this contact to further the interests of the CS&W.[36] Hotchkiss vigorously pursued the Camden possibility.

He sent a map showing a possible extension of his road, and urged a meeting. Camden was willing to discuss the possibility, but his road was leased to the B&O so nothing could be done without the agreement of the management of that company. A direct approach to them failed to achieve the desired conference, partly because the company was too busy restructuring after the acquisition of other railroads, but, more importantly, because of the economic situation.[37]

History was repeating itself. Just as the panic of 1873 frustrated Hotchkiss' attempts to develop coal and iron enterprises along the line of the C&O, the depression of 1893 postponed the development of the Gauley coalfields, and put an end to the Virginia new-town boom. In May, he reluctantly agreed with Camden that little could be done "while financial matters are so disturbed."[38] To John W. Blackburn, stockholder of The Grottoes Company, and soon to be one of its receivers, Hotchkiss wrote, "the times are badly out of joint. All the railways are curtailing their expenses and it is not possible to get them to consider anything new at this time."[39] Nevertheless Hotchkiss was reluctant to give up trying. He was, in fact, so optimistic about the future that he considered a conference with the B&O was worthwhile, if only to learn what that railroad might be disposed to do when the business outlook improved.[40] When, in June, James Bruce, a London financier, showed interest in the construction of the CS&W, it seemed to justify Hotchkiss' view of the temporary nature of the recession, a view he continued to hold throughout the year, fully expecting a great revival of industry in the coming spring.[41] To M. A. Miller, he wrote at the beginning of 1894, "I think there is a decided improvement in prospects and it looks as though now the clouds would break and business resume its ordinary condition."[42] Bruce must have thought the same, for he came to New York and asked for a meeting with Hotchkiss and his associates. Armed with maps, reports, and a letter from Camden assuring him that the WV&P would meet the CS&W at the head of Cherry River, Hotchkiss met Bruce early in April for what seemed to be a promising conference.[43] He returned believing that there was a fair prospect of having something done in the near future.[44] Nothing came of those negotiations and the CS&W was never built as originally envisaged.

By early 1897 the possibility of a road from the Gauley field to tidewater seems to have been abandoned and thoughts were turning strongly to the financially less demanding task of a link with Camden's road. The Gauley Association had now been in existence some seven years, and the stockholders had yet to see some return on their investment. What they did see was a continuing drain through interest payments and taxes on unproductive land. A railroad down Cherry

River to join with the West Virginia & Pittsburgh at the confluence with Gauley River was seen by the Boston investors as a last chance to preserve the property, which otherwise would have to be sold to pay the taxes.[45] On the other hand if they were to be asked for further investment to make a railroad possible they wanted adequate security. Hotchkiss in co-operation with Bell and Catlett put forward proposals which he believed would satisfy the Boston stockholders, but at the same time safeguard his own interests.[46] Hotchkiss was unable to be at the board meeting on February 9, and perhaps for that reason the meeting achieved nothing. The New York and Philadelphia stockholders refused to put any money into the railroad scheme and the Boston men were unable to put up the whole amount needed. Fay considered affairs to be in a critical condition and telegraphed Catlett to come to Boston to help sort matters out before the annual general meeting arranged for February 23. Fay was sick and other influential Boston men were going away. Catlett was not fit enough to travel and Hotchkiss went in his place.[47]

With stockholders widely dispersed in Boston, New York, Philadelphia, and Staunton, concerted action was difficult to achieve. Furthermore there was plenty of opportunity for misunderstandings to arise, a questioning of motives, and lack of trust. A letter to Hotchkiss written shortly after the annual meeting expressed the feelings of the Philadelphia investors.

> I am firmly convinced that the Gauley Co. will get the railroad...and from our Philadelphia sentiment there is no trouble in getting 50,000 to 75,000 or more subscribed here, but no one likes the temper of the Boston men and they think they may as well cool down a little—you know no one cares particularly about having pins stuck into them, nor to be driven about like a pig and the disposition shown at the late meetings in Boston has been anything but pleasant.[48]

That pettiness was extended to Hotchkiss. No longer would he receive any compensation for the use of his office on behalf of the Gauley Association, and Fay instructed that all the reports of Superintendent Rapelje, the engineer working in the field under Hotchkiss, would henceforth be sent direct to him. An impossible situation. Erskine Miller resigned from the board, and there was an expectation among the Boston members that Hotchkiss would follow. Had he done so, the Association would have lost the one man who had the knowledge to further the development of its property.

Hotchkiss' efforts prior to that annual meeting averted a complete breakdown, and real progress was made during the succeeding months toward the building of a railroad down Cherry River. That was to be achieved by the Cherry River Railroad Company financed jointly by the Gauley Association and the Camden interests. By July sufficient progress had been made to permit Hotchkiss to invite Camden's land agent, Mr. R. W. Kelley, to visit Superintendent Rapelje and ride over the proposed line of the road.[49] That invitation was in time to revive Camden's interest. He had been ready for some time to extend his road down the Gauley toward Cherry River, but the slowness of the Gauley Association had sapped his confidence, and he had been thinking of withdrawing from the railroad project altogether. The truth was that Camden had difficulties of his own, otherwise he would have been pushing the Gauley people to get on with a project which would have brought much needed revenues to his West Virginia & Pittsburgh Railroad. His problem was that this road was leased to the B&O which itself had gone into receivership in 1896. So in spite of Hotchkiss' successful efforts to persuade the disparate factions of the Gauley Association to work together to make possible a link with Camden's road, 1897 passed without any written agreement to practical action. In the spring of 1898 Camden's road passed into the hands of the receiver, delaying matters still further, and it wasn't until January 12, 1899, that Camden was able to tell Hotchkiss that the B&O had decided to finance the construction of an extension from Camden-on-Gauley to the mouth of Cherry and a branch up that river toward the Gauley coal.[50] When this letter reached Staunton, Hotchkiss was already desperately ill, and probably never knew that his efforts were about to bear fruit.

At the southern edge of the coal field, the N&W did not cross Flat Top Mountain as early as Hotchkiss or the Clarks expected. Apparently Kimball was content to await the progress of other roads that were being planned to enter the area from a northerly direction. It was not until 1886 that they acted, and instead of climbing the escarpment by way of Crane's Creek, they drove a 3,100-foot tunnel through the coal seam to reach the Elkhorn, a northerly flowing tributary of Tug Fork. That choice effectively negated the early development of the property of the Trans-Flat Top Land Association. Surprisingly it did not deter Hotchkiss, in consort with others, from gaining control of some 60,000 acres of this and adjacent land.

Having reached the Elkhorn, the obvious way to the Ohio was by way of Tug Fork and Big Sandy River, the present route of the N&W, and similar to one that was being considered in 1884. Two years earlier the N&W and Shenandoah Valley railway companies had established a Bureau of Mining Intelligence for the purpose of assessing "the probable amount, quality and value of traffic" the two roads might carry.[51] The Bureau hired Mr. Andrew S. McCreath, chemist to the State Geological Survey of Pennsylvania, to report on the mineral wealth of the territory traversed by the railroads. His second enlarged and revised report of 1884 devoted 24 pages to the Flat Top coal field, and included a map showing the current and possible future routes of the N&W. This map shows that after breaching the mountain in the vicinity of Peter's Gap two routes were under consideration from the headwaters of the Guyandot; one leading to the Kanawha, the other toward Tug Fork and the Big Sandy river.[52]

In the spring of 1888, Hotchkiss reported that N&W engineers were at Louisa to begin a survey up the Big Sandy. He told Mr. Clark that he could not believe for one moment that the railroad company "contemplated the construction of a line down the barren Big Sandy Valley...when it has open to it the rich Guyandot Valley."[53] Both the Big Sandy and Guyandot Rivers were navigable over many miles from their confluence with the Ohio, a fact which had made for such easy access to the timber that much of the forest had already been destroyed. Because of this, Kimball not only abandoned the Big Sandy route, but also the one down the Guyandot River, choosing instead to reach the Ohio by way of Twelve Pole Creek, which dissected the high ground between the other two rivers. That creek was not navigable, and flowed through forests not yet exploited by lumbermen. Its timber could provide an immediate return on the capital expended in the construction of a railroad. Kimball concluded to drive his road along the Tug Fork as far as Pigeon Creek, and thence by Laurel Creek and a tunnel to the West Fork of Twelve Pole. By taking this middle route he believed he would be in the best position to take advantage of the coal and timber resources found in any part of the vast area drained by the three rivers.[54]

About the same time as Kimball was deciding the route of the Ohio extension, Hotchkiss received a telegram telling him that his old friend Hale had secured an option on a large body of land along the Guyandot, but was in need of immediate financial help if he was to hold on to it. Hotchkiss contacted E. W. Clark. To both men this seemed a chance too good to miss, and each put up $5,000 to acquire the option from Abriel A. Low to purchase the so-called Low and Aspinwall tract, 200,000 acres of land lying between the Guyandot and Twelve Pole Creek.[55] They intended to create a coal land association to exploit the coal and timber reserves by the means which had been so successful in the Flat Top region. The first task was for Hotchkiss to set about

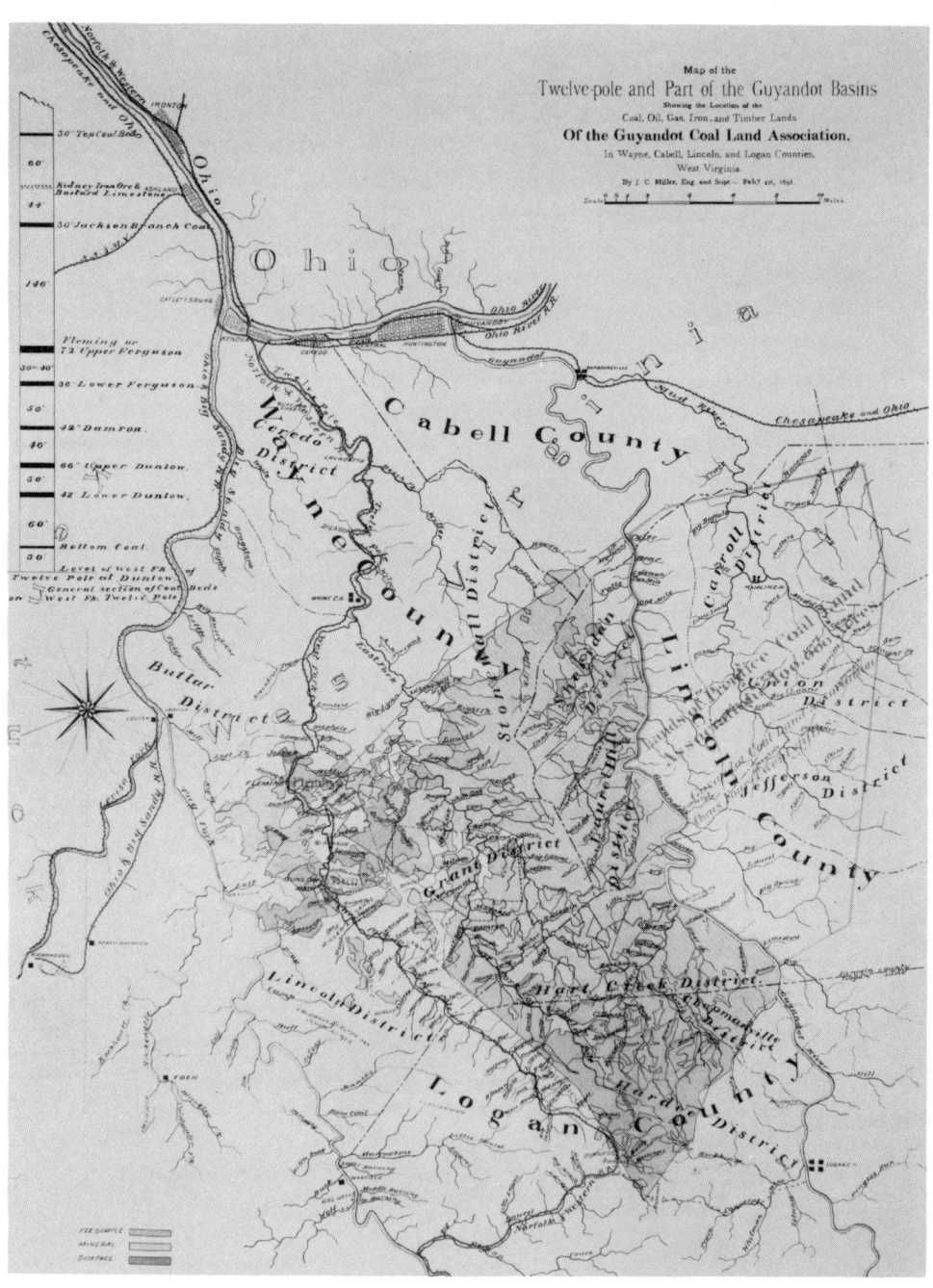

Map of the lands of the Guyandot Coal Land Association. It shows that the Guyandot Valley would have been a more suitable route for a railroad than the west fork of Twelve Pole Creek chosen by the N&W.

Hotchkiss Papers, Box 39, Library of Congress

exploring and mapping the tract. To assist in this he wrote to Charles Eddy, vice-president of the N&W, requesting a tracing of the map of Twelve Pole Creek which had been made following the survey for the railroad extension.[56] He inquired of Professor I. C. White what was known about the geology of the area; particularly Hotchkiss wanted to know about the three or four coal beds that had been reported. Hotchkiss invited White to accompany him on trips through the Guyandot-Twelve Pole region.[57] By the end of April 1889 Hotchkiss' map was at the printers.[58] It showed what both he and Clark already knew, that the mineral resources could be exploited most easily by the building of a railroad up the Guyandot. A railroad alongside the right fork of Twelve Pole Creek would pass through land beyond the western boundary of the Low and Aspinwall tract. Hotchkiss had earlier asked Clark about the prospects for the building of such a road as was proposed by the Huntington & Guyandotte Railroad Company: "You will do me a special favor if you can give me some encouragement about a road up Guyandot River from the Ohio. You informed me when last I saw you that you thought some 40 miles of that road would be made this year."[59]

The explorations with Professor White in May were not encouraging. After "three days of very hard riding—40 miles a day on horseback," Hotchkiss confided his disappointment to Hale; the report about the coal beds was, he said, "*utterly false.*" There was coal there, but not in the condition hoped for. He concluded that they would "have to spend a good deal before we know where we stand."[60] Hotchkiss engaged Harris to make a detailed survey of the coal beds and open them up for inspection. In the meantime he did not intend to reveal his concern to Clark. Indeed, on the same day as he wrote to Hale he told Clark that fuller information would be available from Harris' explorations. "Hope you will have the opportunity to introduce this 'big thing' to Mr Ingalls," the president of the C&O railroad.[61] But Professor White's report contained so little useful information that Hotchkiss suggested to White that he should recall the report and issue a new one following an examination which they would make of the tract after Harris' work was completed.[62] Clark was concerned, and in spite of an enthusiastic report from Hotchkiss, based on Harris' later investigations, he was ready to change his plans. Instead of setting up a Guyandot Coal Land Association on the Flat Top model, he now favored dividing and selling the tract in parts.[63] However, a few months later, influenced as much by Hotchkiss' optimism as by the survey results, he reverted to the original proposal. On October 29, Hotchkiss replied to a letter from Clark: "I am pleased to learn that you have already begun a movement for getting our Guyandot-12 Pole lands into shape." He also said we "must do something quickly, not only in reference to the 200,000 acres but also to the securing of the lands between that and the 12-Pole (R.H.) before they go up with a railway in prospect. Contractors are already going along the line examining the location."[64] That statement reveals the extent of the knowledge which the two men had of the plans of the N&W.

By the end of the year arrangements were completed for the formation of the Guyandot Coal Land Association, financed by E. W. Clark & Co., which purchased the 200,000 acres from Hotchkiss on January 9, 1890, at a price of $600,000, $3 per acre.

Lambie in his history of the N&W suggested that the choice of the Twelve Pole Creek route was influenced by E. W. Clark's interest in the Guyandot Coal Land Association.[65] It is clear that this was not so; on the contrary, the Association's interest would have been much better served had the railroad been built along the Guyandot. By March 1890, subscribers to the Association were being asked to make a further 10% subscription to enable the purchase of more land to bring the holdings up to the expected line of the railroad.[66] The circumstances as they appeared to the Guyandot Coal Land Association were later described in its Fifth Annual Report, February 19, 1895:

> Immediately after the contract for the purchase of these lands was closed and the Association was organized, the Norfolk and Western decided to build this extension, but, to the great disappointment of the Association, so located its route as to make that road of very little advantage to the Low and Aspinwall tract, which had in, and on, it a great abundance of coal and timber, but mainly in the Guyandot and East Twelve-pole basins....
> Apprehensive that others would secure the lands along the railway and between it and your already purchased lands and so prevent their development and deprive the Association of anticipated revenues, purchases were promptly made on the line of the railroad, ...without having time for a careful examination of their mineral resources by the experts of the Association.[67]

It seems that the prospective shareholders were not informed of what its principal promoters had suspected from the time they had secured the option, and knew for certain months before the Association was formed. Such were the business ethics of the time.

At a point close to where it emerged from the tunnel, the railroad approached within 200 yards of the tract, but thereafter was rarely less than a mile from its southwestern boundary. Owners of the intervening land had the power to abstract the highest possible price for the right of way for the construction of branch lines to the tipples of the mines. When, in 1895, such a line was needed to enable another lease to be made near Dingess it cost the Association $28 per acre to acquire the essential 140 acres.[68]

In the first year, purchases of this kind cost the Association over $115,000, half that year's payment for the tract itself. By the end of 1894 over a quarter of a million dollars had been expended in an attempt to adjust to the route selected by the Norfolk & Western.[69] The managers of the Association had no alternative but to develop the tract and this they did with vigor. Even before the purchase was formally completed an approach had been made to J. Craig Miller inviting him to be the Association's chief engineer. He had assisted his father, Captain M. A. Miller, in work for the Trans-Flat Top Association, and was thought by Clark as "just the man for us."[70] In April 1890, a headquarter's site was selected on Twelve Pole Creek, named at Hotchkiss' suggestion, Dunlow, in honor of the previous owner of the Low and Aspinwall tract. Until the house and office were ready Craig operated first from Huntington, and later from Louisa, Kentucky, where the N&W had established an office for its engineers.[71]

The construction of the railroad largely determined the development of the property. That was started from both ends, the line coming south from Kenova being the first to approach the Association's land near a place to be called Flemming. It was around here that prospecting, mapping, and the acquisition of additional land was concentrated during 1890-91. The railroad reached Flemming in August of the latter year, but it was not until the following March that the mine there began to ship coal.[72] Nevertheless, Hotchkiss was optimistic. To Clark he wrote, "Things indicate that we are going to have a very lively season of it, and I think, with proper management, we can get ourselves in good shape during this season."[73] This optimism was as much due to the timber reports he was receiving from Craig as to the coal rumbling into Norfolk & Western cars from Toudy's tipple at Flemming. The sale of timber was a quick and relatively simple way of generating cash, as Kimball had emphasized earlier, so organizing the survey of the land and counting the trees on it was an important part of Craig Miller's job. Hotchkiss spent a good deal of time in the early months of 1892 instructing Craig how these tree counts should be reported. He needed the numbers of trees, classified by species and diameter, a map of the tract, as well as a description including its acreage. Hotchkiss was exacting in his demands, and critical of Craig's reports, pointing out errors in addition and some inadequate descriptions. Even after sending to Craig a specimen report, and expressing the hope that "you will see that your men get all other maps, tables, detailed timber reports &c. so they will be complete and tally with one another," he still found cause for complaint.[74] Indeed Craig never did complete his surveys to Hotchkiss' satisfaction.

Craig Miller had more than enough to do handling the survey teams, buying land, tracing coal outcrops, and looking after the problems of lessees operating coal mines. So when the Association was able to obtain the services of James F. Beattie, a 38-year old Scotsman, a mining engineer with experience as a mine superintendent, Hotchkiss was delighted. This man had been recommended by Professor White, which was recommendation enough. He was married, an accurate surveyor, a skillful draftsman, and as Hotchkiss told Clark, "Don't drink any and habits all good. I think you will find him a jewel as his intelligence is superior to most mine superintendents."[75] Telling Craig about the new mining engineer, Hotchkiss wrote, "I am pleased to learn that he is a good Presbyterian Elder, which is by no means an objection to those of us that believe in that way of getting to Heaven."[76]

So with good timber reports, the school house finished at Dunlow, an interest being shown in the coal at the southern end of the Association's land, a mine producing coal, and a promising mining engineer on the payroll, Hotchkiss seemed to have good reason to be optimistic. But the following month this mood changed. The results of drilling around Flemming were not encouraging, and in June Hotchkiss recommended that no more leases should be made in that area.[77]

In September of 1892 the Ohio extension of the N&W was completed so that traffic in coal was possible not only to the west and northwest, but all the way to the eastern seaboard. The failure of the mines around Flemming and Dunlow made the development of the seams near Dingess at the tunnel all the more important. There the Association would have fared better had not the recession of 1893 intervened. The Pearl Mining Company leased two adjacent tracts totalling 1,200 acres immediately north of the tunnel exit. The coal from their mine proved to be excellent, both as a gas coal, and as a locomotive fuel. At Hotchkiss' suggestion it was dispatched under the name of Logan coal.[78] In spite of the recession the demand for Logan coal was sufficient to require two-shift operation and Hotchkiss was seeking for mining all day and every day, bar Sundays, of course. Mr. Collins, who had operated the mine at Dunlow, had been foolish enough to work his miners on a Sunday. Hotchkiss had expressed his "disapprobation" and extracted a confession from him that he had done wrong. Relating this to Craig Miller, Hotchkiss wrote, "Please see to it that you have no such desecration of the Sabbath any more. Don't tolerate having stores or anything of that sort open on a Sunday. We cannot expect to have good order on our property if we tolerate any such doings, and you will have to take a determined stand in that direction."[79]

The recession made further economies necessary, and Beatty was soon being paid on a retainer basis.[80] By April 1894, the establishment at Dunlow had been reduced to just Craig and his clerk, David Laird.[81] Mr. Toudy's mine at Flemming had failed, partly due to the irregularity of the coal seam, but also from a lack of capital. At Dunlow the coal seam was split by a thick bed of fire clay. This potentially valuable deposit could not be utilized as was hoped, so the mining operations here also proved to be unprofitable.[82] Only the Logan coal showed real promise, but the absence of rights of way to the N&W tracks hampered development.

1894 had been one of the worst years on record for the coal trade, and during its closing months coal was being sold at prices far below the cost of mining and transportation. The accounts for that year showed that the Association was in considerable difficulty which only desperate measures could alleviate. The pressing need was for $59,000 to pay taxes, mortgage interest, and loans. The solution proposed was the creation of another company, later to be called the Mingo Coal Company, which would buy 9-10,000 acres of the Logan coalfield. From the proceeds of this sale enough cash could be generated to pay off the most pressing debts, while the mortgage on the remaining property would be renegotiated to yield yet more funds. By those means it was hoped that the Association could be kept in being until trade improved and the full potential of its lands could be realized. It took the whole of 1895 to put the complex financial package together, but it did not provide a permanent solution to the Association's problem which originated in the choice of Twelve Pole Creek, rather than the Guyandot River as the route to be followed by the N&W Railroad. The Association lingered on to the turn of the century.[83]

The Guyandot River had long provided a route into the Flat Top Mountain area; it was the obvious way to reach the coal-bearing lands owned by the Guyandot Association as well as those controlled by Hotchkiss. Indeed, half the area of land owned by the Guyandot C. L. A., two-thirds of that owned by the Flat Top C. L. A., and all of the Hotchkiss land, lay within the Guyandot basin.[84] As early as 1881 the Ohio & Guyandotte Railroad Company was chartered for the purpose of constructing a railway up the river, but never laid a single rail.[85] Seven years later, the Huntington & Guyandotte Railroad Company was chartered to build a road starting at or near Huntington and running up the Guyandot to the vicinity of Pineville. Construction depended upon Cabell County subscribing $50,000. While the people of Huntington were overwhelmingly in support, the country people were not.[86] The promoters were undeterred by that rebuff and continued to seek capital for the project. In the summer of 1892, Zachary Taylor Vinson, a promoter of this railroad, visited Hotchkiss and discussed the possible route of a railroad up the river starting from Barboursville, West Virginia, and to link with the C&O somewhere on New River. Hotchkiss wrote to the president of the C&O pointing out the significance of such a scheme. "I don't think there is any portion of the country anywhere in the vicinity of your lines that can contribute more than this."[87] Hotchkiss was optimistic enough to advise the Guyandot C.L.A. to purchase lands which would be valuable should the railroad be built up the river.[88] In February of the following year, he persuaded C&O officials to put their engineers to work extending the survey lines from New River across the divide to the Guyandot. The possibility of running the line all the way down the Guyandot to Barboursville was almost certainly talked about.[89] At that time it seemed that the C&O had ample capital to support such a development, but the financial crisis, which was just about to break, put a stop to their railroad-building plans.

The next serious attempt to construct a Guyandot railroad came in 1895 when a charter was granted to the Columbus, Huntington, & Guyandotte Railroad Company to build a road from Huntington up the river to Pineville. With an authorized capital of $2,700,000 that attempt was better positioned to achieve its objectives than previous schemes. In May, Henry Clay Ragland, editor of the *Logan County Banner*, chaired a meeting which was addressed by the promoters, and by General William G. Dacey, who described himself as the agent of a New York syndicate. The purpose of this meeting was to seek support for the proposal that each of the counties through which the road was to be built should subscribe $50,000 to the capital stock. General Dacey said that such a show of confidence was all that the parties he represented needed to guarantee the road's completion by the end of 1897.[90] Subsequently three of the four counties voted in favor of a subscription; only the voters of Lincoln county opposed the idea.[91] The following month approaches were made to C. W. Smith, formerly general manager of the C&O, to be the President of the railroad. The C&O had examined the Guyandot some years earlier, under his direction. At that time, he had recommended the building of a road up that river and now confidently believed "that had the road been built it would have been demonstrated that it was the best and most important feeder of any C&O connection."[92] A meeting of stockholders was convened early in November, and increased the authorized capital to $7,500,000, extended the route to the Virginia line, and changed the name of the company to the Virginias Railway Company. News of these developments was received with enthusiasm by the Guyandot C.L.A. The Annual Report for that year anticipated construction of the first thirty miles from Huntington and up the river to begin in the following spring. "It is probable," wrote the author, "that, sometime during 1896 this road will be open for traffic from the city of Huntington...up to, and for a considerable distance along, and through the lands of this Association...thus opening to lease, to the sale of timber, and to development, a large area of the Association's lands...." Hotchkiss shared this optimistic forecast, telling his friend Hale, "There is very little doubt but that the Virginias Railway up Guyandot will be constructed, the work beginning this year."[93]

The formation of this company meant that Hotchkiss became directly involved in one of the most ambitious schemes of his life, the creation of a railroad which would be in direct competition with the two giants who were moving coal in vast quantities from the New River and Flat Top coal fields.

It was not to be expected that these powerful interests would look kindly on the new company, but would use every resort open to them to frustrate the building of a third coal carrier. It would be difficult to obtain a charter for a railroad to the Virginia coast without attracting the attention of members of the Assembly friendly to the interests of the N&W and the C&O. However, through State Senator J. C. Green, Hotchkiss became aware of the Bland Land Co. charter, and thought this might provide a way of concealing the intentions of the new railroad, at least for a time. This charter allowed the company to build a railroad to connect any lands that it owned, so all that was necessary was for the company to purchase a piece of land at Norfolk, or elsewhere on the seaboard and connect this to another piece of land in Bland county not far from where the Virginias Railway would reach the state line. This charter to an obscure land company could be used as a means of avoiding the attention of "our friends the enemy."[94] The lawyers agreed that a small amendment would suffice to enable the Virginias Railroad to achieve its objects, and a bill was before the Virginia Senate in December.

The plan was nearly shipwrecked by a blunder in drawing up the bill; the existence of an amendment to the original charter had been ignored. Only some quick work by Hotchkiss, Green, and the lawyers, enabled the defective bill to be replaced and a new one put before the Senate committee on January 6. "That committee at once approved the new bill and [Senator Green] had it railroaded through the House on the 11th."[95] All that was now required was for the Bland Land Company to be acquired by the Virginias Railway Company.

This use of the Bland Land Co. charter was entirely the brainchild of Hotchkiss. He had no intention of allowing any one else to interfere, as he wrote Dacey: "I think you can safely leave in my hands all questions pertaining to charters and other matters in Virginia. I can secure what ever we need through my influential friends and by very moderate expenditure probably better than any other person."[96] When the bill went through, Hotchkiss sent his congratulations to Green, saying, "We are under obligations to you that I am sure will be properly appreciated both now and in the future."[97] Green was not seeking any immediate compensation for the aid he was giving to the Virginias Railway, but he did expect to be considered when contracts were being let for its construction. This was not the only bit of political intrigue which Hotchkiss induced Senator Green to engage in on behalf of the railroad.

There were others who owned lands in the Flat Top region or in the upper Guyandot basin which could not be developed until transport was available to move coal or timber. One of these was James T. McCreery. Seeking to achieve control over these lands, Hotchkiss invited McCreery to Staunton for a conference.[98] McCreery showed his lack of interest by replying that he wanted $50 per acre for his land, a suggestion which Hotchkiss said "fairly took [his] breath away." In his opinion, a figure in the region of $12-$15 would have been reasonable; but McCreery had his own plans.[99] He wanted to build thirty miles of railroad from Hinton to Pearisburg to form a link between the C&O and the N&W; from this he planned to build a branch into his lands in the Flat Top coal field. That was a veritable cat-among-the-pigeons of a proposal. It would bring the two major roads into competition, offering a choice of route to coal operators. To Hotchkiss and his friends it was a mixed blessing. In so far as they were concerned with the exploitation of the natural resources, they welcomed it, but as promoters of The Virginias Railroad it posed special problems. Hotchkiss had envisaged that his railroad would descend the Flat Top escarpment by just such a route as McCreery would take for his branch line. Both companies would be competing for rights of way on this section as well as along New River. In that situation it was essential for Hotchkiss to get survey teams on the ground as soon as possible, an action he took even before the formation of the Bland Land Company and its consolidation with the Virginias Railway. The other way to keep ahead was to use his friendship with Senator Green. McCreery's railroad, the Hinton, New River & Western, would have to cross the state line, requiring charters from both Virginia states. He already had one for the West Virginia portion, but was awaiting approval for the one covering the Virginia section. Senator Green delayed the passage of the requisite bill until Hotchkiss had his survey team in place. The situation was made even more complex by the family and business relationship of the lawyer acting for McCreery with the promoter of the Bland Land Company. Martin and Samuel Williams were brothers and partners in the law firm of Williams, Porterfield, and Williams of Pearisburg. Once Samuel became financially interested in the Virginias Railway, Martin could no longer act for McCreery.

The Bland Land Company charter was approved on January 13. On the 17th Hotchkiss was on his way to New York for a meeting with Smith and General Dacey arranged for the 21st. There he had hoped that the charter would be transferred to the railway company, but it was not to be. As he explained to Green,

> Judge Williams came and met us and the lawyers had their usual squabble, the upshot of which was that they drew up a new form of consolidation and the judge has to call another meeting of his stockholders to organize his company, and, as his charter called for a ten days notice about a meeting he had to advertise in the Bland paper. This in a measure will give us away, but I hope the judge will be prompt with his organization so we will lose no time.[100]

The Virginias Railway Company board meeting held next day decided to send a team of surveyors to secure the mountain passes and buy up the rights of way. Hotchkiss wasted no time. While in New York he arranged for Captain J. J. Stack to be in Hotchkiss' office at 8 a.m. the following Monday "to confer...about taking charge of a party to make some surveys along New River in Monroe Co. W.Va. and Giles Co. Va."[101] By the time this meeting took place, Hotchkiss had heard from McCreery that he expected his charter permitting extension of his road into Virginia to pass the General Assembly during the next week. "This," said McCreery, "together with the rights of way we have secured will give us the entire control of the route or line up New River to Pearisburg as well as our line right of way up Bluestone."[102] It was this news which prompted Hotchkiss to ask Green to delay the passage of McCreery's charter through the legislature. Captain Stack was on his way to Pearisburg with his team on the 29th with instructions to start work on the following day. When this proved to be impossible, Hotchkiss impatiently wanted to know the reason why. On that day he wrote to Stack,

I hope to hear from you this afternoon that you got off this morning and will be on the ground at the W. Va. line at about noon today and are already driving stakes along our right of way....The weather is specially favorable for field work and I hope you will provide to work early and late, have your dinners sent to you so you will lose no time during the middle of the day. I shall look for a daily report of progress.[103]

The delay was not of Stack's doing, but was owing to the time taken to assemble local people, including Williams' partner, Porterfield, to assist Stack in securing the rights of way.[104]

Samuel Williams fixed his stockholders' meeting for the 3rd of February, ensuring that the attorney for the Virginias Railway was present so that, as Hotchkiss put it, "after the marriage ceremony is performed [the lawyers] cannot say that the knot was not properly tied."[105] The knot was tied, and on the same day Williams telegraphed the good news to Hotchkiss. The legal framework for a third railroad from Huntington to the sea was in place. There was just the McCreery loose end to clear up. He had been taken by surprise. On February 1 he had visited the New River region to find Hotchkiss' surveyors at work; at Pearisburg he discovered that the Williams were unable to act on his behalf. There was nothing left but to seek that conference with Hotchkiss which he had earlier refused.

Throughout that hectic period of activity there was a veritable deluge of correspondence between the participants, with Hotchkiss at its center keeping everybody informed of developments, sometimes writing three or even four times a day to Senator Green or General Dacey.[106] With the acquisition of the Bland Land Company charter within sight, and McCreery seeking a conference, Hotchkiss arranged to meet Dacey in Washington on February 3 to bring him up to date and agree to the next steps.

The drive that was being given to this enterprise is well illustrated by sixty-seven year old Hotchkiss' time-table for the week beginning Monday, February 3, 1896. At 2:30 a.m. on that day he wrote to Martin Williams: "I have your two letters of the 1st and take time to reply just before leaving for Washington to meet General Dacey at 7 a.m. I expect to get home at 7 p.m. of today and will be here tomorrow, Tuesday, and be glad to meet Mr. McCreery and your brother to talk over New River Ry matters." His train back to Staunton was half an hour late, but he was still in time to chair a meeting of the 'Committee on Extension of City limits.'[107] On Tuesday, McCreery called, but was sent away to cool his heels for the morning while Hotchkiss dealt with his mail. In the afternoon they had their conference, and both went off to Washington that evening to confer with General Dacey the following day. These meetings revealed that McCreery was not averse to the eventual takeover of the Hinton, New River & Western Railroad by the Virginias Railway, provided his board agreed. He was to obtain an agreement which would allow the transfer to take place at a time determined by the Virginias Railway Company. In the meantime that company would assist in getting McCreery's road constructed.[108] Hotchkiss returned to Staunton to relate the outcome to Green. "We came to a satisfactory written understanding about our conflicting interests and we now not only have no objection to the passage of his bill, but would be very glad to have it put through so he can get it as soon as possible, as he will want to secure some rights of way under it quite promptly. Please have its patron stimulated to have the Governor sign it."[109]

The conferences with McCreery had shown that the best interests of both enterprises would be better served by co-operation, and Hotchkiss had to make a complete reversal in his stance toward McCreery. It now seemed sensible to aid McCreery to get on with his Hinton, New River, & Western Railroad and its branch into the Flat Top region. The survey team which had been set up to frustrate McCreery was now to be deployed on his behalf finding a route for the branch line, leaving the New River survey to McCreery's engineers. In sending the new instructions to Stack on February 6, Hotchkiss said, "You will please give publicity, in a guarded way, to this information so that the general public will understand that the Virginias Railway Co. has abandoned the idea of building a railway along New River."[110] The object now was to confuse the C&O and the N&W. Explaining the events of the week to Smith, Hotchkiss claimed, "What we are now doing in furtherance of this contract will thoroughly outwit and deceive the N&W and the C&O....I shall write an article for the *Manufacturer's Record* accompanied by a little map for the purpose of aiding McCreery with his work of keeping the fog so thick along New River that no one, no matter how much interested, can see through it to any objects beyond."[111] A week later his article extolling the importance of the link between the C&O and the N&W was sent for publication as an editorial not attributed to Hotchkiss.

The reversal of the policy toward McCreery, if it did not confuse the C&O, certainly confused the survey team deployed with a speed more in keeping with a military operation against the incursion of a guerilla band than with a peaceful civil engineering work. The fog of war engulfed Hotchkiss' own forces. His new instructions to Stack were unclear, not so much as to where he should operate with his eleven man team, but whether he should await the arrival of McCreery before resuming the offensive. That confusion resulted in unnecessary delay.

It soon became clear that Hotchkiss' spoiling tactics had not worked. Far from diverting the thoughts of the C&O and the N&W from the possibility of an important rival, they interpreted the transfer of the survey team to work for McCreery as indicating a consolidation of the Hinton, New River & Western with the Virginias Railway. Rumors to this effect had reached McCreery, causing him to avoid a planned meeting in New York with the Virginias Railway board. This was seen by that board as an attempt by McCreery to avoid formalizing the agreement reached with Hotchkiss and General Dacey at the beginning of February. At the suggestion of Smith, Hotchkiss disbanded the survey team, instructing Captain Stack to report to Staunton and bring along his instruments, note books, etc. This decision did not distress McCreery, for the close association with the Virginias Railway was viewed with suspicion by the C&O and N&W and was hampering his plans to link Hinton and Pearisburg.[112] To Martin Williams, Hotchkiss said, "Please let everybody know and understand that the Virginias Railway Co. has abandoned your region and that its hope for new railways and consequent prosperity depends on Mr. McCreery and his road and that they should do all that they can to help that."[113]

Thus in the space of a month Hotchkiss had sent out a substantial survey team with clear guidance, switched it to another site in accordance with a new policy, and finally abandoned work altogether. In terms of flexibility and speed of execution it couldn't have been surpassed by "Stonewall" himself.

While all this maneuvering in the interests of the grand design for a third coal carrier was taking place, Smith was making practical progress at the Huntington end of the Guyandot. By that time 25 or more miles of road from Huntington eastward had been located under the direction of Major McKendrew, and was ready to be let to contractors who were considering their bids.[114]

However, there were major problems ahead generated by the political and economic situation that racked the country. This was manifested by an acute shortage of cash which inhibited normal business transactions, and a government policy of protecting the gold reserves, which diverted what money there was into government bonds. The consequence was that funds could not be raised using intrinsically valuable agricultural, timber, or mineral lands as collateral. The solution to the problem was seen by some in the establishment of silver as legal tender in addition to gold. The cry was for the free coinage of silver at 16-1. Broadly speaking "free silver" was supported by the farmers, while the orthodox "sound money" men, wedded to the gold standard, were the financiers and industrialists. In Virginia the silver question very nearly split the Democratic party, but the skillful advocacy of John W. Daniell, and the pragmatic support of Martin, hitherto the spokesman for railroad interests, ensured a majority for the party's presidential candidate, William Jennings Bryan. In the country as a whole the result was otherwise; the Republican, McKinley, was elected.

Where did Hotchkiss stand in that battle, one of the most exciting and colorful since the war, and what was its significance to the Virginias Railway? It might be supposed that Hotchkiss, operating alongside the financiers and the railroad interests, would have supported the "gold bugs." Not so, and not simply because he could not bring himself to vote for the Republican Party. His views were "based upon a thorough and long continued study" as he had so "frequently expressed them in the columns of *The Virginias.*"[115] He had always been a bi-metallist and outspoken in his views, satisfied that not only his own interest, but those of the Virginia states and of their citizens would be best promoted by having in circulation the largest possible quantity of legal tender money. He wanted the restrictions on the lending of money so constructed that investors would "find their best profit not in trading in money, but loaning their money to those developing the country."[116] Even some Republicans were concerned that the efforts of government to protect the gold reserves were inhibiting railroad building. Referring to James L. Caldwell, vice-president of the Virginias Railway, Hotchkiss told a correspondent, "Although an ardent republican in ordinary times I understand that now he is doing all he can to secure the election of Bryan, believing as I do that the interests of those desiring to build railways and who have mineral and timber lands to develop will be best subserved by having the policy Bryan and his party advocate."[117] General Dacey took the other view, saying that the election of McKinley and a gold standard were prerequisites to the construction of the Virginias Railway. He went so far as to promise the voters of West Virginia that within sixty days of a Republican victory he would have 1,000 men at work on the Virginias Railway.[118] Opinions differed as to the effect this had on the vote. Senator Green told Hotchkiss that in his district Dacey's letter was extensively printed and circulated. "The republican speakers referred to it and I assure you it had its effect with the working classes. I trust he will make good his promises."[119] Craig Miller, when asked for his impression, replied that he did not think that General Dacey's letter caused any Democrat to vote the Republican ticket, but all those to whom he had talked were surprised that Dacey should have given such a letter for campaign purposes.[120]

Unwise, unprincipled, though this intervention was it did place a weapon in Hotchkiss' hand to use in furtherance of the railway scheme, and there was a flurry of activity immediately the election was over. He was in New York on November 7 and 8 to confer with Dacey and Smith. He was convinced that work on the railway would soon begin if only because "The republicans recognize that having proclaimed themselves the advance agents of prosperity they will get themselves badly discounted if they don't make the country prosper."[121] To the editor of the *Manufacturer's Record* he wrote, "There is beginning to be, since the election, an apparent condition of affairs that warrants our taking steps to go on with the construction of this road, with a fair prospect of success in our efforts, at an early day. We have reached the conclusion that the opportunity we have been so long waiting for is now within our grasp, and that if we fail to seize it, under existing favorable conditions, we may allow the opportunity to pass by and we be left without the desired results."[122] But early in the new year this optimism began to be eroded. Then, in August, C. W. Smith resigned, ostensibly on the grounds of ill health, but as he remained the President and General Manager of the Pasadena & Los Angeles Electric Railway Company it seems probable that he had given up hope of a successful outcome of the Virginias Railway venture. Hotchkiss continued to provide Dacey with information, and in return Dacey encouraged Hotchkiss in the belief that quiet negotiation was going on behind the scenes. Even in October 1897 he told Hotchkiss, "I believe we will see the whole thing in the most satisfactory and businesslike shape before Christmas and you absolutely relieved from all pecuniary embarrassments."[123] Dacey's sudden death in March 1898, however, revealed a wholly unbusinesslike state of affairs. Hotchkiss told one creditor that the railway company had no funds, and the estate of General Dacey was in the same condition. General Dacey had "entered into a contract with that company for the construction of its road and was authorized to pledge a certain amount of its bonds to secure funds for its construction. He secured on these bonds very substantial sums of money which no one can account for except in part although I doubt not but that he spent them in ways that in his opinion would promote the interests of the railway in the end."[124] One wonders how much went into McKinley's election campaign. To another enquirer Hotchkiss ended the story: "The death of General Dacey deranged all plans about the construction of the Virginias Railway as he had everything pertaining to [it] entirely in his own hands and had so managed it as to leave no one behind to take it up and follow out his plans and it looks as though that scheme would have to be abandoned and a new one inaugurated."[125] Hotchkiss and others who owned land in the Guyandot Basin and the Flat Top region hoped to find someone who would undertake the construction of a railroad on a less ambitious scale, possibly connecting the C&O at Huntington and the N&W on New River.[126] It was not until after Hotchkiss had died that another company was set up to build a railroad up the Guyandot. This was the Guyandot Valley Railway Company incorporated March 1, 1899 to build from near Huntington to near Pineville. It was not until 1904, 13 months after this company had been acquired by the C&O, that the first locomotive, hauling two passenger and two freight cars pulled into the board and batten station at Logan Courthouse.[127] Hotchkiss' dream of a third and independent coal carrier to the tidewater had to wait even longer, until 1909, for a new company with the same name, The Virginias Railway Company, to complete a line to Sewell's Point near Norfolk.[128]

CHAPTER X

"...Is skillful with his pencil

and fond of the duties of a topographical engineer, and withal a gentleman of regular habits."

"His maps are at once a book and a picture."

JUST WHEN JED HOTCHKISS first found an interest in maps is impossible to say, but it was probably early in life. Farmers and land owners needed to understand maps and land survey methods. To provide this knowledge, surveying was commonly included in the curricula of Academies.[1] Whether or not this was the case at the Windsor Academy, we can be reasonably certain that some members of the enterprising Hotchkiss family would have been familiar with its theory and practice. Hotchkiss financed his 1847 walking tour of Virginia by selling maps and atlases.[2] That suggests that maps had a wide appeal within a rural community which had become used to them as means of recording and conveying information in a way more revealing than the metes and bounds of a property deed. His own interest is clearly demonstrated by the entries in his diary: when in Charles Town (West Virginia) he made a point of staying with Mr. James M. Brown, the surveyor of Jefferson county, and when he visited the "small village" of Front Royal, in July 1847, he spent time "examining some old maps."[3] The diary also contains his own sketch maps, "The Vicinity of Weyers Cave," "The Vicinity of Natural Bridge," a map showing the location of "Montecelli," and a plan of the house and gardens.[4]

If he had not received any formal instruction in land surveying before he went to Mossy Creek, then he must have taught himself. Entries in his diary show that he made simple surveys from his early days with the Forrers: Saturday, March 3, 1849, "in the afternoon made a measurement of a small field." Perhaps this was the "Plot of D. Forrer's Meadow" to be found among the Hotchkiss papers at the Library of Congress. He also surveyed and plotted the land he bought in July 1853 from George Craun for the Mossy Creek boardinghouse.[5] All this was elementary, but demonstrated his firm grasp of the principles. To map-drawing he brought better than average drafting skills. The sketches in the walking-tour diary testify to this, as do the flower drawings he made when at Windsor.[6] A small map of Augusta County, drawn when at Mossy Creek, shows an appreciation of certain cartographic ideas. Not only are lines of latitude and longitude shown, but the inner border comprises alternate black and white bands, each representing ten-minute intervals. He used different-sized lettering for different categories of information, and different sizes and combinations of circles to indicate the relative importance of settlements. The map has an outer decorative border.[7] All of this he would have picked up from the atlases and geographies he used in the classroom, and that knowledge, reinforced by the repetition year after year of the basic principles of drawing, surveying, and mapmaking, would make the whole process very nearly second nature. There was, however, another great interest and related skill which Hotchkiss possessed, or developed, that transformed the mechanics of mapmaking into an art form. This was his fascination for topography, his understanding of the shape of the landscape and the geology which determined it. He had been introduced to geology when a boy at Windsor, and the significance of the science was manifest in Lyken's Valley where he taught the coalminers' children. His walking-tour diary is full of references to the rocks he saw and to their significance to farmer or miner. The encouragement of those who supported Mossy Creek Academy, must have been a positive factor too. Forrer was an iron master; McCue, apart from being a farmer on a large scale, also owned land containing exploitable coal. Yet, taking all these

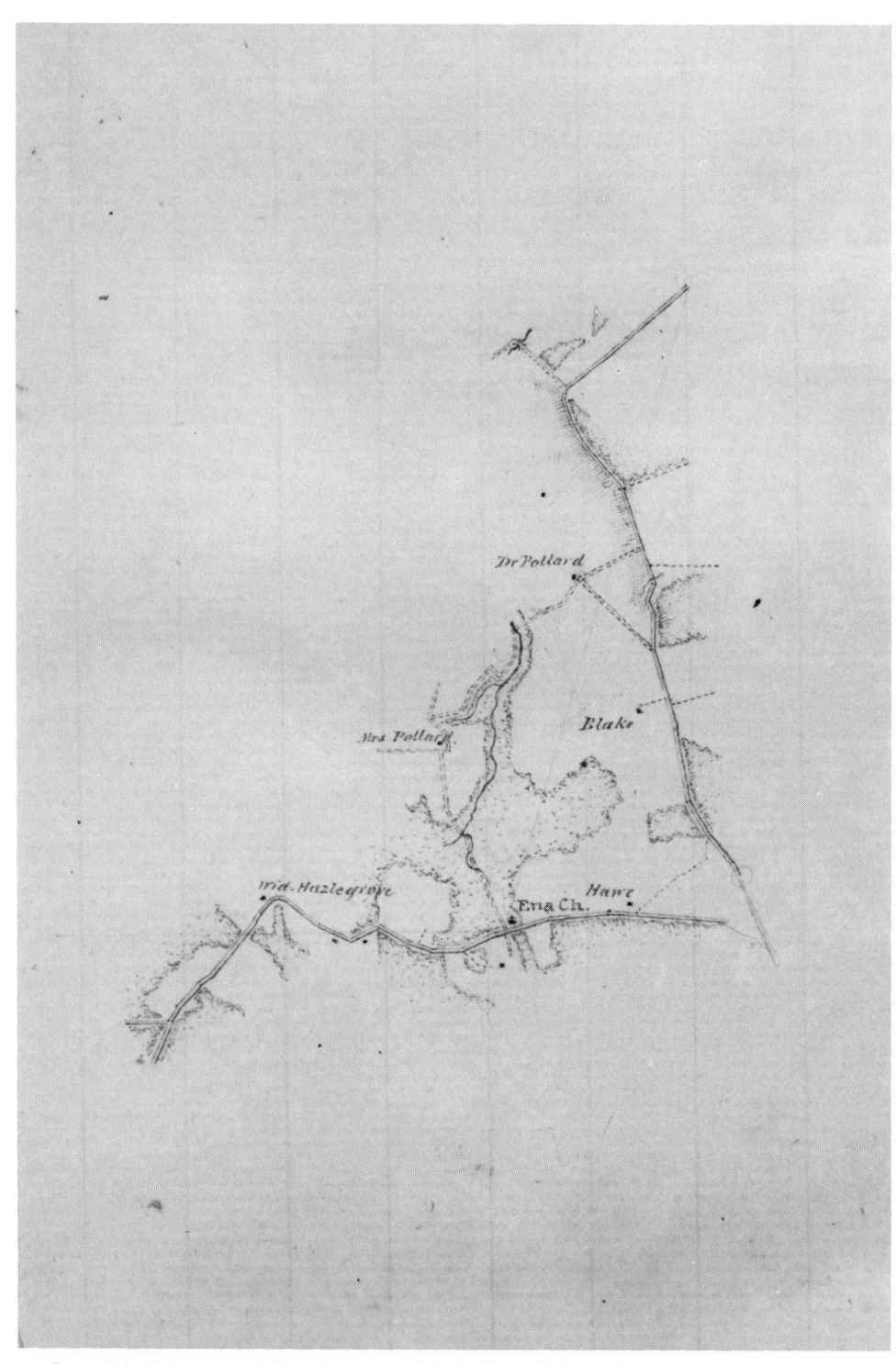

An unidentified sketch found among the Hotchkiss Papers. Included here to illustrate the delicacy of his drawing.

Hotchkiss Papers, Box 39, Library of Congress

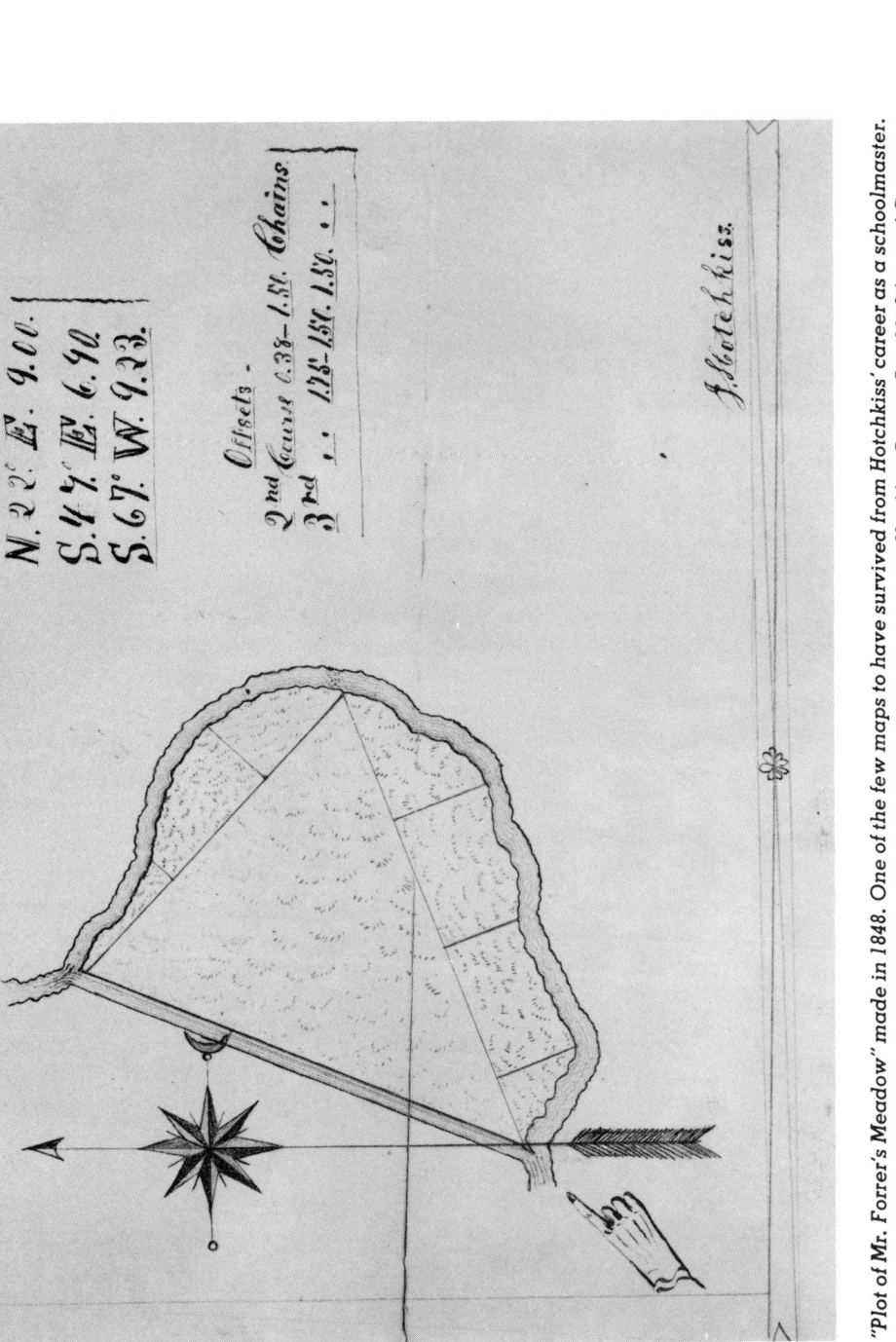

"Plot of Mr. Forrer's Meadow" made in 1848. One of the few maps to have survived from Hotchkiss' career as a schoolmaster.
Hotchkiss Papers, Box 39, Library of Congress

strands together, the drawing skills, the interest in maps, topography, and geology, it is difficult to believe that they could be woven into surveying and cartographic products of such profusion, variety, quality, and importance as emerged from the demands Virginia was to make of him.

It was, of course, the war which revealed Hotchkiss' extraordinary skills, and brought them together to serve a practical end. Both sides entered the conflict with maps inadequate in scale and content for the prosecution of military campaigns, but whereas the Northern armies had the files and information of the Topographic Bureau of the Army Topographic Engineers, the Confederate forces had to make do with what civilian maps were available, supplemented by manuscript maps from the State Archives. For all practical purposes they entered the conflict mapless. Nor was there a serious attempt made to remedy the situation until the Peninsular campaign of 1862, a campaign engaging the armies in country hardly a day's march from Richmond, but where "the Confederate commanders knew no more of the topography than they did about central Africa."[8] Hotchkiss was to tell Henderson, "the Confederates had very imperfect maps of the region around Richmond relying largely upon an old county map of Henrico County and upon what is known as the 9 sheet map of the State both of which are very defective in details."[9] This may have been due to a lack of understanding in the Confederate bureaucracy of the importance of maps, or, possibly, to the higher priority given at the time to the building of fortifications for the defense of the Confederate capital. The lack of maps, and the consequent difficulties faced by Lee in preparing for the confrontation with McClellan, brought about the appointment of Captain Albert H. Campbell to take charge of a map reproduction office which was to become the Topographical Department of The Department of Northern Virginia.[10] Although he put "two or three surveying parties" into the field immediately after being commissioned on June 6, 1862, their work was insufficiently far advanced to be of any help to Lee in the subsequent Seven Days' battle.

Indeed Campbell, for all his efforts, was never able to keep up with the needs of the field commanders. As late in the war as June 1864 when Early's corps left Lee after Cold Harbor and marched toward the Valley, Hotchkiss entered in his diary, "Corrected map of Louisa Co. as we went along." There is evidence to suggest that the failure of Campbell's bureau to provide an adequate service was a source of great irritation to Hotchkiss. He and others lived an uncomfortable and dangerous life, surveying and sketching under fire while Campbell led a comfortable one among the fleshpots of Richmond, or so it seemed.

The lasting impression left with Hotchkiss was of the "large amount of bad work he had done and for the long time he took to do it in." Hotchkiss could never get anything from him unless he sent someone to copy his office maps.[11] So it was the topographical engineers assigned to the field units who provided the major part of the mapping for the marches and engagements of the troops.

The field commanders, particularly those regular officers of the pre-war army, like Lee, who had served in the Engineer Corps, knew the importance of good maps for the successful prosecution of military operations. This recognition extended to commanders of lower formations. Hotchkiss' skill, said General Munford, "was appreciated...by not only the commanding generals, but the subalterns who enjoyed [his] hasty sketches, by day or night."[12]

When Hotchkiss offered his services to the Confederate forces, and was appointed engineer at Camp Garnett, Rich Mountain, Randolph County, on July 2, 1861, he was immediately instructed by the local commander, Colonel Heck, to make a survey of the Confederate positions. He had "nearly completed the necessary triangulations and measurements...and had also by barometrical observations ascertained the height of the points occupied by our forces and had made considerable progress in the drawing of the map..." when his work was interrupted on July 10 by the successful Union attack.[13] Before the retreat from Rich Mountain, Hotchkiss was given no time to recover his notes and maps, so we do not have the result of his first military assignment; we have to make do with a map drawn from memory.[14]

His next important task was given to him by General Lee, who had set up his headquarters at Valley Mountain, some miles to the south. He was directed to prepare a map of all the country from Valley Mountain to Beverley, and of the region northeast up the Greenbrier. Immediately addressing himself to this task, he "gathered information from all directions and corrected the existing maps for immediate use." He then started to make an entirely new map of Tygart's Valley, running northward from Valley Mountain. In making it, he derived very great assistance from a Mr. Conrad, local surveyor and county magistrate. Many years later Hotchkiss recalled his help. "His knowledge of the country was very remarkable. In fact he was a living notebook, giving me courses and distances which enabled me to construct a map of the entire country in front of us that was quite sufficient for all military purposes. Of course this was constructed under great difficulties. My drawing board was the head of a barrel; my seat the half of another barrel."[15] Fortunately, a map based on that work has survived. It was drawn on paper 28 × 15 centimetres over a grid ruled in centimetres and (faintly) half-centimetres; Hotchkiss used colored crayons, brown for relief, blue for rivers, red for roads and tracks, black for lettering. There is no scale or orientation shown, but north is at the top. Apart from the relief shown symbolically by somewhat stiff hachuring, the map is typical of the hundreds he would draw during the next few years.[16] From its appearance it is probably not the one drawn on the barrel. There can be little doubt that it is the fair copy made at Loch Willow the following January after Hotchkiss had been sent home to recuperate from typhoid fever. His account book for this period shows that he charged the Confederate States $5 per day for the equivalent of fourteen days spent in copying a map of Tygart's Valley.[17]

In March 1862, Hotchkiss joined Jackson in the Shenandoah Valley to begin his career as topographical engineer of the Valley District of the Department of Northern Virginia and its successor, II Corps of the Army of Northern Virginia. On the 26th of that month he was ordered by Jackson to make "a map of the Valley, from Harper's Ferry to Lexington, showing all the points of offence and defence in those places." This was the origin of the most famous of the Hotchkiss maps, one that would be the master of many copies made for the marches and battles throughout the length of the Valley. Not that it played any part in Jackson's famous Valley campaign of that year, for it was hardly started before Jackson left the Valley for the Seven Days' battle to save Richmond. Although Hotchkiss immediately started work he was not able to comply with Jackson's request in any systematic fashion, for the situation was so serious after the battle of Kernstown that he was obliged to assist in more immediate tasks. His reconnaissance in front of Jackson's defensive position at Narrow Passage demonstrated to the general that the line could easily be turned, and that a more secure position could be held on Stony Creek. Occupation of this line from April 5 to 16 gave Hotchkiss a chance to start work on the map, but when the enemy renewed his advance, he was again needed for reconnaissance work. This and the associated mapmaking occupied much of his time during the Valley campaign and brought him into close contact with Jackson, who came to rely on him for information on the lie of the lands. Although Jackson had an appreciation of topography as well as an ability to retain a memory of landscape features, Hotchkiss "made a point, though, to be always ready to give him a graphic presentation of any particular portion of the region where operations were going on whenever it was necessary to explain by illustration, making a rapid sketch of the topography in his presence, using different colored pencils etc."[18] There was not always time in that fast moving campaign to draw anything but a quick sketch. Thus, before the battle of McDowell, Hotchkiss

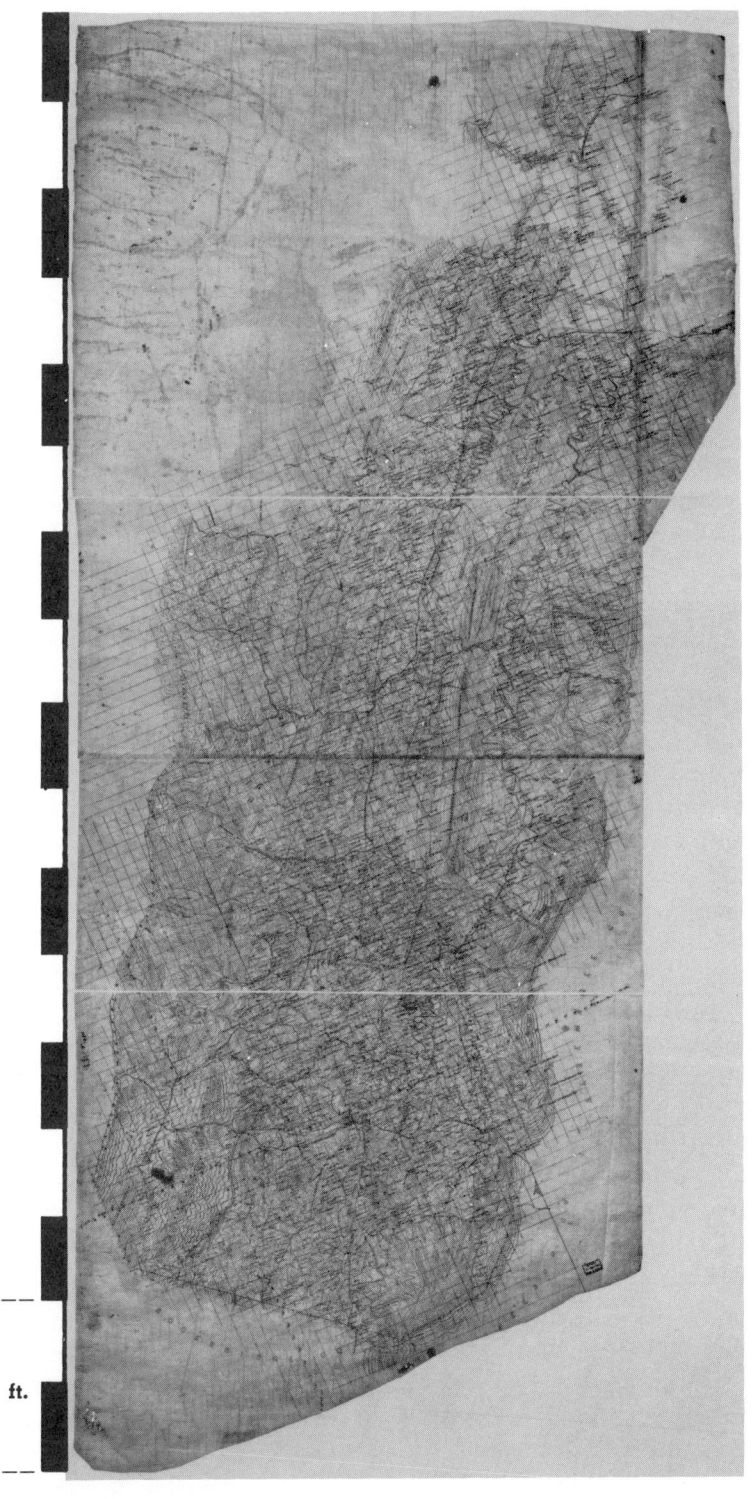

The famous "Map of the Valley," ordered by Gen. Thomas J. (Stonewall) Jackson, **drawn to a scale of 1:80,000, is over 8 ft. long and 3½ ft. wide.** *Library of Congress*
NOTE: EACH BLACK & WHITE SEGMENT REPRESENTS 1 FOOT

reconnoitered the enemy positions, led Jackson to a point where these could be seen, and, with him looking on "made him a map of McDowell and vicinity." So throughout May and half of June he was more actively involved with the mapping for, or of, the battles then taking place than in complying with Jackson's first order. When Jackson marched his troops to Richmond, he ordered Hotchkiss to return to Staunton where he was able to work on the map of the Valley without interruption until ordered to Gordonsville on July 15.[19] There he continued the work until Jackson was ready to start the campaign against Pope and the subsequent invasion of Maryland. By this time he had produced a useful, but incomplete, map. Throughout the war it was in a state of continuous revision; corrections and additions were made as Hotchkiss explored the intricate network of streams of the Valley and the spurs of its mountain borders. As late as April 4, 1865, only days before Lee's surrender, Hotchkiss noted in his diary, "I corrected valley map some."

After the army had recrossed the Potomac following the battle of Antietam, the map assisted Lee in planning his withdrawal up the Shenandoah, for Hotchkiss provided him with a tracing of a portion of it early in October.[20] Hotchkiss then spent much of his time mapping the roads in the Valley, paying special attention to Powell's Fort Valley, a narrow cleft splitting Massanutten Mountain along its length, and to the routes into and out of it. His diary for this period, October 10 to December 1, 1862, records his journeys, his field notebook the sketches he made. This notebook is not only a testimony to his skill and artistry, but provides a record of parts of the Valley for which no satisfactory map was available at that time.[21]

Copies of the whole or, more frequently, parts of the map were used throughout the war by the officers of II Corps, but it is probable that the map in the Hotchkiss Collection is the master-map, which survived the debacle at Waynesboro and was among the maps which Hotchkiss sent to Lynchburg in the care of Robinson in the last days of the war. As we see it now, the map on a scale of 1:80,000 is on tracing cloth, has dimensions 100 × 44 inches, was drawn in red for roads, blue for drainage, with land form and lettering in black, and having a ¾-inch grid. The relief is depicted mainly by form lines, which adequately convey the shape of the landscape in those areas familiar to Hotchkiss, but degenerate into mere symbolism elsewhere. Hachures are employed to a limited extent. Churches and mills are shown by symbols, and there is extensive naming of the occupiers of the dwellings marked on the map. This was a valuable means of identifying location and routes in a sparsely inhabited countryside. A local resident might not be able to read a map, but he would certainly know how to find his neighbor.

It was drawn on three pieces of tracing linen which were glued together to form a continuous sheet. On this long strip Hotchkiss drew the ¾-inch N-S, E-W grid, oriented so that northeast was at the top of the map, thus allowing him to get practically the whole of the Valley onto the yard-wide tracing linen at his disposal. The grid was first drawn in pencil, but was ruled over in ink after the map was finished.

Hotchkiss kept the map rolled, and it was in this form when it was discovered in 1938 by C. Vernon Eddy, who described the opening of the large boxes at The Oaks and seeing the "roll after roll of maps, the long lost and almost forgotten work of Stonewall Jackson's topographical engineer."[22] At Eddy's request the map was mounted by the Library of Congress where it was cut into three parts, base-mounted on paper, and then on muslin to fold.[23]

The map was not constructed from one survey operation, but was a compilation of information from many different sources. What those were the map does not disclose. Some can be inferred from those acknowledged on the map of Augusta County made after the war for the Board of Survey of Washington College. Among these were Wood's *Map of Augusta County, 1820*; J. Heron's *Map of the Shenandoah River, from Surveys, 1832*; J. Anderson's *Survey of the Valley Turnpike, 1838*; and H. D. Whitcomb's *Map of Virginia Central Railroad, n.d.* Not only did he have "all the maps that had been printed prior to the war, but also [was] supplied with manuscript maps from the Archives of Virginia."[24] One of those pre-war printed maps would have been the accurate map of Jefferson County (West Virginia) made in 1852 by his colleague, S. Howell Brown. The extent of new information provided by Hotchkiss has not been researched. Some would have been derived from the reconnaissance and battlefield maps he had been making. Other Hotchkiss additions could be inferred from the contents of the field sketch books which he kept at that time; Hotchkiss would not have wasted time sketching territory for which adequate maps were available.

In the early days of December 1862, when Lee's army was occupying the high ground overlooking Fredericksburg, Hotchkiss was once again required for reconnaissance, and siting good defensive positions. When the battle was over, on December 17, he wrote to his "Dear Little Nellie," a letter in which he included a sketch map, a typical Hotchkiss creation, and almost certainly the first of this engagement.[25] It was not until January 9 that he was asked to prepare a map to assist Colonel Faulkner in writing the report of Jackson's part in the battle, and for this he made use of one made by Jeb Stuart's engineer, Captain Blackford, who had by then surveyed the battlefield.[26]

Winter closed down the military operations. It was the time for report-writing and producing maps of the engagements of the past year.

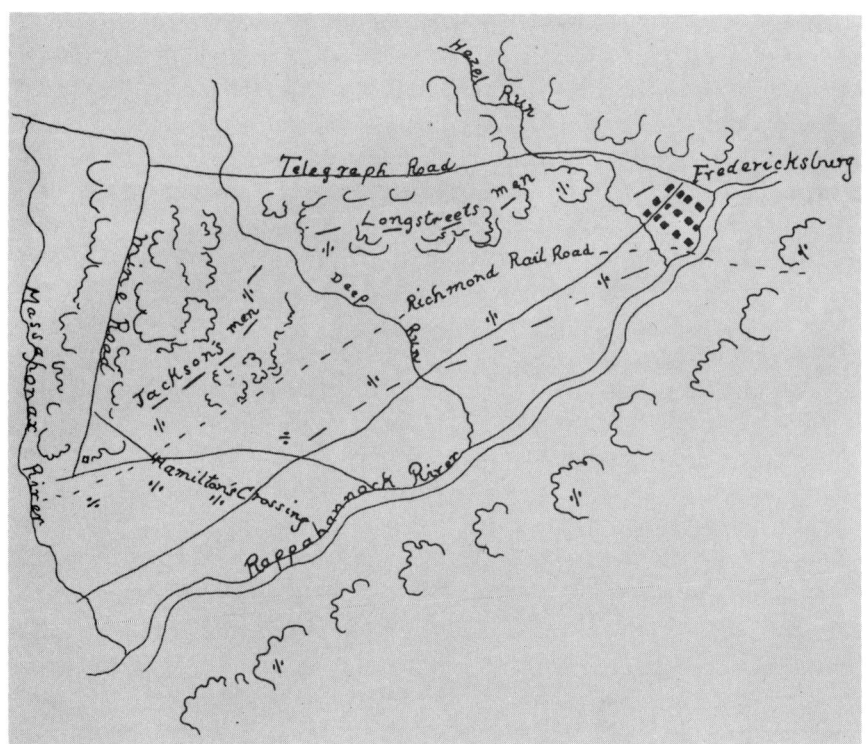

Battle of Fredericksburg. "I must now tell you about a battle we had last Saturday, the 13th of Dec., and I will make a little map for you to look at and see how the armies were located when they fought."
A tracing of this map drawn in the letter to his 9-year old daughter.

While in winter quarters at Moss Neck, Hotchkiss drew maps of Virginia counties—notably Caroline County—battle maps for Jackson's reports of the Valley Campaign from Kernstown to Port Republic, and maps of the defenses along the Rappahannock. Jackson had already told the Secretary of State for War that the facility with which Hotchkiss collected topographical information had been unequalled by any other person he had had with him so far in this war. Now he told Hotchkiss that the map he had made of the route of the army from Franklin to the Battle of Winchester was "a beautifully gotten up map."[27] Jackson was not always immediately satisfied. When the General disputed the location of some of the troops on the map of the Cedar Run battle he sent Hotchkiss to "hunt up the officers that commanded them, so as to get the map correct."[28]

It was not all retrospective work. Lee and Jackson were considering the campaign season which would open in the spring. On February 23, Hotchkiss recorded in his diary, "I got secret orders from the General to prepare a map of the Valley of Va. extending to Harrisburg, Pa. and then on to Philadelphia;-wishing the preparation to be kept a profound secret." The second invasion of the North was being planned. That map had many of the features of the Map of the Valley, but was more finely executed. Relief was shown by hachures in black, roads in red, drainage in blue, and many householders named.[29]

The 1863 season was opened by Hooker and his decisive defeat at Chancellorsville. Immediately after the battle Lee ordered Hotchkiss to make a map of the battlefield.[30] On that occasion he was able to make a proper survey, running lines along the principal roads. Surveying and mapmaking occupied the rest of May and was completed before Lee once again carried the war north of the Potomac. That move started on June 5, and ended with the Battle of Gettysburg at the beginning of July. Whenever the army camped, Hotchkiss would work on the maps needed by his corps commander. Those demands were often pressing. Three days into the move Hotchkiss noted in his diary, "I went to work on a map reaching to the mountains, toward Front Royal, as Gen. Ewell told me that was the route he wished the troops to take tomorrow." When the move was delayed he copied a map of the Valley, which would soon be needed. An advance of 32 miles was followed by a conference to decide the tactics for the capture of Winchester. Hotchkiss advised on the routes the formations should take, then went back to work on the Valley map. Roused at 2 a.m. the following morning he "worked awhile at a map for Gen. Rhodes" before moving off at 4 a.m. On the day after the occupation of Winchester he was ordered to map the battlefield, "so was busy all day riding along the works of the enemy, our lines of march, &c."[31]

One of the purposes of the campaign was to replenish the army with many of its essential stores, food, equipment, clothing, horses. The shortages affected the topographical department no less than any other, so Hotchkiss took advantage of the move to Chambersburg, Pennsylvania, to procure maps, and what he called engineering supplies, presumably drawing paper, tracing cloth, pencils, etc. A similar foraging expedition into Carlisle was interrupted by a call from a testy General Ewell who needed maps to aid him to comply with Lee's order to move to Gettysburg.[32] With that battle over, it was Hotchkiss' job to provide maps of the country back toward Virginia, and at 2 a.m. on the day after Pickett's charge he was doing just that. A few days later he mapped the defensive positions selected to guard the crossing of the Potomac, and when finished "went over to General Lee's and put the ridge for defence on his map."[33] By early August the army was back behind the Rapidan, and Hotchkiss was making maps to illustrate the reports of the campaign.

The death of Jackson, following the battle of Chancellorsville, changed the relationship which Hotchkiss previously had with the higher command; hitherto he had worked entirely to the orders of Jackson. Now, while still the topographical engineer of II Corps, he worked more closely under the direction of Lee's acting chief of engineers, Colonel William Proctor Smith, from whom he received orders given on behalf of General Lee. Under Jackson, Hotchkiss was subordinate to Keith Boswell, the Corps' Chief Engineer, so when the demand for maps was heavy Boswell would provide assistance, sometimes himself, but more often that of Lieutenant Williamson or Sergeant S. Howell Brown. With Boswell dead, and the growing realization of the value of his services, Hotchkiss was provided with help of a more permanent kind. Samson B. Robinson, assigned to him at Gettysburg, became a valued colleague and close friend, and in August he took on a draftsman, H. Von Stenicker, paying him $3 per day.[34] This was the beginning of a Topographical office which developed in skill and renown during the remainder of the war and provided the basis of Hotchkiss' post-war career.

Little military activity took place in Virginia during the remainder of 1863, so that when the maps of the marches and battles of the summer were completed, Hotchkiss and Robinson compiled, copied, or reduced, maps of the counties in which the army was encamped. Even when on three-weeks' leave over Christmas, he had orders to fulfill from Colonel Proctor Smith, including a map of Pennsylvania.[35] No sooner was he back from leave than General Early ordered him to return to the Valley to "reconnoitre for defences."[36] "You will proceed to collect all the material you can for a map of Augusta and Rockbridge from Staunton and Lexington westward and the counties adjoining them on the west."[37] He had to map a section of the Allegheny mountains 100 miles long and 40 miles wide. Hotchkiss replied,

> I brought my assistants along with me, with the consent of Generals Ewell and Lee and I have obtained quarters in Staunton where I can keep them at work and supervise them once a week at least. I have a surveyed map of Rockbridge County and also a survey of portions of Augusta, Bath and Alleghany Counties and I shall have them at once put together by my assistants and so forward the work assigned to me. I am now making tracings of the maps I have, to take along with me, that I may verify them....I need a courier, or cavalryman, to go along with me, it expedites my observations much to have someone to send to ascertain names of houses

&c while I am taking notes and sketching topography &c.[38]

The renting of an office in Staunton not only made life a lot more comfortable for his team, but also had the advantage for Hotchkiss of an easy ride home to Loch Willow to spend Sunday with the family. The three-week reconnaissance in the snow-covered mountains to the west of the Valley provided more map work for the Staunton team, which was further enlarged by the recruitment of Oltmanns in March 1864.[39] By the middle of April the army was again preparing to continue the conflict, the Staunton office was packed up, and the team returned to life under canvas. They exchanged the quiet, steady, perhaps monotonous tasks, of copying and reducing maps for the noisy, dirty, dangerous business of surveying and mapping on the battlefield. For the next six months Hotchkiss was involved in two contrasting campaigns, the bloody killing match as Grant tried, but failed, to destroy Lee's army in a determined attempt to reach Richmond, and General Early's fast moving, brilliant raid toward Washington.

By now there was no aspect of military mapping that Hotchkiss had not experienced: general maps to assist in the development of strategy, and the planning of operations, route maps to help the army move efficiently, maps of reconnaissance expeditions to refine the tactics, maps of defensive positions, and maps to illustrate the reports of the battle. It was in the latter, completed in the comparative leisure of winter quarters, that the Hotchkiss' work was at its most refined, where line and letter were so precisely and finely drawn that it is hard to believe that it was done by hand. It was that skill that allowed Hotchkiss to incorporate so much detail, but at the same time to produce clear, readable products. He was assisted by capable surveyors and draftsmen, Robinson and Oltmanns being the two best known. Perhaps they were the best of his assistants; certainly they were fortunate to join him when he had become established as the foremost military mapmaker of the Army of Northern Virginia. The work of the team reached its professional peak in the last year of the war, as is well illustrated by the *Report of the camps, marches and engagements, of the Second Corps, A.N.V. and of the Army of the Valley Dist., of the Department of Northern Virginia; during the campaign of 1864; illustrated by maps and sketches.*[40] Although this contains 38 different maps, it represents only a small proportion of the survey and cartographic work performed during this campaign. The *Official Records* lists 102 maps "furnished by the topographical engineer office of the Second Corps" for 1864 alone.

Of the enormous output of the war years only a fraction remains today. Much of it was lost in the disaster of Waynesboro, March 2, 1863, where Hotchkiss was only able to save his saddlebags. There is no evidence that he was able to recover the maps left in his wagon though we do know that he made a search for them. Hotchkiss later claimed that he saved all his maps by sending them on the railroad train to Richmond prior to the enemy advance. However, his diary entry for February 28, 1865, reads, "Sent off maps of E. Va. to Engineer Bureau," which certainly suggests that he retained other maps. That those others were lost at Waynesboro is supported by an entry for March 6, "I spent the day at home, fixing up after the losses at Waynesboro." Although this is not specific, we may presume that at this time Hotchkiss only had with him what he could carry, and that his other personal losses would not have warranted a comment. Later he visited the Engineer Bureau and "saw Maj. Campbell about maps, etc." When he left Richmond he got his "boxes to go to Petersburg, but the drayman carried them to the wrong depot."[41] We might speculate that in these boxes were maps which Hotchkiss had recovered from the bureau, maps which he had submitted for the revisions and compilations being made under Campbell's direction, as well as those maps of East Virginia. If so, this could be the origin of Campbell's claim that many of the maps in Hotchkiss' possession after the war were the property of the Bureau.[42] Alternatively his wagon could have been taken to Richmond by Confederate troops after the enemy had moved away, but this seems unlikely. Hotchkiss kept maps at home and had copies of the more important maps stored there for safety, convenience, or for post-war use.

That Hotchkiss was thinking about a future in which he might make commercial use of maps drawn while he was in the Confederate service is indicated when he was in Richmond seeing Major Campbell. He "also saw Gen. Gilmer about the publication of my map."[43] This may have been the Valley map, which Robinson ruled up for reduction on April 1, and Hotchkiss corrected "some," three days later when Confederate resistance was crumbling and Richmond abandoned. Whatever map it was, it seems that he was looking beyond military service. This being the case, it is reasonable to suppose that he would have placed copies of his more important maps at home where they could be recovered in the event of military disaster.

On the last day of March the topographical engineers of II Corps were once again established in Staunton, and while Robinson worked at the reduction of the Valley map, Hotchkiss "spent the day assorting my maps and putting all things in good order." On April 5, four days before Lee's surrender at Appomattox, he "started Robinson, with my maps, to Lynchburg." On the day of the surrender, Hotchkiss was with General Lomax in Lynchburg. While there he arranged for his maps to be sent to Salem. When it was clear that all resistance was at an end he went there for them, secured a wagon, and made for home. On his way he stopped at Lexington and left his maps concealed at the home of the Reverend Ruffner, where they remained until collected by Hotchkiss in July.[44]

His concern with military mapping did not end with the surrender, but continued practically to the end of his life. He was not home long before he was producing maps for Michie on behalf of General Grant, and for the publication with William Allan of their account of the Chancellorsville battle, but his most important contribution to the postwar mapping of the conflict was made over thirty years later when the War Records Office prepared *The Atlas to Accompany the Official Records of the Union and Confederate Armies.* There can be seen some of the more important of the maps produced by Hotchkiss to illustrate reports. The compilers included, for example, "Sketch of the Battle of Winchester, Va., Sunday, May 25th, 1862," "Sketch of the Second Battle of Winchester, June 13, 14, and 15th 1863," "Sketch of the Battles of Chancellorsville, Salem Church and Fredericksburg, May 2, 3 and 4, 1863 prepared by the order of General Lee," and "Sketch of the Battle of Belle Grove...October 19th, 1864." A glance through the list of "Authorities" shows that he has more maps to his credit than any other cartographer, North or South, though it must be mentioned in this connection that, employed as he was, as "Topographer in Office of Publication of Records of Rebellion" he was in a good position to ensure that his work was well represented.[45] The Atlas was first issued in parts, and Hotchkiss esteemed it "a very great honor" that an entire part, part XVII (Plates LXXXI-LXXXV), was devoted to his maps.[46]

In 1874 Congress provided the means "to enable the Secretary of War to begin the publication of the *Official Records of the War of the Rebellion*, both of the Union and Confederate Armies." Real progress, however, awaited the appointment, in 1877, of Lieutenant Colonel Robert N. Scott, who was to devote himself exclusively to this task until his death ten years later. Some time in 1884, Hotchkiss was in contact with Scott and drew attention to the report he had made of the 1864 Shenandoah Valley Campaign and Jubal Early's thrust toward Washington. That report with its many maps had not been sent into the C.S. Engineer Office, but would have been among the archives if Sheridan had not routed the II Corps at Waynesboro in the spring of 1865.[47] From the discussions with Scott, Hotchkiss was encouraged to obtain a quote for the printing of 1,000-3,000 sets of 45 maps with an indication that the War Records Office would pay the bill.[48] Although the report was taken up at that time, the compilation of an atlas of maps to supplement the

Official Records did not begin until First Lieutenant Calvin Duvall Cowells took up the task in 1889, under the direction of the newly formed three-member Board of Publication, whose military member was Major George B. Davis.[49] Cowles approached Hotchkiss in September 1891 with a query about a Hotchkiss 1861 sketch-map of "Camp Garnett and Vicinity."[50] This was the first intimation that Hotchkiss had that an atlas was being compiled, but from then on he was in frequent correspondence with Cowles, and with Davis. The result of this collaboration was a substantial Hotchkiss contribution to the record of Confederate mapping, and remains to this day the largest single collection of Hotchkiss maps to be published.

In 1894 the Federal Government appointed a commission to examine the possibility of acquiring control over the site of the Antietam Battlefield. Its president was George B. Davis who was assisted by General Ezra A. Carmen as expert historian, and by Henry Heth, a former Confederate major general. The first need of the Commission was an accurate map of the battlefield on which to mark troop positions and movements. Naturally, Davis asked Hotchkiss if he was interested. Within days of their conversation he was appointed to the position of expert topographer at a salary of $200 per month. On October 13, 1894, Davis wrote to Hotchkiss: "Matters have moved forward more rapidly than I dared hope when I saw you last week. I am now able to send you an appointment on the Antietam work." He then explained that the immediate task was to get a series of maps into the hands of a lithographer within the next 60 days. Carmen was already at Sharpsburg, Davis and Hotchkiss were to join him on Thursday, October 17.[51] Hotchkiss' reply to this "command" was that he would "report for duty on Wednesday morning." Following this visit to the old battlefield, Hotchkiss set out his scheme for developing the map. It had already been agreed that it should be based on Michler's map in the War Record Atlas.[52] He now proposed that this should be enlarged and cut into four sheets of unequal size, specifying just where the N-S and E-W dividing lines should be drawn. By this means it was possible to contain "a large portion of the active field of operations"- on the northwest, or No. 1, sheet. Initially Hotchkiss had suggested a 4× linear enlargement, but soon concluded that 3× would be sufficient. This would result in a map to a scale of six-inches-to-the-mile, the whole being about four feet square.[53] A month later the No. 1 sheet was ready for the photo-engraver. 500 copies of the map were printed on ordinary map paper, and a further 25 on Whatman's drawing paper, at a total cost of $52.[54] From the larger number, copies were to be sent to state governors and others for annotation of troop positions, the smaller number of more substantial copies being for

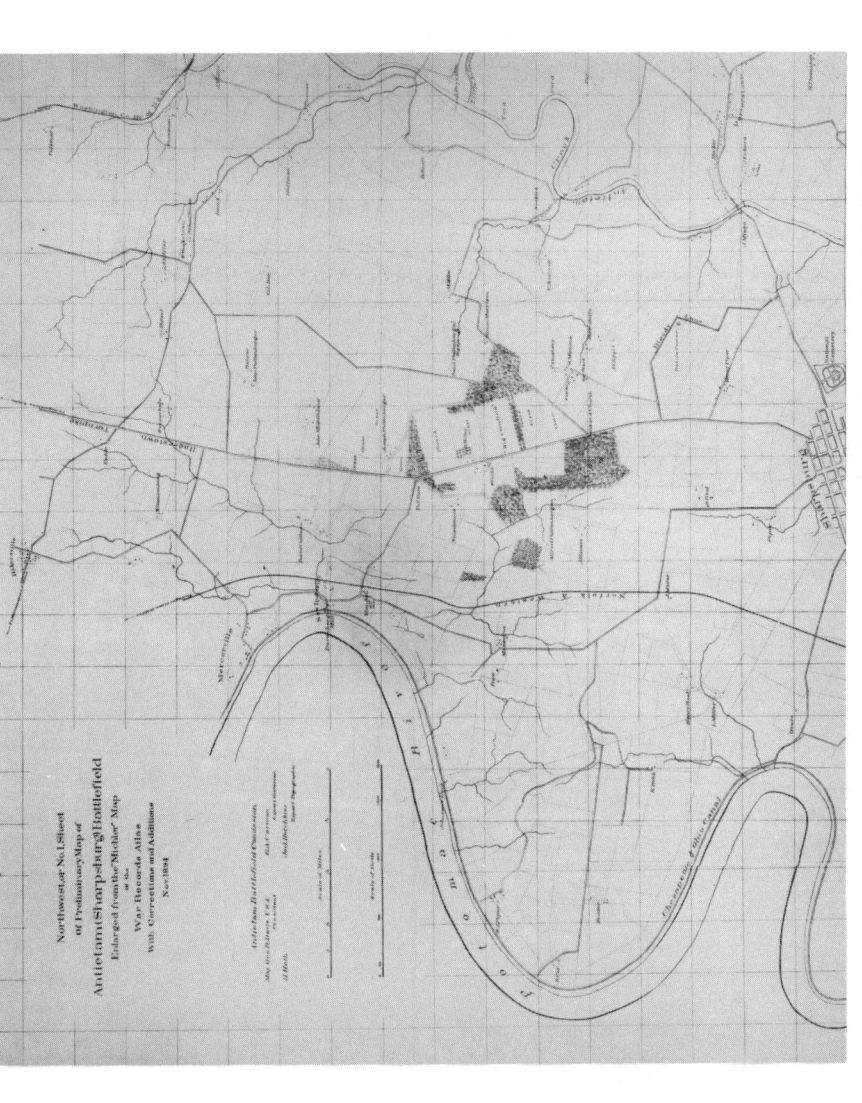

Antietam Battlefield. This map was drawn by Hotchkiss for the Antietam Battlefield Commission. Copies were distributed to State Governors for marking the location of army formations during the battle. On this particular copy Hotchkiss marked his suggestions for a "Battle Avenue" and a "Battle Tower." Both are important features of the present-day battlefield park. *National Archives*

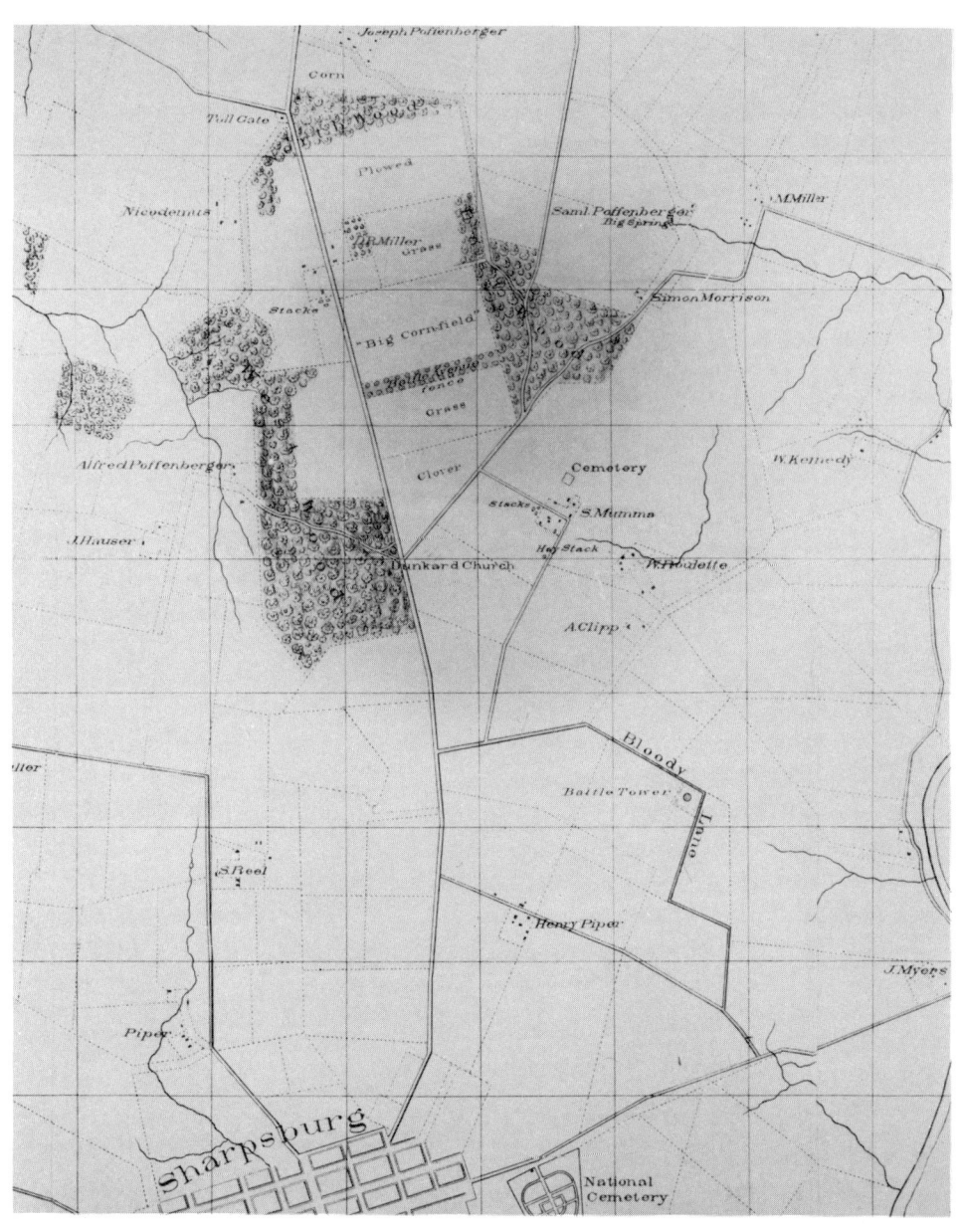

A portion of the Antietam battlefield map showing the proposed Battle Avenue and Battle Tower.

National Archives

the commissioner's own use. One Hotchkiss sent to Davis to show land which he and Carmen recommended should be purchased. They proposed a battle avenue alongside the south fence of "Big Cornfield" as well as the purchase of an acre of land as a site for a battle tower. Both thought these could become among the most attractive features of the battlefield.[55] The southwest, or No. 2, sheet was ready for the printer in January 1895, and at the end of the following month Carmen was ready to put troop positions on the map.[56]

Thus progress had been rapid, even the objective of getting a map to the printers within 60 days had been achieved. But then, toward the end of March, Hotchkiss received a letter from Davis which brought official work to a halt. "When I submitted the estimate for the work at Antietam," wrote Davis, "I set apart $1,200 for the entire expense of the maps, ...I find on examining the abstracts of expenditure that we have already expended nearly $1,700 on that account. This will make it necessary for us to stop....Our existing arrangement will have to come to an end on April 30. I regret it exceedingly."[57] Hotchkiss replied that he would continue to work on the Antietam map at his own expense until completed to his satisfaction. He was unable to fulfill this good intention, but the existence of the manuscript drawing on tracing cloth of *Preliminary map No. 3*, dated July 1895, demonstrates that he did not immediately abandon the project.[58]

Official interest in the work was revived in 1896, and Hotchkiss was determined to play his part. He had discussed his plan with Congressman Henry St. George Tucker, and in a letter dated May 30, 1896, confirmed that he wanted to be a commissioner, but would not apply if Heth was also an applicant. However, he stated, "I want it distinctly understood that if I am not a member of the commission I am to be its official Topographic Engineer." In stating his claim to this position he invoked the support of his long dead heroes. He told Tucker, "This was the battle of R. E. Lee and Stonewall Jackson, one in which each of these great Generals displayed his peculiar and transcendent abilities as a soldier, and I know that if these two had the choosing of anyone to represent them in securing an accurate map of this battlefield, with their men properly located on it, that they would unhesitatingly choose your humble servant for that duty."[59] Tucker twice wrote to the Secretary of War supporting his application, only to be told that Generals Heth and Carmen had been "appointed as members of the Board of Experts in connection with the marking of the battlelines of Antietam. As those gentlemen, with the army member of the Board will be able to attend to all the work yet to be done, and for which a small appropriation was made, it will be impossible to appoint Major Hotchkiss."[60] This denial of the opportunity to honor his wartime comrades must have been a severe disappointment to Hotchkiss.

In the years immediately following the war Hotchkiss was, above all, concerned to provide for his family. His military experience had given him another set of tools for the purpose; these he used to supplement his income from teaching. The gradual emergence of his interest in the economic development of the Virginias has already been described. Suffice it to say that he applied his cartographic skills to enterprises as varied as human activity can be. From individual house plots to whole towns, from small farms to great estates of hundreds of thousands of acres, from cemetery plans to county and state-wide maps. Increasingly, however, his activities came to be dominated by one theme: the development of mineral resources, in particular iron and coal, vital to the emerging industrial economy of the time. In all the vast cartographic activity that this involved, one project was of fundamental importance; the production of the first geological map of the Virginias.

His work on this started with his commission from the state in 1873 to compile *Virginia: A Geographical and Political Summary*, not published until 1876. William B. Rogers colored the base map specially drawn for the purpose at a scale of 24-miles-to-1-inch. This received only limited distribution and was not actively promoted by the sponsoring department. It was left to Hotchkiss to give it wider public notice in 1880 when he had 10,000 copies printed, and it was issued as a supplement to *The Virginias*. From this initial map there evolved a series of geological maps produced at larger and larger scales. The following year he drew for F. J. Kimball, of the Norfolk & Western Railroad, a map, 48 × 72 inches in size, probably on a scale of 8-miles-to-1-inch. This was to decorate the wall of Kimball's office, and it is unlikely that it was anything more than an adequate representation of the main geological features of the state. While this was being drawn, and 35 days of work had been put into it, Hotchkiss received a request for an even larger map "showing the Geographical, Geological, Mineral, and Timber resources of the State and railroad facilities of the State."[61] This inquiry came from the Virginia State Agricultural Society and was the origin of the wallmaps made to a scale of 3.5-miles-to-1-inch which Hotchkiss used to illustrate a variety of themes at the New Orleans Exposition of 1884-5. An edition of 100 of the base maps was printed at a cost of $500, and he was selling hand-colored versions at $50 each early in 1882. Hotchkiss had extracted promises of purchase from 10 of his supporters to ensure that the printing costs were covered. Among the willing purchasers was John W. Powell, director of the U.S. Geological Survey (U.S.G.S.), who was given favorable terms. He got two plain and one colored for $100.⁶² The ten maps derived from this and exhibited at New Orleans were "each mounted in a frame 6 inches wide, each from a different kind or kinds of native Virginia woods handsomely finished to show their character."⁶³ Apart from geology, the themes depicted were railways, each system colored differently, mineral deposits, counties, the natural grand divisions, relief, hydrography, rainfall, temperature. Also exhibited was the new edition of the 24-miles-to-1-inch map, the one to accompany *Rogers' Geology of the Virginias*. This showed for the first time the Permian area of West Virginia.

As judged from the description of the geological map exhibited at New Orleans, one example of the map currently in the Library of Congress is very similar in its coloring. The coloring of the map to accompany *Rogers' Geology of the Virginias* had been a matter of some discussion between Hotchkiss and Mrs. Emma Rogers. In 1882 the U.S.G.S. had adopted a range of colors to identify on their maps the outcrops of different geological formations. Mrs. Rogers reluctantly agreed to the use of the new scheme instead of the beautiful coloring of Mr. Rogers' choice "which we so carefully studied together."⁶⁴ She was later reassured when told that the scheme of colors "is likely to be in good taste and harmonious in arrangement as it is in the hands of Mr. Holmes...an artist of some distinction."⁶⁵ However, Hotchkiss found the new colors "abominable," so, much to the pleasure of Mrs. Rogers, he changed his mind.⁶⁶ To this she responded, "I cannot say that I regret to return to the colors of *our map*, for the harmonious tints were surrendered with a pang and even in the specimen of the U.S. colors the shocking blue and purple offend the eye."⁶⁷ The coloring of the map displayed at the New Orleans Exposition and of one of the Library of Congress maps is in accordance with the U.S.G.S. scheme, while the one on view at the Virginia Polytechnic Institute (V.P.I.) uses the colors preferred by the Rogers. The map at the V.P.I. was bought from Mrs. Rogers and is presumably the one Hotchkiss colored for her in 1882.⁶⁸

Of greater scientific interest would have been the geological map which Hotchkiss and Rogers had always wanted to produce, from the time of their first collaboration. Rogers had in mind a map at a scale of 10- or 12-miles-to-1-inch,⁶⁹ but when Hotchkiss told him of a publisher's wish that he prepare a map of Virginia and West Virginia at the larger scale of 4-miles-to-1-inch Rogers commented, "I would prefer either this or better still a reduction to one half."⁷⁰ Nothing came of these discussions, but in March 1882 Rogers wrote to Hotchkiss (using his wife as a scribe) that "now he is released from the cares of

M.I.T." he hoped in conjunction with Hotchkiss and others to produce the kind of map they had talked of in the past.[71] The following month Professor and Mrs. Rogers stayed with Hotchkiss for a few days after Rogers had attended the meeting of the National Academy of Sciences in Washington. The two men discussed the project and shortly afterwards "decided to prepare and publish a new Geological and Topographical Map of Virginia and West Virginia, on a scale of 8-miles-to-1-inch."[72] Hotchkiss claimed that this map would be far more accurate and complete, both topographically and geologically, than any hitherto published. Unfortunately Rogers died (May 30, 1882) before anything was done. His widow, having resolved to reprint Rogers' reports of the Virginia Geological Survey and to carry out her husband's wishes in the matter of the publication of the map, wrote to Hotchkiss in August seeking his assistance. From the correspondence between them over the following years it is clear that Hotchkiss gave Mrs. Rogers considerable help in her project, for he was as anxious as she to see that the work of the late Professor Rogers was made available to those having an interest in Virginia's development. In particular he undertook to continue the work on the map to accompany the publication of *Rogers' Geology of the Virginias.* They entered into a formal agreement in October 1882 "to publish at joint expense and share equally any profits or losses an edition of 1,000 copies" of the map.[73] Although the book was not available for printing until late in 1884, Hotchkiss had not completed the map and the book was published with only the new edition of the small scale map prepared for the *Summary of Virginia.* Referring to the larger geological map in her Preface to the reprint Mrs. Rogers wrote, "Delays caused by waiting for important topographical surveys now in progress, have made it impossible to publish this map at present, but it is hoped that it will not be long delayed." Although Hotchkiss wrote to Mrs. Rogers on August 7, 1885, that he would probably get the map in shape early next year, and was discussing the project with Powell in 1886, there is no evidence that the map was ever published, and no manuscript is known to exist.[74]

Hotchkiss' aim was always to present geological and mineral information to a public, sometimes a few hundred potential purchasers of a piece of real estate, sometimes a few thousand who would invest in a railroad or subscribe to a coal land association, or to the tens of thousand who attended the New Orleans Exposition, but he always seems to have had an urge to reach a wider public, a desire to be a map publisher. He indulged his fancy shortly after the war when he published the circular map *35 miles around Richmond.* (See p. 97) This was printed by C. Bohn of Richmond. The contract provided for royalties to be paid every six months. But nine years later, Hotchkiss wrote with remarkable restraint, "Is it not time for us to have a settlement—I think so now that *nine years* have passed and I will be obliged to you for a statement of account *according to contract.*"[75] That experience seems to have persuaded him that success as an independent map publisher was unlikely. However, as we have seen was the case with the Board of Survey of Washington College and the *Southern Planter and Farmer*, he continued to seize every opportunity to get his maps into print. His journal *The Virginias* provided him with the best opportunity for putting maps before the public, and was liberally illustrated with them either within the text or as supplements. Apart from the geological map, other notable maps were *Map of The Shenandoah Valley showing the location of The Shenandoah Valley Railroad*, scale 1/400,000, 1880; *Topographical Map of the Flat-top Mountain Coalfield*, scale 3-miles-to-1-inch, 1882; and *Geological Map of the Potomac Basin West of the Blue Ridge*, 1882.

A venture which occupied a great deal of time and temper was the preparation of the maps for the *Historical Atlas of Augusta County, Virginia* published by Waterman, Watkins & Co., Chicago, in 1885, who first approached Hotchkiss in April or May 1883. He offered to draw maps of ten valley counties and their magisterial districts ready for the engraver on the basis of $1 per square mile.[76] At some time during the next twelve months they must have come to an agreement by which Hotchkiss was to prepare certain maps in a form suitable for the lithographic printing process. Then in June 1884, when Hotchkiss was well into the task and had two men employed correcting and revising maps, Waterman's changed their mind and wanted to use photolithography. This seems to be the beginning of an acrimonious correspondence which continued until the Atlas was completed. At first Hotchkiss was prepared to do the additional work required by the change, provided of course he was paid for it. Almost immediately he had second thoughts, writing that he had not the time to do so, not even he was paid ten times as much.[77] Whether for that reason or not, the publishers reverted to the original plan.

It was not long before there was more trouble. Waterman's continually complained of Hotchkiss' slowness. Hotchkiss was always endeavoring to influence the printing process, stipulating the style of lettering to be used, and even suggesting which engravers the publishers should employ. He strongly recommended Bien for the job, saying, "They are the best engravers in the country."[78] Waterman's were not prepared to take his advice, and there followed a whole series of criticisms from Hotchkiss. In September 1884, having received a proof of the map of

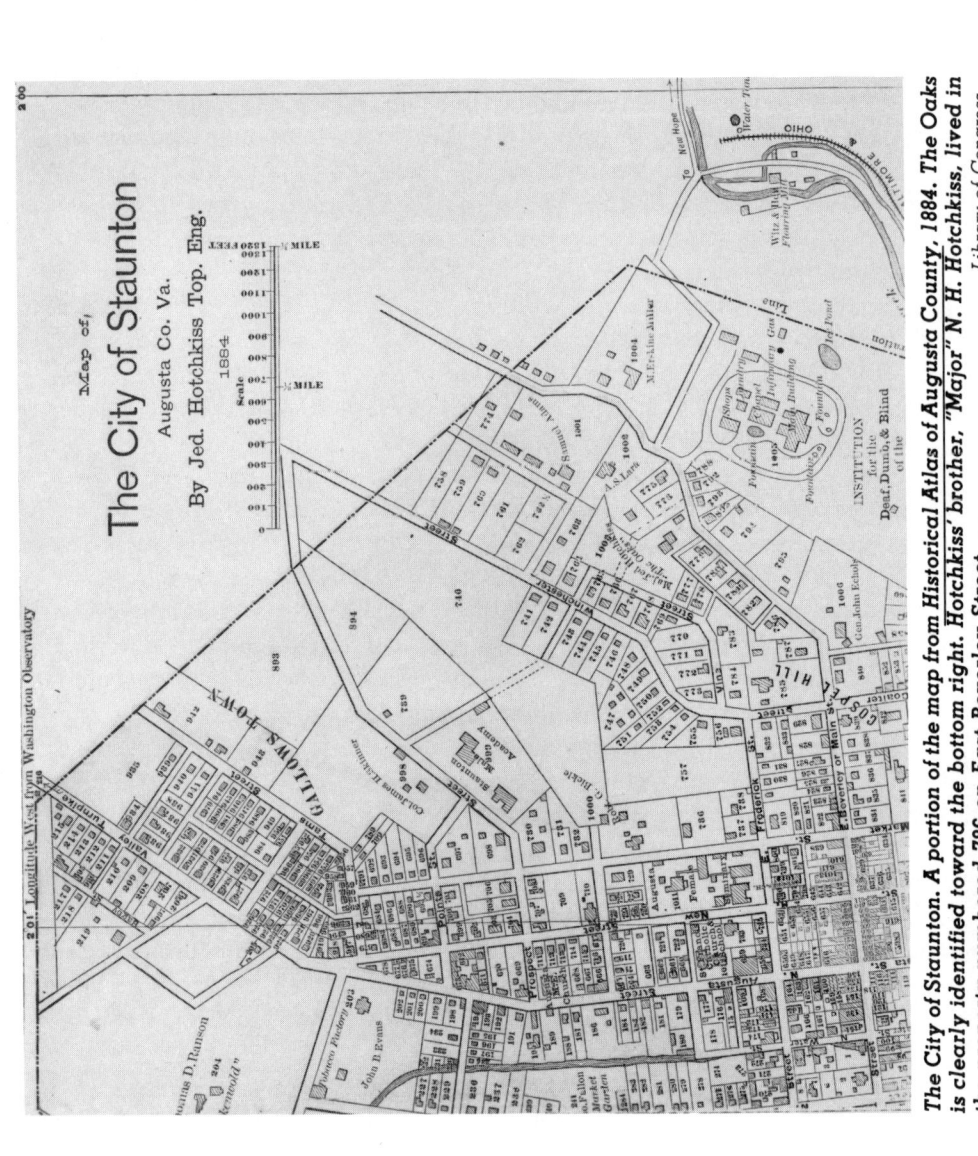

The City of Staunton. A portion of the map from Historical Atlas of Augusta County, 1884. The Oaks is clearly identified toward the bottom right. Hotchkiss' brother, "Major" N. H. Hotchkiss, lived in the property numbered 786 on East Beverley Street.

Library of Congress

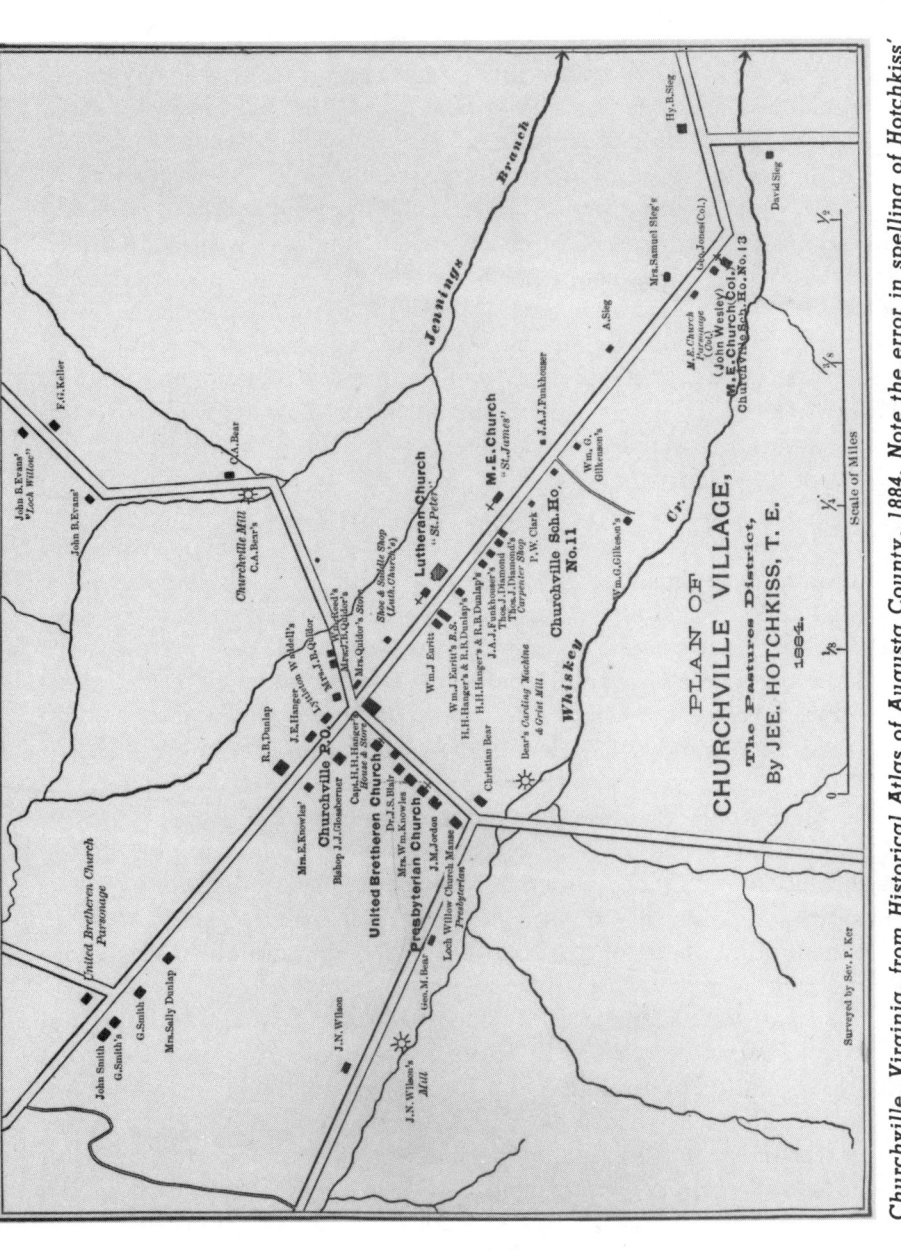

Churchville, Virginia, from *Historical Atlas of Augusta County*, 1884. Note the error in spelling of Hotchkiss' christian name which escaped his critical eye. The Loch Willow property is shown at the top of the map.

Library of Congress

the Middle River District, Hotchkiss wrote, "I hope you have asked your engravers to send me a copy of Beverley Manor as soon as completed. I must say to you frankly that *I do not like this work at all* it is about the worst map work I ever saw, and I am prepared to be seriously disappointed when I see the sample of Beverley Manor...." He even asked that his name be erased from the map title: "I *cannot* afford to appear as the author of maps having this appearance."[79] Worse was to follow. The engravers badly damaged one of the maps so that the work had to be done all over again. An exasperated Hotchkiss wrote, "In an experience of 30 years I never had a burnt map or one used up past remedy before."[80] When Waterman's complained that the Staunton map was too crowded he replied, "Of course it is crowded as it has over 1,100 properties on it, but a *good engraver* can make a handsome map of it and *no other can.*"[81] His assessment of the printers employed by Waterman's was summarized in the letter accompanying the return of proof sheets of five District maps.

> In all my long experience in correcting proofs I have never found the equal of these for downright perversity and general badness. They do not hesitate to change copy in every sort of way and omit whatever suits them to omit....You ought to make them clean up and finish the maps and return to me two copies of each when completed, with all my copy and proofs, so I can see if correct, before they are printed, for they cannot be trusted to make corrections.[82]

If all this was not enough, two weeks later on February 24, 1885, Hotchkiss had good reason to berate one of the principals of the publishing house. Once again the printers had made alterations without consulting him, but this time they did seek the authority of Mr. Watkins who, instead of discussing the matter with Hotchkiss, went elsewhere to confirm the name of a particular mountain.

In an address made to the Society of Arts of the Massachusetts Institute of Technology in 1882, following the death of Professor Rogers, Hotchkiss had proposed that the highest summit in the "grand Appalachian Ranges" should be called Mount Rogers. At the time this point was thought to be Elliott Knob, a prominent mountain peak west of Staunton, Virginia, with a height of 4,448 feet. Hotchkiss took the opportunity afforded by the publication of the atlas of Augusta County to introduce the new name of Mount Rogers. This was to be printed boldly above the old name, still to be retained, but placed within brackets. Without consulting Hotchkiss, the publishers erased Mount Rogers and reverted to the old name. Hotchkiss was incensed, especially as it had been widely accepted in scientific circles that his proposal should be adopted. He insisted that his instructions must be adhered to, and declared that he, and he alone, was responsible for the contents of the map.[83]

Hotchkiss won his battle with the publishers, but could not defeat nature. In 1891 that means of honoring Virginia's great geologist was secured for all time when Rogers' name was given to the summit of a ridge in southwest Virginia in what is now Mount Rogers National Recreation Area.[84]

Nor were his troubles confined to the maps, for it was part of the agreement that he would provide a description of the topography of the county, a description which he could not condense into the two pages hoped for by the publishers.[85] Whatever his difficulties with the publishers, we can only be grateful to Hotchkiss for his part in the production of a record of the human geography of Augusta County for the mid-1880s.

There was one final irony in all this trouble with the publishers and printers: his name on the map of the village of Churchville, his home for many years, was incorrectly spelled as JEE HOTCHKISS.

The nineteenth-century maps of Virginia were compilations of the various county maps that existed at the time. Indeed, in the absence of an institution charged with the task of conducting a state survey, that was the only expedient available to publishers. As the county surveys had been conducted at different times, and varied widely in quality, the derived state map fell far short of the standard that could have been achieved. Contrary to what might be thought, the creation of the United States Geological Survey in 1879 did not bring about an immediate improvement in this situation.

Prior to 1879, the Federal government assumed responsibility for the charting of the coastline, and for the survey of the public domain west of the Appalachian mountains, but left the mapping of the land within state boundaries to the discretion of state governments. Five years of bitter debate about who should be responsible for mapping and who should direct the new agency culminated in the formation of the U.S. Geological Survey. Powell, the second director of the Survey, extended its role to cover not just the lands in the public domain, but those of the individual states. He did that by the simple expedient of having the phrase "and to continue the preparation of a geological map of the United States" added to the wording of the 1882 Sundry Civil Expenditure Bill. It didn't matter that such a map had not even been started!

Hotchkiss strongly favored that extension. Leaving to their governments the responsibility for topographical and geological mapping of the land within the states' boundaries had meant forty years of neglect in Virginia. In July 1882 he wrote, not only to Powell, but also to Congressman Paul and to Senator William Mahone, urging an increase in the appropriation to the U.S.G.S. to permit it to operate within the states. When the appropriation was increased by $100,000, Powell thanked Hotchkiss for his "kind and efficient aid in behalf of the Survey."[86]

For his chief geographer, who would organize the field work and supervise the mapmaking, Powell appointed Henry Gannett. Gannett, familiar with Hotchkiss' activities, his leading role in the promotion of Virginia's natural resources, and his cartographic output, made a visit to the Hotchkiss office in February 1883 to browse among the maps and borrow those of interest to him.[87] As a result the U.S.G.S. made an official offer "for the privilege of making copies of all the map material in your possession embraced in the Mountain and Piedmont region of Virginia and West Virginia." For this the Survey offered to pay Hotchkiss $1,250 and a similar sum for the balance of his material relating to the eastern part of Virginia.[88] The copies were to be made photographically, and it was part of the deal that Hotchkiss would have his maps returned together with a photographic copy. In all, 53 maps of the western part of the Virginias were borrowed by the Survey, only a small proportion being Hotchkiss' work. Other important material, included, for example, Claudet Crozet's original survey of the Staunton and Parkersburg Turnpike. Of his own work, *Augusta County* took pride of place on the list of the first batch of thirty maps sent on July 4, 1883. Wartime maps which may have been drawn by Hotchkiss or compiled under his supervision were attributed simply to C.S. Engineers. These included what was probably his famous map of the Shenandoah Valley at the 1/80,000 scale.[89] In 1885, when Hotchkiss had completed his new 1-inch-to-1-mile map of Augusta County for Waterman, Watkins, & Co., he sent it along to Gannett to be photographically reduced to ⅓- and also ¼-inches-to-the-mile and asked for two or three copies at each scale. He expected Gannett to do this "for the sake of getting copies of this new map for your collection." At the same time Hotchkiss promised to send him a copy of Rogers' *Geology of the Virginias.*[90]

It was not just a one-way process. In 1890 when writing to Professor I. C. White about the prospects for buying land, Hotchkiss was able to say, "Confidentially I obtained from the Geological Survey office, by paying the men to work them up outside office hours, advance sheets on an inch scale of the map of the Gauley region. These I have redrawn and will send to the photo-engraver and have three hundred sheets printed for our own use; some of them I will send you."[91] This seemingly unorthodox procedure was conducted quite openly, and

Hotchkiss received a bill on U.S.G.S.-headed paper from Charles E. Cook "for services 50 hours @ 50¢ per hour," which Hotchkiss paid on February 18, 1890.[92] On the whole though, it was the Survey which benefitted more from Hotchkiss' interest in its activities. Thus in the summer of 1892, after a week exploring along East River Mountain in Tazewell County, he wrote privately to Gannett: "Of course I took along your map of that region for use, and feel it my duty to a highly valued friend to call your attention to the fact that, in reference to the region I went over, this map is wholly unreliable; in fact is ridiculously wrong, and I would not give out any more sheets of it until it has been thoroughly revised." Because there was the possibility in the near future of mineral development in the area, Hotchkiss advised Gannett to "immediately have that region gone over and revised, especially the part between the crest of East River Mountain and the Clear Fork of Wolf Creek. I cannot conceive what your topographers were doing when there to have secured such results."[93]

In 1893 there was considerable Congressional dissatisfaction with Powell, which primarily stemmed from the vested interests of senators of Western states who disliked his notions on the management of desert areas. Doubt was cast not only on Powell's future as the Director of the Geological Survey, but on the Survey itself. The possibility that it would be disbanded dismayed Hotchkiss, who campaigned on its behalf. He had a long conversation about this with Senator Blackburn of Virginia. He wrote to fellow Stauntonian, Henry St. George Tucker, Democratic representative in Congress, "I hope Congress will not abolish the Geological Survey, but will reorganize it with a definite line of duty....Our District and State have much benefitted by the topographical work of the Survey, and now they can be greatly benefitted if its whole force can be turned over to what we call 'Economic Geology.' The only way such a result can be obtained, though, will be by having *clearly defined requirements as to work and publication set forth in Statute.*"[94] Although there were cuts in the appropriation for the Survey in 1893, the Survey survived, but the following year Powell was succeeded as director by Charles D. Walcott.

Hotchkiss had a particular reason at that time to be dismayed at the prospect of the abolition of the Survey. His endeavors to have made a proper survey and map of Virginia stretched back at least to the days of Robert E. Lee and Washington College's Board of Survey. Now there was a real hope of this coming about. Late in 1893 he was in correspondence with a Mr. R. U. Goode of the U.S.G.S. about such a project, one in which Goode had taken the initiative by writing to Hotchkiss to outline his ideas and to seek comment. Hotchkiss replied immediately and was candid with his criticism of the current U.S.G.S. maps, remarking on the lettering, a subject on which he had very decided views, the lack of place names and public roads. He had some interesting observations to make about the depiction of relief. His only objection to the scheme put up by Goode was to the proposal to use contours for this purpose. "If introduced they should be only those at 500 feet intervals. Everyone that uses the maps published by the Geological Survey objects seriously to the contours. They confuse the map and are of necessity conjectural and therefore of no use. I think you would give far more satisfaction if you would simply shade the prominent mountains and ridges omitting all contour lines because of the present state of our knowledge in reference to them but putting in small but plain Arabic figures the known altitudes of prominent points."[95]

As for lettering, Hotchkiss made his usual points, stressing his dislike of block and open letters, and preferring always the use of upper-case for the initial letter of a name followed by lower-case letters. He told Goode that he had

> succeeded in getting the Geological Survey to introduce, in part, the scheme of caps and lower case, greatly to the advantage of their maps, but I consider it a great defect in them that the names of the counties are run on as they are. They cover too much space on the map and are difficult to find. The question ought always to be *"Which is the better form for use?"* and that should be unhesitatingly adopted. No name should be extended by large spacing. Another great mistake is the putting the names of some rivers in capitals. It will add immensely to the value of your map, I am satisfied from a long experience in making and publishing maps, to adopt this rule of putting no words in capital letters, not even in the title, and rigidly following it. I am having maps of all sizes made constantly and find that they give satisfaction because of this method of lettering. I look upon it as one of the most important things in any map.[96]

When Hotchkiss learned that Goode held similar views to his own on the depiction of mountain topography he was prepared to do all he could to promote Goode's plans. The largest demand for the sort of map Goode had in mind would be from the public schools where the potential demand was about 10,000 copies, so Hotchkiss lost no time in interesting the State Superintendent of Public Instruction in the project.[97] In spite of this, and the lobbying of members of the Virginia Assembly, nothing came of that initiative.

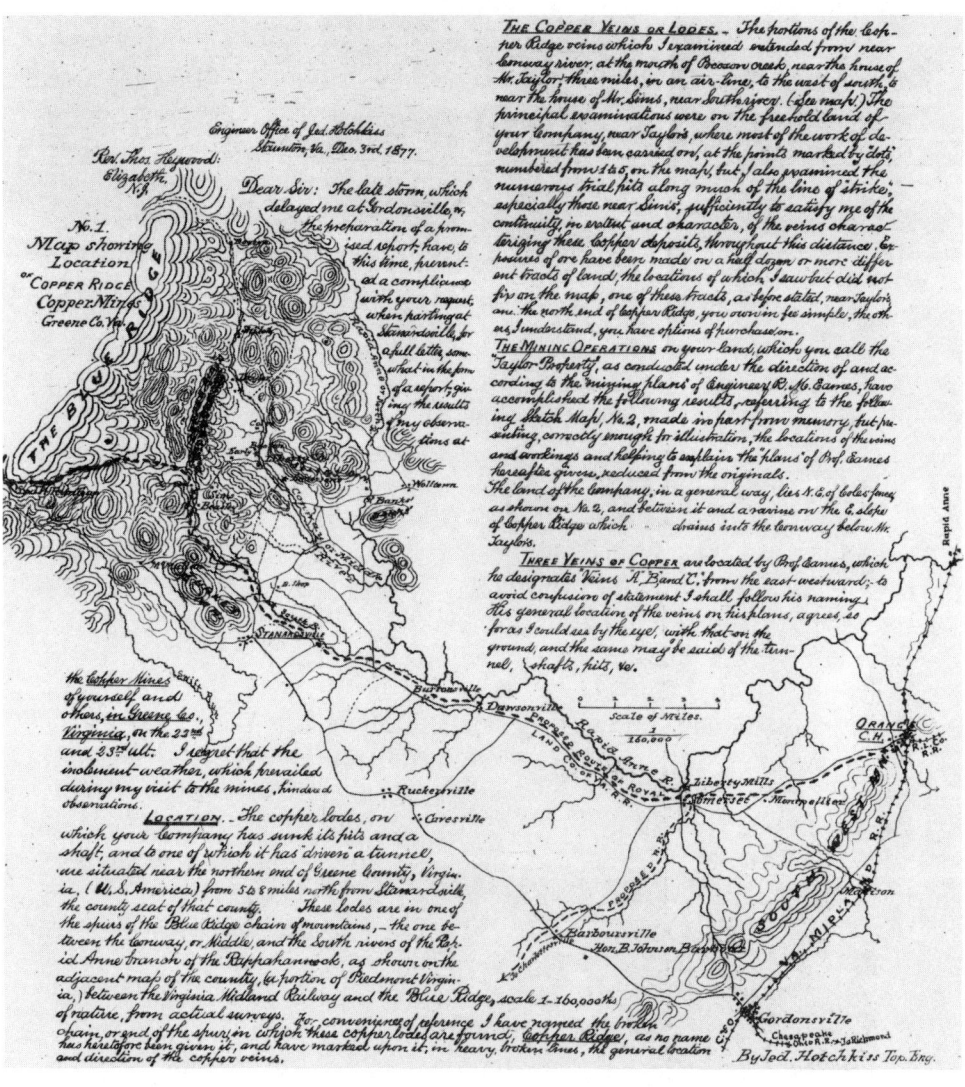

Page 1 of a letter to the Reverend Thomas Heywood, December 3, 1877. This is typical of the way in which Hotchkiss reported on small commissions; map and text complimented each other.

Hotchkiss Papers, Box 3, Library of Congress

Before his death, Hotchkiss made one more attempt to have a proper survey and map made of the Commonwealth. This time he wanted Virginia to follow the example of other states by making this a joint venture with the U.S.G.S. To assist in survey work, and to ensure that the wishes of individual states were considered, the U.S.G.S. was prepared to make co-operative arrangements with state surveys where they existed. The methods and conduct of the field work was under U.S.G.S. control, with the state reserving the right to inspect, approve, or condemn the work. Funding was shared between the national and state agencies.[98] Agreements for the making of co-operative topographic surveys had been entered into by seven states, including Virginia's neighbors, Maryland and North Carolina. In spite of Hotchkiss' efforts to publicize the resources of the Virginias, or perhaps because he had been too successful in this self-imposed task, Virginia had not reinstated its Geological Survey (disbanded in 1841), and, in the view of Hotchkiss and his friends, had suffered as a consequence. Thus Professor White wrote to Hotchkiss to offer the opinion that both West Virginia and Virginia had allowed themselves "to be outstripped in the industrial pursuits by neighboring ones with far less mineral and natural resources, simply because the world at large knows nothing officially concerning them."[99] Notwithstanding the spirit of retrenchment that pervaded the Assembly at this time, Hotchkiss had, in December 1897, written to the newly elected Governor, J. Hoge Tyler, suggesting that Virginia should imitate the example of New Jersey which for more than 60 years had conducted a geological survey at moderate expense, a mere $10,000 per annum.[100] To assist in the financing of the proposal, Hotchkiss recommended that the Department of Agriculture should be disposed of, and the office of railroad commissioner be done away with, and the railroads be asked to contribute the money saved to the support of the survey. At his instigation a bill was presented to the Assembly's House Committee on Finance to establish a state geologic and economic survey. The bill was introduced to the committee by Silas N. Walker of Augusta, who invited Hotchkiss to address its members. This he did at considerable length, persuading them to forward the bill to a joint session of the finance committees of the two houses of the Virginia Assembly. There was widespread sympathy for the objects of the bill, but no money, a situation that was mirrored by the outcome; the bill was passed, but without an appropriation to implement it.

The volume and variety of Hotchkiss' cartographic output defies a summary. Wherever a map would aid understanding, then a map was provided. It was the supreme form of communication, to which written and spoken words were usually subordinate, for no quantity of print could convey the information so meaningfully. His many lectures were illustrated by maps which he drew in chalk on a blackboard, more accurately a blackcloth, which he carried with him. On occasion he was used by others lacking drafting skills to draw a map as the lecturer developed his theme. This facility to use the map as a method of communication is most clearly demonstrated in some of the letters and reports to his colleagues and clients. In these the map is not relegated to a separate sheet, but is an integral part of the message, the script embracing the map.[101] It is in these letters that we see most clearly the special talent, the fluency of expression that was Hotchkiss in his chosen, self-taught, self-created language.

Truly, "His maps are at once a book and a picture."[102]

CHAPTER XI

Family and Friends

ALTHOUGH SOLITARY in many of his ways, and independent in his actions, Hotchkiss had no difficulty in making friends. How otherwise would he have become part and parcel of the Mossy Creek community? He did not go there intending to stay. He stayed because he found his life there agreeable. He could have used his earnings from tutoring the Forrer children to pay for higher education for himself. But instead he invested his time and treasure in the people he had come to know by chance. True, there was much in the physical surroundings to attract and keep him. It was a beautiful country, shaped by an intriguing geology which generated a fertile soil for cultivation by a hard-working and God-fearing population. He was living in the home of a man who depended upon the soil and the rocks for his livelihood. He was living in a house built in Revolutionary times, on a site that had been a source of iron from the earliest days of white settlement in the Valley.

To the young Hotchkiss it was a place that stimulated the many strands of his imagination and curiosity. True, he brought with him something not immediately available to the people of Mossy Creek, his booklearning and experience as a teacher, limited though those were. They were good reasons for his coming to stay for a time, but to become such a part of the community as he did, required more. To attract so many to the closing exercises of the Mossy Creek Academy after his resignation, to address this crowd in the way he did, demonstrates not only the confidence he had in himself, but also the rapport which he had with his neighbors, the most prominent of whom clubbed together to pay off the debts he had incurred in their interest. It is clear that Daniel Forrer was fond of Hotchkiss, and treated him as one of the family. The prominence of the Forrers in the district ensured that he had the necessary introductions, but the way in which the new acquaintanceships developed depended on Hotchkiss and the impression he made. All the developments at Mossy Creek indicate that he made a deep impression, and was held in high esteem.

In the army he was respected for his skills as a topographer, admired for his knowledge, relied upon for the conscientious performance of his duties. Colonel Jonathan M. Heck, reporting on the operations in West Virginia for May 24 to July 13, 1861, referred to him as "Professor Hotchkiss, my engineer," a soubriquet acknowledging his profession as a pedagogue.[1] His diary shows that he readily established good relationships with his colleagues. He was a great talker, and throughout his life got involved in conversation with whomever he happened to be travelling at the time. Stonewall Jackson thought Hotchkiss talked too much, but this, from a man who could ride all day alongside one of his staff officers without uttering a word, can hardly be accepted as a reliable assessment.

His closest friend before he settled at Mossy Creek was Ralph McKune. The nature of that friendship has to be gleaned from the few items that remain. During the summer vacation of 1851, when Hotchkiss visited his relatives around Windsor and Binghamton, he met Ralph to settle up their affairs outstanding since the walking tour. Hotchkiss recorded, "Today Ralph and I settled up our affairs and passed receipts—we have also divided the [geological] specimens collected in Virginia. We have had dealings for five years and all things have been conducted with the greatest good feelings between us."[2] Within a year Ralph was dead. How much this influenced Hotchkiss in his decision to stay in Virginia we cannot know, perhaps only that it removed a reason for returning North. It did, however, have a major effect on his future because it made Sara available to be his wife.

From the evidence, it is difficult to see his marriage as any other than one of convenience, an arrangement that suited Hotchkiss and

Mossy Creek Academy. It was only proper that he should marry, and display a stable, conventional domestic scene to parents of prospective students. To Sara it would have brought some consolation for the loss of her beau. That is not to say that Hotchkiss was anything other than a loving husband and dutiful father. He was nothing if not conventional in these matters; but there existed the clearly separated functions of husband and wife, and there is no evidence that Hotchkiss made use of Sara's intellectual abilities in any of his business activities. He worked long hours, and had done so since a boy. Only Sundays would have been available for family discourse; on that day business would have been forbidden and conversation would have been of the "improving kind." Sunday school and church twice a day did not leave a lot of time even for that. Nevertheless he showed to his wife and family the care and affection that would be expected of a man who was by nature concerned about the wellbeing of his fellows. The most moving of his diary entries was made when in England with Nellie, an entry made on Sara's birthday, Sunday, February 14, 1875. By this time it was clear to Hotchkiss that his English expedition had been a failure, and he had been away from home seven months. "My wife's birthday—God grant she is well and in good spirits—I fear she is not—and what is worse and harrows my soul is wanting some things—God grant me a speedy deliverance from present troubles and may I learn from them." Nellie was staying with Lady Antonio Brady in Stratford, East London, and after church Hotchkiss went there for lunch. In the afternoon father and daughter had an opportunity to talk matters over, "but we both nearly shed tears over home and long to get there."

If Ralph had not died, would the pull from the north have been strengthened just sufficiently to prize Hotchkiss from Virginia? And what then of the future? Certainly not service with the Confederates, no acquaintance with Lee, Jackson, Stuart, Early, and a host of other Confederate commanders, no friendship with Keith Boswell, William Allan, Christian W. Oltmanns, and Samson B. Robinson.

Of those, Robinson secured a special place in the affections of the Hotchkiss family. Whenever the Army of Northern Virginia was within riding distance of Loch Willow, and duty permitted, Hotchkiss would bring Robinson home for a glimpse of homely domesticity, a welcome break to the hardship of the field. Thus, when Hotchkiss was setting up his topographical office in Staunton during the winter of 1863-4 prior to his reconnaissance for General Early, Robinson accompanied him to Loch Willow.[3] The following Christmas there were gathered at Loch Willow, Colonels William Allan and Proctor Smith as well as Oltmanns and Robinson.

FAMILY AND FRIENDS   225

The experiences of Hotchkiss and Robinson had remarkable similarities. Both had been teachers, both were self-taught surveyors and mapmakers, both had travelled far from their family origins, and both had become attached to their adopted states, Hotchkiss to Virginia, Robinson to Louisiana.[4]

Robinson had sought adventure as an escape from unhappiness, Hotchkiss accepted adventure as an unavoidable companion of war. By the time of Lee's surrender, both had had enough, and were anxious to get on with their lives. Each respected the other for his skills, so it was natural that Robinson should join Hotchkiss in his teaching and mapmaking activities until he was able to get back to Louisiana. The success of those activities and the attachment which grew between him and the Hotchkiss family prolonged Robinson's residence in Staunton. But by the end of 1866 he felt that he could make the move with a clear conscience, and in January 1867 he made the tiring five-day journey to New Orleans.[5]

There is no evidence of a friendship developing between Hotchkiss and any other person that was as close as that between him and Robinson, but plenty to show that his friendly, generous nature, was extended to all his associates. Sometimes it was stiffened by a sense of duty, especially where the friend fell short of the standards of behavior he thought proper. Oltmanns provides an example of this. Although Hotchkiss more than once commended Oltmanns as a draftsman, it is clear from correspondence, that Oltmanns was deficient in some other respect, whether it was drink, or a lack of diligence cannot be divined. It seems that he could not always be relied upon, and when Hotchkiss' own interests were at stake other help was sought.[6]

Hotchkiss kept in touch with many of his war-time associates, and the surviving correspondence shows the high regard that accompanied their friendship for him. That friendship was renewed and strengthened in the Nineties when Hotchkiss was helping Colonel Henderson with his biography of Jackson. The unselfish, unstinted help that he rendered the biographer of his hero abundantly illustrates those characteristics which endeared him to so many. Apart from one day exploring the Port Republic battlefield, all their contact was by letter, but it was such that Henderson was able to write to Dr. Hunter McGuire, "In the first place I hope my dear old friend Hotchkiss has by this time quite recovered under your care and that you have given him a new lease of life. I wish you would send him over here. I will promise to look after him and give him 'the mixture' three times a day! I shall hope for good news of him very soon. He has been very kind to me, and I have the most affectionate regard for the grand old rebel.'"[7]

His friendship with Professor Rogers and his wife Emma was characterized by the same warmth. William Barton Rogers had succeeded his father as Professor at the College of William and Mary, Williamsburg, in the year in which Hotchkiss was born. As we have seen, he was the main source of Hotchkiss' knowledge of Virginia geology, and his inspiration in the search for, and development of, its mineral resources. He extended his friendship to Rogers as to a much-loved teacher, having him stay in his home and arranging excursions on the C&O railroad to see the progress made since his pioneer surveys of the 1830s. In turn Emma and Sara became friends, and invitations to the girls to visit Boston followed. Hotchkiss' reverence for Rogers was given practical form in the assistance he gave Mrs. Rogers in the editing and reprinting of her husband's reports and other papers on the geology of the Virginias. It was given symbolic form by his proposal to name the highest peak in the Appalachian chain within Virginia's boundaries, Mount Rogers.

To his business partners he showed the same friendship, extending himself to ensure that they were properly informed, giving them accurate, reliable information which generated the confidence necessary for friendship as well as business. Those with whom he worked in that way are too numerous to mention here. Many have already been encountered in previous chapters: Sir Antonio Brady, who provided much needed hospitality to Hotchkiss and Nellie in London; J. P. Hale of Charleston, West Virginia; Captain M. A. Miller; J. H. Bramwell; E. W. Clark; F. J. Kimball; and Professor I. C. White. These were just a few of those to be numbered among his friends, all coming into his life through business.

As his influence, and the number of his important acquaintances grew, so did the demand by others for him to use his contacts on their behalf. Whenever Hotchkiss felt justified in doing so he was happy to help in this way. These services ranged from securing railway passes for Professor White, so enabling him and his students to conduct their field work in the coal regions of West Virginia, to providing work in his survey parties to young men of his own family, or of those of his friends; from providing references to employees leaving his service, to writing to John W. Powell, head of the U.S.G.S., on behalf of the son of a state functionary. Employing young men, sons of relatives and acquaintances was a fairly safe way of discharging his obligations, and at the same time protecting his reputation. Sometimes these engagements were successful, if only in the long term, as with David Humphreys; others did not work out.

Of a totally different kind was the help given to a young lady attending the Augusta Female Seminary. Replying to a letter from J. T. Richards "in reference to the daughter of your friend who is at Miss Baldwin's school," Hotchkiss said, "[We] will soon look her up and for your sake will see what we can do to break the monotony of her stay away from home."[8]

While there is much in the surviving record describing the wide-ranging interests from which can be inferred his relationships with those with whom he did business, there is little which allows us to create a picture of the domestic scene. Before the marriage, first of Anna, then of Nellie, the evidence is particularly sparse. Domestic life is rarely noteworthy, especially if it conforms to the rules of contemporary society. Before the war, life at Loch Willow must have been hectic, especially when the school was in session. During the war, with the opposing armies fighting their destructive way up and down the Valley, it must often have been frightening. The post-war years were no less worrisome, but the fear had gone.

By 1870, Hotchkiss' brother, Nelson, who was the travelling agent for the Richmond & York River Railroad, and for the C&O, had moved his family to Staunton. In 1874 he bought a house on East Beverley Street, not far from The Oaks, so once again the two families were neighbors, and were able to give each other support in times of difficulty.[9] The two brothers were very different in character. Nelson was essentially a front man; Jed's friendly, warm sincerity was in Nelson exaggerated to a bluff geniality which earned for him some remarkable notices in the Staunton press. "That steam engine in pantaloons," the *Staunton Spectator* once described him. "The indomitable and ubiquitous agent...with his capacious Meerschaum, puffing, as usual, volumes of fragrant smoke, the sublimation of A. M. Lyon's & Co's best brand, Sultana."[10] He did, however, put his larger-than-life personality to good use on behalf of the state by organizing an excursion to Virginia for the editors of Northern newspapers. Jed Hotchkiss assisted in this, accompanying the party on its journey by special train over the C&O R.R. to White Sulphur Springs, and bringing a serious note to an otherwise convivial occasion.[11] This trip was regarded as very successful and received "many complimentary notices by the members of that excursion party."[12]

While Hotchkiss was in London seeking capital to develop the resources along the line of the C&O, his brother, "the ubiquitous Maj. N. H. Hotchkiss," was on the special train taking the official party to the ceremony of laying the last rail, and driving the last spike in the link between Richmond and the Ohio.[13]

Jed Hotchkiss may not have been entitled to use the rank of Major, but he had certainly earned it. On the other hand his brother had been a Yankee sympathizer during the war, and had actually been exempt from service in Company D, 160th Regiment, Virginia Militia, "as being disabled from the disease Scrofula."[14] Nelson's use of the title must have irritated Jed, for in 1884 he publicly demonstrated its spurious nature in the key to householders numbered on his map of Staunton, where it was contained within quotation marks.[15] Sara may not have been upset by this affectation of her brother-in-law—it was common enough—but she was by his pipe smoking, sufficiently so for Hotchkiss to record in his diary for Sunday, June 18, 1871, "Nelson came up & sat awhile Sara complaining with sore eyes."[16]

Whatever Hotchkiss might have thought of his brother, he was a fond and helpful uncle to his nieces and nephews. The youngest, Stiles, born at Loch Willow in 1860, he employed for a time to assist with the publication of *The Virginias*, but he was a rogue, utterly unreliable, and was eventually voted an outcast by the family.[17] In contrast, his brother, Elmore Delos, became a highly respected freight agent for the C&O. Of the nieces, Lora married J. Taylor Ellyson, prominent in the Democratic Party, later to be Mayor of Richmond and Lieutenant Governor of the state. Olive also settled in Richmond as Mrs. Hezekia Jordan, but Sarah remained unmarried and eventually took over her father's Staunton house.[18]

Hotchkiss had known the influential J. Taylor Ellyson before his marriage to Lora, and frequently asked his advice, or sought his help, as for example, when the liquor interests in Staunton attempted to change the local option law, and in lobbying the Virginia Assembly in support of an appropriation for a map of the state.

Hotchkiss' mother continued to live in Windsor, New York, for as long as she was able, but in November 1879 moved to Staunton to make her home with Nelson.[19] This tenacious and God-fearing woman, from whom Jed Hotchkiss seems to have derived his strong sense of duty and discipline, died in 1883. This was a tragic summer for the family, for less than a week before the old lady's death, Nelson's wife Harriet also died. But this decade brought some happiness as well as sadness to the family. For Hotchkiss it was the decade in which his proselytizing on behalf of Virginia started to bear fruit. For Anna and Nellie it was to see themselves begin new lives as married women.

On Thursday, November 26, 1885, Anna was married in the Second Presbyterian Church, Staunton, to Allan Moore Howison, merchant of Roanoke, but not until 1894 was a child born who was to survive; this was Ellen who inherited the vigor of the Hotchkiss line.[20] In the intervening period the couple returned to Staunton where Allan was employed first by a dry goods firm, then by his father-in-law as treasurer of The Grottoes Company, and, later, as a clerk with the Gauley Coal Land Association.

Whether Allan ever rued the day he became a Hotchkiss employee, as well as a son-in-law, is not on record, but it could not have been an easy life, unless by nature he was particularly placid and devoid of ambition. In return for the security of The Oaks, he yielded to an exacting master. Hotchkiss kept business and family matters entirely separate and made it clear to his son-in-law that he must do the same. Allan was treated in the same way as other employees and not as being in a privileged position as son-in-law.[21]

Nellie was married on the last day of June 1886. It was a brilliant occasion, Staunton society was out in force enjoying an open-air reception on the lawn in front of The Oaks and being entertained by the Stonewall Band.[22] The bridegroom, a widower, S. Thomas McCullough, attorney from Annapolis, Maryland. During the war he had sided with the South and served with the Second Maryland Infantry. With them he saw action at Gettysburg, was wounded and taken prisoner. As befitted an attorney of those days, he was a good orator, and used this skill to embellish the heroic Confederate record at post-war memorial meetings.

The marriage day was brilliant, the prospects bright, but the reality was different. There were no children, and Tom McCullough had a drinking problem which was to destroy him. We can only imagine the slowly developing misery that enveloped Nellie. When should she tell the family, did they know, or guess there was something wrong? What would her father say, how would he react? All her life she had heard him rail against the evil of "ardent spirits." Within a year of the marriage Hotchkiss knew that his daughter was being treated "very badly," and brought her home to The Oaks. Tom followed and made a "contrite confession of his wrong doing of which he seemed to have no knowledge."[23] He stayed with the Hotchkisses, by whom he was "received in a spirit of forgiveness" for nearly a month before he returned to Annapolis.[24] It was Hotchkiss' suggestion that he should alternate short periods there attending to business, with similar periods of relaxation at Staunton. In the meantime, Nellie remained with her parents. Hotchkiss wrote to Tom's brother, Allan McCullough: "I am afraid we do not any of us realize fully the condition of your brother. *There is no questioning the fact that he has a constant craving for stimulants and that he has no present power to resist this craving....*It is equally evident that he *must have* first class medical treatment."[25]

Attacks of delirium became increasingly common, so when in

March 1894 he had "three violent outbreaks of ungovernable passion, accompanied by threats of violence to almost every member of the family as well as to himself," Hotchkiss decided that the time had come to send him to the Western State Hospital in Staunton.[26] There was no real hope for him and he died suddenly without pain on April 20, 1897. He was buried in Thornrose Cemetery, Staunton, in a grave to be marked by a neat granite block carrying the inscription "The wages of sin is Death, but the gift of God is eternal life thro' Jesus Christ our Lord."

In the midst of all this misery and financial strain there was one bright and joyful event, the successful birth of a daughter to Anna. Ellen Moore Howison was born on October 10, 1894, and immediately became the focus of family interest. She was doted on by mother, namesake aunt, and grandmother. Even Hotchkiss was so enthused by being a grandparent that he actually wrote a letter to the 18-month-old child.[27] His thoughts at this time must have been directed toward a future beyond his own, for, quite unsolicited, he proffered advice to his nephew on the education of Elmore's sons, suggesting that they should attend Pantops Academy near Charlottesville. He excused his intervention by saying, "Your boys are the only ones who will transmit the name of our family & therefore I have in them a very peculiar interest & take pride in watching their growth & development."[28]

There can be little doubt that Hotchkiss would have liked a son of his own. His interest in the family history would certainly have generated a wish to see the Hotchkiss line extended through him, and this seems to be confirmed in his letter to Elmore. To some extent Nellie seems to have been treated as the son he never had. She accompanied him to England and she went with him to New Orleans when he had charge of Virginia's mineral exhibit at the Exposition in 1884. Anna does not seem to have had quite the same degree of attention. This impression could be a false one derived from the absence of data rather than existence of positive evidence to support it. However, the possessiveness shown by Nellie in later life toward her father's maps, papers, and house contrasts with Anna's more rational approach, and is suggestive of a particularly close bond between them. Of course she had every reason to be grateful to her father for the support he had given her during her difficult first marriage, but this was no more than a responsible parent would extend, if it were possible to do so. Anna too had benefitted from that parental solicitude.

The apparent difference in the treatment of the two daughters could be entirely due to Anna's poor health. Family health was a subject of frequent reference in the Hotchkiss correspondence. Sara was never very well at any time after Anna's birth, and her ill health contributed to

Hotchkiss' decision to leave Mossy Creek and set up the select school at Stribling Springs, where she could take the waters. "My wife has not been well, but is better now," or some such phrase recurs time and time again.[29] To his nephew, Walter C. Reddy, he wrote in March 1892, "We have been having a regular hospital here. Annie has now been sick for nearly 10 weeks, and is now just getting to sit up a little. Your Aunt Sara has also been in bed for a week, but is now able to sit up."[30]

As for his own health it can only be described as excellent. Only someone with a robust constitution could pursue such a punishing schedule year after year as he did. True there were days when he was prostrated with headache, probably the consequence of overwork, or stress. For example, stress is the best explanation for his headache on a Sunday in July 1872. He wrote in his diary, "Spent the day at home reading &c.—having a headache from being up with my wife last night."[31] Simple loss of sleep would not have bothered Hotchkiss, he needed very little. It was not unusual for him to work until past midnight before taking the train to Washington for a breakfast meeting, or to get up at 4 a.m. to travel to some piece of real estate. In spite of the general impression of good health given by his energetic life, there are indications that Hotchkiss did suffer from a long-standing medical problem. The suggestion that, as a child, he was weaker than his brothers, may have its origins in the bouts of pain that he then suffered. When commiserating with a friend who was once again on the sick list, he wrote, "I have a fellow feeling for you as I went through that for years when a boy, and if there is any excruciating torture I had it, and you are having it now."[32] It is probable that Hotchkiss suffered from attacks of renal colic. Certainly he thought this to be his problem and toward the end of his life sought relief by drinking copious drafts of "Alkavis," supplied directly from "The Church Kidney Cure Co." He told them he was well satisfied that he had derived great benefit from their product, but it had not cured the problem, for the symptoms had returned after finishing the last bottle of his present supply.[33] His medical condition deteriorated and in May 1897 a haemorrhage began which in spite of the ministrations of his doctor could not be halted. Another opinion being needed, Hotchkiss wrote to his old friend and war-time colleague, Dr. Hunter McGuire. He must have advised treatment which brought about some improvement, but finally recommended an operation to remove a stone from his bladder. At the beginning of September of the following year Hotchkiss was in New York during a spell of exceptionally hot weather and returned home "badly used up." During the following weeks he suffered a great deal from his bladder, and so arranged to see Dr. McGuire again. He was admitted to St. Luke's

Hospital and a stone "2½ inches long by an inch wide and an inch thick" removed. There followed a week in hospital in the care of Miss Anderson's "young lady nurses" and a further few weeks convalescing at home, during which he wrote to McGuire, "Thanks to your great skill and unremitting attention to me while in your admirable St. Luke's Home I am speedily recovering my strength and spending a little time each day in my office bringing up arrears in correspondence."[34]

Hotchkiss was now 70 and, despite his optimism, the serious operation must have undermined his general health so that when in the new year of 1899 he fell victim to the "grippe" his body was unable to ward off a mastoid infection, and he died on January 17.

Hotchkiss had always wished for a happy funeral service. That was conducted at The Oaks on the afternoon of the 19th, and by choosing three appropriate hymns, "There is a land of pure delight," "How blest the righteous when he dies," and "Servant of God, well done," the grieving family did their best to fall in with his desires in death as they had always done in life. The private service over, the coffin was escorted to Thornrose Cemetery by the Stonewall Jackson Camp, Confederate Veterans, where the "Rev. Dr. James P. Smith, the only surviving member of Jackson's staff pronounced the benediction, while the setting sun shone on the mound of fragrant flowers, the waving flags and the mourning assembly of devoted relatives and neighbors."[35]

CHAPTER XII

Assessment

TEACHER, SOLDIER, surveyor, mapmaker, geologist, land speculator, author, editor, churchman, historian, all of those he was, and more. Ingalls, President of the C&O railroad, said of him, he "knows more about more different things than any man I ever saw."[1] The acquisition of knowledge on his own, and its dissemination, were the common factors in all that he did. They were essential attributes of the classroom teacher, but they were important characteristics of his other careers. As a soldier he served his generals in a reconnaissance role, as well as a self-educated topographical engineer. He discovered the lie of the land and the location of enemy formations; he conveyed this information in oral, written, or graphic form. As a self-taught geologist his major contribution was the creation of geological maps summarizing the discoveries of others, compacting a mass of information into two dimensions. As land speculator he sought to discover the true area and the resources of land offered for sale, then produced a description and map to aid the prospective purchaser. As historian he searched for the truth of Civil War events, and made his knowledge known through his writings and those of others. As a churchman he learned and taught the Scriptures. When he lectured it was to inform as well as entertain, and because he was skilled in the art, he entertained while he informed. There was nothing he liked doing more than telling what he knew, unless it was to find out more things to tell.

His main characteristic was his curiosity about the physical world. This was innate, and apparent during his childhood and youth. Combined with his other talents of a retentive memory, diligence, drafting skills, a sense of the importance of events, and a desire to communicate, he was well endowed for a life as a teacher. When we invest these attributes with the religious and moral teachings of home, church, and school, expose the man to the world as it was, we find that his life, though varied in content, was consistent, unvarying, in its living.

He went to Virginia in 1847 on vacation, to see what the place was like, to satisfy his curiosity. He stayed because he was offered a job, and found the place, the people, and the life congenial. He found an outlet for his talents, and no need to return to Windsor, or to go anywhere else for that matter. Had there not been a war he would have continued as a school teacher, for he had already achieved something of a reputation for the quality of his schools.

Because he was from New York State, a state with many prominent in the abolitionist cause, and all opposed to slavery, it was assumed that he too, the son of a Beecher, was an abolitionist. With his upbringing, his nature, he must have given considerable thought to the problem. Because his family did not understand how he could live in a slave-owning society, he had to justify himself. He was satisfied that there was much Scriptural material accepting the notion of the ownership of one man by another. As a reader of the *Staunton Spectator* he was helped by the series of 16 letters over the name "NOVANGUS" published January to May 1852. The writer, who claimed to be a Northerner settled in western Virginia, sought to demonstrate that Scripture gave an affirmative answer to the question, "Can a master have a right of property in his slaves, which will justify him holding them like other property for his own benefit?" The writer concluded that on the evidence of the Scriptural testimony, slaveholding could not be in itself sinful. Whether Hotchkiss was influenced by these letters, beyond being guided by its long list of references to book, chapter, and verse, we do not know, but a letter from his mother in 1859 makes it clear that he had come to the same conclusion.[2] What I am sure we can accept is that Hotchkiss would never condone the ill-treatment or exploitation of slaves. As we have recorded in earlier chapters he hired slaves to help at Loch Willow and retained his own personal servant during the war. All this could have been the quiet acceptance of the mores of the society in which he was now living. However, when we consider his stand against drink, his fight against secularizing the Sabbath, his strong religious convictions, and his careful study of contentious matters, it is reasonable to conclude that he found no fundamental objection to the peculiar institution, and none to the way he found it operating in the Valley. Long after the matter had been settled, he wrote of "The humane and kindly character of African slavery in Virginia...eloquently testified by the fact that during the civil war almost without exception the slaves remained faithful and loyal to their masters."[3]

To suggest that he was an abolitionist at heart, accepted slavery expediently, and fought for the Confederacy only under pressure from his neighbors, is to deny the very nature of the man. He could have opted out as his brother did; he could have returned to the North. He did neither; he stood by his adopted state to defend it against those who sought to impose their own fanatic solution upon a difficult social and economic problem.

When Lincoln precipitated the war, Hotchkiss was 32, the rules governing the conduct of his life well-established, rehearsed daily in the class room. There could be no possibility of teaching one thing, practicing another, and still retaining the respect of the community. That respect had been shown in abundance when mounting debts nearly drove him from Mossy Creek. He entered upon his military career with a strong sense of discipline, a capacity for hard work, and a devotion to accuracy and detail which ensured valuable service to his commanders whatever the nature of his duties.

What he brought in addition to those personal qualities were a knowledge of the fundamental principles of surveying, a facility to draw, and a unique understanding of the structure of the countryside as he derived it from the study of its geology. He was to apply this theoretical knowledge in the most unforgiving of circumstances, on the battlefield. His services to Jackson were a major factor in that general's success. Within days of joining Jackson he demonstrated that the defensive position at Narrow Passage was vulnerable, and reconnoitered a better line on Stony Creek. From then on Jackson recognized that he had an officer who knew what he was about. When he wanted something done of critical importance, he learned that he could rely on Hotchkiss. We need only to recall the blockading of the passes through the mountains after the battle at McDowell, or the leading of Taylor's division to flank the Federal guns at the battle of Port Republic. Hotchkiss served other commanders in the same loyal and skillful way, bringing to the task his special knowledge to discomfort the enemy, as, for example, his direction of the night march to a crossing of the Shenandoah to surprise and rout two corps of Sheridan's army camped alongside Cedar Creek.

What military service gave to Hotchkiss was a rapid development from theory into practice. From the elementary application of basic mathematics to a practical problem performed as a school exercise, or from simple plans for himself and his neighbors, his mapmaking was transformed into the finest exposition of the art. From the delineation of a few hundred square yards it became the presentation of hundreds of square miles of territory on which the fate of thousands was determined. It was important to him in another respect. For the first time in his life he was in an organized environment which was not a school. He had to learn to manage and motivate men, not children. He had to learn to live in the company of men with very different ideas, morals, and standards from his own, men who could not be told to do this or that like pupils at Loch Willow. By the end of the war he had control of his own small team of topographical engineers, an experience which was to be of value in later life. He had learned some management skills. Above all he derived enormous benefit from working closely with Jackson. Jackson's devotion to duty, his loyalty to Lee, his uncompromising discipline, his religious faith, supported and reinforced Hotchkiss' own principles. Jackson's success as a military commander demonstrated the correctness of these principles, and was an inspiration to Hotchkiss, not merely in performing his war-time duties, but throughout his life. "Never take any counsel of your fears" was a Jackson phrase which came readily to his mind. For him to liken someone's singlemindedness or determination to that of Jackson, was praise indeed.

Nothing in his post-war writings suggests that Hotchkiss regretted his support for the Confederate cause. It had cost him dear. He shared the hardship of all Southerners, but with the added burden of a divided family. Not until the '80s, twenty years after the war had ended, is there evidence of a visit to Windsor. It was his brother, Nelson, the pacifist, who kept in touch with the northern relatives. When their mother could no longer look after herself, and moved to Staunton, it was with Nelson she stayed, not Jed.

It was not his intention to do other than to return to his profession when the war ended, but the schoolroom was now too confining. He had enjoyed the outdoor work, and could not settle into academic life again. Out of the variety of survey jobs he performed during the immediate post-war years, coupled with his geological knowledge, grew a mission: the exploitation of the natural resources of the Virginias. He pursued it with missionary zeal. The iron, coal, and timber were God's gifts to man, there for his benefit if only he had the wit to use them. When mildly upbraiding a landowner who had neglected to develop the iron ore underlying his property he referred him to the parable of the talents.[4] The two minerals, coal and iron ore, were the mainspring of industrial expansion, of progress. Hotchkiss believed in progress. The extraction of these from mine and quarry was self-evidently a noble purpose, which could only benefit mankind. Not for him or his contemporaries the environmental doubts of later generations. He did not, could not, foresee that the opening up of the vast coalfields of West Virginia would have appalling consequences for the miners and their families in the Appalachians.

But there was one ill of exploitation he did see. It was already evident. While for all practical purposes, coal and iron ore deposits could be described as being inexhaustible, it was not apparent that this could be more properly said about timber. Far from it. As the railroads extended their tracks along the bottoms of the rivers and creeks to seek the tipples of the mines, the hillsides were denuded of all saleable timber. For land developers the timber paid the taxes until the land could be leased for mining. Furthermore, woodlands were being destroyed by fire and pest. In those cases where Hotchkiss had influence, he attempted to confine lumbering to trees over 18 inches in diameter, leaving the smaller and younger trees to mature. He also recognized that by looking upon trees as a crop, timber could be truly inexhaustible. To Clark in 1892 he wrote, "As for selling trees down to 5 inches in diameter, that is a nonsense. Under no circumstances should we sell young trees....I do not think we should allow a tree of any sort to be cut that is less than 18 inches in diameter and if we manage our forests as they should be managed we can have there a perpetual crop of timber for generations."[5] Independently, he was advocating practices which were to be given much publicity further to the south. After seeing Gifford Pinchot's report on the management of the great forests of the Biltmore Estate near Asheville, North Carolina, in 1894 he wrote to him, saying that he too had been endeavoring to carry out similar ideas on the millions of acres of West Virginia forests in which he had an interest.[6] The importance he attached to timber had earlier been shown by the assistance he had given to Professor Charles S. Sergent following the census year of 1880. Sergent was the special agent charged with reporting on the forest resources of West Virginia. The funds allocated for his task were insufficient. In particular no map summarizing his findings could be published out of public funds. Hotchkiss sought the help of Senator Davis, but eventually persuaded Kimball of the N&W to pay for the printing of a map to be issued as a supplement to

The Virginias, May 1883.

The Virginias, the New Orleans Exposition of 1884, the World Fair of 1892 at Chicago, and the 9th edition of the *Encyclopaedia Britannica,* were only the more obvious lecterns from which to expound his faith in the industrial potential of the Old Dominion. Whenever an opportunity occurred to promote Virginia he seized it. Whenever funds were needed to assist in the development or assessment of the state's assets he was available to lobby Senators, Congressmen, or industrialists. His continuing efforts to secure funds for a thorough survey of the state are witness to that, as is also his successful appeal to Clark for the modest sum required by Professor Fred P. Dewey, curator of metallurgy at the Smithsonian Institute in Washington. Dewey had been making comparative analyses of the cokes derived from West Virginia and Pennsylvania coals; he wanted to do more tests using apparatus developed in England and not in his possession. Hotchkiss asked Clark for the necessary $150. Through Clark, contributions were made by two coal companies whose names Hotchkiss did not disclose in order to avoid future accusations of bias.[7]

Missionary zeal brought him close to direct political involvement. Correctly, Hotchkiss recognized that the industrial potential of the nation could only be realized if imports of iron and steel were curbed. Only behind a properly constructed tariff wall could the investment in furnaces, mines, and railroads proceed at a satisfactory rate. For the consumer such tariffs meant higher prices than would otherwise be necessary; most Virginians, being farmers, were consumers of manufactured goods, and the agrarian interest dominated the Democratic party. That provided a dilemma for Hotchkiss. Because it was impossible for him, a Confederate veteran, to support the Republican party, the advocate of protection, he therefore offered himself in 1884 to the voters of the Tenth Congressional District as an independent candidate for the 49th Congress. It was a short-lived diversion, and he was easily persuaded to return to the right path. When tariffs on iron and coal were again under threat he worked hard for their retention, but this time by lobbying politicians, addressing Congressional committees, and writing to governors. The Silver question got him to the hustings, not as a candidate, but as a speaker on behalf of the Democratic party, and its presidential candidate, Bryan. Politics, however, were not for Hotchkiss, his interest in government being only in what it could do to assist industrial development. Whenever government intervened to regulate business, as in the case of the Interstate Commerce Commission and the railroads in 1898, he was vociferous in his condemnation.[8] It is perhaps in this outburst, and in his response to the proposal to appoint an inspector of mines, that he can be accused of using his prestige in the interests of capital to the detriment of those (other than the carriers of coal) dependent upon the railroads, or of labor in the mines. He told Senator Green, "We have absolutely no use for such an officer, and it will add unnecessarily to the expense of the state. Such an officer would be a nuisance to every mining enterprise in the state."[9] Because in this he was but a creature of his class and time, we should not lessen our appreciation of the integrity he brought to his great service to his adopted state.

"To tell the story of Victorian Britain and leave religion out...impresses us as an example of blatant disregard of the evidence."[10] The same can be said of the Hotchkiss story. Religion permeated his whole being. His was not the narrow sectarian kind. Although a Presbyterian he was quite prepared to go to mass in a Roman Catholic church, and considered it foolish for the different denominations to go to the expense of building separate churches when the sizes of the congregations were insufficient to maintain either the building or the preacher. Nevertheless, the specific instructions of the church were to be complied with. He shared with Jackson the great worry of waging war on the Sabbath, but although the erosion of Sunday observance by the necessities of military campaigning became a commonplace, his attitude never changed.

His post-war diary shows that he avoided Sunday travelling if at all possible, preferring to be away from home if he were unable to get back to Staunton on a Saturday. He opposed the opening of the caves at Shendun on Sunday, and wrote to Ruffin, his successor as president of The Grottoes Co., "I sincerely regret to hear that visitors are being admitted to the Cave on Sunday. It is not only contrary to the public sentiment of this community, but is in violation of the laws of the State....It will bring to Shendun a class of people that will do us no good, no matter how much money they may bring there,...."[11] Similarly he castigated a manager for operating a mine on a Sunday. He usually went to church both morning and evening, and taught a bible class as well. When he was unable to get back to Staunton, he attended a church wherever he happened to be at the time.

Although most of his religious life was of the private kind, he did become involved in public campaigns which had lasting consequences. Soon after his return home from England in 1875 he became the spokesman for a small group within the Presbyterian congregation in Staunton which was dissatisfied with the progress being made by the church in recruiting adherents. Their solution to this was to create the Second Presbyterian Church, which came into being in November 1875.

Hotchkiss played a full part in its subsequent development, becoming an elder in 1881, and its Sunday school superintendent in 1890.

In 1891 the Lexington Presbytery, which administered the church over a large part of Virginia and West Virginia, was anxious to "establish a first class school" at Elkins, West Virginia. Hotchkiss was appointed secretary to the committee charged with this task. In this role he labored in an adverse financial climate to raise funds, and used his business connections to maintain the interest of Senators Davis and Elkins, who were major benefactors. That phase of the project was abandoned after the death of Hotchkiss, but with the return of more favorable conditions, Davis and Elkins College was founded in 1903.[12] As a mark of Hotchkiss' interest, his widow donated, in 1907, a gift of books from his library and a cabinet of minerals.[13]

Religion was not an "out of hours" activity. The establishment of a church and Sunday School at Dunlow was at least as important as opening up the mines. There was, Hotchkiss said, "a great field for spiritual harvesting along the N&W."[14] He expected the Guyandot C.L.A. and its employees to play an active part. When Hotchkiss applied his talents to the development of Virginia's resources he believed he was working out God's purpose.

His integrity—deep rooted in his religious upbringing, reinforced by his years as teacher, fundamental to the practice of a surveyor— earned for him the respect of his contemporaries. It showed itself in small matters as well as large. When he was offered travelling expenses on a visit to Boston to address the Society of Arts in honor of William B. Rogers, he refused them on the grounds that he was in the city anyway on other business.[15] To a correspondent who had offended him, Hotchkiss was quick to demonstrate his credentials as an expert on West Virginia lands, and went on to write, "We claim to be business men of standing and integrity, and employ only such men to look after our affairs and we seek to deal with those having similar views."[16] He had the same high expectation of those who worked for him as he demanded of himself. He also believed that nothing was impossible for an intelligent man, provided he had the will to do it. Craig Miller had not been quite the superintendent that had been expected, but when Craig had to assume day-to-day control at Dunlow, Hotchkiss wrote, "I have abiding faith that you can do all that we want done and do it efficiently, speedily and economically if you will *will* so to do."[17] He expected his son-in-law to master the intricacies of title deeds, although his previous experience had been in a dry-goods store, and as a clerk.

Duty was a guiding principle. It required Hotchkiss to stick at the job in hand to the limits of his physical ability. It required him to maintain the alcoholic Tom McCullough, although his behavior was deeply offensive and embarrassing. Those who worked for him were expected to accept the same code.

None of this meant that he was stiff, remote, censorious; it was simply that he had a firm core of beliefs that enabled him to bring to every problem a consistent technique for their solution. Harry Frazier, consulting engineer of the Chesapeake and Ohio, published in 1938 his *Recollections* of working with that railroad. From boyhood he had known Major Hotchkiss, and remembered him as "an interesting character, a delightful conversationalist, a charming lecturer and a man of commanding presence."[18] Travelling by railroad was an opportunity to talk to fellow passengers on Virginia's progress or potential as seen from the car windows. It seems highly probable that he actually looked to see who was travelling on the cars, take a seat beside them, and engage in useful conversation.

One such occasion serves to demonstrate his enthusiasm for presenting information in his favorite way, his concern for an employee, and the expectation that his travelling companion took the conversation as seriously as he did. Travelling to Washington toward the end of August 1896, Hotchkiss met Mr. H. W. Fuller on the train. Fuller, the General Passenger Agent of the C&O, was just the companion Hotchkiss would enjoy. The conversation turned to the possibility of producing a tourist map of the railroad, showing points of interest along the route, and possibly accompanied by a guide book. Hotchkiss seized on this as both an interesting project wholly consistent with his mission of publicizing Virginia, and a solution to a problem which was bothering him. Only the week before he had discharged his draftsman, Frank Anschutz, who had been working for him on the Virginias Railway project. That job was finished and Hotchkiss had nothing more for him to do. Now here was an opportunity to re-engage him. Hotchkiss was convinced that Fuller was equally enthusiastic about the project, for they had talked about $75 a month as the cost of preparing the map. As soon as he returned to Staunton, Hotchkiss invited Anschutz back to the drawing board. Only eight days into September Hotchkiss wrote to Fuller recalling their conversation.

> I at once wrote to my draftsman and he reported on the 4th. inst and has already made good progress in the preparation of the map reaching from Washington to Charlottesville with the railway running through the middle of it and reaching each way from the railway an average distance of 15-16 miles and so taking in all historical points and objects of interest that would attract the attention of an inquisitive traveller riding on your trains.

Progress was such that he would soon require a personal interview with Fuller.[19]

This breath-taking enthusiasm, and more particularly the precipitate action, reveals an aspect of his character quite different from the one we might be tempted to ascribe to an upright Presbyterian gentleman moving in cautious business circles. No letter of confirmation of the understanding reached on the train journey, no outline of the specifications of the map, no statement as to expected costs; he just got on with it, the assumption being that he had already got Fuller's complete agreement. It is a reminder of that letter to his daughter, Nellie, in which he referred to a want of caution as being a family trait.

Perhaps it was this lack of caution which was at the root of his financial difficulties. Time and time again he was let down by his associates, or those with whom he was doing business. The Valley Railroad, Pliny Fisk, Charles Easton, Maximilian Low. Somehow he did not manage to hold these people to their agreements, and the liabilities which Hotchkiss incurred remained unsettled for many years. The cost of Ansted's work should have been paid by Pliny Fisk, but it was to Hotchkiss that Ansted looked for recompense. In spite of his plea to Ansted not to take legal action, judgment was obtained against Hotchkiss in 1877. As Hotchkiss had warned, there was no possibility of the money being paid at that time. In 1883 he offered Ansted's executors $1,000 worth of 6% bonds in the Rorer Iron Company, saying to his friend Captain Thomas D. Ranson, the attorney for the Ansted estate, "I earnestly desire to affect a fair settlement of my debts, and have never sought to get rid of them by bankruptcy or other means."[20] This offer was ignored. Eventually in 1887 when the debt, through accrued interest and legal costs, had more than doubled from the original $1,200 to $2,256.96, a compromise was reached and Hotchkiss paid 60% of it.[21]

Hotchkiss' financial affairs, by our standards, were chaotic, but not in any way out of the ordinary at that time. Transactions, more often than not, were conducted on credit, each being a link in a chain of deals, notes due one party to a deal were used as payment to the other. Payment of a particular creditor could be dependent upon settlement between many such debtor/creditor pairs. The lack of cash was universal in Virginia during the Nineties. In 1891, Lieutenant Governor J. Hoge Tyler reported that in his store in the southwest of the state hardly more than $50 in cash had passed over the counter during the preceding year.[22]

The consequences of the Panic of 1893 made the Nineties a particularly bleak time for Hotchkiss. A check he made out in September 1893 in favor of E. W. Clark & Co. for $31.25 and which was returned dishonored was annotated "A protest—showing how troubles came along in 1893." A month later he was due to repay his bank $1,000, but hoped for an extension of time, but the bank required his indebtedness to be reduced by $250, an impossibility for Hotchkiss.[23] His accounts at this time were in such disarray that a check to his son-in-law was worthless before Allan received it.[24] It seems that he was depending on a check from M. Erskine Miller to keep his bank account in credit.[25] By the beginning of 1896 Hotchkiss' income was so severely curtailed that he had to discontinue subscriptions to societies and journals. *The Northwestern Lumberman* was one such journal to whose editor he had to confess that he could not afford to take it any longer. That the editor offered to waive the subscription indicates the esteem he had for Hotchkiss.[26]

Money, whether in the form of land, credit notes, or cash was not the prime motive, or inspiration, for his enormous outpouring of effort; had it been, surely he would have used his talents differently. He was inspired by the potential benefit to Virginians of developing the natural resources of the Old Dominion. The thirty years up to his death were devoted in one way or another to the realization of this potential, and his efforts alone brought into the two Virginia states millions of dollars of investment.

This element of public spirit showed itself in other forms. Some were linked to his Presbyterian faith—his support of the Temperance movement, the Local Option Bill, and the Y.M.C.A.—others to the memory of the Confederate cause. But others stood alone as actions of a man simply concerned with the well-being of the community in which he lived.

In the midst ot the hectic activity associated with the Virginias Railway, he returned from a conference in Washington with General Dacey to chair a meeting of Staunton citizens who wished to have the city boundaries extended.

During the same month he found time to involve himself in such diverse matters as the "unfortunate condition of things at our D.D.&B. Institution, and the lack of funds for the gauging of Virginia's rivers."[27] Short of money though he was, he could still think of presenting to his fellow citizens a museum of Natural History, his ability to do so dependent on the sale of large interests in West Virginia lands.[28]

This optimism is revealed time and time again in his correspondence: in 1879 as signs of a change in the business life of the nation began to show; in the midst of the crisis of affairs of The Grottoes Company; even in 1893. To J. C. Green he wrote in May of that year, "Of course we can do nothing just now with the present condition of the Iron Market and the Money Market...[but] this is the time for us to get ready so we can take advantage of the change for the better which is sure to come in the near future."[29] In 1894, "I think there is a decided improvement in prospects and it looks as though now the clouds would break and business activity resume its ordinary condition since the people have gotten tired waiting for spooks to disappear and for the quack medicine that Congress is dispensing in the shape of silver bills and the Wilson Tariff."[30]

This optimism for the future seems to have obscured his view of the more immediate problems. The sale of the Elkhorn lands in 1884, for example, put Hotchkiss in a position of eliminating his minor debts, but he continued to invest in real estate and never secured complete freedom from his creditors. He was continually pressed to pay his bills; frequently Staunton shopkeepers had to take out a summons before he settled quite trivial debts, even for one as low as $3.50.[31] With all his assets in property, major debts could not be discharged until a large sale had been affected. One of these debts dated from 1865, his investment in the short-lived National Express and Transportation Company, when it was finally settled in 1901 it amounted to $5,426.[32] It was not until 1903, four years after his death, that Sara finally settled his affairs, by which time she had paid out a fraction over $26,000. Even so, there still remained a substantial sum to be realised from the sale of the North Flat Top lands. While Hotchkiss had difficulty in the Nineties in finding a few dollars in cash, Sara received something in excess of $55,000 when these lands were sold in 1905/6.

When we consider his competence in so many different activities, most of them requiring meticulous attention to detail, his apparent mismanagement of his accounts is something of a surprise. It was not a flaw in his integrity; there was no question of him trying to avoid payment. Ironically his failure came from optimism, lack of caution, dogged belief in the eventual success of mineral development in Virginia, long-sightedness that could not always focus sharply on short-term matters of less moment.

Compared with the achievements, these deficiencies were indeed trivial, no more than hair-line cracks in otherwise sound endeavor, minor defects of major virtues.

Jedediah Hotchkiss toward the end of his life.
Mary Baldwin College, Staunton, Virginia

Epilogue

THE MAPS

Considering the enormous output of the Hotchkiss offices during the post-bellum years, it is surprising how little of that work is known to have survived. Much of it may have been widely dispersed. Maps of mineral properties would have been sent to those who commissioned them. They may still be languishing in attorneys' offices, or in family and company archives.[1] When Hotchkiss produced a report and a map to aid a sale several hundred copies would be printed for distribution, but he would have kept the manuscript. His sense of history, and the importance he attached to his work, encouraged him to hoard rather than to discard. The quantity of textual material that has survived testifies to that.

After 1889, he had two places in which to store his maps and papers, the large safe in The Oaks, and his office detached from the house. It is reasonable to suppose that the safe would hold those out of date documents not frequently consulted. Some of these would be maps, certainly the Civil War maps, but the maps of mineral properties, some covering many square miles of the Virginias, he probably retained in his office to be used for other purposes. He would not have started another survey if he could trace part of an existing map. It could be that there was a greater destruction of maps following his death than of the more easily stored documents. On the other hand, it might have been simpler to leave the maps in the cabinets in the office while removing to the house-safe the notebooks, letterbooks, diaries, and files. In which case the maps could have survived until the office building was demolished (ca. 1907), then destroyed or dispersed at that time.[2] In either case, the maps that did survive remained neglected in The Oaks for over thirty years.

Although, in the recollection of the last surviving member of Hotchkiss' family, his granddaughter, Ellen Howison Christian, some interest had been shown in the maps by the Library of Congress in 1920, the earliest documentary evidence of this is a reference in the Library's correspondence index file to a letter dated October 5, 1928, from Mrs.

Christian's mother, Mrs. Allan M. Howison of Staunton, on the subject of Jed Hotchkiss.[3] The first letter known to exist is one dated October 26, 1928, in which Colonel Lawrence Martin, head of the Division of Maps, replied to one from Mrs. Christian, "It is very gratifying to learn of the existence of the collection of maps owned by the late Major Hotchkiss."[4] About the same time, but presumably prior to this correspondence, Martin had asked C. Vernon Eddy, Librarian at The Handley Library, Winchester, Virginia, whether he had any information as to the whereabouts of the Hotchkiss maps. He in turn approached Elmore D. Hotchkiss, Hotchkiss' great-nephew, from whom he learned that the maps were stored at The Oaks in Staunton. Although Martin had told Mrs. Christian that the Library of Congress was interested in buying the maps, or, if the family was unwilling to sell, to make photostat copies of them, and Eddy had suggested this to Elmore Hotchkiss, nothing came of those approaches at the time.[5] In fact no serious attempt was made even to see the maps until 1937, although Martin had inquired of Eddy in 1933 whether there had been any further developments "in connection with the project of borrowing and photostating the Jed Hotchkiss maps." A casual conversation at a dinner in Staunton caused Eddy to take up the matter again and led to a meeting with Mrs. Christian at The Oaks on March 29, 1938. There Eddy was shown into what has been described as "the largest private walk-in safe in Augusta County."[6] In it were two long boxes fastened by wrought iron hoops and padlocks which, in the absence of keys, had to be broken open to reveal "roll after roll of maps."[7]

How it came about that ten years were to elapse before most of these were deposited in the Library of Congress is a story of a family problem exacerbated by the selfishness of the renowned Richmond newspaper editor, historian and biographer of Lee, Dr. Douglas Southall Freeman.[8]

To understand that little drama it is necessary to know something about the two principal actresses involved; Nellie Hotchkiss Holmes, Hotchkiss' elder daughter, then 81, and her niece, Ellen Howison Christian. Between those two there was a generation gap of gigantic proportions. Nellie had been brought up in a strictly regulated household, the very essence of propriety where the God of work was indistinguishable from the God of all creation; Ellen, the only surviving daughter of Nellie's sister, Anna, had been doted on by both, married toward the end of World War I, and took to the liberated Twenties as if they had been created especially for her. Nellie revered her father, this reverence turning to idolatry with age. She thought that her niece did not have that deep interest which she should have. To Ellen, who was only four years old when her grandfather died, he and all his works were just history, and she could only say that her aunt's criticisms were not "quite true."⁹ With the death of her mother in 1929, the Hotchkiss property, including The Oaks, was jointly owned by herself and her aunt, a situation which both regarded as a mere legal convention. Both behaved as if the property was wholly possessed by Aunt Nellie, she with the assurance of age and the "knowledge" of what father would have wished, Ellen resentfully and fearful of the displeasure of her second mother.

Shortly after Ellen, without consulting her aunt, had agreed that the boxes of maps could go to The Handley Library in Winchester, and Eddy was sorting through this treasure trove, Nellie was being enchanted by another altogether grander prospect. In an excited letter to her niece she told the story of Freeman's visit to her in Charleston, South Carolina:

> His suggestion is this: get all the maps, reports, letters, the typed Diary and similar mss in one room. Then he will send *his* right hand man, reliable and honest and good along this kind of work for him (Dr. Freeman). Then the Dr. will come in person and see what he can suggest and *do*! With the *Diary* see if there is enough *other* matter to make a *book*, which he will do for us. I feel like giving him a hug and kissing his knees. He says papa's place is one of *greatness* all over the reading historical world—such maps no one else prepared.

She instructed Ellen to put the map chest in the parlor of The Oaks and "get all the papers from the dressing-room closet, wardrobe, and trunk now in sister Anna's former dressing room." She had visions of working alongside Dr. Freeman when he made his own examination.¹⁰

Of course this put Ellen in a fix, and she tried to stop Eddy from completing the cataloging of the maps. Fortunately she had second thoughts, and then sought to persuade Freeman to have all the material from The Oaks deposited for examination in The Handley Library. Freeman would have none of this. Wanting to have easy, complete, and essentially private access to all the Hotchkiss material, he proposed that it should all be sent to the Confederate Memorial Institute—the Battle Abbey—in Richmond. This proposal being happily accepted by Aunt Nellie, Ellen had no option but to comply. The papers, notebooks, and the diaries were removed from The Oaks to Richmond, where they were joined by the maps when Eddy completed the cataloging a month later. A quick examination of all the documentary material convinced Freeman that there was "in the Hotchkiss papers sufficient material to justify a new edition of Henderson, if not a new biography of Jackson. Needless to say also, there is opportunity for a fine memorial of Major Hotchkiss. The nature and scope of this memorial I am now pondering."[11] A week of pondering produced the following in a letter to Nellie:

> I can not say as yet whether to advise you to have a biography written...My new book, *Lee's Lieutenants*, is to contain sketches of about 25 or 30 of the most impressive figures among those who fought under General Lee. To some of these men, of course, a total of not more than 5 or 6 pages will be given...I am convinced Major Hotchkiss deserves a place in this book...Such a sketch will not take the place of a biography, but...it may inspire some writer to undertake a biography. I am very happy to feel that your great father so fully measures up by every standard to the great men of the Confederacy that I can treat him, however briefly, in this new book.[12]

Eddy had been fearful all along that there was "something hollow about Dr. Freeman's promises," and made the obvious comment to Ellen Christian that there was "a vast difference between writing a biography of your grandfather and a 'short sketch' of him in a book about Lee and his Lieutenants."[13] Nellie was not dismayed; she was enchanted by the great man who charmed her by his attention, hospitality, and reverence for her father. In those circumstances there was nothing Ellen could do but wait until she had sole control of the family property. Until then her grandfather's maps, so recently disinterred from the vault in The Oaks, would remain interred in "the tomb-like structure" of Battle Abbey.[14]

Seven years were to pass before Ellen was able to consider the final disposition of the maps and papers. When Aunt Nellie died at the age of 92 in April 1947, Ellen lost no time in writing to Mr. Eddy and Dr. Freeman; Eddy immediately approached the Library of Congress to determine whether that institution was still interested in acquiring the maps. Freeman made every effort to retain them in Richmond while acknowledging the right of Mrs. Christian to dispose of her property as she thought fit. A visit by Eddy to Battle Abbey revealed that while "a half dozen or more had been removed from the boxes and were on display in cases around the wall of the room" there were "no facilities for the close study or scrutiny" of the maps. This visit, with its attendant frustrations, and petty indignities, graphically described by Eddy in a letter to Ellen, convinced her of the need to remove the material as soon as possible to The Handley Library, a place where they could be prepared for inspection by prospective purchasers.[15]

There were only a few libraries which would have both the interest in this collection of maps and papers, or the resources with which to buy them. The Handley Library would have been an appropriate location, sited as it is in Winchester, a Valley town closely associated with Jackson and II Corps of the Army of Northern Virginia, but it could not possibly afford the sum which this collection was likely to be worth. Eddy had, nevertheless, expressed the hope that some items could be retained. Particularly there was one item that he did "most heartily crave," namely the long map of the Shenandoah Valley. Apart from the Library of Congress, only the Virginia State Library, in Richmond, and the Alderman Library at the University of Virginia were likely to have the requisite combination of funds, interest, and the expertise to hold and use such a collection. Quite fortuitously, Francis L. Berkeley, Jr., Curator of Manuscripts at the Alderman Library, learned of the existence of the Hotchkiss maps shortly after their return to Winchester, and wrote to Mrs. Christian, "This library would covet the opportunity to consider their purchase."[16] In this way both the Library of Congress and the Alderman Library became rivals for the honor of housing this unique assemblage of Civil War material and much more besides. Their interest was heightened by the closer examination made when their experts, defying severe weather and snow-blocked roads, were at last able to get to Winchester at the end of January 1948. Clara Le Gear, one of the trio from Washington, who later cataloged the maps, remarked to Eddy that they were "marvellous" examples of cartography and doubted if any one now living could do such work.[17] Mr. Wylie, of the Alderman Library, wrote, "It would be a catastrophe, I think, if the collection were in any way dispersed." While acknowledging that it was "peculiarly appropriate that the personal papers and manuscript maps of one of America's foremost cartographers should go" to the Library of Congress, he pointed out the advantages of locating them in the midst of "scholars constantly working on research projects, publications, monographs, biographies, etc."[18]

The first to make a bid was the Library of Congress, an offer so generous that their rival acknowledged that Mrs. Christian could do no other than accept it. Except for four items left at The Handley Library, all the material that had been at Battle Abbey was bought by the Library of Congress for $4,100.[19] The Alderman Library had to make do with a consolation prize in the shape of other maps, papers, letter books, and relics which had either been bequeathed to Ellen by her Aunt or had escaped the roundup at The Oaks in 1938. Of the four maps left in Winchester, three were an outright gift by Ellen to Mr. Eddy "as

Librarian of The Handley Library." The fourth, the map of the Shenandoah Valley, remained the property of Mrs. Christian, but was "allowed to stay...as a loan, in consideration of your deep interest and courtesy to me in connection with the discovery and disposal of my grandfather's maps and papers."[20] It was her intention that it should remain in Winchester until Eddy's death, after which it would join the collection in the Library of Congress. This it did in 1964, Eddy having died in October of the previous year. Of the other three, the most impressive, perhaps historically the most important, is the map of parts of Pennsylvania, Maryland, and Virginia on a scale of 1:160,000 already referred to. (see p. 199) For sheer beauty, clarity, and skill of execution, however, it is surpassed by the *Sketch of the Battle of Winchester, Va., Sunday May 25th. A.D. 1862*, drawn on a scale of 2-inches-to-1-mile which formed the basis of Map #2, Plate LXXXV of the *Atlas to Accompany the Official Records.*

Toward the end of August 1948 a press release announced that original Confederate war maps were among the significant items in the Hotchkiss Collection recently acquired by the Library of Congress. The collection was stated as containing some 475 maps, of which 275 were manuscript. Acknowledgement was made to the part played by C. Vernon Eddy in locating the maps, listing them, and negotiating for their eventual safe-keeping. In November of the same year Clara Le Gear published an article on the map collection in the *Library of Congress Quarterly Journal of Current Acquisitions*, and in 1951 published a catalog of the collection. This, with a few minor corrections, has been included in *Civil War Maps. An Annotated List of Maps and Atlases in the Library of Congress.* Second Edition, compiled by Richard W. Stephenson (Washington: Library of Congress, 1989).

Today many of Jed Hotchkiss' surviving maps are a valuable part of the rich collection of Civil War maps in the holdings of the Library of Congress' Geography and Map Division. They are especially important for the study of Confederate operations in Virginia, and, because of the profusion of householders' names on many of the maps, valuable in genealogical research. For many, they are appreciated as outstanding examples of the cartographic art.

Endnotes

Endnotes to Chapter I

1. "Sketch of the life of Jed Hotchkiss of Staunton, Virginia," H.P., 57/657.
2. Lester J. Capon, *Atlas of early American History. The Revolutionary Era 1760-1790*, Princeton University Press, 1976: 96; Marjory B. Hinman, "The Birth of Windsor," in *Historical Essays of Windsor*, compiled and edited by Marjory B. Hinman and Bernard Osborne, Windsor, N.Y. 1976: 1.
3. William Allison Patent, February 26, 1789, Deed Book 1:47, Broome County, N.Y.
4. Deed Book 11:424, November 27, 1828, Broome County, N.Y.
5. *Biographical Review: Sketches of the Leading Citizens of Broome County*, Boston, Biographical Review Publishing Company, 1894, contains references to various members of the Hotchkiss family, including Stiles, in the entries *William Wallace Hotchkiss:* 13, and *Charles B. Hotchkiss*: 343.
6. Diary, H.A., Box 1.
7. Jeanette Hotchkiss to Jed Hotchkiss, August 3, 1852, H.A., Box 1.
8. Marjorie Wood, "Presbyterian Church," in *Historical Essays of Windsor*, 215; *Sketches of Leading citizens*: 13.
9. Jed Hotchkiss to Nellie Hotchkiss, November 18, 1877, H.A., Box 1.
10. Testimonial from J. T. Hotchkiss M.D., September 27, 1846, H.P.
11. *Sketches of Leading Citizens*; 344.
12. Jeanette Hotchkiss to Jed Hotchkiss, August 3, 1852, H.A., Box 1.
13. Diary, December 27, 1845, H.A., Box 1.
14. Diary, November 30, 1845, H.A., Box 1.
15. Holly Gardinier, "Our Educational System," in *Historical Essays of Windsor*.
16. Diary, December 2, 1845, H.A., Box 1.
17. Diary, H.A., Box 1.
18. Two manuscript copies of *Autumn Wreath* are in H.A., Box 5.
19. H.P., 49/661.
20. Journals of Jed Hotchkiss, April 26, 1847 to August 2, 1847, and August 3, 1847 to March 3, 1848, H.P., 1/030-202.
21. Elizabeth Brown Pryor, "An Anomalous Person: Northern Tutor in Plantation Society," *Journal of Southern History*, XLVIII (No. 3, 1981): 363-392.
22. *Ibid.*, 385.

23 Address to "Friends and Fellow Citizens," June 20, 1856. H.P., 50/420.
24 Undated newspaper clipping, H.P.; Kathleen Bruce, *Virginia Iron Manufacture in the Slave Era* (1930); John W. Wayland, *Historic Homes of Northern Virginia, 1937*: 240-243; John D. Capron, "Virginia Iron Furnaces of the Confederacy," *Virginia Cavalcade*, (Autumn, 1967): 10-18.
25 December 7 and 13, 1847. Journal of Jed Hotchkiss, August 3, 1847 to March 3, 1848, H.P., 1/101-202.
26 Journal of Jed Hotchkiss, December 11, 1847; February 5, April 29, May 13, and 14, 1848; *S.S.*, April 26, 1848, carries an advertisement for Van Amburgh & Co's menagerie.
27 *S.S.*, February 25, 1849, an advertisement, "Colored Daguerreotypes, R. Platt—rooms at New Building adjoining Virginia Hotel likenesses taken."
28 Jed Hotchkiss to George Hotchkiss, September 24, 1849. A copy of this letter was found at Deerfield at the former home of Hotchkiss' granddaughter, Mrs. Ellen Christian. It is now in the Hotchkiss Collection, Mary Baldwin College Archives, Staunton, Virginia, hereafter referred to as H.C.
29 Journal, H.P., 1/030-097; Bertha M. Rothe, ed., *Daniel Webster Reader*, 1956: 112-125.
30 Address to "Friends and Fellow Citizens," loc. cit.
31 *Ibid.*
32 B. M. Smith to Jed Hotchkiss, June 20, 1856, H.P.
33 Jeanette Hotchkiss to Jed Hotchkiss, August 3, 1852, H.A., Box 1.
34 "Specification of Work & Materials for the Erection of an Academy at Mossy Creek, Augusta County, Virginia," September 18, 1852, H.P., 60/770-774. The Constitution of Mossy Creek Academy is set out in a deed dated December 22, 1855, Deed Book 75: 417, Augusta County Courthouse, Staunton, Virginia.
35 From his letter of resignation February 22, 1856, H.P., 58/153.
36 Leaflet dated July 1853, announcing opening of Mossy Creek Academy on August 29, 1853; Advertisement in *S.S.*, July 6, 1853; editorial comment, *S.S.*, July 20, 1853.
37 Address to "Friends and Fellow Citizens," loc. cit.
38 *Ibid.*
39 "Rules and Requests of Mossy Creek Academy," H.P., 60/787.
40 Catalogues, Mossy Creek Academy, loc. cit.
41 Elwood B. Cubberley, *The History of Education* (Boston: Houghton Mifflin Company, 1948): 699.
42 Deed, December 22, 1855, Deed Book 75: 417.
43 Deed, December 20, 1855, Deed Book 75: 559.
44 Letter of Resignation, February 22, 1856, H.P. 58/153.
45 *Ibid.*
46 May 8, 1856, letter from Wells Fargo—New York & California Express Co., in answer to a request from Jed Hotchkiss, H.A., Box 1. A similar

letter written by I. W. Raymond, and bearing the same date and quoting passage rates to San Francisco, was among the papers found at the former home of Hotchkiss' grand-daughter, Mrs. Ellen Christian, at Deerfield, Virginia, and now in the H.C.

47 *S.S.*, June 25, 1856.

48 W. H. Ruffner, *Rockingham Register*, July 18, 1856; Deed, July 10, 1856, Deed Book 76/251, Augusta County Courthouse, Staunton, Virginia. The gentlemen were J. Givens Fulton, John Craun Sr., J. H. Ervine, G. W. Crawford, G. H. Ervin, R. H. Robertson, Nailer Oder, J. T. Brodt, D. N. Van Lear, Thomas Reeves, George Craun, Andrew Grist, Jacob Sanger, Robert A. Curry and John Earhart. It may be significant that Daniel Forrer, Benjamin Estil, A. B. Rogers, and C. R. Gibbons, all trustees of Mossy Creek Academy, are not among this list. J. Marshall McCue is also absent from the list, but had already assumed part of the Hotchkiss debts and thus was a party in the execution of the deed of trust.

49 Jeanette Hotchkiss to Jed Hotchkiss, August 3, 1852, loc. cit.

50 Sara Ann Comfort, daughter of John Comfort and Anna Bridgman, born February 14, 1833, at Lanesborough, Susquehanna County, Pennsylvania, H.P., 57/340; *Eighth Annual Catalogue...Wyoming Seminary*, Kingston, Pennsylvania, annotated "Graduated July '53 S.A.C." H.A., Box 4. Sara Comfort's diploma from Wyoming Seminary is also in the H.A., Box 4.

51 H.P., 57/340. Jed Hotchkiss' niece, Lora, writing to Ellen Christian, September 16, 1933, said "Uncle Jed and Aunt Sara were married...in our father's new home...I was quite old enough to remember the wedding cake frosted with sugar," H.C.

52 H.P., 57/340.

53 Jed Hotchkiss to Rev. H. W. Gilbert, November 2, 1886, H.P., 22/585.

54 July 10, 1857, Deed Book 77:163, Augusta County Courthouse, Staunton, Virginia.

55 *S.S.*, June 29, 1858, carried the following advertisement for a Classical School at Stribling Springs: "The subscriber will open a Classical, Mathematical, and Scientific School at the above named place, on the 27th September next (after the close of the Springs' season)...The school will be under the control of Mr. J. Hotchkiss."

56 Lora to Ellen Christian, September 16, 1933, H.C.

57 Details of the Loch Willow house from the manuscript diary and autobiography of Alansa M. Rounds, copyright John M. Irvine, 1992, a copy of which is in the Martha Grafton Library, Mary Baldwin College, Staunton, Virginia.

58 I have not located the deed relating to the purchase of Loch Willow from the Commissioner, James Cochran, but from promissory notes in H.A. Box 1, it is clear that Nelson Hotchkiss bought the property for $12,000 on March 10, 1859. A memorandum of an agreement between Nelson H. Hotchkiss and William H. Ruffner made March 29, 1859, is recorded in Deed Book 81: 388, Augusta County Courthouse, Staunton, Virginia. This shows that Ruffner provided security for the first payment and in turn was secured by the funds arising from Nelson's eventual sale of his Hale's Eddy property.

59 Catalogue of Loch Willow School, H.P., 60/744. What may be part of the mineral collection is now located in the H.C. on loan from the Public Library, Staunton, Virginia.
60 Promissory note, March 29, 1859, H.A., Box 1.
61 Deed conveying Loch Willow Farm etc. to David Fultz, January 28, 1860, Deed Book 79: 271, Augusta County Courthouse, Staunton, Virginia;
62 H.P., 58/002, H.A. Box 1.
63 Jed Hotchkiss to Rev. H. W. Gilbert, November 2, 1886, H.P., 22/585.
64 The Wilmot Proviso is emphasized here because it is a useful starting date for the final descent into war and one which happens to coincide with Hotchkiss' departure from Windsor, N.Y.
65 Alansa M. Rounds manuscript diary and autobiography, loc. cit.
66 Jed Hotchkiss, *Virginia; a Geographical and Political Summary*, 1876: 3.
67 *Staunton Vindicator*, February 20, 1891.
68 *S.S.*, July 4, 1855.
69 Lydia Hotchkiss to Jed Hotchkiss, December 13, 1859, H.A., Box 1.
70 *S.S.*, December 20, 1859, January 17, 1860.
71 *S.S.*, August 28, 1860.
72 *S.S.*, November 6, 1860.
73 *S.S.*, December 4, 1860.
74 John L. Peyton, *History of Augusta County, Virginia*, 2nd ed: 230.
75 *S.S.*, April 23, 1861.

Endnotes to Chapter II

1 H.P., 1/419, 57/674-5.
2 Hotchkiss, *C.M.H.*, III: 43.
3 *C.M.H.*, III: 45.
4 *C.M.H.*, III: 46.
5 H.P., 1/419.
6 "Report of Mr Jed. Hotchkiss, Topographical Engineer, Confederate Services, of events from July 2 to 14," dated January 18, 1862, *O.R.*, II: 261.
7 Diary, H.P., 1/420.
8 Diary, July 22, 1861, H.P., 1/420.
9 Hotchkiss does not explain why he resigned the adjutancy or why he refused Jackson's request. We can only speculate that he wished to retain the freedom of action of a civilian specialist able to offer his services wherever he chose.
10 Diary, H.P., 1/421.
11 Diary, H.P., 1/421.
12 *Tygart's Valley W. Va. Made at Valley Mt. 1861 from Jacob Conrad's Memory. J. H.* Area Table #754-85, Alderman Library, University of Virginia.
13 *Make Me a Map of the Valley, The Civil War Journal of Stonewall Jackson's Topographer*, edited by Archie P. McDonald (Dallas: Southern Methodist Press, 1973) 10. Hereafter the title of this publication is abbreviated to *C.W.J.*

14 To the 6,000 Jackson had in June, must be added Edward Johnson's 3,000, and R. S. Ewell's 8,000. The reader must keep in mind that in the vocabulary of the Shenandoah Valley, "up" means to the south, toward Staunton and Lexington, and "down" means to the north, toward Harper's Ferry and Pennsylvania.

15 "Battle of McDowell. Personal Incidents," H.P., 40/003; C.W.J.: 38 et seq.; C.M.H., III: 231.

16 "Battle of McDowell. Personal Incidents," loc. cit.

17 "Fremont's Pursuit of Jackson in the Shenandoah Valley. The Journal of Colonel Albert Tracey, March-July 1862," ed. Francis F. Wayland, Va. Mag. of Hist. & Biog. 70 (1962): 164 and 332.

18 C.W.J., May 18, 1862, "Gen. R. S. Ewell reached our camp about daylight this morning and had a long consultation with the General."

19 C.W.J., June 2, 1882.

20 C.M.H., III: 255.

21 C.W.S., June 8, 1862, "Gen Ewell managed his troops admirable." [sic]

22 C.M.H., III: 258.

23 C.M.H., III: 262; Jed Hotchkiss to Col. G. F. R. Henderson, May 23, 1895, H.P.

24 C.M.H., III: 264.

25 C.M.H., III: 287.

26 C.W.J., July 15, 1882.

27 These two corps were formerly the separate armies of Fremont and Banks. The loss of independent command caused Fremont to resign; he was replaced by Franz Sigel. Banks remained to serve under Pope.

28 The battle of August 9, 1862, is usually referred to as the battle of Cedar Mountain, but Hotchkiss recorded in his diary: "By request of Gen. Jackson I made a sketch of the battle field and suggested the name for the battle, Cedar Run, which the General adopted." The map of the battle reproduced in the *Atlas to accompany the Official Records of the Union and Confederate Armies*, Plate LXXXV, No. 4 also uses this name.

29 C.W.J., September 18, 1862.

30 This battle is often portrayed as a Union victory. Lincoln chose to regard it as such, and used it as the opportunity to issue the Emancipation Proclamation. Only in the sense that Lee could no longer carry the war further into the enemy's territory, but had to withdraw to Virginia, can it be so regarded. With a maximum of 40,000 men, Lee had fought McClellan's 87,000 to a standstill, and even after terrible losses was prepared to resist an assault by as yet uncommitted Union troops. Henderson was scathing of McClellan's performance. "The principle of mutual support was utterly ignored....He had still to grasp the elementary rule that the combination of all arms against a single point is necessary to win battles." Peter J. Parish, *(The American Civil War*: 189) contrasting the performance of the opposing commanders, wrote, "Incredibly Lee stood his ground next day and even contemplated a counterattack. Even more incredibly, with his massive superiority, McClellan did nothing." Parish called this battle, "this half success for the North where complete victory was possible."

31 Officially, Hotchkiss was still a civilian. An order had been issued that all civilians attached to the army were to be conscripted into the army. Hotchkiss had been asked to select the company in which he wished to be enrolled. See Chapter III.
32 Diary, February 27, 1863. Lora to Ellen Christian, September 16, 1933, H.C.
33 John B. Baldwin to Jed Hotchkiss, April 22, May 16, 1863, H.P., 49/184 and 186.
34 C.W.J., January 21, 1863; Jed Hotchkiss and William Allan, *The Battlefields of Virginia. Chancellorsville*: 11.
35 C.W.J.
36 Jed Hotchkiss to Hunter McGuire, October 8, 1898, H.P. 15/677.
37 C.W.J., May 2, 1863.
38 Jed Hotchkiss to Hunter McGuire, October 8, 1898, loc. cit.
39 C.W.J., May 2, 1863.
40 C.W.J., May 3, 1863.
41 Jed Hotchkiss to Col. G. F. R. Henderson, January 12, 1898, H.P., 14/671.
42 G. F. R. Henderson, *Stonewall Jackson and the American Civil War*, Centennial Edition (New York: Longmans, Green & Co. 1961): 706.
43 Jed Hotchkiss to Col. G. F. R. Henderson, December 15, 1897, H.P., 14/563.

Endnotes to Chapter III

1 C.W.J., July 3, 1863.
2 C.M.H., III: 401-410.
3 C.W.J., July 4, 1863.
4 This volume contains a copy of *True Courage, a Discourse Commemorative of Lieut-General Thomas J. Jackson* by Rev. R. L. Dabney, D.D., 1863; a copy of *Discourse on the Life and Character of Lt. Gen. Thos. J. Jackson (CSA)*, by Francis H. Smith, read before the Board of Visitors, Faculty, and Cadets, VMI, July 1, 1863; as well as a pencil sketch of Jackson drawn by Hon. A. R. Boteler, July 29, 1862. To the inside of the front cover is attached the letter from Cooke to Hotchkiss dated August 19, 1863. It is to be found in the Manuscript Department, Alderman Library, University of Virginia.
5 "Sketch of C. W. Oltmanns Life," an obituary notice, *The News*, Staunton, September 17, 1897. Newspaper clipping in H.P.
6 Bruce Catton, *Never Call Retreat* (London: Victor Gollanz Ltd., 1977): 364.
7 C.M.H., III: 476.
8 C.W.J., July 20, 1864.
9 C.M.H., III: 505.
10 While Hotchkiss spells it "Edenburg," it is "Edinburg" today, and so pronounced with a short "E."

11 *C.W.J.*, December 21, 1864.

12 *C.W.J.*, January 2, 1865.

13 All quotations hereafter, unless otherwise noted, are from *C.W.J.*

14 In Hotchkiss' diary this is identified as the home of B. F. W. Harlan. On the "Map of the Valley," Hotchkiss Map Collection #89, there is a house shown on the ridge in the expected position with the name "Harland" adjacent to it.

15 H.P., 57/604.

16 Archie P. McDonald, "The Illusive Commission of 'Major' Jedediah Hotchkiss," *Va. Mag. of Hist. & Biog.* 75 (1967): 181-185.

17 Jed Hotchkiss to Hon. Geo. W. Randolph, Secretary of War, September 19, 1862, H.P., 49/136.

18 *C.W.J.*, March 5, 1863.

19 *C.W.J.*, March 14, 1863.

20 *S.S.*, September 19, 1865.

21 *S.S.*, May 15, 1866.

22 *S.S.*, September 12, 1865.

23 Memorandum of a contract, May 29, 1868, University Library, Washington and Lee University.

Endnotes to Chapter IV

1 Diary, H.P.

2 H.P., 50/236.

3 June 21, 1865, H.P., 58/004; July 12, 1865, H.A., Box 1.

4 July 11, 1865, H.P., 40/207.

5 Diary, July 20-August 3, 1865; August 7-19, 1865, H.P., 2/485-8; Jed Hotchkiss Account Book, H.P., 53/237.

6 Diary, August 4, 1865, H.P., 2/487, September 6, 1865, H.P., 2/488. The Diary locates the property at the corner of Lewis and Water Streets, but this must be an error. Hotchkiss' map of Staunton, 1870, shows Water Street as running **parallel** to Lewis Street, along the line of the present Central Avenue. An examination of property deeds revealed that in 1858 Waddell bought a quarter-acre "lot, house and appurtenences" located at the corner of Water and **Frederick** Streets. This he sold to Eliza B. Garber in December 1865, who in turn sold it to Beverley P. Reese in 1869. The Hotchkiss map shows property at this corner as being owned by Dr. Reese. Further, an advertisement in the *Staunton Spectator*, October 3, 1865, reads, "L. Waddell Jr. offers a house and lot in Staunton for sale $3,500. The property is rented out for 11 months, and possession cannot be given at present. My address is Churchville, Augusta County, Va." In his diary for September 18, Hotchkiss records, "Mr. W. H. Waddell moved out to Churchville, to the 'Loch Willow' house I had occupied, as I moved in." (H.P., 2/490.) Although some inconsistencies remain to be explained, it does seem likely that the house and school were located on property at the northwest corner of modern Frederick Street

and Central Avenue. Accepting this conclusion transfers the problem to the diary entry itself. The 1865 diary in the Library of Congress is not the original, but a typed copy; it is possible that the error occurred during transcription, for it seems unlikely that Hotchkiss would make a geographical mistake of this kind.

7   *S.S.*, September 12, 1865.
8   S. B. Robinson to D. F. Boyd, September 22, 1865, Archie P. McDonald, "Samson B. Robinson: An Englishman in Louisiana," *La. Hist.* 7 (Spring 1966): 152.
9   *S.S.*, September 19, 1865; Jed Hotchkiss Account Book, September 29, 1865, H.P., 53/230.
10 L. Rowland to Jed Hotchkiss, August 29, 1865, H.P., 49/219.
11 C.W. Oltmanns to Jed Hotchkiss, October 19, 1865, H.P., 49/195.
12 Diary, October 23, 1865, H.P., 2/492.
13 Alexander H. H. Stuart to Gov. Francis H. Pierpoint, October 25, 1865. John B. Baldwin to Gov. Francis H. Pierpoint, October 25, 1865. John Echols to Colonel D. H. Strother ("Porte Crayon"). H.P., 49/144-146.
14 Diary, October 26 and 27, 1865, H.P., 2/492.
15 Peter S. Michie to Jed Hotchkiss, December 29, 1865. H.A., Box 1.
16 *C.M.H.*, III: 939, Hotchkiss Papers, 45/728.
17 Charles Hotchkiss Osterhout, "A Johnny Reb from Windsor N.Y." *Courier Magazine.* 4 (1955): 20-23; Jerry B. Thomas, "Jedediah Hotchkiss, Gilded Age Propagandist of Industrialism," *Va. Mag. of Hist. & Biog.* (1976): 189-202; Archie P. McDonald, *Make Me a Map of the Valley.* McDonald appears to have combined the diary record with the *Virginia Biography* statement.
18 *Boston Traveller*, November 20, 1886, H.P., 58/642.
19 H.P., 58/509.
20 H.P., 57/671-678. On October 25, 1886, Hotchkiss acknowledged a letter from Thomas F. Anderson of the *Boston Traveller*, and told him that the biographical sketch would be sent in a few days. H.P., 22/584.
21 A copy of this letter is owned by Charles English, Windsor, N.Y.
22 Campbell Brown to Jed Hotchkiss, August 18, 1865, H.P.
23 Thomas Lafayette Rosser, Papers, Alderman Library, University of Virginia.
24 G. W. Hotchkiss to Jed Hotchkiss, July 10, 1865, H.A., Box 1.
25 S. Howell Brown to Jed Hotchkiss, H.P., 49/218.
26 *Staunton Vindicator*, November 18, 1864.
27 Douglas Smith, *Virginia during Reconstruction 1865-1870: A Political, Economic, and Social Study.* Ph.D. Thesis, University of Virginia, 1960, quoting *Report of the Joint Committee on Reconstruction*, 39th. Congress, 1st. Session, *Part II Virginia*, 68, Testimony of Douglas Gray of Augusta County.
28 *Staunton Vindicator*, September 1, 1865.

29 Whitelaw Reid, *After the War: A Southern Tour:* 323. (First published 1866, reprinted as Harper Torchbook edition, Harper and Row, New York, 1965); John Richard Dennett, *The South as it is: 1865-1866*, being the reports of the special correspondent to *The Nation*, brought together by Henry M. Christian (The Viking Press, 1965)

30 *S.S.*, September 11, 1866.

31 *S.S.*, October 3, 1865; P. Tams, "Address delivered at the Annual General Meeting of the Augusta County Historical Society, November 9, 1964," *Augusta Historical Bulletin* 1 (1965): 20.

32 Robert R. Jones, *Conservative Virginia. The Post War Career of Governor James Lawson Kemper*: 33-38. Unpublished Ph.D. Thesis, University of Virginia; *S.S.*, September 26, 1865. On October 28, 1865, Jed, "Took 5,000 stock in the new U.S. Express Co.," and on November 4, paid 1% of his subscription. Diary H.P. 2/492-3. January 2, 1866, Hotchkiss' note in lieu of payment of 5% of subscription to the stock endorsed by Col. M. G. Harman and signed by W. H. Tams and Hugh W. Sheffey, H.A., Box 1.

33 McDonald, *loc. cit.*

34 Jed Hotchkiss Account Book, H.P., 53/230 et seq., Diary, November 25, 1865, H.P., 2/494.

35 Diary, November 7, 1865, H.P., 2/493.

36 Agreement between Harman and Hotchkiss, March 17, 1866, H.A., Box 1; *S.S.*, May 11, 1866. Staunton City Deed Book 5: 142, July 13, 1868, records the purchase for a $50 down payment and a bond of $4,250 payable in one year, or in eight installments plus interest.

37 Wm. Allan to Jed Hotchkiss, September 20, 1866, H.P., 49/211.

38 Jed Hotchkiss to General Smith, December 13, 1865, Virginia Military Institute Archives.

39 *S.S.*, March 5, 1867; D. Van Nostrand to Jed Hotchkiss, H.A., Box 1.

40 *S.S.*, January 29, February 26, April 2, April 30, May 28, 1867.

41 Jed Hotchkiss to George Hotchkiss, September 24, 1849. A copy of this letter was found in June 1985 in the former home of Hotchkiss' granddaughter, Mrs. Ellen Christian, at Deerfield, Virginia, and now in the H.C.

42 *S.S.*, January 30, February 27, April 10, 1866, May 28, 1867. Allen W. Moger, "Railroad Practices and Policies in Virginia after the Civil War," *Va. Mag. of Hist. and Biog.* 1951: 424.

43 *S.S.*, March 26, July 16, 1867.

44 *S.S.*, July 2, 1867; March 3, July 28, November 3, 1868; H.P., 50/514.

45 *S.S.*, April 30, 1867; H.P., 50/514.

46 J. M. Curry, *A Brief Sketch of George Peabody and a History of the Peabody Fund through Thirty Years*, 1898; *S.S.*, July 16, August 27, 1867.

47 Jed Hotchkiss to H. W. Gilbert, November 2, 1886, H.P., 22/585.

48 Jed Hotchkiss Account Book, H.P., 53/230 et seq.

49 H.A., Box 1.

50 Charles S. Bundy, "Some Recollections of Windsor," *The Echo*, No. 18, 1909. Copies of this map are held by the Library of Congress and the Alderman Library, University of Virginia.
51 H.P., 50/509 et seq.
52 H.A., Box 1; *S.S.*, November 19, 1867.
53 H.A., Box 1. Miller was employed almost continuously from November 1868 until August 1869.
54 Board of Trustees of Washington College, "Records of Minutes," June 17, 1868; "Memorandum of Contract, June 29, 1868," University Library, Washington and Lee University, Lexington, Virginia.
55 Under the Morrill Land Act the Federal Government gave each state 30,000 acres of the public domain for the support of schools of agriculture and mechanical arts. Assignment of the land or its proceeds to specified institutions was left to the states.
56 Francis H. Smith to Matthew F. Maury, October 19, 1868, quoted in Peter C. Thomas, *Matthew Fontaine Maury and the Problems of Virginia's Identity, 1865-1873*; Francis Leigh Williams, *Matthew Fontaine Maury-Scientist of the Sea*: 449-469.
57 *S.S.*, November 3, 1868.
58 R. E. Lee to Maj. J. Hotchkiss, December 14, 1868, University Library, Washington and Lee University; President's Report to the Trustees of Washington College, June 22, 1869, University Library, Washington and Lee University.
59 R. E. Lee to Maj. J. Hotchkiss, October 20, 1868, University Library, Washington and Lee University.
60 President's Report to the Trustees of Washington College, June 17, 1870. University Library, Washington and Lee University; Diary, January 2, 1870, H.P., 2/503.
61 Letter headed "Farmville, April 14, 1870," and signed F.N.W., in a collection of newspaper clippings, H.P., 60/009.
62 General G. W. Custis Lee, President's Report to the Trustees of Washington College, University Library, Washington and Lee University.
63 Contract with *Southern Planter and Farmer*, February 10, 1871, H.P., 58/074-5. On one of the Memoranda pages of Hotchkiss' diary for 1871 there appears the following, "County maps for Farmer & P 1st. Louisa, 2nd Buckingham, 3rd Orange, 4th Hanover, 5th Surry, 6th Rockbridge, 7th Culpeper, 8th Albermarle, 9th Pr. Edward; Hotchkiss Papers, 2/610. In addition to the five published maps, Earl G. Swem, "Maps relating to Virginia," *Bulletin of the Virginia State Library*, Vol. 7, 1914, includes one of Lunenburg County, bearing a similar title. A copy of this map is among the collection of Hotchkiss maps held by the Alderman Library. Hotchkiss prepared texts to accompany the maps of Hanover County (Diary, April 28, 1871), Surry County (Diary, May 23, 1871), Prince Edward County (Diary, June 16, 1871); *S.S.*, June 13, 1871, "June issue [of the *Southern Planter and Farmer*] contains a map of Surry County. The map is prefaced by a very interesting sketch of Surry Co. from its formation in 1652/53 to present time."

64 Chilton C. Pearson, "William Henry Ruffner: Reconstruction Statesman of Virginia," *South Atlantic Quarterly*, XX (1921) 29-30, 138.

65 "Official Appointment as County Superintendent of Schools for the County of Augusta, September 22, 1870." H.P., 52/443. Hotchkiss resigned in March 1871 (Diary, March 6, 1871), H.P., 2/557.

66 H.A., Box 7; Diary, March 20, 1872, H.P., 2/657.

67 There are a number of references in the Hotchkiss Papers to William Gearing's drinking, e.g. in his Account Book, H.P., 53/222, et seq. Here it is recorded that William lost a number of days at work by being drunk at the end of November and the beginning of December 1865.

68 *S.S.*, November 3, 1868.

69 William Cauper, *The Life of Claudet Crozet*, Appendix C; James Poyntz Nelson, *The Chesapeake and Ohio Railway*, "An address given before the Railway Men's Improvement Society, January 27, 1916,": 16.

70 Douglas Smith, *loc. cit.*: 62.

71 James Poyntz Nelson, *loc. cit.*: 15.

Endnotes to Chapter V

1 Jed Hotchkiss to "My Beloved Daughter," November 27, 1872, H.A., Box 1.

2 *S.S.*, November 12, 1872.

3 *S.S.*, February 18, 1873.

4 *Journal of the Society of Arts*, February 21, 1873.

5 David Thomas Ansted (1814-1880). Professor of Geology at King's College, London, 1840-53, Fellow of the Royal Society, 1844. From 1853 onward he was much concerned with the practical applications of geology to mining, engineering, and water supply. Consequently he was much in demand as a consultant. In 1853 he visited the Kanawha River and examined the area to the south of that river drained by its tributaries, Armstrong, Cabin, and Coal creeks.

6 *The Times* (London), March 1, 1873.

7 *Ibid.*, September 12, 1873.

8 *Mining Journal*, September 27, 1873.

9 Sir Antonio Brady (1811-1881) was a civil servant with the Admiralty, which he joined at age 17 and rose to the head of the contracts department in 1869. He retired on a special pension in 1870 and was knighted by Queen Victoria at Windsor in June of the same year. He was an amateur geologist who made a valuable collection of mammalian remains from the brickearths of the Thames valley. After his retirement he devoted himself to social, educational, and religious reform.

10 Contract between Sir Antonio Brady and Pliny Fisk, April 14, 1873, H.P., 16/547; Jed Hotchkiss to Messrs. Mason, Justice, and Bowron, April 15, 1873, H.P., 16/541; Jed Hotchkiss to Sir Antonio Brady, June 10, July 4, 1873, H.P., 16/604, 638; *S.S.*, June 10, 1873, reported "Large Sale—Messrs. H. Forrer & Co. have sold Elizabeth Furnace to Sir Antonio Brady of England for $200,000. This sale was effected by Major Jed Hotchkiss, and it is considered the best iron property in Virginia. Sale conditional."

11 Jed Hotchkiss to Charles Easton, May 14, May 31, 1873, H.P., 16/583, 598; Charles Easton to S. A. Miller, June 22, 1873, H.P., 6/263; Charles Easton to Jed Hotchkiss, July 11, 1873, H.P., 6/259; telegram to Charles Easton from Miller and Hotchkiss, July 17, 1873, H.P., 6/263.

12 *S.S.*, March 25, 1873, reported the sale of porcelain works to a "company of English gentlemen" one of which "was extensively engaged in the Terra Cotta business in England." *S.S.*, May 20, 1873, reported "Mr. Easton has left for England to bring over the workmen...for Porcelain works."

13 Jed Hotchkiss to Frederick Easton, July 23, 1873, H.P., 16/666.

14 Jed Hotchkiss to William Easton, June 25, 1873, H.P., 16/628.

15 Jed Hotchkiss to Edward Sidgwick, November 5, 1873, H.P., 17/014.

16 The property was divided into three lots and sold at public auction in July 1875. The Selma Mansion and 32.7 acres were bought for $5,850 by John N. Hendren; Jed Hotchkiss to W. P. Isaacson, July 26, 1875, H.P., 6/455.

17 Jed Hotchkiss to Charles Easton, July 14, 1873, re contract with John T. Boston, the purchaser of the timber on Oak Hill estate for $6,042.50. H.P., 16/649.

18 Charles Easton to Jed Hotchkiss, November 25, 1873, and reply, H.P., 6/293.

19 For an account of the panic of 1873 see Allan Nevins, *Emergence of Modern America, 1865-1878*, Chapter XI, (New York: The MacMillan Company, 1927); Harold Underwood Faulkner, *American Economic History*, 6th ed: 584-9 (New York: Harper and Brothers, 1949) For contemporary accounts see Cornwallis, "History of the Crisis," *Lippincott's Magazine* XIV, December 1873, reprinted in F. Flugel and H. U. Faulkner, *Readings in Economic and Social History*: 688 (New York: Harper and Brothers, 1929); "An Englishman's View," *Bankers Magazine* XXXIII (November 1873): 993-5; and *The Times* (London) October 7, 1873.

20 For accounts of the Virginia debt problem see C. Van Woodward, *Origins of the New South, A History of the South*, Vol. VI (Baton Rouge: Louisiana State University Press, 1953): 92; Nelson M. Blake, *William Mahone of Virginia* (Richmond, 1935): 137 et seq.; Allen W. Moger, *Virginia: Bourbonism to Byrd 1870-1925* (Charlottesville: University Press of Virginia, 1968); Robert R. Jones, *Conservative Virginian: The Post War Career of Governor James Lawson Kemper*, unpublished Ph.D. thesis, University of Virginia, 1964.

21 Ansted, D. T., "Account of a Recent visit to the Coal and Iron Fields of Virginia," *Journal of the Society of Arts*, January 30, 1874.

22 Jed Hotchkiss to Henry Forrer, January 15, 1873, H.P., 17/075-6. Of the 6,605 acres of the Elizabeth Furnace Estate, the Forrers had undisputed title to 5,771.7 acres.

23 From a copy of Joseph Grubb Patent, October 15, 1795, H.P., 50/228.

24 Jed Hotchkiss to Sir Antonio Brady, February 26, 1874, H.P., 17/324-6.

ENDNOTES — PAGES 118 TO 125

25 Jed Hotchkiss to W. L. Nicholson, March 29, 1875, H.P., 17/122-7. M. A. Miller's report on his survey of the Cabin Creek lands in the form of a letter to Messrs. Swann and Knight, Trustees, January 6, 1874, H.P., 35/179-202.

26 A biographical sketch of John P. Hale, which first appeared in W. S. Laidley's *History of Kanawha County*, is reprinted in the 2nd (1931) and 3rd editions of *Trans-Allegheny Pioneers*, by John P. Hale, first published in 1886. The salines or salt manufactories exploited the underground deposits of salt by means of artesian wells. The brine was evaporated, using the abundant coal as fuel.

27 Jed Hotchkiss to Pliny Fisk, March 30, 1874, H.P., 17/181-4.

28 Diary, January 10-16, 1872, H.P., 2/646.

29 Jed Hotchkiss to Pliny Fisk, January 7, 1874, H.P., 17/....

30 Jed Hotchkiss to Pliny Fisk, June 1, 1874, H.P., 17/249-253.

31 Jed Hotchkiss to M. Harvey Effinger, March 11, 1874, H.P., 17/155.

32 Jed Hotchkiss to J. Byrd, April 11, 1874, H.P., 17/212.

33 Jed Hotchkiss to Major William M. Tate, Secretary to the Baldwin Augusta Fair, June 6, 1874, H.P., 17/412. See p. 105, above.

34 Jed Hotchkiss to Pliny Fisk, June 11, 1874, H.P., 17/270.

35 Jed Hotchkiss to John T. Cowan, written in the "Office of Sir Antonio Brady, 114, Cannon Street," July 6, 1874, H.P., 17/286-289.

36 Jed Hotchkiss to Pliny Fisk, June 29, 1874, H.P., 17/276-9.

37 Diploma to Nellie M. Hotchkiss, June 16, 1874, H.C.

38 Jed Hotchkiss to Capt. I. A. Welch, May 3, 1873, H.P., 16/596.

39 *Daily Courier*, May 29, 1874, reports the formation of this company with Hotchkiss as one of its directors.

40 *S.S.*, December 19, 1871.

41 Board of Immigration of the State of Virginia to General Assembly of Virginia, January 13, 1874, and Jed Hotchkiss to the Board of Immigration, December 31, 1873. Both in Senate Document No. 5, 1874.

42 William Barton Rogers to Jed Hotchkiss, September 20, 1873. H.P., 6/279,

43 Jed Hotchkiss to John T. Cowan, July 6, 1874, H.P., 17/286-289.

44 Jed Hotchkiss to Pliny Fisk, July 28, 1874, H.P., 17/308.

45 Jed Hotchkiss to Pliny Fisk, July 31, 1874, H.P., 17/316.

46 Jed Hotchkiss to Donald Allen, July 29, 1874, H.P., 17/313-5.

47 Nellie bought for twopence *The Sights of London*, and marked in it those she wished to visit; some have dates beside them. Her copy is in H.C.

48 Jed Hotchkiss to John Echols, July 27, 1874, H.P., 17/305.

49 Jed Hotchkiss to John T. Cowan, September 4, 1874, H.P., 18/500.

50 This journey took them to Birmingham where they met Hotchkiss namesakes, then to Belfast to attend the British Association meeting. A circuitous return route included Edinburgh, Melrose, and finally, Abbotsford to see the tomb of Sir Walter Scott.

51 Jed Hotchkiss to Major T. J. Kirkpatrick, September 17, 1874, H.P., 18/551.

52 Jed Hotchkiss to Major J. T. Kirkpatrick, March 27, 1875, H.P., 17/319.
53 Jed Hotchkiss to Pliny Fisk, September 10, 1874, H.P., 18/516-523.
54 Jed Hotchkiss to John T. Cowan, September 29, 1874, H.P., 18/566.
55 Jed Hotchkiss to J. G. Martien, March 11, 1874, H.P., 19/11-14.
56 Jed Hotchkiss to Major T. J. Kirkpatrick, March 27, 1875, H.P., 17/319.
57 Jed Hotchkiss to P. P. Barbour, September 4, 1874, H.P., 18/497.
58 Jed Hotchkiss to Major A. D. Robertson, April 22, 1892, H.P., 28/022.

Endnotes to Chapter VI

1 Data from London *Times*, January 27, 1875; May 7, 1875; July 1, 1875; August 21, 1878. *"Poor's Manual of Railroads of the United States,"* and *Annual Reports of the American Iron and Steel Federation.*
2 Jed Hotchkiss to John T. Cowan, March 17, 1875, H.P., 17/321.
3 Commissioners appointed April 1, 1875, on behalf of the creditors, who were joined by D. T. Ansted and Wm. M. Dunlap on June 2, 1875, Deed book 12: 358 and 428 Augusta County Courthouse, Staunton, Virginia.
4 Jed Hotchkiss to Professor D. T. Ansted, September 10, 1875, H.P., 18/673-6.
5 Hotchkiss drew up the sale document, "Commissioners' Sale of Thirty Valuable Building Lots." This included a location map, and a plan of the lots on Oak Hill (now Sears Hill) at a scale of 100ft-to-one-inch.
6 Statement No. 1, September 6, 1875. Report of Commissioners of sale of lots, March 11, 1878, H.A., Box 1.
7 Receipt for $1,354.17 paid "in settlement at authorized compromise of 60% of the judgment (Hustings Court of Staunton, September 1877) of the Executors of D. T. Ansted decd against said Hotchkiss." H.P., 58/104.
8 Jed Hotchkiss to W. H. Stable, June 29, and July 1, 1875, 18/620 and 622; Jed Hotchkiss to J. B. Peck and C. J. Johnston, July 1, 1875, H.P., 18/621.
9 Jed Hotchkiss to Pliny Fisk, April 10, 1875, H.P., 18/592.
10 Jed Hotchkiss to John T. Cowan, May 12, 1875, H.P., 17/4??.
11 Jed Hotchkiss to Pliny Fisk, May 14, 1875, H.P., 17/434.
12 Jed Hotchkiss to Sir Antonio Brady, May 31, 1875, H.P., 18/607.
13 Jed Hotchkiss to Pliny Fisk, June 10, 1875, H.P., 18/618.
14 Jed Hotchkiss to J. Taylor Ellyson, October 15, 1875, H.P., 19/049.
15 Jed Hotchkiss to Judge E. R. Watson, April 27, 1875, H.P., 8/596.
16 Jed Hotchkiss to John T. Cowan, May 3, 1875, H.P., 19/031.
17 Jed Hotchkiss to William Parr Isaacson, June 28, 1875, H.P., 17/466.
18 Jed Hotchkiss to Edgar Whitehead, March 30, 1875, H.P., 17/334; April 19, 1875, H.P., 19/028; May 5, 1875, H.P., 19/033.
19 Cornelius J. Heatwole, *History of Education in Virginia*: 236-239.
20 Programme of Teachers Institute, Abingdon, Virginia, October 5, 1875, H.P., 61/035.

21   Jed Hotchkiss to W. H. Ruffner, September 17, 1875, H.P., 18/660.
22   Jed Hotchkiss to Prof. W. Stevens, May 8, 1876, H.P., 19/090; Jed Hotchkiss to K. P. Battle, June 16, 1879, H.P., 19/248; Jed Hotchkiss to Prof. H. H. Smith, August 15, 1879, H.P., 19/287; Jed Hotchkiss to Prof. J. A. Smith, August 16, 1879, H.P., 19/290.
23   Jed Hotchkiss to J. H. Grabill, March 12, 1877, H.P., 19/128.
24   Jed Hotchkiss to A. Hoen, November 25, 1876, H.P., 6/537.
25   "Report on Guys Run Iron Lands," H.P., 37/218-226.
26   Jed Hotchkiss to Rev. Thomas Heywood, December 3, 1877, H.P., 60/662, 19/151.
27   S.S., May 16, 1876.
28   H.P., 50/592.
29   See correspondence March 3 to July 2, 1877, H.P., 19/119-142.
30   April 4, 1879, H.P., 19/239.
31   Archives, Virginia Military Institute, Lexington, Virginia.
32   Eleven-page report and map, H.P., 18/152-63.
33   Jed Hotchkiss to D. S. Cook, March 7, 1877, H.P., 19/121.
34   Jed Hotchkiss to E. A. Packer, March 12, 1877, H.P., 19/127.
35   London *Times*, October 17, 1877; J. M. Swank, *Annual report of the American Iron and Steel Association*, 1879; London *Times*, June 9, 1880.
36   S.S., June 18, 1878.
37   Jed Hotchkiss to Messrs. W. M. & C. J. Fields, May 13, 1878, October 21, 1878, H.P., 19/157 and 170. The report was issued as a 72-page pamphlet in an edition of 500; it included a map at a scale of 1/40,000 showing the location of the four tracts making up this 31,000 acre estate.
38   James M. Swank, Ann. Rep., *Am. I&S Assn.*; London *Times* June 9, 1880.
39   Jed Hotchkiss to John T. Cowan, October 10, 1879, H.P., 17/511.
40   Jed Hotchkiss to L. N. Ketcham, November 21, 1879, H.P., 17/560.
41   Jed Hotchkiss to E. A. Packer, February 5, 1879, H.P., 19/185.

Endnotes to Chapter VII

1   Jed Hotchkiss to H. T. Douglas, February 11, 1879, H.P., 19/192.
2   Jed Hotchkiss to D. E. Strasburg, February 5, 1879, H.P., 19/186.
3   Jed Hotchkiss to Samuel Coit, August 25, 1879, H.P., 19/299.
4   *The Virginias* V (1884): 36.
5   *The Virginias* address book, H.A., Box 7.
6   *The Virginias* I (1880): 104.
7   *The Virginias* I (1880): map inserted between pages 104 and 105.
8   The United States Geological Survey was formed in March 1879.
9   *The Virginias* III (1882): 181.
10 *Ibid.*, VI (1885): 33; III (1882): 119.
11 S.S., August 8, 1876.

12 *The Virginias* I (1880): 86.
13 William Barton Rogers, *Report of the Geological Survey of the State of Virginia for the year 1836*: 137.
14 C. H. Ambler and F. P. Summers, *West Virginia, the Mountain State*, 1958; Thomas Jefferson, *Notes on the State of Virginia*, ed. William Peden (New York; W. W. Norton & Co., 1972): 28.
15 Rogers, *Report of the Progress of the Geological Survey*, 1836: 117-124.
16 Frederick J. Kimball, 1844-1903. In 1862, Kimball joined the engineering department of the Pennsylvania RR. After eight years experience, including two spent in the workshops of the London & Northwestern Railway at Crewe, England, he became a partner in the Philadelphia banking house of E. W. Clark & Company. In 1879 this company organized the Shenandoah Valley Construction Company with Kimball as chairman. Two years later the bankrupt A.M.&O. was purchased by E. W. Clark & Co. and renamed the Norfolk & Western Railroad. In the same year the Shenandoah Valley RR made junction with the N&W at Big Lick, the future "Magic City" of Roanoke. Kimball was president of SVRR from 1881 to 1885, vice president of the N&W, 1881-1883, its president, receiver or chairman, from then until his death in February 1903. See Joseph E. Lamie, *From Mine to Market. The History of coal transportation on the Norfolk & Western Railway*, (New York University Press, 1954) 19-25.
17 Jed Hotchkiss to F. J. Kimball, October 9, 1879, H.P., 17/510.
18 F. J. Kimball to Jed Hotchkiss, November 4, 1880; Jed Hotchkiss to F. J. Kimball, November 6, 1880, H.P., 18/254-261.
19 F. J. Kimball to Jed Hotchkiss, November 8, 1880, referred to in Jed Hotchkiss to F. J. Kimball, November 15, 1880, H.P., 18/263.
20 Jed Hotchkiss to F. J. Kimball, November 15, 1880, H.P., 18/263-271.
21 Jed Hotchkiss to F. J. Kimball, April 14, 1881, H.P., 18/295-9. The map is to be found in Folder C1 in the Special Collections Division, Newman Library, Virginia Tech., Blacksburg, Virginia.
22 Jed Hotchkiss to F. J. Kimball, April 14, 1881, H.P., 18/295-9.
23 Jack M. Jones, *Early Mining in Pocahontas, Virginia*, (Lynchburg: Jack M. Jones, 1983)
24 Supplement to *The Virginias* for June and July, 1882.
25 Jones: 25.
26 Harriet Eliza Lathrop, foreword by Helen Lathrop Thompson, 1948, unpublished account in the possession of the Pocahontas Coal Company, Bluefield, Virginia.
27 *The Virginias*, IV (1883): 50.
28 Lambie: 34; Jones: 26.
29 Jones: 32.
30 Lambie: 24; Ronald D. Eller, *Miners, Millhands and Mountaineers*, University of Tennessee Press, Knoxville, 1982: 51-52, 71-73; Jerry Bruce Thomas, "Coal Country: The rise of the Southern Smokeless Coal Industry and its effect on Area Development, 1872-1910," University of North Carolina, Chapel Hill, Ph.D. Thesis 1971: 77-79.

31 F. J. Kimball to Jed Hotchkiss, April 7, 1884, H.P., 7/253.
32 Jed Hotchkiss to C. W. Smith, March 25, 1885, H.P., 21/693.
33 Jed Hotchkiss to Editor, *Industrial South*, December 28, 1885.
34 Jed Hotchkiss to Gen. James McDonald, March 14, 1886, H.P., 23/063.
35 Jed Hotchkiss to R. H. Edmonds, Editor, *Manufacturers Record*, March 14, 1886, H.P., 23/069.
36 Professor Eggleston to Jed Hotchkiss, June 24, 1881, H.P., 7/042.
37 A. S. McCreath to Jed Hotchkiss, June 8, 1881, H.P., 7/039.
38 *The Virginias* IV (1883): 66.
39 *The Commonwealth*, June 9, 1880.
40 *The Virginias*, VI (1885): 3. See Chapter X.
41 Hotchkiss was not much interested in politics, and became involved on only a few occasions in his life, but during the presidential campaign of 1896, he explained to C. W. Oltmanns that he played an active part on that occasion "because I considered it my duty both as a citizen and as a Christian so to do." He went on to say, "No old Confederate can find any possible excuse for voting the republican ticket or that of its allies." October 31, 1896, H.A., Box 8.
42 August 18, 1884. Independent Candidate for Congress. A card addressed to the voters of the 10th. Congressional District. H.P., 58/480.
43 Newspaper clippings, H.P., 58/484.
44 F. J. Kimball to Jed Hotchkiss, September 22, 1884, H.P., 7/600.
45 Jed Hotchkiss to Messrs. A. Hoen & Co. August 12, 1887, H.P., 23/278; Jed Hotchkiss to Col. J. M. McCue, January 25, 1888, H.P., 24/169.
46 Jed Hotchkiss to Professor I. C. White, February 4, 1888, H.P., 24/190.
47 Jed Hotchkiss to Mrs. Wm. B. Rogers, February 3, 1888, H.P., 24/185.
48 January 16, 1888, H.P., 24/160.
49 Jed Hotchkiss to G. H. Wetherell, May 5, 1888, H.P., 24/296-8.
50 Jed Hotchkiss to Board of Directors, Augusta National Bank, July 3, 1888, H.P., 24/383.
51 Jed Hotchkiss to Board of Directors, Valley National Bank, December 12, 1888, H.P., 24/520.
52 "The Oaks" was accepted into the National Register of Historic Places and as a Virginia Landmark in 1979. It was the second private residence in Staunton to be so honored. Fletcher Collins, Jr., *The Oaks. A Room-By-Room Inventory, Descriptive and Historical*, Staunton, Virginia, 1991 (unpublished).

Endnotes to Chapter VIII

1 3rd meeting Washington April 27-29, 1886, "The Value of Topographical Knowledge in Battles and Campaigns, with Blackboard Illustrations," H.P., 60/509.
2 e.g. "Military Surveyors during the Civil War," February 26, 1892; "The Battle of Fredericksburg," Jed Hotchkiss to G. F.R. Henderson, May 20, 1895, H.P., 11/361.

3   e.g., in June 1879 he delivered 13 lectures to the Teachers Institute in Chapel Hill, North Carolina, the last being about Jackson's Valley campaign to "which the whole community turned out to hear."
4   *Virginia Free Press*, June 21 and 28, 1893. H.P., 61/145.
5   H.P., 61/148.
6   *S.S.*, October 22, 1878.
7   Jed Hotchkiss to Colonel G. F. R. Henderson, December 22, 1892, H.P., 30/248.
8   C. B. Ryan to Jed Hotchkiss, May 28, 1894, H.P., 31/618; Jed Hotchkiss to A. E. White, June 4, 1894, H.P., 31/625.
9   R. W. Stephenson, *Civil War Maps*, 2 ed. (Washington: Library of Congress, 1989): 550.8.
10 *Morgantown Weekly Post*, June 23, 1888; H.A., Box 1.
11 American Historical Association, Vol II No. 1, Report of the Proceedings, Third Annual Meeting, Washington, D.C. April 27-29, 1886.
12 Jed Hotchkiss to Gen. Jubal A. Early, March 25, 1886, H.P., 22/510.
13 H.P., 8/093.
14 Jed Hotchkiss to Clarence H. Bell, August 30, 1886, H.P., 22/456.
15 Jed Hotchkiss to Major H. Fortescue, October 27, 1890, H.P., 27/379; Jed Hotchkiss to Hon. H. St. George Tucker, January 28, 1896, H.P., 33/096.
16 Gilbert Thompson, born Blackstone, Mass., March 21, 1839, died Washington, D.C., June 8, 1909; served with the Battalion of Engineers, U.S. Army. In 1864 he was assistant engineer at H.Q. Army of the Potomac. See Marcus Benjamin, *Memorial Papers of the Society of Colonial Wars in the District of Columbia*. No. 5, 1910. An account of the meeting and the contrasting styles of the lecturers appeared in *The Washington Post*, February 27, 1892.
17 Jed Hotchkiss to Wm. N. McDonald, November 22, 1892, H.P., 30/202; Jed Hotchkiss to Gen. Marcus J. Wright, Jan. 1893, H.P., 30/351.
18 Jed Hotchkiss to Editor, So. Hist. Soc. Papers, March 1885, H.P., 21/707.
19 Jed Hotchkiss to Major George B. Davis, September 29, 1892, H.P., 30/114.
20 George Francis Robert Henderson, 1854-1903, commissioned in the York and Lancaster Regiment in 1878, and served in the Egyptian campaign of 1882. In 1892, he was appointed Professor of Military Art and History at the British Army's Staff College, a position he occupied until the outbreak of the Boer war. He was regarded as a fine writer and a learned soldier. London *Times*, March 7, 1903.
21 Jed Hotchkiss to W. L. Chase, March 28, 1892, H.P., 27/654; March 30, 1892, H.P., 27/663, 9/101-134.
22 December 22, 1892, H.P., 30/248.
23 Jed Hotchkiss to W. L. Chase, March 28, 1892, H.P., 27/654.
24 G. F. R. Henderson to Jed Hotchkiss, February 23, 1893, H.P., 9/397.
25 Jed Hotchkiss to G. F. R. Henderson, May 23, 1895, H.P., 11/373.

26 *Ibid.*
27 Jed Hotchkiss to G. F. R. Henderson, April 26, 1895, H.P., 11/286.
28 *Ibid.* For further evidence in support of Hotchkiss' assessment of Kyd Douglas, see Dennis E. Frye, *Civil War*, 1991, Vol. IX No. 5, p. 40.
29 Jed Hotchkiss to T. T. Munford, October 22, 1897, H.P., 49/239.
30 General T. T. Munford to Dr. Benjamin Blackford, November 30, 1898, H.P., 16/115.
31 R. L. Dabney to Jed Hotchkiss, May 7, 1896, H.P., 12/469; S. J. C. Moore to Jed Hotchkiss, May 19, 1896, H.P., 12/516 and May 25, 1896, H.P., 12/545; D. C. Humphreys to Jed Hotchkiss, August 2, August 24, 1896, H.P., 13/088.
32 Jed Hotchkiss to Dr. H. H. McGuire, November 13, 1890, H.P., 27/386.
33 March 14, 1895, H.P., 11/173.
34 *Stonewall Jackson and the American Civil War*, was published in October 1898 by Longmans Green & Co., 2 vols., price 42s.
35 Jed Hotchkiss to Capt. Thos. Ellett, June 16, 1892, H.P., 28/148.
36 August 3, 1891, H.P., 27/555.
37 H.P., 14/125.
38 Jed Hotchkiss to Clement E. Evans, January 3, 1898, H.P., 14/622.
39 H.P., 15/608.
40 Jed Hotchkiss to Clement A. Evans, August 17, 1898, H.P., 15/487.

Endnotes to Chapter IX

1 Memorandum of Agreement, January 21, 1890, H.P., 37/005.
2 Jed Hotchkiss to Professor I. C. White, November 13, 17, & 26, 1890, H.P., 27/385, 393, & 400.
3 Jed Hotchkiss to M. E. Ingalls, April 29, 1891, H.P., 27/453.
4 Jed Hotchkiss to J. T. Richards, May 21, 1891, H.P., 27/476.
5 *Johnson Newlon Camden: a study in individualism.* Festus P. Summers, 1937, Chapter XVII.
6 Jed Hotchkiss to J. N. Camden, August 20, 1891, H.P., 27/572.
7 Jed Hotchkiss to Professor I. C. White, October 20, 1891, H.P., 28/486.
8 Jed Hotchkiss to E. W. Clark, May 24, 1890, H.P., 27/285.
9 Jed Hotchkiss to R. W. Harris, June 24, 1890, H.P., 27/236.
10 Jed Hotchkiss to Trustees, September 24, 1891, H.A., Box 7; Jed Hotchkiss to J. H. Bramwell, September 24, 1891, H.P., 28/428.
11 January 10, 1892, H.P., 28/692.
12 Jed Hotchkiss to J. H. Bramwell, January 2, 1892, H.P., 28/681; Jed Hotchkiss to E. D. Hotchkiss, March 11, 1892, H.P., 27/622.
13 March 7, 1892, H.A., Box 7.
14 Jed Hotchkiss to H. H. Fay, April 23, 1892, H.A., Box 7; Jed Hotchkiss to J. S. Russell, May 12, 1892, H.P., 28/058; Jed Hotchkiss to J. H. Bramwell, May 13, 1892, H.P., 28/069.

15 Jed Hotchkiss to H. H. Fay and M. E. Miller, November 25, 1892, H.A., Box 7.
16 January 30, 1893, H.A., Box 7.
17 Jed Hotchkiss to C. P. Williams, March 31, 1892, H.P., 27/661.
18 Jed Hotchkiss to Professor D. C. Humphreys, April 24, 1890, H.P., 27/171.
19 *Spring Report of the Condition of The Grottoes Co.*, March 1, 1891, H.P., 37/112.
20 Jed Hotchkiss to E. E. Denniston, May 19, 1890, H.P., 27/203; Jed Hotchkiss to E. W. Clark, May 24, 1890, H.P., 27/205.
21 Jed Hotchkiss to F. E. Randall, July 26, 1890, H.P., 27/317.
22 Jed Hotchkiss to C. P. Williams, July 29, 1890, H.P., 27/321.
23 Jed Hotchkiss to J. H. Taylor, October 22, 1890, H.P., 27/372.
24 *S.S.*, March 20, 1891.
25 *Rockingham Register*, March 27, 1891.
26 *Staunton Vindicator*, April 3, 1891.
27 "A Word of Explanation to the Stockholders of The Grottoes Company." Jed Hotchkiss et al. August 13, 1891.
28 *Shendun News*, September 17, 1891.
29 Jed Hotchkiss to D. Lowenburg, December 16, 1891, H.P., 28/656.
30 H.P., 37/129.
31 Jed Hotchkiss to J. W. Rumple, May 13, 1892, H.P., 28/064.
32 Jed Hotchkiss to Judge Jos. Christian, May 28, 1892, H.P., 28/104.
33 Jed Hotchkiss to M. A. Riffe, May 30, 1892, H.P., 28/108.
34 Jed Hotchkiss to Annette Jordella, August 24, 1892, H.P., 30/050.
35 *Acts of the General Assembly*, Chapter 72, page 109, Session of 1891, approved January 22, 1892.
36 Jed Hotchkiss to H. G. Davis, April 25, May 12, 1892, H.P., 28/030, 055.
37 Jed Hotchkiss to J. N. Camden, April 12, 1893, H.P., 30/503; Jed Hotchkiss to R. H. Catlett, April 12, 1893, H.P., 30/505; Jed Hotchkiss to J. K. Cowan, April 28, 1893, H.P., 30/533.
38 Jed Hotchkiss to J. N. Camden, May 17, 1893, H.P., 30/576.
39 Jed Hotchkiss to J. W. Blackburn, May 18, 1893, H.P., 30/581.
40 Jed Hotchkiss to J. N. Camden, May 17, 1893, H.P., 30/576.
41 James Bruce to Jefferson Chandler, June 24, 1893; Jed Hotchkiss to Jefferson Chandler, July 8, 1893, H.P., 30/689; Jed Hotchkiss to Charles Catlett, October 14, 1893, H.P., 31/097.
42 January 2, 1894, H.P., 31/403.
43 Jed Hotchkiss to J. N. Camden, April 6, 1894, H.P., 31/554; J. N. Camden to Jed Hotchkiss, April 8, 1894, H.P., 36/112; Jed Hotchkiss to J. N. Camden, April 18, 1894, H.P., 31/574.
44 Jed Hotchkiss to Gov. A. B. Flemming, April 12, 1894, H.P., 31/558.
45 Stephen M. Weld to M. Erskine Miller, Jan. 29, 1897, H.P., 13/560.

46 R. H. Catlett to H. H. Fay, February 2, 1897, H.P., 13/590.
47 Telegram, H. H. Fay to R. H. Catlett, February 17, 1897, and reply, H.P., 13/647.
48 March 2, 1897, H.P., 13/682.
49 J. N. Camden to Jed Hotchkiss, July 22, 1897, H.P., 14/200; John Rapelje to Jed Hotchkiss, August 5, 1897, H.P., 14/260.
50 Summers: 522-3.
51 Preface to *The Mineral Wealth of Virginia tributary to the lines of the Shenandoah Valley and Norfolk and Western Railroad Companies*, Andrew S. McCreath, 1883.
52 Andrew S. McCreath, *The Mineral Wealth of Virginia tributary to the lines of the Norfolk and Western and Shenandoah Valley Railroad Companies*, 1884: 105-129.
53 Jed Hotchkiss to E. W. Clark, April 27, 1888, H.P., 24/288.
54 F. J. Kimball to Vivian, Gray & Co., February 16, 1889, quoted by Joseph T. Lambie, *From Mine to Market: The History of Coal Transportation on the Norfolk and Western Railway*, (N.Y. University Press, 1954), 123-4.
55 Jed Hotchkiss to J. P. Hale, March 7, 1889, H.P., 24/616; E. W. Clark & Co. April 16, 1889, credit $5,000 to Jed Hotchkiss for an undivided half interest in the purchase of the option, H.P., 8/365; Jed Hotchkiss to J. P. Hale, April 20, 1889, H.P., 24/700.
56 March 23, 1889, H.P., 24/651.
57 March 23, 1889, H.P., 24/650.
58 Jed Hotchkiss to J. P. Hale, April 20, 1889, H.P., 24/700.
59 March 23, 1889, H.P., 24/650.
60 May 27, 1889, H.P., 25/028.
61 May 27, 1889, H.P., 25/029.
62 Jed Hotchkiss to I. C. White, quoting Edward Ilsley, June 13, 1889, H.P., 25/051.
63 Jed Hotchkiss to E. W. Clark, July 24, 1889, H.P., 25/114.
64 H.P., 25/235.
65 Lambie: 124.
66 H.P., 37/447.
67 Guyandot Coal Land Association, *Fifth Annual Report year ending 1894*, February 20, 1895, "Comparative Statement of Expenditures, 1890-1894," H.P., 37/428.
68 E. W. Clark to J. C. Miller, March 12, 1895, H.P., 11/162.
69 G.C.L.A., *Fifth Annual Report*.
70 E. W. Clark to Jed Hotchkiss, December 23, 1889, H.P., 8/479.
71 G.C.L.A., *Second Annual Report*, 1891, H.P., 37/300-319.
72 Jed Hotchkiss to H. J. Toudy, March 24, 1892, H.P., 29/089.
73 Jed Hotchkiss to E. W. Clark, March 11, 1892, H.P., 29/080.
74 Jed Hotchkiss to J. C. Miller, January 29, 1892, H.P., 29/053.
75 March 7, 1892, H.P., 29/029.

76 March 9, 1892, H.P., 19/080.
77 Jed Hotchkiss to E. W. Clark, June 12, 1892, H.P., 29/141.
78 Jed Hotchkiss to E. W. Clark, October 11, 1893, H.P., 29/322; Jed Hotchkiss to F. J. Kimball, October 14, 1893, H.P., 31/099.
79 May 12, 1892, H.P., 29/127.
80 Jed Hotchkiss to James F. Beattie, October 14, 1893, H.P., 29/328; G.C.L.A., *Fourth Annual Report, for year ending December 31, 1893.*
81 G.C.L.A., *Fifth Annual Report.*
82 Jed Hotchkiss to J. P. Hale, November 22, 1893, H.P., 31/171.
83 The Annual General Meeting, February 28, 1900, was presented with a plan for winding up the Association and settling its affairs.
84 Jed Hotchkiss to J. C. Maben, June 24, 1892, H.P., 28/171.
85 Spelling of Guyandot; United States Commission on Geographical Names, October 1, 1895, Henry Gannett to Jed Hotchkiss, February 15, 1896, H.P., 33/402.
86 Edwin A. Cubby, *The Transformation of the Tug and Guyandot Valleys: Economic and Social Change in West Virginia, 1888-1921*, Ph.D. Dissertation, Syracuse University, 1962: 213-4.
87 Jed Hotchkiss to M. E. Ingalls, June 25, 1892, H.P., 28/178-9.
88 Jed Hotchkiss to E. W. Clark, July 28, 1892, H.P., 29/196.
89 Jed Hotchkiss to Z. T. Vinson, February 24, 1893, H.P., 30/402.
90 Cubby: 221.
91 *Ibid.* 222.
92 C. W. Smith to Jed Hotchkiss, August 3, 1895, H.P., 11/611.
93 G.C.L.A., *Sixth Annual Report, year ending December 31, 1895*, H.P., 37/621; Jed Hotchkiss to J. P. Hale, February 7, 1896, H.P., 33/110.
94 Jed Hotchkiss to C. W. Smith, November 21, 1895, H.P., 33/149.
95 Jed Hotchkiss to C. W. Smith, January 13, 1896, H.P., 33/246.
96 November 28, 1895, H.P., 33/158.
97 Jed Hotchkiss to J. C. Green, November 27, 1895, H.P., 33/157 and January 13, 1896, H.P., 33/249.
98 December 4, 1895, H.P., 33/049.
99 Jed Hotchkiss to J. T. McCreery, December 11, 1895, H.P., 33/188.
100 Jed Hotchkiss to J. C. Green, January 27, 1896, H.P., 33/272.
101 January 23, 1896, H.P., 33/274.
102 J. T. McCreery to Jed Hotchkiss, January 25, 1896, H.P., 33/278.
103 January 30, 1896, H.P., 33/307.
104 Martin Williams to Jed Hotchkiss, January 30, 1896, H.P., 33/312.
105 Jed Hotchkiss to Campbell and Holt, January 29, 1896, H.P., 33/297.
106 E.g., to General Dacey on February 14, 1896, H.P., 33/376.
107 Jed Hotchkiss to W. G. Dacey, February 4, 1896, H.P., 33/332 and 12/168; "Petition to enlarge the boundaries of Staunton...," H.P., 33/100.

108 Jed Hotchkiss to C. W. Smith, March 11, 1896, H.P., 33/490.
109 February 6, 1896, H.P., 33/340.
110 H.P., 33/344.
111 February 7, 1896, H.P., 33/352-3.
112 J. T. McCreery to Jed Hotchkiss, March 2, 1896, H.P., 33/448-9.
113 March 4, 1896, H.P., 33/450.
114 Jed Hotchkiss to John H. Wright, February 29, 1896, H.P., 33/438.
115 *The Virginias* IV, April, August, 1883.
116 Jed Hotchkiss to Hon. Wm. G. Worley, October 31, 1896, H.A.
117 Jed Hotchkiss to C. A. Stebbins, October 15, 1896, H.P., 13/226.
118 Cubby: 226.
119 November 12, 1896, H.P., 13/267.
120 J. C. Miller to Jed Hotchkiss, November 12, 1896, H.P., 13/286.
121 Jed Hotchkiss to J. C. Green, November 9, 1896, H.P., 13/248.
122 Jed Hotchkiss to R. H. Edmonds, November 7, 1896, H.P., 13/252.
123 W. G. Dacey to Jed Hotchkiss, October 1, 1897, H.P., 14/420.
124 Jed Hotchkiss to L. S. Foster, April 25, 1898, H.P., 15/170.
125 Jed Hotchkiss to A. T. Shoemaker, May 25, 1898, H.P., 15/260.
126 Jed Hotchkiss to C. B. Hite, June 28, 1898, H.P., 15/323.
127 Cubby: 231.
128 Jerry Bruce Thomas, "Coal Country: The Rise of the Southern Smokeless Coal Industry and its Effects on Area Development, 1872-1910." Ph.D. Thesis, University of North Carolina, 1971.

Endnotes to Chapter X

1 Cubberly: 463 and 697.
2 Sketch of the life of Jed Hotchkiss, loc. cit.; Journals of Jed Hotchkiss, April 26, 1847 to March 3, 1848, H.P., 1/030-097, 101-202.
3 J. M. Brown was the father of S. Howell Brown, who served with Hotchkiss in the Army of Northern Virginia, see pp. 1, 37, 40, 50.
4 H.P., 1/091, 113, 142.
5 Deed Book 73: 296, Augusta County Courthouse, Staunton, Virginia.
6 H.A., Box 6.
7 Journal, March 5, 1848, H.P., 1/208.
8 Colonel H. V. Canan, "Maps for the Civil War," *Armor* 65 (No. 5, 1956): 36.
9 H.P., 31/336-341.
10 James L. Nichols, "Confederate Map Supply," *Military Engineer* (1954): 29.
11 Jed Hotchkiss to C. W. Oltmanns, November 29, 1893, H.P., 31/186.
12 General T. T. Munford, August 17, 1896, H.P., 13/051.

13 See chapter II.
14 *O.R.*, II: 261.
15 Jed Hotchkiss to General Fitz. Lee, October 22, 1891, H.P., 45/351-8.
16 The use of a metric grid was unusual. The grid was not drawn by Hotchkiss, but was lithographically printed on the paper he used. It seems probable that the paper was from a school exercise book.
17 H.P., 53/190.
18 Jed Hotchkiss to Colonel G. F. R. Henderson, May 24, 1892, H.P., 28/092.
19 Jed Hotchkiss to Colonel G. F. R. Henderson, April 18, 1895, H.P., 11/260.
20 October 7-8, 1862.
21 Hotchkiss map collection, Library of Congress.
22 Everard Kidder Meade, "Maps and other Papers of Major Jed Hotchkiss, C.S.A." *Proceedings of the Clarke County Historical Association*, VIII (1948): 57.
23 Private communication from Mr. R. W. Stephenson, Geography and Map Division, Library of Congress.
24 Jed Hotchkiss to Colonel Thomas M. Anderson, November 22, 1892, H.P., 30/187.
25 H.A., Box 1.
26 *C.W.J.*, January 9-12, 1863.
27 *C.W.J.*, March 12, 1863.
28 *C.W.J.*, April 6, 1863.
29 Clara E. LeGear, *Hotchkiss Map Collection*, first published 1951, reprinted in *Civil War Maps. An Annotated List of Maps and Atlases in the Library of Congress* (Washington: Library of Congress, 1989), H156.

  I doubt whether this is the *original* map. In the border appear the names S. Buckholtz, J. A. Wilson, C. W. Oltmanns, and the initials B.H.H., L.F., C.W.O. C. W. Oltmanns and J. A. Wilson did not join Hotchkiss until long after Gettysburg; March 25, and December 21, 1864, respectively. There was a considerable amount of copying required to meet the needs of many subordinate commanders, and it is at least possible that this particular map is one compiled from a number drawn since Jackson's first request made at Moss Neck.
30 *C.W.J.*, May 6, 1863.
31 Hotchkiss Map Collection, Library of Congress, #155.
32 *C.W.J.*, June 28, 1863.
33 *C.W.J.*, July 10, 1863.
34 *C.W.J.*, August 13, 1863.
35 *C.W.J.*, January 4, 1864.
36 *C.W.J.*, January 16, 1864.
37 Major General J. A. Early to Captain Jed Hotchkiss, January 20, 1864, H.P., 49/168.

38 January 21, 1864, H.P., 49/169.
39 Diary, March 25, 1864.
40 Hotchkiss Map Collection, #8.
41 *C.W.J.*, March 17, March 20, 1865.
42 Albert H. Campbell to Jed Hotchkiss November 25, 1892, H.P., 9/303.
43 *C.W.J.*, Saturday, March 18, 1865.
44 *Report of Operations of Second Corps and of Army of the Valley District, Army of Northern Virginia, C.S.A. During Campaigns of 1864-5* by Jed Hotchkiss, Top. Eng. Including *Supplemental Report on the Operation of the Valley District, A.N.V. from November 14, 1864 to April 12, 1865*, made from my notes taken during the period, but written up September 30, 1892. H.P., 49/002-069; *C.W.J.*, April 16, 1865; Diary, July 5-6, 1865, H.P., 2/483-4.
45 H.P., 30/427. The Atlas contains 57 of his maps plus 60 "Sketches Accompanying Journal of Capt. Jed. Hotchkiss, C. S. Army."
46 Jed Hotchkiss to George B. Davis, Aug. 7, 1893, H.P., 30/705.
47 Jed Hotchkiss to Captain C. D. Cowles, September 14, 1891, H.P., 28/391.
48 June 20, 1884, H.P., 21/392.
49 Richard Sommers, Introduction to *The Official Military Atlas of the Civil War* (New York: Arno Press, 1978)
50 *Atlas*, Plate II, 6.
51 George B. Davis to Jed Hotchkiss, October 13, 1894, National Archives. Q.M. General Record Group 92.
52 *Atlas*, Plate XXIX, 2.
53 Jed Hotchkiss to George B. Davis, October 20 and 22, 1894, National Archives, Q.M. General Record Group 92.
54 Authorized by General Heth, November 24, 1894, *Ibid.*
55 Jed Hotchkiss to George B. Davis, November 30 and December 13, 1894, *Ibid.*
56 Jed Hotchkiss to George B. Davis, January 10, 1895. George B. Davis to Jed Hotchkiss, February 23, 1895. *Ibid.* Nos. 1 and 2 sheets printed by Norris Peters and mounted as one map, with manuscript additions of names of residents and some topography, are filed under #111 in the Hotchkiss Map Collection, Library of Congress.
57 George B. Davis to Jed Hotchkiss, March 25, 1895. National Archives. Q.M. General Record Group 92.
58 Hotchkiss Map Collection #113, Library of Congress. A printed copy of this map also exists, Library of Congress, Geography and Map Division file 245.6.
59 National Archives of the United States, Q.M. General Record Group 92.
60 George B. Davis (By direction of Secretary of War) to H. St. George Tucker, July 2, 1896. *Ibid.*
61 Colonel Robert Beverley to Jed Hotchkiss, June 6, 1881, H.P., 7/038.
62 September 2, 1882, H.P., 19/336. The full title of the map was *Hotchkiss' Centennial Geological, Mining and Railway Map of the Virginias.*

The Geology that of the Virginia State Survey by Prof. Wm. B. Rogers 1835-41 corrected by later observers. Staunton, Va. 1881. Several versions of this map are to be found in the Geography and Map Division of the Library of Congress and one adorns a wall in the Geology Department of the Virginia Polytechnic Institute at Blacksburg. For an account of Hotchkiss' role in publishing geological maps based on the work of Professor Rogers see Peter W. Roper, "Jed Hotchkiss and the Geological Map of Virginia," *Earth Sciences History,* v 10 no. 1, 1991.

63 *The Virginias,* 1885: 4.

The woods used were (1) White Oak, (2) Black Walnut, (3) White Walnut, (4) Poplar, (5) Ash, (6) White Pine, (7) Persimmon and Lime, (8) Yellow Pine, (9) Maple and Cherry, (10) Cedar. Staunton craftsmen, H. J. Lusbaugh and Frank Prufer, respectively, made the frames and mounted the maps.

What eventually happened to the ten maps is unknown. After the exposition the maps were in the custody of Virginia's Commissioner for Agriculture, Colonel Randolph Harrison, but in 1887 Hotchkiss arranged for them to be loaned to Randolph-Macon College at Ashland, Virginia, where they remained until the summer of 1893, when he asked for them to be sent to him for revision before being exhibited at the World's Fair in Chicago. Due to an administrative error they never reached Hotchkiss, but were delivered back to the Commissioner of Agriculture. A year later Hotchkiss suggested that the maps should go to the Richmond Chamber of Commerce. There is no evidence that they ever did so, nor of their fate after this time. Jed Hotchkiss to Colonel Randolph Harrison, August 27, 1887, H.P., 24/018; Jed Hotchkiss to Captain T. C. Morton, July 10, 1893, H.P., 30/696; Jed Hotchkiss to Dr. W. W. Smith, President, Randolph-Macon College, Ashland, July 10 and August 7, 1893, H.P., 30/393 and 30/709; Jed Hotchkiss to Captain Richard Irby, Secretary, Randolph-Macon College, August 12, 1893, H.P., 31/010; Jed Hotchkiss to Secretary McCleod, Governor's Office, September 4, 1893, H.P., 31/021; Jed Hotchkiss to R. A. Dunlap, Secretary, Chamber of Commerce, Richmond, January 15 and 18, 1894, H.P., 31/418 and 432.

64 Mrs. W. B. Rogers to Jed Hotchkiss, March 10, 1883, H.P., 7/305.

65 Mrs. W. B. Rogers to Jed Hotchkiss, quoting Professor Marsh. March 16, 1883, H.P., 7/308. Wiliam Henry Holmes, 1846-1933, artist, anthropologist and archaeologist, was an outstanding illustrator of scientific subjects. From 1880-84 he was on the staff of the U.S. Geological Survey.

66 Jed Hotchkiss to Mrs. W. B. Rogers, May 29, 1883, H.P., 21/135.

67 May 31, 1883, H.P., 7/397.

68 Mrs. W. B. Rogers to Jed Hotchkiss, August 2 and 19, 1882, H.P., 7/134 and 139.

69 W. B. Rogers to C. T. Smith, March 6, 1875, H.P., 6/389.

70 W. B. Rogers to Jed Hotchkiss, April 3, 1875, H.P., 6/404.

71 March 15, 1882, H.P., 7/106.

72 *The Virginias* 1882: 65, 149; *S.S.*, May 9, 1882.

73 October 11, 1882, H.P., 40/667-8.

74 Jed Hotchkiss to Mrs. W. B. Rogers, August 7, 1885, H.P., 21/765; Mrs. W. B. Rogers to Jed Hotchkiss, January 11, 1887, H.P., 8/145-7.

75 August 7, 1875, H.P., 18/658.
76 Jed Hotchkiss to N. R. Waterman May 5, 1883, H.P., 21/123.
77 July 7, 1884, H.P., 21/422.
78 August 13, 1884, H.P., 21/496. Hotchkiss used the words "engravers" and "engraving" very loosely as synonyms of "printers" and "printing." Julius Bien was a lithographer, not an engraver.
79 September 8, 1884, H.P., 21/518.
80 January 2, 1885, H.P., 21/618.
81 January 5, 1885, H.P., 21/624.
82 February 13, 1885, H.P., 21/644-5.
83 Jed Hotchkiss to Watkins, February 24, 1885, H.P., 21/660.
84 Hotchkiss, who, once again, had not been consulted, was unhappy with this choice of feature, not because he disputed the survey data, but because, unlike Elliott Knob, it was "inconspicious from any point of the great lines of travel." Furthermore it was in the Blue Ridge formed from "the old, or Archaen rocks to which Professor Rogers devoted but a small portion of his time during his great survey of Virginia. His reputation as the 'Father of American Geology' was established by his observations and reports on the Paleozoic rocks west of the Blue Ridge." Jed Hotchkiss to the editor of the *Richmond Dispatch*, June 28, 1894, H.P., 31/316-7.
85 Jed Hotchkiss to N. R. Waterman, February 25, 1885, H.P., 21/661.
86 August 16, 1882, H.P., 7/139.
87 Henry Gannett to Jed Hotchkiss, January 29, 1883, H.P., 7/256; Jed Hotchkiss to W. G. Kerr, February 2, 1883, H.P., 21/056; Henry Gannett to Jed Hotchkiss, January 14, 1884, H.P., 7/493.
88 May 26, 1883, H.A., Box 1.
89 H.P., 21/146-7.
90 March 12, 1885, H.P., 21/675.
91 March 8, 1890, H.P., 27/095.
92 The receipted bill is annotated on the back "for the Gauley map." H.P., 26/495.
93 June 9, 1892, H.P., 25/123.
94 January 14, 1893, H.P., 30/320.
95 December 12, 1893, H.P., 31/204.
96 December 15, 1893, H.P., 31/218.
97 Jed Hotchkiss to R. U. Goode, January 17, 1894, H.P., 31/427.
98 Memorandum, Relative to Co-operative Topographic Surveys, H.P., 43/110-115; C. D. Walcott to Jed Hotchkiss February 9, 1898, H.P., 43/119-124.
99 February 8, 1898, H.P., 43/095.
100 December 13, 1897, H.P., 14/558.
101 e.g. Jed Hotchkiss to Rev. Thos. Heywood, Dec. 3, 1877, H.P., 60/662.
102 General T. T. Munford to Benjamin Blackford, November 30, 1898, H.P., 16/115.

Endnotes to Chapter XI

1 *O.R.*, Series I, vol. 2, 256.
2 Diary, September 1, 1851, H.P., 1/348.
3 *C.W.J.*, January 23, 1864.
4 Samson Biddulph Robinson was christened in February 1825 in the parish church of Bunny, Nottinghamshire, England. He was the son of the village schoolmaster and succeeded to this position when his father died in 1848. The school taught, inter alia, "a superior kind of Penmanship, Mapping and Planning," and for those particularly requiring it, "Practical Land Surveying." Some time between 1849 and 1853 he emigrated to Central America, but was in Louisiana in 1861 when he joined the 7th Louisiana Infantry. Robinson died in Baton Rouge, La., August 14, 1870.
5 S. B. Robinson to Jed Hotchkiss, Jan. 1867, H.A., Box 1.
6 October 17, 1874, H.P., 18/030.
7 July 16, 1897, H.P., 14/192.
8 February 24, 1893, H.P., 30/403.
9 *Staunton Vindicator*, June 5, 1874.
10 *S.S.*, February 7, 1871.
11 Diary, May 26-29, 1871, H.P., 2/570-1.
12 *S.S.*, June 13, 1871.
13 *S.S.*, January 28, 1873.
14 Exemption Certificate, February 18, 1862, H.A., Box 1.
15 Historical Atlas of Augusta County, Waterman, Watkins & Co., Chicago, 1885.
16 H.P., 2/574.
17 Jed Hotchkiss to D. W. Russell, June 10, 1887, H.P., 23/201.
18 At the time of Nelson's death in 1891, Olive Jordan was living at Shendun. Edward L. Hotchkiss (1856-1893), Nelson's second son, conveyed 322 East Beverley Street to his sister May 12, 1891, Deed Book 5: 559, Augusta County Courthouse, Staunton, Virginia.
19 *S.S.*, November 18, 1879.
20 Wedding Invitation, H.A., Box 1.
21 Jed Hotchkiss to Allan M. Howison, July 14, 1892, H.A.
22 Newspaper clipping, H.A., Box 4.
23 Jed Hotchkiss to H. M. Murray, May 26, 1887, H.P., 23/169.
24 *Ibid.*
25 May 31, 1887, H.P., 23/175.
26 Jed Hotchkiss to Allen McCullough, March 30, 1894, H.P., 31/548.
27 Jed Hotchkiss to My dear little Grand daughter, July 17, 1896, H.A., Box 3.
28 August 26, 1896, H.A., Box 8.

29 Jed Hotchkiss to S. B. Robinson, April 8, 1867, " 'Is there any letter from Mr. Robinson?' Correspondence between Jedediah Hotchkiss and Sampson B. Robinson," A. P. McDonald, *West Virginia History*, (1972): 408.

30 March 25, 1892, H.P., 27/646.

31 Diary, July 14, 1872, H.P., 2/677.

32 Jed Hotchkiss to J. C. Green, October 29, 1891, H.P., 28/499.

33 Jed Hotchkiss to The Church Kidney Cure Co., May 2, August 1, 1896, H.A., Box 8.

34 Jed Hotchkiss to Hunter McGuire, June 14, 1897, H.A., Box 8; Jed Hotchkiss to J. C. Maben, September 5, 1898, H.P., 15/560; Jed Hotchkiss to Hunter McGuire, October 5, 1898, H.P., 15/667; Jed Hotchkiss to A. T. Shoemaker, November 22, 1898, H.P., 12/006; Jed Hotchkiss to Miss Anderson, n.d. H.A., Box 3; Jed Hotchkiss to Hunter McGuire, November 14, 1898, H.P., 49/271.

35 Obituary, *The Echo*, (Windsor Academy magazine) 1899.

Endnotes to Chapter XII

1 *Staunton Vindicator*, May 29, 1891.

2 December 13, 1859, H.A., Box 1.

3 *C.M.H.*, III.

4 Jed Hotchkiss to Jacob Wissler, Liberty Furnace, November 30, 1880, H.P., 17/810.

5 January 1, 1892, H.P., 28/675.

6 May 15, 1894, H.P., 31/602.

7 Jed Hotchkiss to E. W. Clark, November 3, 1885, H.P., 21/785; Jed Hotchkiss to Prof. S. F. Baird, November 28, 1885, H.P., 21/799.

8 Jed Hotchkiss to Editor *Manufacturers' Record*, Baltimore, January 24, 1898, published January 28, H.P., 47/082.

9 February 7, 1896, H.P., 33/108.

10 Walter Arnstein, Michael Bright, Linda Peterson, Nicholas Temperley, Recent Studies in Victorian Religion, *Victorian Studies*, 33 (1989): 149.

11 September 14, 1891, H.P., 28/395.

12 Minutes of the Lexington Presbytery, September 5, 1891 to October 21, 1899; *The Diamond Jubilee History, Davis and Elkins College*, Thomas Richard Rom. 1980.

13 Letter of thanks from Henry A. Converse to Mrs. Hotchkiss, October 24, 1907, H.A., Box 3.

14 Jed Hotchkiss to Rev. S. D. Boggs, December 23, 1892, H.P., 30/254.

15 Jed Hotchkiss to S. W. Hobman, November 22, 1882, H.P., 20/595.

16 Jed Hotchkiss to Col. G. W. Bennett, April 21, 1892, H.P., 28/018.

17 Jed Hotchkiss to J. C. Miller, September 14, 1893, H.P., 29/316.

18 *Recollections*, (C&O RR, 1938): 60.

19 September 8, 1896, H.P., 13/119.

20 April 20, 1883, H.P., 20/624.
21 Receipt for $1,354.17, signed T. D. Ranson, June 23, 1887, H.P., 58/104.
22 Allen W. Moger, *Virginia: Bourbonism to Byrd, 1870-1925* (Charlottesville: University Press of Virginia, 1968), 160, quoting *Richmond Dispatch*, February 18, 1891.
23 Jed Hotchkiss to W. P. Tamms, October 2, 1893, H.P., 31/076.
24 Jed Hotchkiss to A. M. Howison, October 10, 1893, H.P., 31/085.
25 Jed Hotchkiss to R. W. Burke, October 10, 1893, H.P., 31/087.
26 Jed Hotchkiss to the editor of the *Northwestern Lumberman*, January 2 and 9, 1896, W. B. Judson to Jed Hotchkiss, January 4 and 9, 1896, H.P., 33/072.
27 Jed Hotchkiss to Hon. J. N. Stubbs, February 20, 1896, H.P., 33/120; Jed Hotchkiss to J. C. Green, February 29, 1896, H.P., 33/124; Jed Hotchkiss to General James A. Walker, MC, February 29, 1896, H.P., 33/125.
28 Jed Hotchkiss to Professor Henry A. Ward, December 6, 1895, H.P., 33/052.
29 May 24, 1893, H.P., 30/588.
30 Jed Hotchkiss to M. A. Miller, January 2, 1894, H.P., 31/403.
31 Among a list of Summons' H.P., 57/680 et seq.
32 H.A., Box 3.

Endnotes to Epilogue

1 For example, in 1991, the Virginia State Library and Archives acquired from such a source, "Map of the lands of the Longdale Iron Company, situated in Allegheny, Bath, Botetourt and Rockbridge counties, Virginia, showing the lines of the original patents and of the inclusive survey, embracing 22,013 acres from surveys by Jed. Hotchkiss, Top'l Engineer Staunton, Va., assisted by John A. McGuffin. June 1870. Scale 1/20,000."
2 Up to 1907, the property valuation records in Staunton show two buildings on The Oaks lot, numbers 344 and 346, in 1908 only one, viz. 344. This property number was changed to the current number, 437, in 1911.
3 Private Communication, R. W. Stephenson, Geography and Map Division, Library of Congress.
4 Library of Congress correspondence files.
5 C. Vernon Eddy to Major E. D. Hotchkiss, October 29, 1928, Library of Congress correspondence files.
6 Private Communication from Dr. Fletcher Collins, Jr., the present owner of The Oaks.
7 Meade, loc. cit.
8 For a full account of the discovery of the Hotchkiss maps, see Peter W. Roper, *The Winchester-Frederick County Historical Society Journal*, IV (1990): 1-27.
9 Mrs. R. E. Christian to C. Vernon Eddy, January 29, 1940. This is one of 141 letters written between March 30, 1938, and April 27, 1964, by

the principal persons involved in the disposal of the maps. They were found by the present writer at the former residence of Mrs. R. E. Christian at Deerfield, Virginia, and are now located in H.C. Correspondence cited hereafter, unless stated to the contrary, is from this collection.

10 Mrs. G. S. Holmes (Aunt Nellie) to Mrs. R. E. Christian, May 25, 1938.
11 D. S. Freeman to Mrs. G. S. Holmes, July 11, 1938.
12 D. S. Freeman to Mrs. G. S. Holmes, July 19, 1938.
13 C. Vernon Eddy to Mrs. R. E. Christian, July 26, 1938.
14 C. Vernon Eddy to Mrs. R. E. Christian, July 17, 1947. "It is my opinion that your grandfather's memory would be more enhanced by having the maps in the Library of Congress than stored in a tomb-like structure as the Battle Abbey in Richmond."
15 C. Vernon Eddy to Mrs. R. E. Christian, August 4, 1938.
16 Francis L. Berkeley, Jr. to Mrs. R. E. Christian, November 17, 1947.
17 C. Vernon Eddy to Mrs. R. E. Christian, February 18, 1948.
18 J. Cooke Wylie to C. Vernon Eddy, February 13, 1948.
19 Mrs. R. E. Christian to Alton H. Keller, Chief, Order Department, Library of Congress, June 14, 1948.
20 Mrs. R. E. Christian to C. Vernon Eddy, June 14, 1948.

Bibliography

Ambler, Charles H. and Summers, Festus P., 1958, *West Virginia, the Mountain State.* Englewood Cliffs, NJ.

Bean, W. G., 1968. "Stonewall Jackson's Jolly Chaplain, Beverley Tucker Lacy." *West Virginia History.*

Bean, W. G., 1970. "Captain James Keith Boswell." *Virginia Cavalcade.*

Bean, W. G., 1970. "The Valley Campaign as revealed in the letters of Sandie Pendleton." *Va. Mag. Hist. & Biog.*

Blake, Nelson M., 1935. *William Mahone of Virginia, Soldier and Political Insurgent.* Richmond.

Booker, A. Brooks, 1949. "History of the Academies of Augusta County, Virginia." M.A. thesis, University of Virginia.

Brock, William R., 1973. *Conflict and Transformation.* New York.

Bruce, Kathleen, 1930. *Virginia Iron Manufacture in the Slave Era.* (Republished 1968 in Reprints of Economic Classics. New York.)

Canan, H. V., 1956. "Maps for the Civil War." *Armor.*

Capon, Lester J., 1976. *Atlas of Early American History. The Revolutionary Era, 1760-1790.* New York.

Capron, John D., 1967. "Virginia Iron Furnaces of the Confederacy." *Virginia Cavalcade.*

Cash, W. J., 1941. *The Mind of the Old South.* New York.

Catton, Bruce, 1961. *The Coming Fury*, New York.

Catton, Bruce, 1963. *Terrible Swift Sword.* New York.

Catton, Bruce, 1965. *Never Call Retreat.* New York.

Chambers, Lenoir, 1959. *Stonewall Jackson.* New York.

Collins, Bruce, 1985. *White Society in the Antebellum South.* New York.

Corgan, James X., 1982. *The Geological Sciences in the Antebellum South.*

Couper, William, 1936. *Claudius Crozet: Soldier, Scholar, Educator, Engineer (1789-1864.)* Charlottesville.

Couper, William, 1952. *History of the Shenandoah Valley.*

Craven, Avery O., 1953. *The Growth of Southern Nationalism.* (*A History of the South*, Vol. VI. Ed. Wendel H. Stephenson and E. Merton Coulter.) Baton Rouge.

Craven, Avery O., 1969. *Reconstruction: the ending of the Civil War.*

Crenshaw, Oliver W., 1969. *General Lee's College: The Rise and Growth of Washington Lee University.* New York.

Cubberly, Elwood P., 1934. *Public Education in the United States.* Boston.

Cubberly, Elwood P., 1948. *The History of Education.* Boston.

Cubby, Edwin A., 1962. "The Transformation of the Tug and Guyandot Valleys: Economic and Social Change in West Virginia. 1888-1921." Ph.D. thesis, Syracuse University.

Cubby, Edwin A., 1965. "Timbering Operations in the Tug and Guyandot Valleys in the 1890s." *West Virginia History.*

Curry, J. L. M., 1898. *Sketch of George Peabody and a History of the Peabody Education Fund.*

Davis, George B., Perry, Leslie J., Kirkley, Joseph W., 1891-1895. *Atlas to Accompany the Official Records of the Union and Confederate Armies*, compiled by Calvin D. Cowles. Washington. Reprint 1978 with introduction by Richard Sommers. New York.

Dennett, John R., 1965. *The South as it is: 1865-1866.* New York.

Eaton, Clement, 1961. *The Growth of Southern Civilisation, 1790-1860.* New York.

Edwards, Newton and Richey, Herman G., 1947. *The School in American Social Order.* New York.

Eller, Ronald D., 1982. *Miners, Millhands and Mountaineers: Industrialisation of the Appalachian South 1880-1930.* Knoxville.

Faulkner, H. U., 1952. *American Political and Social History.* New York.

Fishwick, Marshall W., 1959. *Virginia: A New Look at the Old Dominion.* New York.

Flugel, F., and Faulkner, H. U., 1929. *Readings in Economic and Social History.* New York.

Foster, Gaines M., 1987. *Ghosts of the Confederacy: Defeat, the Lost Cause, and the Emergence of the New South.* New York.

Franklin, John H., 1961. *Reconstruction after the Civil War.* Chicago.

Frazier, Harry, 1938. *Recollections.* Huntington.

Freeman, Douglas S., 1942. *Lee's Lieutenants: a Study of Command.* New York.

Frye, Dennis E., 1991. "Riding with Stonewall." *Civil War* Vol. IX No. 5.

Gillenwater, Mack H., 1972. "Cultural and Historical Geography of Mining Settlements in the Pocahontas Coalfields of South West Virginia 1880-1930." Ph.D. thesis, University of Tennessee.

Good, Harry G. and Teller, James D., 1973. *A History of American Education.* New York.

Hale, John P., 1886. *Trans Allegheny Pioneers.* 3rd edition 1971 edited by Harold J. Dudley. Raleigh, NC.

Heatwole, Cornelius J., 1916. *A History of Education in Virginia.* New York.

Henderson, George F. R., 1898. *Stonewall Jackson and the American Civil War.* London. (Centennial Edition, 1961, New York.)

Hinman, Marjory B. and Osborne, Bernard, 1976. *Historical Essays of Windsor.* Windsor, New York.

Hitchcock, William S., 1981. "The Limits of Southern Unionism: Virginia Conservatives and the Gubernatorial Election of 1859." *Journal of Southern History.*

Hotchkiss, Jed and Allan, William, 1867. *Chancellorsville.* New York.

Hotchkiss, Jed, 1899. *Confederate Military History, III, Virginia.* Atlanta.

Hughes, Jonathan, ...*American Economic History.* 2d Edition, 1987. Glenview, IL.

Hughes, Sara S., 1979. *Surveyors and Statesmen: Land Measuring in Colonial Virginia.* Richmond.

Jones, Jack M., 1983. *Early Coal Mining in Pocahontas, Virginia,* Lynchburg, VA.

Jones, Robert R., 1964. "Conservative Virginian: The Post War Career of Governor James Lawson Kemper." Ph.D. thesis. University of Virginia.

Klein, Maury, 1968. "Southern Railroad Leaders, 1865-1893: Identities and Ideologies." *Business History Review.*

Knight, Edgar W., 1941. *Education in the United States.* Boston.

Lambie, Joseph T., 1954. *From Mine to Market. The History of Coal Transportation on the Norfolk and Western Railway.* New York.

Lawson, Sidney B., 1941. *Autobiography and Reminiscences of Sidney B. Lawson MD: Fifty Years a Mountain Country Doctor.* Logan, W.VA.

Maddex, Jack P., Jr., 1970. *The Virginia Conservatives, 1865-1879.* Chapel Hill.

MacMaster, Richard K., 1987. *Augusta County History.* Staunton, VA.

McDonald, Archie P., 1967. "The Illusive Commission of 'Major' Jedediah Hotchkiss." *Va. Mag. Hist. & Biog.*

McDonald, Archie P., 1972. " 'Is there any letter from Mr. Robinson?' Correspondence between Jedediah Hotchkiss and Samson B. Robinson." *West Virginia History.*

McDonald, Archie P., 1973. *Make Me a Map of the Valley: The Civil War Journal of Stonewall Jackson's Topographer.* Dallas.

McPherson, James M., 1982. *Ordeal by Fire. The Civil War and Reconstruction.* New York. Alfred A. Knopf.

McPherson, James M., 1988. *Battle Cry of Freedom. The Civil War Era.* New York. Oxford University Press.

Meade, Everard K., 1948. "Maps and other Papers of Major Jedediah Hotchkiss, C.S.A." *Proceedings of the Clarke County Historical Association.*

Merrill, George P., 1924. *The First Hundred Years of American Geology.* New Haven.

Moger, Allen W., 1951. "Railroad Practices and Policies in Virginia after the Civil War." *Va. Mag. Hist. & Biog.*

Moger, Allen W., 1958. "Industrial and Urban Progress in Virginia from 1880-1900." *Va. Mag. Hist. & Biog.*

Moger, Allan W., 1968. *Virginia: Bourbonism to Byrd, 1870-1925.* Charlottesville.

Munroe, James P., 1904. *William Barton Rogers, Founder of M.I.T.* Charlottesville.

Nelson, James P., 1927. *The History of the Chesapeake and Ohio Railway Company: Its Antecedants and Subsidiaries.* Richmond.

Nevins, Allan, 1947. *Ordeal of the Union.* New York.

Nevins, Allan, 1950. *The Emergence of Lincoln.* New York.

Newby, I.A., 1978. *The South, a History.* New York.

Nichols, James L., 1954. "Confederate Engineers." *Military Engineer.*

Nichols, James L., 1957. "Confederate Engineers." *Confederate Centennial Studies, No. 5, 1957.* Tuscaloosa, Ala.

Nye, R. B., 1974. *Society and Culture in America 1830-1860.* New York.

Owsley, Frank L., 1949. *Plain Folk in the Old South.* Baton Rouge.

Parish, Peter J., 1975. *The American Civil War.* New York.

Pearson, Charles C., 1921. "William Henry Ruffner: Reconstruction Statesman of Virginia." *South Atlantic Quarterly.*

Pepper, Charles M., 1920. *The Life and Times of Henry Gassaway Davis.* New York.

Peyton, John L., 1882. *History of Augusta County.* Staunton, VA.

Philips, P. Lee, 1896. *Virginia Cartography.* Washington, D.C.

Potter, David M., 1976. *The Impending Crisis 1848-1861.* New York.

Pryor, Elizabeth Brown, 1981. "An Anomalous Person: Northern Tutor in Plantation Society." *Journal of Southern History.*

Reid, Whitelaw, 1866. *After the War: A Southern Tour.* Reprinted as Harper Torchbook edition, 1965. New York.

Rice, Otis K., 1965. "Coal Mining in the Kanawha Valley to 1861: A View of Industrialization in the Old South." *Journal of Southern History.*

Rogers, Emma S., ed., 1884. *A reprint of annual reports and other papers on the geology of Virginias by the late William Barton Rogers, LL.D., etc.* New York.

Rothe, Berth M., Ed., 1956. *Daniel Webster Reader.*

Sanchez-Saavedra, E. M., 1975. *A Description of the Country: Virginia's Cartographers and their Maps.* Richmond.

Schlebecker, John T., 1971. "Farmers in the Lower Shenandoah Valley, 1850." *Va. Mag. Hist. & Biog.*

Sewell, Richard H., 1988. *A House Divided: Sectionalism and Civil War, 1848-1865.* Baltimore.

Simkins, Francis B. and Roland, Charles P., 1972. *A History of the South.* New York.

Sizer, Theodore R., 1964. *The Age of the Academies.* New York.

Smith, Douglas, 1960. "Virginia during Reconstruction, 1865-1870: A Political, Economic and Social Study." Ph.D. thesis. University of Virginia.

Stephenson, Richard W., 1989. *Civil War Maps: An Annotated List of Maps and Atlases in the Library of Congress.* Washington.

Storer, John F., 1955. *The Railroads of the South 1865-1900: A Study in Finance and Control.* Chapel Hill.

Summers, Festus P., 1937. *Johnson Newlon Camden: A Study in Individualism.* New York.

Swank, J. M., *Annual Report of the American Iron and Steel Association.*

Swemm, Earl G., 1914. *Maps Relating to Virginia in the Virginia State Library and other Departments of the Commonwealth.* Richmond.

Tanner, Robert G. 1976. *Stonewall in the Valley: Thomas J. (Stonewall) Jackson's Shenandoah Valley Campaign Spring 1862.* New York.

Terrell, John U., 1969. *The Man who Rediscovered America. A Biography of John Wesley Powell.* New York.

Thomas, Jerry B., 1971. "Coal Country: The Rise of the Southern Smokeless Coal Industry and its Effect on Area Development." Ph.D. thesis, University of North Carolina.

Thomas, Jerry B., 1976. "Jedediah Hotchkiss, Guilded Age Propagandist of Industrialism." *Va. Mag. Hist. & Biog.*

Thomas, Peter C., 1982. "Mathew Fontaine Maury and the problem of Virginia's Identity, 1865-1873." *Va. Mag. Hist. & Biog.*

Turner, Charles W., 1946. "Virginia Central Railroad at War, 1861-1865." *Journal of Southern History.*

Turner, Charles W., Ed., 1955. "A Virginia Small Farmer's Life after the Civil War: The Journal of William J. Hart 1871-1873." *Va. Mag. Hist. & Biog.*

Wayland, Francis F. Ed., 1962. "Freemont's Pursuit of Jackson in the Shenandoah Valley: The Journal of Albert Tracy, March-July, 1862." *Va. Mag. Hist. & Biog.*

Wayland, John W., 1937. *Historic Homes of Northern Virginia.* Staunton, VA.

Wert, Jeffry D., 1987. *From Winchester to Cedar Creek: The Shenandoah Campaign of 1864.* New York.

Williams, Frances L., 1963. *Mathew Fontaine Maury-Scientist of the Sea.* New Brunswick.

Woodward, C. Van, 1951. *Origins of the New South. (Vol. IX, A History of the South.* Ed. Wendell H. Stephenson and E. Merton Coulter.) Baton Rouge.

Index

Alderman Library, acquires Hotchkiss maps and papers, 250
Allan, W.: 78, 95, 224
  foundation of postwar co-operation, 51
  sets up real estate business, 84, 87
  co-author with Hotchkiss of *Chancellorsville*, 92, 94, 151
  cashier, First National Bank, Staunton, 93
  professor of Applied Mathematics, Washington College, 99
American Association for the Advancement of Science, Albany meeting, 11
American Historical Association, 153
American Institute of Mining Engineers, 145
Anderson, Brig. Gen. Richard H., at Battle of Chancellorsville, 54
Anderson, Major Robert, at Fort Sumter, 26
Anschutz, Frank H.:
  engaged by Hotchkiss, 162
  joins Rapelje in the Gauley survey, 163
  re-engaged, 241
Ansted, Professor David T.:
  supports Hotchkiss' view of Virginia's mineral wealth, 110
  visits Hotchkiss, 114
  address to the Society of Arts, 114-15
  sues Hotchkiss, 127-28
  biographical note, 262 n. 5
Antietam Battlefield Commission, 204-8
  map for, illustrations, 205, 206
Atlas to Accompany the OR's, 203-4
Augusta Female Seminary:
  Hotchkiss and Robinson on the faculty of, 87
  Nellie Hotchkiss completes education at, 121
Augusta County, Virginia:
  militia, 34
  map of for General Grant, illustration, 89
  fair, 96, 100, 105, 120
  map of for Board of Survey, 102, illustration, 101
  Historical Atlas of, 211-15, maps from illustrated, 213, 214
Augusta Lee Rifles, 31
Averell, Maj. Gen. William W., 71

Baldwin, John B., 53, 87, 95, 96
Baldwin, Mary J., 84, 87
Bancroft, George, praises Hotchkiss lecture, 153
Banks, Maj. Gen. Nathaniel P.:
  attacks Jackson at Stony Creek, 36
  link up with Fremont prevented, 1, 40
  defeat by Jackson, 41-43
Baylor, William S., 34
Beattie, James T., engaged by Guyandot CLA, 176
Beauregard, Pierre Gustave T., shells Fort Sumter, 26
Bell, Henderson M.:
  promoter of the Gauley CLA, 160
  director of The Staunton Development Company, 164
  promoter of The Grottoes Company, 287
  incorporator of C.S.&W. Railroad, 292
Bell, John, constitutional Union Party presidential candidate, 28
Berkeley, Francis L. Jr., and the Hotchkiss collection of maps and papers, 250
Beverley, W.Va., Confederates retreat through, 29
Big Sandy River, W.Va., possible route for N&W's Ohio extension, 171
Bird, Mark, co-founder of Mossy Creek Iron Works, 9
Blackburn, John W., 168
Blackford, Col. William W., map of Battle of Fredericksburg, 197
Bland Land Company, 179, 180, 181
Boswell, Capt. Keith: 224
  accompanies Hotchkiss on reconnaissance, 41
  killed at Chancellorsville, 57
  recommends Hotchkiss for commission, 83
Bowron, James, 110
Boyd, David, 93, 95
Boylan, Frank, 97
Brady, Sir Antonio:
  chairs meeting at Society of Arts, 111
  visits to Virginia, 111, 120
  partner in purchase of real estate, 111, 124
  personal support of Hotchkiss, 226
  biographical note, 262 n. 9

INDEX 291

Bramwell, J. H.: 226
  promoter of Gauley CLA, 160
  promoter of The Grottoes Company, 164
Brodt, J. T., Associate Principal, Mossy Creek Academy, 13
Brown, James M., surveyor of Jefferson County, 189
Brown, John, 25, 27
Brown, S. Howell: 54, 57
  and the blocking of Dry Run Gap, 1, 40
  assists Hotchkiss in destruction of Shenandoah bridges, 37
  at Fredericksburg, 50
  letter to Hotchkiss re map of the Valley, 92
  map of Jefferson County (W.Va.), 197
Brown's Gap, Blue Ridge:
  arduous march to, 39
  army camps there after Port Republic battle, 46
  proposed railroad through, 167
Bruce, James, 168
Bryan, William Jennings, 185
Bundy, Charles S., 97
Burnside, Maj. Gen. Ambrose E.:
  attacks Fredericksburg, 50
  "Mud March," 53

Cabin Creek, W.Va.: 110, 111, 128
  negotiations with Charles Easton, 111
  survey, 116, 118, 119
  map of (Illustration), 117
Caldwell, James L., 185
Camden, Johnson N.:
  and the Gauley Coal Land Association, 161
  and the W.V.&P. Railroad, 161, 167
Cameron, Simon, Secretary of War, calls out militia, 26
Campbell, Capt. Albert H.:
  appointment, 192
  Hotchkiss critical of, 193
  on origin of Hotchkiss' collection of maps, 202
Campbell, Prof. John L., 136
Camp Garnett:
  Hotchkiss drives wagon to, 28
  Federal attack on, 29
  Survey by Hotchkiss, 29, 193, 204
Carmen, Gen. Ezra A., 204, 207
Catlett, Richard H.:
  as promoter of Gauley CLA, 160
  as promoter of The Grottoes Company, 164

as incorporator of the C.S.&W. Railroad, 167
Chancellorsville, Va.:
  battle of, 54-57
  survey of battlefield by Hotchkiss, 59, 199
Chase, William L., 155
Churchville, Va.:
  Hotchkiss moves to in 1859, 20
  Hotchkiss opens school in Temperance Hall, 86
  map of, 213
  See also *Loch Willow*
Churchville Cavalry:
  at blockade of Dry River Gap, 1, 40
  mobilized, 27
  at Camp Garnett, 29
  retreat to Monterey, 31
Christian, Ellen Howison:
  heirlooms, vi; birth, 228; disposes of Hotchkiss maps and papers, 246-51
Civil War:
  origins, 22-26
  start of, 26
  Virginia secedes, 27
  battles and campaigns, Kernstown, 35, 36; Valley Campaign (1862), 35-45; McDowell, 1, 39-40; Winchester (1862), 41, map of, 42; Cross Keys, 44; Port Republic, 46, map of, 45; Seven Days, 47; Antietam, 48; Cedar Run, 48, 64; Manassas (second), 48; Fredericksburg, 50, map of, 198; Chancellorsville, 54-57; Gettysburg, 60; Wilderness, 67; Cold Harbor, 68; Valley campaign (1864), 69-78; Winchester (1864), 72; Fisher's Hill, 73-74; Cedar Creek, 75-78
  effect on Staunton and the Shenandoah Valley, 93
Clark, Edward C.: 226
  secures option on Low and Aspinwall lands, 171
  and the Guyandot CLA, 173
Clark, E.W. & Co.:
  finances N&W RR, 140
  and the Ohio extension of the N&W RR, 170-71
  and the Guyandot CLA, 174
Coal Land Associations:
  Flat Top, 144, 177
  Gauley, 160-63, 168-70
    formation of, 160
    need for railroads, 160
    Hotchkiss manager of surveys, 160, 162
    surveys for, 162-63

"Fay Association," 160
"Robinson Association," 160
Guyandot,
   map of (illustration), 172
   mapping and surveys for, 173
   formation of, 174
   adverse effect of route of N&W RR, 174-75
   Hotchkiss optimism, 176
   collapse of, 177
   restructuring, 177
   and the Virginias Railway, 179
Coal mines and mining:
   Hotchkiss' early introduction to, 6, 9, 89
   in West Virginia, 138-44
Constitutional Union Party, supported by the Hotchkiss brothers, 25
Coe, W. W., 143
Confederate Military History, 154, 158
Confederate veterans, 157
Cooke, John Eston, 64
Council of Foreign Bondholders, reaction to Virginia's debt problem, 110, 115, 126
Cowan, John T.:
   and the Cabin Creek Lands, 119, 120, 121
Cowells, Calvin Durall, and the *Atlas to Accompany the O.R.'s*, 204
Crawford, James, 94
Crawford, Col. John H., 34
Crawford, Thomas, 22

Dacey, Brig. General William G.:
   and the Virginias Railway Company, 178, 180, 182, 184, 185
   supports Republican Party, 185
   death, 186
Daniel, John W., champion of "Free Silver," 185
Davis and Elkins College, W.Va., 240
Davis, Major George B.:
   and the publication of War Records, 155
   and *The Atlas to Accompany the O.R.'s*, 204
   as president of Antietam Battlefield Commission, 204
Davis, Henry G., 167, 237, 240
Davis, Jefferson, 26
Dixon, Thomas, 3
Doolittle, John, early settler on Susquehanna, 3

Dry River Gap:
   blockade of, 1, 40, 235
   map showing, 32
Dunlow, W.Va.:
   date founded and origin of name, 175
   failure of mines at, 177

Early, Maj. Gen. Jubal A.: 34
   at Gettysburg, 62-63, 64
   at Winchester, 69, 72
   Valley Campaign (1864), 69-78
   threatens Washington, 71
   at Fisher's Hill, 73
   and battle of Cedar Creek, 75-78
   address to the Army of the Valley, 77-78
   routed at Waynesboro, 80
   orders Hotchkiss to reconnoiter in Allegheny Mountains, 200
Easton, Charles, abandons purchase of Cabin Creek, 112, 113, 242
Easton, William:
   as owner of "Selma," 109
   death of daughter, 113
   financial affairs, 112-13
   influence on Charles Easton, 112
   sale of "Selma," 113, 126, 129-30
   writes offensive letters to Hotchkiss, 113
Echols, Bell & Catlett, 94, 99
Echols, John, 95, 96, 126
Eddy, Charles, 173
Eddy, C. Vernon, and the Hotchkiss collection of maps, 197, 247-51
Education of southern children by tutors, 8
Elkins, Stephen B., 240
Elizabethville, Pa., 6, 7, 8
Elizabeth Furnace, 97, 99, 111, 116
Ellyson, J. Taylor, 129; weds Hotchkiss' niece, 225
Evans, Gen. Clement, 75, 158
Everett, Edward, vice-presidential candidate, 25
Ewell, Maj. Gen. Richard Stoddert: 34, 60, 63
   confers with Jackson on plan to defeat Banks, 41
   at the Battle of Cross Keys, 44
   assumes command of II Corps, 59
   requires maps of Spottsylvania Campaign, 92

Faulkner, Charles James, report writing for Jackson, 51, 197
Financial Panic of 1873:
   effect on Hotchkiss' attempts to raise capital, 113

INDEX

briefly described, 114
Financial recession, 1893; effect on railroad construction, 168, 177
Fisk, Pliny:
  intervention in sale of Elizabeth Furnace, 111
  and Cabin Creek, 112, 119
  and the financial panic of 1873, 114
  failure to pay for Ansted's services, 114, 127, 242
  finances Hotchkiss' second visit to England, 120
  partner in purchase of real estate, 120, 124
Flat Top Coalfield, 138-45, 171-77, 179
Fleming, W.Va., 175
  failure of mines at, 176
Fontaine, Col. Edmund, 106
Forrer:
  Daniel, 7, 94, 97, 189, 223
  Elizabeth, 9; furnace named after, 97
  Henry, 7, 8, 22, 111
  Mary, 10
  Samuel, 10, accused of desertion, 52; at Mossy Creek after Gettysburg, 65
Forests:
  as a cash generator, 171, 175
  tree counts on Guyandot CLA, property, 175
  conservation, 237
  resources of West Virginia, map of, 237
Fort Sumter, S.C., bombardment of, 26
Franklin, W.Va.:
  road from blockaded, 1, 40
  Jackson pursues Union forces toward, 36
Frazier, Harry, opinion of Hotchkiss, 241
Fredericksburg, Va.:
  battle of, 50-51
  map of the battlefield, 197, illustration, 198
Freeman, Douglas Southall, and the Hotchkiss papers, 247-49
Fremont, Brig. Gen. John C.:
  junction with Banks prevented, 1, 40
  at Cross Keys, 44
Fuller, H. W., 241

Gannett, Henry, borrows maps from Hotchkiss for U.S.G.S. use, 147
Garnett, Brig. Gen. Robert S., commands Confederate forces in northwest Virginia, 29
Gearing, William 22, 54, 69, 79, 81, 86, 105, 262 n. 67

Gilbert, Rev. Hiram M., pastor, Presbyterian Church, Windsor, N.Y., 5
Gilmer, Brig. Gen. Jeremy F., 202
Goode, R. U., and a proposed map of Virginia, 218-20
Gordon, Maj. Gen. John B.:
  at Gettysburg, 60
  at Battle of Cedar Creek, 75-76
Graham, Rev. Dr. James R., 157
Grant, Gen.-in-Chief Ulysses S.: 96
  and the Wilderness Campaign, 67-69
  crosses James River, 69
  instructs Sheridan to destroy Early, 71
  "scorched earth" policy, 71
  and the Hotchkiss maps, 87-92, 203
Green, J. C. (Virginia State Senator), and the Virginias Railway Company, 179, 181, 183, 185
Grinnan, Oswald F.:
  at Loch Willow School, 20
  organizes Ready Rifles of Augusta, 27
Grottoes Company, The:
  Hotchkiss president of, 164
  general managers of, 164, 166
  new board voted in, 165
  other presidents of, 165, 166
  problems of, 165
Guyandot Valley, as railroad route, 171

Hale, Dr. John P.: 226
  association with Hotchkiss, 118, 124
  accompanies Hotchkiss to England, 120
  secures option on Low and Aspinwall land, 171
Hale's Eddy, N.Y., 4; Jed Hotchkiss and Sara Comfort married at, 19
Handley Library, The, and the Hotchkiss maps, 247, 248, 249, 250-51
Harpers Ferry, W.Va., 7, 25; map of, 70
Harman, Col. Michael G.: 95, 97
  at Potomac crossing after Gettysburg, 63
  after defeat at Fisher's Hill, 74
  engages Hotchkiss to survey land, 86
  sets up National Express and Transportation Co., 93
  sells half interest in "The Oaks" lot to Hotchkiss, 94
  president of Valley Railroad Company, 96
Harris, R. W., 162, 173
Heck, Jonathan N., 29, 193, 223
Henderson, Colonel George F. R.: 192
  his biography of "Stonewall" Jackson, 154-57
  visits Port Republic with Hotchkiss, 156

gratitude to Hotchkiss, 157
tribute to Hotchkiss, 225
biographical note, 269 n. 20
Heth, Henry, and the Antietam Battlefield Commission, 204, 207
Heywood, Rev. Thomas, map of property, 131, illustration, 219
Hill, Maj. Gen. Ambrose Powell: 34
at Chancellorsville, 56
appointed to command of III Corps, 59
at Gettysburg, 62
at Bristoe Station, 65
Hoge, John B., 99
Holmes, William Henry, 209, 277 n. 65
Hooker, Maj. Gen. Joseph:
replaces Burnside, 53
at Chancellorsville, 54-57
Hotchkiss:
Amraphel, 3, 4
Anna,
birth, 19
death, 248
Hotchkiss maps and papers, 247
ill with scarlet fever, 38
marriage, 228
Carver, 5
Charles, 148
David, 3
Ellen May (Nellie),
birth, 19
death, 249
Hotchkiss maps and papers, 247-49
ill with scarlet fever, 38
marriage, 229
with father in England, 121, 125
Elmore D., 230
Frederick, 4
George (1), 3, 4
George (2), 4
Gideon, 3, 4, 5
Giles, W., 92
Jeanette, 5, 11-12, 18, 19
Hotchkiss, Jedediah
Biographical details:
antecedents, 3-4; birth, 3; education, 5-6; leaves Windsor, N.Y., 6; walking tour, 6-8; founds Mossy Creek Academy, 11; marriage, 19; children, 19; at Stribling Springs, 19; founds Loch Willow school, 20; joins Confederate army, 28; returns to teaching, 86; moves to Staunton, Va., 87; abandons teaching to begin career as topographical and mining engineer, 97, 105; attempts to raise capital in England, 110, 124; publicizes Virginia's resources, 122, 134-38; stimulates coal mining in West Virginia, 140-44, 160, 171-77; attempts to create third coal carrier, 163, 167-68, 179-87; president of The Grottoes Co., 164-65; death, 232
Civil War:
appointed adjutant of Augusta County Militia, 34, blockades mountain passes, 1, 40; escorts Jackson's ambulance, 57; paroled, 82; status, 82-4
History: intention to write, 51; aid to Henderson, 154-7; Confederate Military History, vol. III, 154, 158
Lectures on: 91, 151-54
Service at/in: Rich Mountain, 28-31; Valley campaign (1862), 36-62; McDowell, 39; Cross Keys, 44; Port Republic, 46; Maryland campaign, 48; Fredericksburg, 50; Moss Neck, 51; Chancellorsville, 54-57; Gettysburg, 60; Wilderness campaign, 67; Valley campaign, (1864,) 69-78; Cedar Creek, 74-7; Waynesboro, 80
Development of resources:
Cabin Creek, 110, 111, 116, 118, 119; seeks investment in England, 110, 124; Authority on, 122, 147; Flat Top coal field, 140-44; as Special Agent for 10th Census, 145-46; Gauley C.L.A., 160-70; The Grottoes Co., 164-65; Guyandot C.L.A., 171-77; Virginias Railway, 179-87
Financial affairs:
state of, 120, 124-25, 127, 128, 129, 244; improvement in, 148; comments on, 242-43
Health:
during Civil War, 31, 44, 49, 65, 69; final illness, 232
Maps and mapping, civil:
early interest in, 10, 189; skills, 35, 189; publication of, 97, 210-215; Board of Survey, Washington College, 100-2; in the Southern Planter and Farmer, 103; geologic, 123, 137; variety of, 131, 208; methods, 162-63; for New Orleans Exposition, 208-9; in The Virginias, 211; and the U.S.G.S., 215-20; campaigns for State survey, 217, 220; cartographic style, 218

INDEX 295

Maps and mapping, military:
  illustration, 30; Tygart's Valley, 31, 34, 192-94; McDowell, 39, 194, 196; Winchester (1862), illustration, 42; Winchester (1863), 60, 199, illustration, 61; Rich Mountain, 193; Shenandoah Valley, 194, 196-7, illustration, 32, 195; Powell's Fort Valley, 196; Fredericksburg, 197; Chancellorsville, 199; Allegheny Mountains, 200; Valley campaign of 1864, 201; variety of, 201; Antietam Battlefield Commission, 204-08
Opinions on:
  intoxicating liquor, 12, 38; education and the role of teacher, 16-18; religion, 16, 18, 52, 237, 239; slavery, 23, 234-5; secession, 24; Confederate defeat at Gettysburg, 62-63; Early's defeat at Waynesboro, 64, 80; surveying of real estate, 116; financial crises, 132, 243-4; politics, 147, 238; Sunday observance, 176, 239; "Free Silver," 185; conservation of timber resources, 237; government, 238
Personal qualities: 4, 9, 116, 160, 182, 223, 224, 229, 235, 236, 240-44
Publications:
  Chancellorsville, 94; in Scribner's Monthly, 107; address to the Society of Arts, 110; Virginia: A Geographical and Political Summary, 122-24, 130; Hotchkiss' Geography of Virginia, 130; The City of Staunton, 131; The Virginias, 134-37, 144
Teaching and related Activities:
  Elizabethville, Pa., 6; Mossy Creek Academy, 11, 12, 13-18; Stribling Springs, Va., 19-20; Loch Willow, Churchville, Va., 20-22; Augusta Female Seminary, Staunton, Va., 87; Superintendent of Augusta County Schools, 104; Agent for textbooks, 104-5; Teachers' Institutes, 130; Davis and Elkins College, 240
Hotchkiss,
  Jesse T., 4, 5
  Lydia Beecher, 3, 4, 228, 236
  Nelson, 3, 20, 52, 227, 228, 236
  Sara Comfort, 19, 79, 230

  Samuel, 3
  Stiles (1), 3, 4
  Stiles (2), 228
Howison, Allan M., 239
  as secretary of The Grottoes Company, 164
  weds Anna Hotchkiss, 228
Howison, A. M., Mrs., and the Hotchkiss maps, 247
Humphreys, David C., 157, 162, 226
  survey of Shendun site, 164
Huntington, Colis P., 106, 107

Imboden, Brig. Gen. John D., 27
Immigration Convention, 122
Ingalls, Melville E., 161, 173, 233

Jackson, Brig. Gen. Henry R., 31
Jackson, Maj. Gen. Thomas J. (Stonewall), 1, 2, 4, 22, 34, 48, 50, 224, 235
  appointed commandant of Harpers Ferry, 27
  orders Hotchkiss to make "Map of the Valley," 34
  Valley campaign, 35-45
  narrow escape at Port Republic, 44
  respect for Hotchkiss, 47, 235
  at Chancellorsville, 54-56
  mortal wounding, 56
  death, 87
  demands accuracy in maps, 198
Jackson, Lt. Col. William L., 29
James River Canal, 81, 106
Jennings' Gap:
  Federal cavalry at, 38
  Hotchkiss directs army through, 41
Jefferson, Thomas, 138
Johnson, Maj. Gen. Edward:
  at West View, 38
  wounded at Battle of McDowell, 39
  on the Rapidan, 66
Jones, Rev. Dr. J. W., 157
Jordan, Capt. Macon, cavalry escort on mission to destroy Shenandoah bridges, 37
Justice, Philip S., 111

Kanawha:
  City, 118, 125
  salines, 106, 108
Kelley, Col., 156
Kelley, R. W., 170
Kernstown, Va., 35
Kershaw, Maj. Gen. Joseph B., 76
Kimball, Frederick J., 2, 226
  and the development of the Flat Top coal field, 138, 140

portrait, 139
appointed First Vice-president of the N&W RR, 140
finances Hotchkiss' route map of Shenandoah Valley Railroad, 140
tributes to Hotchkiss, 142, 148
and the Ohio extension of the N&W RR, 170
finances map of W.Va. forests, 237
Know Nothing Party, supported by Hotchkiss, 25

Le Gear, Clara, and the Hotchkiss Map Collection, iv, 251
Lee, Maj. Gen. Robert E., 24, 34, 47, 48, 50, 54, 63, 64, 67, 81
  at Valley Mountain, W.Va., 1861, 28, 31, 34, 193
  at Chancellorsville, 54-58
  reorganizes Army of Northern Virginia, 59
  at Gettysburg, 60-62
  and the Wilderness campaign, 67-69
  surrenders at Appomattox, 82
  and Board of Survey of Washington College, 84, 99-102
  requests battlefield plans, 92
Letcher, John:
  response to Lincoln's call-out of militia, 26
  calls out Augusta Co. militia, 34
Library of Congress, and the Hotchkiss maps and papers, 246-7, 249, 250
Lilley, Robert D.:
  drills company of Home Guard, 27
  commands Augusta Lee Rifles, 31
Lincoln, Abraham:
  orders call-out of militia, 26
  presidential election of 1860, 26
  reaction to occupation of Fort Sumter, 27
Loch Willow, 1, 24
  school, 20-22, 28, illustration, 21
  purchased, 20
  slaves at, 22
  inventory, 22
  threat to, 38, 52
  farm sold, 52
Logan Coal, 176, 177
Lomax, Maj. Gen. Lunsford, 81
Longstreet, Maj. Gen. James, 50, 59, 63
Loring, Maj. Gen. William W.:
  appoints Hotchkiss Lieutenant of Engineers, 31, 82

orders Hotchkiss to map Tygart's Valley, 31
Low, Abriel A., 171
Low and Aspinwall tract, 171
Low, Maximilian, 125, 242
Lowel Institute, 153

Maury, Matthew Fontaine, 100
McClellan, Maj. Gen. George B.:
  and the "Philippi Races," 29
  in West Virginia, 29
  commands Army of the Potomac, 36
  and the battle of Antietam, 49, 296 n. 30
McCreath, Andrew S.:
  and the Staunton meeting of American Institute of Mining Engineers, 145
  reports on mineral wealth adjacent to N&W RR, 171
McCreery, James T., and the Virginias Railway, 180, 181, 182, 183, 184
McCue, J. Howard, 65, 89
  Hotchkiss property conveyed to, 15
McCullough, Allan, 229
McCullough, S. Thomas:
  marries Nellie Hotchkiss, 229
  death, 230
  drinking problem, 229-30
McDowell, Va., 1, 36, 39, 196
McGuire, Dr. Hunter H., 56, 64, 156, 225, 231
McKendrew, Maj., 184
McKinley, William, elected President, 185
McKune, Ralph H.:
  with Hotchkiss at Elizabethville, Pa., 6
  with Hotchkiss on walking tour, 6-7
  completes business with Hotchkiss, 18, 223
  death, 19
McLaughlin, Robert, 154
"Map of the Valley," see under *Hotchkiss, Jedediah, Maps and Mapping, military: Shenandoah Valley*
Maps and Mapping, see under *Hotchkiss, Jedediah*
Martin, Colonel Lawrence, and the Hotchkiss maps, 247
Mason, Amasa, 111
Massanutten Mountain:
  military significance of, 36
  as observation point, 38, 41, 43, 75
Maury, Matthew Fontaine:
  as Professor of Physics at VMI, 100

INDEX
297

meets Lee at White Sulphur Springs, W.Va., 100
VMI's Physical Survey of Virginia, 100, 102
Meade, Maj. Gen. George; replaces Hooker, 60; at Mine Run, 66
Michie, Gen. Peter S., requests maps from Hotchkiss, 87, 94, 97, 203
Michler, Nathaniel, map of Antietam battlefield, 204
Miller, Henry, founds Mossy Creek Ironworks, 9
Miller, M. Erskine:
  and the Gauley CLA, 160, 169
  and the Staunton Development Company, 164
  as incorporator of the CS&W RR, 167
Miller, J. Craig, 185
  engaged as Chief Engineer, Guyandot CLA, 175
  and tree counts, 175
Miller, Capt. M. A., 99, 168, 175, 226
Miller, Rev. W. H., 5
Milnes, Hon. William, 97, 138, 140
Milroy, Maj. Gen. Robert H., defeat and pursuit by Jackson, 1, 36
Mingo Coal Company, 177
Monterey, Va., Gen. H. R. Jackson at, 55
Moore, Maj. Samuel J. C., 157, 158
Morrill Act, 100
Moss Neck, Va., Jackson's winter quarters, 1862-3, 51
Mossy Creek, Va., v, 7, 8, 9;
  Ironworks, 9
  Church, 10, 12
  Academy, 11, 12, 13-18, 19, illustration, 14
  Boarding House, 13
Mount Rogers, Va., named in honor of Professor W. B. Rogers, 214-15
Munford, Maj. Gen. Thomas T., 47, 82, 156
  appreciates Hotchkiss' skills, 193

Narrow Passage Creek, Va., vulnerable as defensive position, 35
National Express and Transportation Co., 93, 244
National Geographic Society, Hotchkiss lectures at meetings of, 151, 153
Nelson, Jordan, 142
New Orleans Exposition, 208
Newspapers and periodicals:
  Baltimore Gazette, 110

  Coal Trade Journal, 145
  Commonwealth, 147
  Industrial South, 144
  Journal of the Society of Arts, 110
  Logan County Banner, 178
  Manufacturers' Record, 145, 183, 186
  Mining Journal, 111
  New York Bulletin, 111
  North Western Lumberman, 243
  Richmond Dispatch, 152
  Richmond Enquirer, 94
  Richmond Whig, 102, 103
  Rockingham Register, 165
  Scribner's Monthly, 107
  Shendun News, 165
  Southern Planter and Farmer, 103
  Staunton Spectator, 12, 25, 26, 27, 90, 93, 94, 100, 110, 227, 234
  Times (London), 110, 132
  Valley Virginian, 92
  Virginia Free Press, 152
Nicholson, W. L., 97, 118
North River, Va., crossed by bridge of wagons, 41

Oaks, The, v, 94, 148
Official Records (OR), publication of, 203
Oltmanns, C. W.:
  with Hotchkiss during the war, 67, 201
  postwar work with Hotchkiss, 94, 97, 225

Pack, Augustus, 111
Page Valley, Va.:
  military significance of, 36
  Jackson uses to outflank Banks, 41
  Hotchkiss observes Federal movements in, 43
Peabody, George, and the Education Fund, 96, 130
Pearl Mining Company, The, 176
Pechin, Edmund C., as general manager, The Grottoes Company, 166-67
Pendleton, Alexander Swift ("Sandy"),
  provides Hotchkiss with transport, 34
  romance with Kate Corbin, 51
  and John Esten Cooke's Life of Jackson, 64
  with Hotchkiss selects winter camps, 66
  mortally wounded, 73
Philippi, W.Va., Confederate retreat through, 29
Pickett, Maj. Gen. George Edward, at Gettysburg, 62
Pinchot, Gifford, and forest management, 237

Pocahontas, Va.:
  building of, 143
  first delivery of coal from, 143, 159
  mine explosion, 144
Pope, Maj. Gen. John:
  appointed to command "Army of Virginia," 47
  suppression of, 48
Population data, blacks in Tidewater, the Valley, and Staunton, 24
Port Republic, Va.:
  church at, 7
  march to prior to battle of McDowell, 38
  Jackson escapes capture at, 44
  Hotchkiss and the Battle of, 44-46, 235, map of, 45
Powell, John Wesley:
  as director of U.S.G.S., 147
  buys Hotchkiss' large Geological Map of Virginia, 208
Presbyterian Church
  Windsor, N.Y., David Hotchkiss donates land for, 4
  Mossy Creek, Va., 7, 10, 12
  Staunton, Va., 239

Ragland, Henry Clay, 178
Railroads:
  AM&O, 120, 140
  B&O, 168, 170
  C&O, 106-108, 109, 160, 161, 178
  Covington & Ohio, 96
  CS&W, 167, 168
  Cherry River, 170
  Columbus, Huntington & Guyandotte, 178
  Guyandot Valley Railway Company, 187
  Hinton, New River & Western, 180, 183, 184
  Huntington & Guyandotte, 173, 177
  Kanawha & Michigan, 161
  Louisa, 106
  Manassas Gap, 95
  N&W, 170, 183, 184
    formation of, 140
    New River Division, 142
    and the Virginia new town boom, 163, 164
    Ohio extension, 170, 171
  Ohio & Guyandot, 177
  Orange & Alexandria, 69, 93
  Richmond & York River, 227
  Shenandoah Valley:
    linkup with AM&O, 140
    map of for Kimball, 140
  South Side, 81
  Valley, 95, 121, 164, 242
  Virginia Central: 80
    Jackson's use to deceive enemy, 39
    operating after Civil War, 93, 95
    extended as C&O, 106
  Virginias Railway Company, 160, 179-87
  Virginia & Tennessee, 140
  WV&P, 161, 167, 168, 169, 170
  WVC&P, 167, 169
Ramseur, Maj. Gen. Stephen D., 71
Randall, Frank E., as general manager of The Grottoes Co., 166
Rapelje, John, 169, 170
  engaged as superintendent of Gauley survey, 162
  Hotchkiss' appreciation of, 163
Richmond, Va.,
  perceived importance to Union, 35
  peninsular campaign, 47
Rich Mountain, W.Va.:
  Hotchkiss joins Confederate forces at, 29
  Hotchkiss leads retreat from, 29-30
  Hotchkiss surveys Confederate position at, 29, 193
Ristow, Walter, iv
Rives, Hon. William C., 96
Robinson, Samson Biddulph, 64, 224, 225
  joins Hotchkiss' topographical team, 65, 200
  with Hotchkiss postwar, 82, 86, 87, 93, 97
  return to Louisiana, 95, 225
  biographical note, 279 n. 4
Rodes, Maj. Gen. Robert E., 72
Rogers, Emma, 209, 210
Rogers, William Barton:
  Hotchkiss' first meeting with, 11
  and the geological map of Virginia, 123, 137, 208, 209, 210
  visits Hotchkiss, 210
  death, 210
  Geology of the Virginias, 210
  friendship with Hotchkiss and family, 226
Rosser, Brig. Gen. Thomas L., 76, 78, 81, 92
Rowland, L., 87
Royal Land Company of Virginia, 131, 133
Ruffin, Edmund S., as president of The Grottoes Co., 165, 166
Ruffner, Rev. William H.,
  attends sale of Hotchkiss property, 18

INDEX

safeguards Hotchkiss maps after Lee's surrender, 82, 203
as superintendent of Public Instruction, 103-4
at Teachers' Institutes with Hotchkiss, 130
Rumple, J. W., as president of The Grottoes Co., 166

Salling, John P., 138
Scott, Col. Robert N., and the *OR's*, 203
Sergent, Prof. Charles S., 237
Sears, Barnas:
 settles in Staunton, 96
 agent for Peabody Fund, 96, 130
 joint owner with Hotchkiss of building lots, 128
Shenandoah
 ironworks, 6, 7, 22, 37, 86, 97, 132
 River, destruction of bridges across, 37
 Valley:
  Hotchkiss' first visit to, 7
  settles in, 11
  joins Jackson in, 34
Shendun, 160
 lots laid out, 165
 optimism over future of, 167
 see also *Grottoes Co., The*
Sheridan, Gen. Philip:
 "scorched earth" policy, 71, 74
 defeats Early, 72-80
Shields, James, threat to Jackson at Port Republic, 44
Sitlington's Hill, W.Va.:
 Hotchkiss finds route for artillery, 39
 Hotchkiss sketches battlefield, 40
Slavery, issue, 9, 22
Slaves:
 Hotchkiss' first sight of, 7
 employed at Loch Willow, 22
 Alansa Rounds' reaction to, 24
Smith, Rev. B. M., 11
Smith, C. W., and the Virginias Railway, 178, 183, 184
Smith, Francis:
 provides Hotchkiss a contact with publisher Van Nostrand, 94
 distrust of Hotchkiss, 100
 engages Maury as Professor of physics at VMI, 100
Smith, Rev. Dr. James P., 232
Smith, Col. William Proctor, 78, 79, 200, 224
Society of Arts (London), Hotchkiss' address to, 110
Sopwith, Thomas, FRS, 110

Stack, Capt. J. J., makes surveys for the Virginias Railway, 181, 183, 184
Staunton Development Co., 164
Staunton Spectator, see under *Newspapers and periodicals*
Staunton, Va.:
 postwar recovery, 95
 Hotchkiss pamphlet on, 131
 extension of city limits, 182
Sterrett, Alansa Rounds, 23-24
 Capt. Francis F., 1, 27, 29, 40
Stone House, Windsor, N.Y., 3, illustration, 2
Stonewall Jackson Camp No. 25, 157
Stony Creek, Va.:
 Hotchkiss recommends defensive line along, 35
 Bank attacks, 36
Stribling Springs, Va.: Select school at, 19-20
Stuart, Alexander H. H.:
 opinion leader in Augusta County, 25, 132
 intercedes on behalf of Hotchkiss, 87
 presides over Immigration Convention, 122
Stuart, Maj. Gen. J.E.B., 49, 54, 58, 62, 64, 84
Sunday observance, 176, 239
Surveying, (see also *Mapping*):
 as an Academy subject, 188
 by Hotchkiss, see under *Hotchkiss, Jedediah*

Taliaferro, William B., at Battle of McDowell, 40
Taylor, Maj. Gen. Richard, 46
Thompson, Gilbert, 153, 269 n. 16
Tracey, Albert, on effect of blockade of Dry Run Gap, 40
Tucker, Henry St. George, 207, 217
Tucker, John Randolph, 147
Twelve Pole Creek, 171, 173
 map of, 172
 survey by N&W engineers, 174
Tygart's Valley, W.Va., Hotchkiss' map of, 31, 34, 193-94, illustration, 30

U.S.G.S.:
 formation of, 215
 borrows maps from Hotchkiss, 216
 and a Virginia state map, 217-18
 co-operation with State Surveys, 220

Vinson, Zachary, T., 178
Virginia:
  secedes from the Union, 27
  significance to the Confederacy, 35
  debt problem, effect on English investment, 113
  Board of Immigration, 122
  geological map of, 137, 208-10
  new town boom, 161, 163
Virginia Development Company, 166
Virginia: A Geographical & Political Summary, 102, 122, 124, 137, 208
Virginia Military Institute (VMI), 22, 27, 100, 102, 136
Virginias Railway Company, see under Railroads
Virginias, The:
  advertising in, 135
  aims of, 134, 135
  and the sale of real estate, 136
  maps in, 136
  gives publicity to Rogers' work, 137
  records Flat Top coal field development, 144
  ceases publication, 144
  reports Pocahontas mine explosion, 144

Walker, Brig. Gen. John G., 48
Walker, Dr. Thomas, 138
War Records office, 203
Waterman, Watkins & Co., and the *Historical Atlas of Augusta Co.*, 211-15
Washington, DC:
  Hotchkiss visits, 10
  Jackson's perceived threat to, 36
  Early's threat to, 71
Washington College, Board of Survey, 84, 99-102
Washington, George, 106
Waynesboro, Va.:
  Early's defeat at, 71
  Hotchkiss escapes from, 80-81
Webster, Daniel, oration of, July 4, 1851, 11
Welch, Capt. Isiah A., engaged by Hotchkiss for survey work, 122, 138, 142, 143
Wharton, Brig. Gen. Gabriel C., 76, 78, 80
White, Professor Israel C.:
  and the Gauley Coal Land Association, 161
  reports on Low and Aspinwall tract, 173
  on lack of maps of Virginia and West Virginia, 220

White, T. J., acquires Hotchkiss interest in Mossy Creek Academy, 19
Wickham, Brig. Gen. William C., 106
Williams, Martin, 181, 184
Williams, Samuel, and the Bland Land Company, 181, 182
Williams, Porterfield & Williams, attorneys for McCreery, 181
Williamson, Col. T. H., 39, 136
Wilmot, David, "proviso," 23
Wilson, Hinkle & Co., 105
Winchester, Va., Battles of, see under *Civil War*
Winder, Brig. Gen. Charles S., 46
Windsor, N.Y.,
  founding of, 3
  Presbyterian Church, 4
  Academy, 5, 6
Winslow & Wetherell, 148
Winthrop, Robert C., 96
Wright, A. D., 164
Wylie, J. Cooke, and the Hotchkiss map collection, 250

YMCA, 152, 243